The Resurrection A Biblical Study

THE RESURRECTION

F. X. DURRWELL, C.SS R

THE RESURRECTION

A Biblical Study

translated by
ROSEMARY SHEED

and with an introduction by
CHARLES DAVIS, S.T L.

SHEED AND WARD
NEW YORK

Originally published as
La Résurrection de Jésus, mystère de salut,
by Editions Xavier Mappus, Paris and Le Puy

NIHIL OBSTAT
CAROLUS DAVIS, S.T.I.
CENSOR DEPUTATUS

IMPRIMATUR
E MORROGH BERNARD
VIC GEN

WESTMONASTERII, DIE 2A AUGUSTI, 1960

The *Nihil Obstat* and *Imprimatur* are a declaration that a book or
pamphlet is considered to be free from doctrinal or moral error It is
not implied that those who have granted the *Nihil Obstat* and
Imprimatur agree with the contents, opinions or statements expressed

Library of Congress Catalog Card Number 60-15679

Manufactured in the United States of America

TRANSLATOR'S NOTE

The system of numbering followed in Scriptural references
is that of the *Bible de Jérusalem*

CONTENTS

CONTENTS

CHAPTER VII · THE PROGRESS AND CONSUMMATION OF THE PASCHAL MYSTERY IN THE CHURCH .

PREFACE TO THE SECOND EDITION

The favourable reception accorded the first edition of this book suggests that its theme is one that fills a need for many. I have therefore decided to see what further work I can do on it I have not had enough free time to make all the improvements I could have wished, but I have tried at least to make this new edition easier to read, in the hope of reaching a wider public.

I have said more, though still not perhaps enough, about the eschatological aspect of Christ's glory, and stressed the "fullness of being" contained in that glory, which makes our Lord the principle of the world as well as its end. Since it is not a practicable possibility for me to undertake a "Theology of the Holy Ghost in the New Testament", I have sought to clarify and develop certain ideas about the Holy Ghost; I hope this may supply material for anyone wishing to set about writing such a book.

Without wanting to exert pressure on the reader's judgement or personal preferences, I should like to draw his attention to two vital truths which emerge from studying the resurrection of Christ: the fact that the death and resurrection remain forever actual in Christ in glory, and the identification of the Church with Christ in glory, not merely in one body with him, but actually in the act of his death and glorification. These two complementary truths seem to me to be among the most fruitful of all towards an understanding of the Church, her life and her sacraments

Finally, I must express my profound gratitude for the kindness with which so many theologians have welcomed the first edition of this book. I am especially pleased that so many have given their unreserved approval to the method of scriptural enquiry I have tried to follow; I think it is one which can do much to enrich our understanding of the Christian mystery.

FOREWORD

Not so long ago theologians used to study the Redemption without mentioning the Resurrection at all. The fact of Easter was made to yield its utmost value as a piece of apologetics; but no-one thought of examining it in itself as one of the inexhaustible mysteries of our salvation.

Christ's work of redemption was seen as consisting in his incarnation, his life and his death on the cross. The theologians stressed the note of reparation, of satisfaction, of meritoriousness in that life and death, and generally they went no further. When the Resurrection was mentioned, it was not so much to give it any part in our salvation as to show it as Christ's personal triumph over his enemies, and a kind of glorious counterblast to the years of humiliation he had endured to redeem us. In short, Christ's resurrection was shorn of the tremendous significance seen in it by the first Christian teachers, and relegated to the background of the redemptive scheme. Such blindness naturally impoverished the whole theology of the Atonement.

Yet all that was needed was to listen to St. Paul, who says categorically:

> And if Christ be not risen again, your faith is vain, for you are yet in your sins. (1 Cor. xv. 17.)
> Christ died for all . . . died for them, and rose again. (2 Cor. v. 15.)
> Who was delivered up for our sins, and rose again for our justification. (Rom. iv. 25.)

This book was born out of my excitement over these key-texts of St Paul, and a wish to share with others this tremendously helpful realization of the mystery of Easter.

During the years I have been pursuing my meditations and studies, the theme of Christ's resurrection has suddenly come to the fore in theological thought. A proper return to the origins of

Christian thought has speeded the rediscovery of this mystery.[1] In
the history of the Church's spirituality, the new realization of the
Resurrection will undoubtedly come to be seen as the chief event of
our day.

A number of works on Scripture and the liturgy have thrown
light on different doctrinal aspects of Christ's resurrection. One
recent book[2] offers an extremely important documentary study of
the whole Easter message. The author has, however, imposed limits
on himself which mean that he does no more than make an approach
towards a full doctrinal synthesis For some years now it has been
my wish to make this synthesis.[3]

In Scripture, there are two possible methods of doctrinal research.
One may try either to analyse what the sacred writer is thinking,
or to grasp the Christian reality underlying the inspired text.

The first is the historian's way. It sets out to follow the conscious
thought of the author, to go deeper, it will look for the historical
origins of that thought, and trace its progress and completion. It
must draw no conclusions which cannot be proved to have been in
the conscious mind of the sacred writer, for its job is simply a sort
of stock-taking.

When we are concerned with analysing the teaching of any book
of human wisdom, this is the only legitimate method. But the
Apostles were not wise men, their claim was that they were witnesses. They had not created a system, but had simply seen certain
events and lived a new reality. They are recording those events and
expressing that reality.

Hence it is quite legitimate for the exegete to carry his investigation as far as those truths and that reality. He is not exceeding his
brief if, not content with merely collecting and verifying the
accounts, he seeks to establish the nature of the truths to which they
bear witness. A study that goes beyond the actual words of the

---

[1] I use the term "rediscovery", for an exactly similar return to the beginning had earlier led Condren, Olier, Bossuet, Thomassin and others to the
heart of the Easter mystery. But they were too narrow in taking the idea
of sacrifice as their only biblical basis; and further, this theology did not catch
the attention of the age in which they lived.

[2] J Schmitt, *Jésus ressuscité dans la prédication apostolique*, Paris, 1949

[3] There is such a synthesis in German It is by the Protestant theologian,
W Kunneth· *Theologie der Auferstehung*, Munich, 1933. The ideas in it are
excellent, though interspersed with a good many philosophical considerations.
The book is hard to come by, and I myself have only recently seen it Cf too,
A. M Ramsey, *The Resurrection of Christ*, London, 1946

Apostles in an effort to grasp the Christian reality itself presupposes
a faith in that reality and is no longer a purely historical theology;
it remains, however, a biblical theology, for its concern is only with
the Christian mystery as expressed in the Bible. It submits to the
discipline of historical theology, and only from the most precise
handling of the text does it arrive, by reconstructing the thought of
the sacred writer, at the contemplation of the Christian mystery.

This second sort of exegesis can, thanks to its faith in the Christian
reality, in some cases see beyond the partial sense of an individual
text and, by fitting various texts together as their inner essence
dictates, effect a synthesis which the writers of the Bible did not
express and may not even fully have realized. This does not mean
that such a synthesis exists only in our minds; it exists in the
Christian mystery, and the Apostles grasped the various aspects of
it, but made no attempt to set it out as an organized system.

The term "biblical" is usually reserved for the historical theology
of Scripture.[4] Must it be denied to the theology I have just described?
In the immense house of Catholic exegesis there are many man-
sions. I hope I am not over-bold in claiming house-room for a book
in which I have tried to follow the principles stated above.

The scheme of this work was dictated by the end in view. Historical research into the doctrine of the Resurrection would have
called for an individual discussion of each sacred writer in a series
of separate treatises Theological research into revealed truth per-
mits of a study linking together the different aspects of the mystery.
But if a work is to claim the title of a biblical study it must look at
those aspects steadily with the eyes of the sacred writers.

My introductory chapter will set out the redemptive nature of
the Resurrection, and cast some light on the sacred writers' teaching on the subject.

Chapter II will establish the relationship of the Resurrection with
the two other truths of the Redemption—the coming to earth of the
Son of God, and his death.

Chapter III will pinpoint the special role the Resurrection plays
in our salvation—the bursting into the world of the Holy Spirit.

Chapters IV to VII analyse the effects of the Resurrection first

----

[4] Biblical theology has always been ranged with historical theology, for the
only other theology that has been recognized is speculative theology Cf.
F. Prat, *The Theology of St Paul*, London, 1926-7, vol i, p 1.

in Christ himself (Chapter IV), and in the Church born out of its Saviour's resurrection (Chapter V); then in the Church's paschal life—both in itself (Chapter VI) and in its history (Chapter VII).

Chapter VIII will describe the ways in which that paschal life spreads throughout the world.

And the last chapter will picture the mystery of Easter in its fulfilment in heaven.

This is my method. A study of purely historical theology might have been of greater interest to specialists. But I intend my book for those who are bearing witness all over the world to the death and resurrection of Christ, to all the Apostles of the Lord Jesus. It has been their insistence that spurred me on and prevented my allowing the task to be crowded out by other work.

I offer these pages to the world with the strongest sense of their inability to express the incomparable splendours of the risen Christ. Yet the encouragement of such recognized masters as Père Congar and Père Dillenschneider gives me reason to hope I may not have laboured in vain.

"For God, who commanded the light to shine out of darkness, hath shined in our hearts, to give the light of the knowledge of the glory of God, in the face of Christ Jesus " (2 Cor. iv. 6)

I

THE RESURRECTION OF CHRIST A MYSTERY
OF REDEMPTION

There is a widespread idea that the Resurrection is an epilogue; that the whole mystery took place on Calvary, and the drama was brought to its close at the ninth hour on Good Friday. Easter simply tells us of the fate of our hero after his great adventure His work done, he must come back to life, for "it was impossible that he should be holden by it". (Acts ii. 24)

But Scripture sees the history of our redemption differently.

1. What the Old Testament Has to Tell Us

In the Old Testament, God outlined the salvation that was to be fulfilled in Israel in the fullness of time. He showed himself as the God who saves from death, man's salvation is seen as a life coming from God

Various psalms[1] speak of sufferings similar to Christ's and a providential salvation like his resurrection Generally the singer is recounting the suffering and salvation of himself, of the just in general, or of the Chosen People. Pursued by his enemies, Iahweh's follower goes from suffering to suffering to the very gates of Sheol But his prayers and the justice of his cause call for divine intervention and God rescues him when the trial is at its height. All these psalms express a twofold movement of descent and re-ascent, a kind of rough sketch of a death and a resurrection.

The New Testament gives us the exegesis of most of these psalms We see that God's thought looked further than the just man in the Old Law and reached forward to Christ in his messianic sufferings and his triumph.[2] For the Apostles, these texts were alive with

[1] Ps XVI, XXII, XXX, XXXI, XXXV, XL, XLI, XLV, LVI, LXIX, CII, CIX, CXVIII.
[2] Cf Matt xxii. 42ff.; Luke xxiii. 46; John ii. 17; xiii 18; xv 25, Acts i 20; ii. 25–8; Rom xv. 3; Heb x 5–10.

foreboding, with a presence outside themselves; the just man who
suffers, and is saved by Iahweh is, as it were, understudying Christ;
he bears Christ's lineaments and his voice has a messianic ring, so
that Christ's followers see in him their Master's face and hear the
sound of his voice. With Christ as exemplar it became legitimate to
apply to him alone texts which in their context applied to the
prophets or the singers of Israel, or to phases of the race's history.[3]

If one accepts this charismatic exegesis, while continuing to give
full value to the historical sense of the texts, it is clear that Israel,
throughout its story, is God's prophet of what is to come, prophesying even more by its history than by the words of its psalmists and
prophets. It is a wholly divine way of foretelling the future. Israel
often did not fully recognize its own being, nor understand its own
words. The people of Israel were a messianic people bearing within
themselves God-given seeds of hope, and what they said about themselves and the things that were happening to them were later to be
recognized as describing future events or a man not yet born. When
the flower came to open out, the Apostles would apply to it all that
had been said of the seed, unfolding as they saw fit the hidden riches
of the texts.[4]

Thus the New Testament saw the salvation that was constantly
being renewed for the Israelites as a foretelling of the salvation that
was to come once and for all; the just man, with his cries of anguish
and then his words of triumph, was to them the voice of Christ in
suffering and then in the joy of his resurrection. (Acts ii. 25–8.) The
Apostles saw his death and resurrection heralded in the Old Testament far more clearly than any modern exegete. (Luke xxiv. 26ff.,
44ff.; 1 Cor. xv. 3–4.)

In the Old Testament, salvation consisted in the intervention of
God called down by prayer; suffering did not save, but was the evil
from which the just man was to be saved. God came to his assistance;
he brought him back to life, established him in complete happiness

[3] Matt xxi 42ff., Luke iv 18 (though this perhaps applies primarily to
Isaiah); John xiii. 18
[4] The psalmists of Israel certainly possessed, at least vaguely, this vision of
faith concerning the inmost nature of their national history Psalm XLV, for
instance, which bestows messianic honours on a king descended from David,
shows this, and Psalm LXXXVII praises ancient Sion as the metropolis of the
nations To them the messianic era was to be simply "the perfecting of the
theocracy of Israel". (L Dennefeld, "Messianisme", *Dict. Théol. Cath*,
col 1405), the blossoming of its inmost essential being Cf. L Desnoyers,
Histoire du peuple d'Israel, Paris, 1930, vol III, pp 305–28

(Ps. XVI), and the assembly of the people resounded with God's praises (Ps XL, LXIX, CII). Psalm CXVIII declares that on the day made by the Lord his people, till then despised and rejected, will become the cornerstone of the house of all the nations built by God. Israel's world-wide destiny is to be accomplished in a salvation that comes after a humiliation.

Of all the psalms about the just man suffering, Psalm XXII must be given a special place for its extraordinary messianic richness. Yet one feels that the writer himself must have lived through what he is describing, for to us now it seems hard to think that anybody could express such intense sorrow merely in someone else's sufferings.[5]

But the hero it sings is a man of such importance that his fate concerns all nations, even to the ends of the earth, and his deliverance brings with it the conversion of all—which is the hope of messianic times. The description of the trial and liberation contains more than the story of this one sufferer; it takes on messianic proportions. Then, too, it displays such incredible beauty of character: innocence without boasting, gentleness in face of the most appalling cruelty, serene abandonment into God's hands; this just man far surpasses any ancient writer one could name and is comparable in stature only with the Servant of Iahweh. Psalm XXII is more clearly one of the Servant's psalms than any of those whose theme is the just man who suffers. Even if it does express the sufferings and hopes of the author himself, the intensity and completeness of its religious and messianic feeling must put it among the greatest things written to foretell the coming of Christ.

It does not speak in so many words of death and resurrection, but of mortal suffering and a miraculous deliverance. So terrible is the unhappy man's lot that he comes near to despair. His life is over; he is "poured out like water"; his hands and feet are pierced, his bones scattered. His executioners are already casting lots for his clothes. Yet suddenly the dying man's soul exults in the certainty of a new fullness of life: God has stepped in, and has raised him up when he was as good as dead.

The period of suffering gains no merit, either for the hero himself or for anyone else, except in that it is in answer to his own anguished

---

[5] This argument is by no means conclusive, and it remains possible that this psalm may be directly messianic. Cf L. Dennefeld, "Messianisme", col 1505ff.

cries that the sufferer is set free. His deliverance, on the other hand, has universal repercussions. It calls forth thanksgiving throughout creation. The hero himself intones Iahweh's praises in the great assembly. He offers a sacrifice of thanksgiving at which he invites the poor to eat and be filled. The horizon grows, and not merely the assembly of Israel, but all nations are drawn into the chorus of praise; they were once led astray, but they have seen this deliverance and remembered God, and now return to him from the ends of the earth Nor is this saving power limited to the present moment, but spreads over the generations to come and shines back into the distant past: "And even they who sleep in the earth shall adore him, and those who go down to the earth and have no more life shall fall down before him. . . . My seed shall serve him. There shall be declared to the Lord a generation to come: and the heavens shall show forth his justice to a people that shall be born." (Verses 30–32.)[6] The deliverance of this just man casts its light on those who sleep in the earth, and those yet to be born into life; it awakens the one and summons up the other, to praise God

Thus the just man's salvation is at once the starting-point and the cause of thanksgiving. Although the rendering of verse 30 is by no means certain, it is clear that the results of this deliverance have assumed huge proportions which can only be appreciated in the light of New Testament revelation: Israel and all the nations, future generations, and no doubt the inhabitants of Sheol too, are gathered into the liturgy of praise arising out of the just man's deliverance.

But richer even than Psalm XXII is the last song of the Servant of Iahweh (Isa. lii. 13–liii. 12)—sometimes called the "Passion of Our Lord Jesus Christ According to Isaiah". This text can quite definitely be applied to no-one but Christ.[7] Its closeness to the story of the Passion is remarkable, and even more remarkable are the profound intuition of what caused the Passion to come about and the vision of what its effects were to be. It is our earliest theology of the Redemption.

The structure of the song is a familiar one: a descent followed by

---

[6] Cf the new Latin psalter by the professors of the Pontifical Biblical Institute; F. Nötscher, *Die Psalmen*, Würzburg, 1947, p 39. For a justification of this rendering, cf A Vaccari, "Psalmus Christi Patientis et de Morte Triumphantis", *Verb. Dom.*, 20 (1940), 101–4

[7] Israel as a whole bears the title of Iahweh's Servant Even in this text the title has a certain collective sense, but that is because the great Just Man stands for the whole nation whose sins he is expiating.

a sudden exaltation. But in this case the descent ends explicitly in death, and the exaltation really is a resurrection.[8] The cause of the exaltation is the death: it is precisely as a result of his humiliations that he is lifted up again. (liii. 10–12.) Unlike those of the just man of the Psalms, the Servant's sufferings are not simply due to the wickedness of men; they are part of a redemptive plan. The sufferer expiates crimes he has not himself committed—the crimes of his many brethren—and just as the humiliations touch him personally because he has put himself in the place of sinners, so too the glory which the humiliations win for him is turned to the profit of his brethren. Having made expiation for men, "he leads them to the glory he has won for himself through his humiliations."[9] The Servant's work, then, does not end with his suffering, for this is only one of two stages in it; it expiates and merits, but God's plan for mankind is fulfilled in the glorified Servant: "If he shall lay down his life for sin, he shall see a long-lived seed, and the will of the Lord shall be prosperous in his hand." (liii. 10) The glory of the Servant is specifically bound up with our salvation, but only because it follows an expiative death to which it is linked as effect to cause.

The effects of the return to life are defined with some precision. This resurrection is not simply a coming back to life, but an elevation to a richer life altogether: the Servant "will lengthen his days" (liii. 10), and there seems no special limit to their length.[10] He will see the light and be filled. (liii. 11) He will rejoice in that life-giving light from the face of God which the more spiritual of the Psalms saw as the reward granted to the just man after his sufferings, his fullness of life and everlasting satisfaction.[11]

[8] From verse 8 of ch liii the Servant is dead and buried. The resurrection is not mentioned in so many words in the Massoretic text, but the life the Servant leads after his death, and his action upon the nations, presuppose it Verse 10, in which the passage from humiliation to glory takes place, is thought to be a corruption, and may once have stated the resurrection more clearly. (Cf. J Fischer, *Das Buch Isaias*, Bonn, 1939, vol. II, p 137) For verse 11, the Massoretic text gives, "Because of the sufferings of his soul, he shall see and be filled " What shall he see? Here again it seems likely that the text is incomplete The Septuagint gives, "He shall see light." The manuscript found in the Judaean desert in 1947 says more definitely, "He shall see the light"; "to see the light" means "to live" or "to return to life". (Job. iii 16, 20; xviii. 18; Ps. xlix. 20; lvi. 14.)

[9] E. Tobac, "Isaïe", *Dict., Théol. Cath* , col. 76

[10] According to the Semitic way of thought, this can be interpreted as meaning a life lasting forever. The phrase "He will lengthen his days" expresses duration without fixing any limits.

[11] Ps. lxxiii. 23ff ; xvi. 11; xvii. 15.

The Servant's personal triumph will bring with it the triumph of God's cause: "The will of the Lord shall be prosperous in his hands." We know what that will was from the other Servant songs. to establish justice among the nations (xlii 1, 4), to bring back Jacob, to be a light to the Gentiles and to bear the salvation of God to the ends of the earth (xlix 5ff.). In this phase of his new life the Servant was to have descendants, and in so spiritual a context this must clearly mean a great religious family growing up round him as generation succeeds generation. He shall justify many by his knowledge[12]—that knowledge akin to the faith of the New Testament, whereby both mind and heart cleave to God, which Jeremiah held to be the psychological basis of the religious life under the new covenant. (Jer. xxiv. 7; xxxi. 34.)

Because the Servant has borne their sins, God will give him "many men for his share, and multitudes for his spoils". (liii. 12.) He shall have dominion over those for whom he offered his sacrifice of expiation. This dominion to be exercised by the humble Servant is the last picture we get from this tremendous text.

2. What the Synoptics Tell Us

The synoptic tradition appears to give the Resurrection something of a background role in the mission of the Son of Man. This indicates a remarkable historical objectivity in these authors, who have set down only the essential facts in a teaching in which the glorification of Christ holds first place.

To them their message consisted in announcing the imminent coming of the Kingdom. In the early days of Christ's ministry, the whole Gospel could be summed up in a concise formula: "The time is accomplished, and the Kingdom of God is at hand: repent and believe the gospel." (Mark i. 15.) Christ's preaching was a continuation of the messianic prophecy of the ancients, in which the idea of the Kingdom predominated The personal role of the Son of Man was to be herald of the Kingdom, and leader of the people into this world of greater reality.

Access to the Kingdom was gained through a penitent heart, through faith in the Kingdom, and through Jesus its prophet; it was open to publicans and harlots if they were stirred by the ex-

[12] Another rendering is, "He will nourish them with his knowledge " In either case the Servant's knowledge is to be shared as a means of salvation

hortations of Christ or John the Baptist. For a long time the only conditions for entry were conversion, faith, and obedience to the Law in the perfect manner indicated by the Sermon on the Mount. (Matt. v. 20ff.)

But gradually a new element was revealed as being an integral part of Christ's mission. From the time of Peter's confession at Caesarea, he was constantly showing his disciples the necessity of his coming death. (Matt. xvi. 21.) It is clear from his insistence that his death must be an essential part of the messianic scheme. Our Lord explains this when he says that he is "come . . to give his life a redemption for many". (Matt. xx. 28; Mark x. 45.) On the eve of his death, he was to tell them the meaning of that redemption · it was the "blood of the new testament which shall be shed for many [Mark xiv. 24] unto remission of sins". (Matt. xvi. 28.)

At the same time he began to tell them in so many words something which had been outlined earlier (Matt. viii. 22; x 38ff.)—the fact that they must unite themselves to him and his destiny so that, having lost their lives for his sake, they might find them again when he returned in the glory of the Kingdom. (Matt. xvi. 24–8.)

From then on these two themes run side by side in his preaching. The heralding of the imminent coming of the Kingdom remains as important as ever, but now that these things are about to happen, it takes second place to the heralding of his death (Matt. xx. 22ff.)

A third theme, essential to both, serves as a link between them— the Resurrection, closely bound up with the Son of Man's twofold mission to announce the Kingdom and to die for many.

At first we find the Resurrection coupled with Christ's death in the messianic scheme. Only rarely is that death mentioned without it.[13] In the three solemn predictions of the Passion that the Synoptics give us, the Resurrection comes as the crowning point in Christ's life.[14] Our Lord gives a threefold rhythm for his destiny: the Son of Man is rejected by his people and given over to the Gentiles; he is tortured, humbled, killed; he rises on the third day.

The Resurrection is not given as the last act of the Passion simply to brighten the picture by a gleam of light. In our Lord's eyes his resurrection was as much part of his mission as his death; it was involved in his messianic destiny: The Son of Man must die and

[13] Christ's death is announced alone in Luke ix 44; Matt xxvi. 2 In Luke xvii. 25 the Resurrection is implicit, though not stated.
[14] Matt xvi 21; xvii. 22; xx 17ff

rise again. Death was to be one phase in a falling and rising movement "He must...be put to death and the third day rise again"
(Matt. xvi. 21ff.). "It is written that Christ must suffer and rise
again from the dead." (Luke xxiv. 46)

No doubt that recurrent *must* was meant to dispel the scandal of
the Cross; but it also brings together death and resurrection in the
messianic scheme as two realities which are successive in themselves,
but all of a piece in God's plan, two phases in the accomplishment
of one destiny.

There is no redemptive significance to be got from these formulae,
either for Christ's death or for his resurrection, except in so far as
both are fulfilling a plan of God's. We learn from other texts that
Christ's death has a redemptive value; but what of the Resurrection?
Here too the link is hard to perceive The two events follow each
other, but the nature of their relationship remains hidden in the
mystery of God's plan, which unites them.

Our Lord's words to the disciples on the road to Emmaus give a
new twist to the idea they already had· "Ought not Christ to have
suffered these things and so to enter into his glory?" (Luke xxiv. 26.)
The Resurrection is not merely a return to life, but a glorification.
Death and resurrection are no longer merely things existing side by
side, but essentially linked together. His entry into glory fulfilled
the demands of prophecy, but in a different sense from his death.
The disciples already believed that the Scriptures foretold Christ's
glory; our Lord had to show them that it was necessary for him
first to die, that the glorification of the Messiah must come as the
climax of a passion. The Vulgate renders the original text with
complete faithfulness: "Ought not Christ to suffer thus *in order to*
enter into his glory?" Death was the preliminary condition, the
glory the ultimate object.

Our Lord had previously said that he would give his life as a
ransom for many; here he was showing this giving as directed
towards his glory. We may believe that in his mind the entry into
glory had redemptive repercussions since it came as the final point
of a passion which was to be a ransom for men. But such a conclusion, which is suggested by placing the two texts side by side,
goes beyond the soteriology of the Synoptics. It was not until
St. Paul's theological reflection was applied to the facts that the
relationship between Christ's resurrection and death came to be seen
in its true place in the Redemption. Here the line of thought is

simpler and fits in with the pattern the Synoptics saw · the entry into glory constitutes the inauguration of God's kingdom The two disciples have placed all their hopes in the prophet of Nazareth. (Luke xxiv. 21.) Far from disappointing their expectations, his death has fulfilled them, by introducing Christ into the true glory of the Messiah.

Thus with the Synoptics, our Lord's resurrection fits into the scheme of the Kingdom, as does his death. It inaugurates the Kingdom, while his death is a necessary preamble to it.

The life of the risen Christ, as described in the closing chapters of the three gospels, develops along the lines we expect · the Resurrection realizes Christ's coming as Messiah. Henceforth he possesses all the power that is needed to establish the Kingdom. He gives the Apostles the mission of winning all nations to him through preaching and baptizing: "All power is given to me in heaven and in earth. Going therefore, teach ye all nations." (Matt. xxviii. 18ff.; Mark xvi. 15ff.)

St. Luke, at the end of his gospel—of which Acts i. 3–8 is a continuation—sees the Resurrection as the end of Christ's life on earth and the beginning of the history of the Church. As far as written statements went, Christian life was already bound up with the story of the Resurrection (Luke xxiv. 46–9; Acts i. 3–8). During the forty days before the Ascension, Christ spoke of the Kingdom of God (Acts i. 3); he promised to send "the promise of the Father" (Luke xxiv. 49; Acts i. 4) upon the Apostles, that promise given long ago, the Spirit whose outpouring, so the Prophets tell us, was to characterize the time of the Messiah. He then enjoined his disciples to teach all nations. He did not tie them to any one existing kingdom; his kingdom was, as it were, beginning from scratch, and though its teaching started in Jerusalem, the centre of the Chosen People of old, not only pagans, but Jews too, must be converted before they could enter it. (Luke xxiv. 47.)

Thus the Resurrection unites the two streams of doctrine that flow from Christ's mission; it belongs to both the theme of the Kingdom, and the theme of the necessary death. The explanation of Christ's death is to be found in the ransom it provides and also in the Resurrection, to which it is the prelude. It is the Resurrection which brings the Kingdom of God into the world. Our Lord's death, his glorification and the coming of the Kingdom, are linked together. But it might be better to speak of the Resurrection as

following necessarily upon Christ's death rather than as bound up
with it, for the link between them remains unexplained and the
character of that death does not seem to take any development as
redemptive from the happening of the Resurrection. It is easier to
understand the relationship between the Kingdom and the Resurrection; the fact that the latter is an "entry into glory" suggests
the coming of a king; Christ says that he now has "all power", and
shows that he can now fulfil the messianic promise of the Father.
But even here the theological elements do not fit together to form
a system; the sending of the Holy Ghost, the fullness of power, the
sending of the Apostles and their baptizing in the name of that
power—all these are loosely grouped round the Resurrection, but
have no essential link with each other.

If we consider the conclusions of these three gospels, the primitive
teaching is something like this: Christ has died and risen again
according to the Scriptures, the Messianic age has come. The idea
of a redemptive death is touched upon, and the remission of sins
in Christ's name is promised to those who do penance. (Luke xxiv.
47.) But the Kingdom and Resurrection theme takes first place.

3. The Earliest Teaching

Two historical sources have preserved for us in their original
form the thought of the Apostles about Christ's resurrection:
the First Epistle to the Corinthians (xv. 3–5), and the Acts. (ii. 22–
36; iii. 12–26; iv. 10–12; x. 34–43.)

Of the two, the text from St. Paul was the earlier to be made
public. "For I delivered unto you first of all, which I also received:
how that Christ died for our sins according to the Scriptures: And
that he was buried, and that he rose again the third day according
to the Scriptures: And that he was seen by Cephas; and after that
by the eleven." This formula represents an earlier tradition which
Paul had himself received, and which must therefore date from
before his conversion. It sees an expiatory value in Christ's death,
but merely states the Resurrection as a fact, though its importance
is indicated by giving witnesses to prove it. Must we conclude from
this that the early teaching did no more than state the fact? The
Resurrection could not have been coupled with Christ's death as
the root of all teaching ("I delivered unto you first of all...") had
it not been extremely significant.

We cannot take the silence of this particular text to mean that no appraisal was made of the value of the Resurrection. There could be one very simple explanation of why St. Paul chose to pass it over at that time doctrinal understanding of the resurrection of Jesus was not yet complete enough to be expressed in as succinct a formula as was used to sum up the purpose and meaning of his death, which was so much less complex and easier to state.[13]

In the Acts of the Apostles, St. Luke records a series of discourses given by St. Peter to the Jews shortly after the Resurrection, and one given some time later to pagans.

From a literary point of view, and in their basic thought, these texts are related to Luke's account of the instructions given by Christ to the Apostles during his forty days of glory on earth.

In the first discourse, among his brethren, St. Peter is concerned with fixing upon a substitute for Judas who must at the same time be an irrefutable witness of Christ's resurrection He lists the conditions which the candidate must fulfil to "be made with us a witness of his resurrection" (i. 22), it is therefore a paschal message that the Apostles are preaching.[14]

At Pentecost, St. Peter established the Christian *kerygma* with a proclamation of the resurrection of Jesus of Nazareth, and this was to remain the focal point of his teaching All the Jews knew, at least by hearsay, the story of the prophet; they knew he had died on the Cross; what the Apostle had to do was assure them of the Resurrection. (ii. 24–32; iii 15.) In this first statement, the expiatory value of the death of Jesus does not appear; the Apostle is simply concerned to dispel the scandal of the Cross; he recalls God's plan (ii. 23; iii 18), which certainly suggests a mystery.

The Resurrection itself is immensely rich in both personal significance for our Lord and messianic impact. It is primarily a glorification of the crucified Jesus. "The God of our fathers hath glorified his servant Jesus, whom you indeed delivered up". (iii. 13.) All the prophecies concerning the time of the Messiah come together and are fulfilled in it. Jesus of Nazareth is the Messiah; his resurrection is proof of the fact, and is the opening of the "last days" (ii. 17): "Let all the house of Israel know most certainly, that God hath

[13] In the Epistle to the Romans, theological thought about our Lord's death and resurrection had become clear enough to be explained in a single perfectly balanced formula. (iv 25)
[14] Cf J Schmitt, *Jésus ressuscité dans la prédication apostolique*, Paris, 1949

made both Lord, and Christ, this same Jesus whom you have crucified." (ii. 36.) "This is the stone which was rejected by you the
builders, which is become the head of the corner." (iv. 11.)

After the curing of the cripple at the Beautiful Gate, St. Peter
enlarges on this theme: the time spoken of by Moses, and all the
Prophets from Samuel on, has come, and God has sent his servant
Jesus to the sons of Abraham, bringing all the blessings promised
to their ancestor. (iii. 22–6.) The time of perfection has of course
not yet come, the time "of refreshment", "of the restitution of all
things"; but this final plenitude, when Christ must return to the
world, is assured to the Israelites by his present glory, for henceforth
Christ is their Messiah and is promised to them.

The special mark of the risen Christ, which shows him to be
the Messiah, is his power to dispose of the riches of the Holy Spirit.
(ii. 33.) The pouring out of the Spirit is the sign that "the last
times" are come (ii. 16ff.), and contains all the blessings of the
promise; the Spirit is the substance of the promise. (i. 4–8; ii. 33.)

Christ's use of his power is not in accord with the current
messianic ideas. The era starting with the Resurrection is marked
by a new relationship between God and his people And from now
on it is Christ who is to form the intersection of this relationship;
so much so that all Israel's communication lines with God, and
their only road to salvation, must pass through him. "This is the
stone which was rejected by you the builders, which is become the
head of the corner. Neither is there salvation in any other. For there
is no other name under heaven given to men whereby we must be
saved." (iv. 11–12.)

Salvation is primarily defined in the negative, as the remission of
sins: "Him hath God exalted with his right hand . . . to give repentance to Israel and remission of sins." (v. 31.) The risen Christ
brings Israel the blessing promised to Abraham in the guise of the
grace of conversion and absolution. (iii. 25–6.) To the forgiveness
of sins in his name (ii. 38; x. 43), our Lord adds the charismatic
gift of the Spirit. (ii. 33, 38.)

On the threshold of the Apostles' teaching, the glorification of
Christ appears as an essential, as the key mystery which opens the
messianic era. It is the starting-point for the salvation of mankind;
not that salvation comes in the very power and glory whereby God
raises Christ and in him the whole world—this was a Pauline idea
not present in these beginnings of theology; but rather, that this

power opens up the messianic era and puts salvation at the door of whoever will call on the name of this Jesus "that God hath made both Lord, and Christ". (11. 36.) The idea of his death as an expiation is perhaps beginning to take shape when the Apostle proclaims that God's forgiveness is granted in the name of Jesus, but it is not stated. The principle of our salvation is Christ glorified at God's right hand after his death at the hands of the Jews

4. The Theology of the Fourth Gospel

The Gospel of St. John[17] is a story lived during the youth of the Evangelist, but seen in the light of some fifty years of Christian life and contemplation—contemplation of Christ's divinity, and a religious experience lived chiefly in the liturgy of the sacraments.

With him the work of salvation is not seen in the framework of the Kingdom of God, as it is with the Synoptics. He does not leave out this aspect; there is a slight movement towards it in the early chapters (i. 49; iii. 3, 5), but the Kingdom it envisages is rather abstract in nature compared with the concrete ideas of the Synoptics: it is the Kingdom of Truth. (xviii. 37.) Salvation is enlightenment. It is the work of the Word who is the Light. To us, it is knowledge, of Christ and of God in Christ. (xvii. 3.) But it is not the knowledge got from a simple handing on of ideas; it results from the light taking possession of a man (1 John v. 20), for the light is life in the Word, and salvation is a sharing in that life. To have it, man must lay himself open by the voluntary act of faith which places his entire person in the light. Infidelity, resistance to the light, is the great sin whereby man remains in the darkness of death.

The incarnation of the Word is the central mystery of our salvation; through it the life-light has penetrated mankind in the person of Christ, and whoever cleaves to Christ by believing in his words has passed from darkness to light, from death to life. "He that believeth in the Son hath life everlasting." (111. 36; vi. 40.) The

---

[17] It is quite proper to place St John's teaching here, before that of St Paul A longer theological incubation preceded the writing of the last Gospel than took place in the Apostle of the Gentiles; its thought grew to maturity, nourished by a long experience of Christian life, whereas Paul's epistles are giving witness to a theology still in process of development. In spite of this "the Gospel of the Spirit" takes us back further, because of the exact historical memories in which the theology was born

Redemption is already complete in the Incarnation; up till its final consummation in the resurrection of the dead, salvation is effected by the Incarnation and by faith.

This soteriology is in the strongest contrast to the Pauline conception of redemption through a death of expiation; indeed it seems almost in flat contradiction to it if, as some would wish,[18] the whole of the Evangelist's thought could be enclosed in the somewhat simplified scheme I have just outlined. But we also find St. John, who at first appears to disagree with St. Paul, seeming to contradict himself, by declaring most emphatically the necessity of Christ's death for the salvation of men (despite the fact that in this so-called Johannine system, the Incarnation by itself is sufficient principle of redemption). "It is expedient for you that one man should die for the people... And this he spoke not of himself: but being the high priest of that year, he prophesied that Jesus should die for the nation. And not only for the nation, but to gather together in one the children of God, that were dispersed." (xi 50–2.) The First Epistle of St. John returns to this idea and puts it in a theological form (iv. 10.)

It is not hard to find other things in St John that are incompatible with the idea of a redemption merely through the Incarnation and faith—for instance, the part played by Christ's flesh (vi. 52), the expectation of a coming glorification (xvii. 1), the highly developed sacramentalism throughout the fourth gospel, the importance of the Holy Spirit's role (iii 5ff.), the fact that Christ had to go before the Holy Spirit could be sent. (xvi. 7.)

1. THE BODILY HUMANITY

It has often been pointed out that this is at once the most speculative and the most concrete of all the gospels; the things that have happened form a historical reality with a body and soul and a doctrine, and John sees himself as their true witness; Christ is presented in a spirituality quite beyond our reach (viii. 58), yet he is most palpably physical. (iv. 6; xx. 27.)

This dualism governs the whole of the Johannine theology of salvation. From the start it stresses the vital part played by the bodily humanity of the incarnate Word. The Word was made flesh

[18] For instance, R Bultmann, *Das Evangelium des Johannes*, Göttingen, 1941

so that the life-light could come to us through that flesh and be given to us by it. John tells us that the Word was made "flesh" because, as a Semite, he conceived man as an essentially corporeal being to be identified by his "bodiliness". The life which was in the bosom of the Father is made manifest to us in a Christ whom "our hands have handled" (1 John i. 1ff.), and it is the Word himself we are touching in his flesh. St. John is both the most heavenly and the most earthly of the Evangelists. No-one has shown better how sublime are the sources of our salvation—in the bosom of the Father from which the Word has come; and no-one brings so close to us the way in which the life of the Word is given for mankind—in that part of Christ which is lowest and nearest to the earth, his flesh. (vi.) That is why he found the Docetist doctrine so intolerable (1 John iv. 2ff.)

It is significant that while Mark opens his account of our Lord's preaching with the announcing of the Kingdom (i. 14ff.), and Luke, the Evangelist of the Spirit, starts with Isaiah's promise of the Spirit that is to come and with Christ's declaration that this is now being fulfilled (iv. 18ff.), John places at the very beginning of Christ's public life a statement about his body, the temple of the new era (ii. 19, 21). This somatic theology reaches its climax in Chapter VI. Here the importance given to the flesh is so great that the statements indicating the absolute necessity for contact with the physical Christ can be placed level with those which demand that the light of the Word be accepted by faith (cf. vi. 54 and iii. 36; vi. 40). The story of our Lord's life on earth concludes with the emphatic statement that John himself had witnessed water flowing from Christ's body as well as the blood of the Passion—a significant point coming at the end of a gospel which had so often talked of water bringing salvation. (iii. 5; iv. 10ff.; vii. 38; ix. 7.)

Indeed, we can say that the body of Christ, together with the Word, forms the centre round which the whole account revolves. This will seem no exaggeration to anyone who studies the nature of worship as seen in the fourth gospel,[19] for the place and source of Christian worship is none other than this body, the temple of the new People of God.

[19] The liturgical and sacramental nature of the fourth gospel is brought out very well by O. Cullmann's *Early Christian Worship*, London, 1953, pp. 37–116. E Stauffer, in *Die Theologie des N T.*, Stuttgart, 1941, speaks of John as "the liturgist of the Apostles" (p 181.)

The mystery of the Incarnation has set up God's true tabernacle among men: "The Word was made flesh, and dwelt [set up his tabernacle] amongst us, and we saw his glory." (i. 14.) Christ's flesh is God's tent set up among us with the Word dwelling in it, and in it we have seen the *doxa*, the light-giving glory of God's presence. The gospel opens with this vision and remains lit up by it throughout.

When Nathaniel, astounded by our Lord's knowledge of him, cried, "Rabbi, thou art the Son of God, the King of Israel!" Christ answered, "Greater things than this shalt thou see .. Amen, amen, I say to you, you shall see the heaven opened, and the angels of God ascending and descending upon the Son of man." (i. 50-51.) The allusion to Jacob's ladder is obvious. The patriarch had cried upon waking, "Indeed, the Lord is in this place, and I knew it not .. How terrible is this place! this is no other but the house of God and the gate of heaven." (Gen. xxviii. 16-17.) The disciples will see heaven opened above the Son of Man and the angels ascending and descending between him and heaven; it goes without saying that this is a terrible place, the house of God and gate of heaven.

Christ began his public life by reaffirming the dignity of the Temple; he declared that the temple of his body was to succeed the temple made of stone (ii. 19-21.) Unlike those of the Synoptics, this gospel goes on to develop almost entirely within Judea, in the area made sacred by the Temple [20]

The body of Christ bears a ritual character which marks it out as destined for sacrifice. John the Baptist pointed to Christ, saying, "Behold the Lamb of God." (i. 29, 36.) One wonders whether this was because our Lord was the servant of God given as a victim for our sins, or rather an allusion to the lamb of sacrifice, the paschal lamb in particular. John's words do not really tell us. But the Evangelist who is recounting them has his own clear ideas on the subject in his account of Christ's death he makes a point of recalling the sacrifice of the paschal lamb. (xix 36.)

The sacramentalism so characteristic of the fourth gospel is enshrined in the theology of the body and the whole framework of worship. This has been pointed out before: "Saint John is a deeply spiritual man. God is spirit, and those who adore him must adore

---

[20] When Christ did preach in Galilee, it was only because of the opposition of the Jews in Judea (iv. 1-3; vii. 1); but Judea was Christ's natural sphere of action in the fourth gospel

him in spirit and in truth, but he is also a great sacramentalist "[21]
We are born of God by faith in the Word (i 12), we are born of
light (xii 36), we live by faith (iii. 15; vi 47); yet we are also given
light by bathing in water (ix. 5, 7), we live by bread that comes
down from heaven (vi. 50–52), we are born of water and the Holy
Ghost (iii. 5) symbolized by water drawn from Christ (vii. 37ff.).
That these means used for our salvation are so material strengthens
the gospel's theme of redemption through the body, which runs
parallel with the theme of the life-giving light, and salvation through
knowledge And, too, these sacraments are very closely linked with
Christ's body: in the Eucharist it is Christ's body itself that we are
given, and in baptism we are acted upon by the Holy Ghost (iii. 5)
who flows out of that body. (vii. 38–9.)

ii. THE PASSAGE THEME

This somatic theology all tends towards the mystery of Easter:
there is a paschal theme running alongside the theme of the Incarnation, its path often hard to trace, moving by symbols and fugitive
allusions with the intuitive thought of St. John, whose richness is
to be felt rather than analysed.

Knowing the subtle genius of this Apostle, we can hardly think
it coincidence that his gospel should unfold against the backcloth
of the Exodus,[22] that exemplar of the paschal mystery. The Word
"has set up his tabernacle amongst us" (i. 14) just as God encamped
among the Jews; Christ must be lifted up like the serpent (iii. 14);
he has come down from heaven like manna, and will become our
food (vi. 48ff.); his followers will be refreshed by him as by the
rock in the desert (vii. 37); they will follow him as the Israelites
followed the pillar of fire (viii. 12).[23] Christ is the paschal Lamb.
(xix. 36)

If this mention of the Exodus is to remind us of a very definite
plan, then clearly St. John saw the paschal mystery of the

---

[21] J Huby, *L'Évangile et les évangiles*, 2nd ed , Paris, 1940, p 236.
[22] Cf. J Daniélou, "Bulletin d'histoire de la théologie sacrementaire",
Rech Sc Rel., 34 (1947), 370, *Sacramentum Futuri*, Paris, 1950, p. 139.
[23] The image suggests this recollection; Christ is the light of mankind in
the same way as the pillar of fire was, rather than as the sun is; we do not
follow the sun. A number of commentators connect this statement of our
Lord's with the liturgy for the Feast of the Tabernacles, which would relate
it even more closely with the Exodus.

Exodus as being repeated and perfected in the Word made flesh. He signposts his account by indicating the paschs that occurred during our Lord's public life (ii. 13, 23; vi. 4; xi. 55, xii. 1; xiii. 1). He does this so often that it imparts to the story a definite sense of direction.[24]

All the allusions to the Mosaic Pasch converge upon the consummation of Christ's life on earth. The idea of the tabernacle, suggested in the prologue (i. 14), is carried further in ii. 19 to become a prophecy of Christ's death and resurrection; the brazen serpent brings the idea of Christ's being lifted up (iii. 14) and thus of the Cross; manna is none other than his flesh offered for us (vi 50-2), and only after he is glorified will Christ become the rock at which the faithful are to be refreshed (vii 39). The mention of each of the first two paschs is followed by a veiled announcement of the coming death and glorification (ii. 19, vi. 51, 62); the third is spoken of just before the account of the end of Christ's life (xii. 1, 7, xiii. 1); but in his death the lamb is immolated, the Pasch is complete. (xix. 36.)

In the day of Christ's life this is the sublime hour, his hour *par excellence*, the moment of a leavetaking, of a journey and a return, and thus of an exodus. Long before his death, he spoke of it as the major thing he was to do The Evangelist purposely connects this hour and this journey with his allusions to the Pasch, when he writes, "Before the festival day of the pasch, Jesus knowing that his hour was come, that he should pass out of this world to the Father . . ." (xiii. 1.) The Bible tells us (Exod. xii. 11) that the word "pasch" means "the passage of the Lord".[25] At last the true pasch, Christ's pasch, his passage and his hour, has come. Whereas the Synoptics point out the paschal nature of the Last Supper, and note its taking place on the evening when the lamb was eaten, the fourth gospel passes over it in silence, and fixes Christ's death at the hour when the lambs were slain, going on to indicate that Christ was the paschal Lamb. (xix. 36.)

The theme of a passing and a transformation runs, often almost imperceptibly, all through the sayings and miracles of our Lord. It is one of the constants in this very variegated gospel. To enter

[24] Preisker (*Th. W N T*, vol. ii, p 331), sees in this repeated reference "an eschatological intention", "an allusion to the paschal lamb"
[25] The word was taken in different senses Josephus understood it as the passage of the angel over the children of the Jews (*Jewish Ant*, ii, xiv 6); Philo understood it as the passing through the Red Sea (*De Spec leg.*, ii, 145)

the Kingdom, one must pass from the order of the flesh to that of the spirit. (iii. 5.) The Temple will be destroyed and rebuilt (ii. 19), and in future people are not to adore in Jerusalem but in spirit and in truth. (iv. 21–3.) On the seventh day (carefully reckoned by the Evangelist—i. 19, 29, 35, 43; ii. 1) from the point at which the gospel starts, our Lord arrives at Cana after a hard and hurried walk. This was for a special reason. The seventh day is a day of accomplishment, according to the mystical scheme of numbers which John knew so well: the fullness of reality was to begin. Christ, bridegroom of the Church (iii. 29; Apoc. xix. 7; xxi. 9; xxii. 17), makes his appearance amid the festivities of a wedding, already with his first disciples, and accompanied by his mother who, in John's mind, summed up the whole Church in her person. (Apoc. xii.; John xix. 26ff.) It was a tremendous moment for our Lord, and brought to his mind that great and unique hour yet to come.[26] But that hour was still in the future: "Woman, my hour is not yet come"—it is only prefigured, in this earthly marriage and the miracle he was going to perform. At the level of the sign, our Lord did what his mother wished; at the level of the reality, he must wait for the Hour to come. That was when the real transformation would take place.[27]

This was the first sign worked by our Lord, the bright dawn of his messianic glory. (ii. 11.) The symbolism of this first miracle and its definite pascal bearing must guide us in our interpretation of the

[26] It was part of Christ's psychology to associate ideas, to move from an earthly to a heavenly reality All things and events were naturally evocative to his profoundly intuitive mind More than once his hour suddenly came before him as if he had turned a corner that brought him face to face with it with a sort of almost physical directness which at once disturbed and exalted him. (ii. 19; xii. 20–32; xiii. 30ff.) When this happened what he said was not intended to be immediately understood, for his thought moved quicker than his listeners could follow.
There can be no doubt that in this case he spoke of his great hour, and not of the miracle he would perform: the Johannine phraseology can have no other sense.

[27] Maximus of Turin, *Hom. XXIII, De Epiphania Domini*, vii, P L., lvii, 275· "He was undoubtedly promising the glorious hour of his passion, that wine of our redemption, which was to bring life to all." J Jeremias, *Jesus als Welt-vollender*, Gutersloh, 1930, p 29· In the symbolism of the Bible "the miracle of Cana is the first manifestation of Christ's sovereignty as renovator of the world" "A new reality was to succeed the old economy." P Benoit, *Bulletin R.B.*, 56 (1949), 153ff Cf F M Braun, *La Mère des fidèles*, Paris, 1953, p. 69.

later passages, which are equally simple and spontaneous in style,
but filled by the Evangelist with inner meaning.[28]

The Evangelist gives us the key to his mind in the number seven
which governs the arrangement of the whole book.

The miracle of Cana, where six pots of water were changed into
wine, was the first of a series of six.[29] What, then, is the seventh?
For, by the symbolism of numbers, six is an incomplete number,
indicating an imperfect reality. The seventh is the one that matters.
The six miracles are to be seen in the light of a seventh of which
they are merely the earthly signs. While several miracles took place
on a seventh day (Cana), at the seventh hour (iv. 52), or on the sabbath day (v. 10; ix. 14), Christ's solemn work was accomplished in
the setting of a solemn seventh day, the "great sabbath day".
(xix. 31.)

Alongside the signs, other landmarks stand along the way and
indicate its direction: the liturgical feasts. There are six of them.[30]
But the seventh is the one that matters: the true paschal feast with
Christ as the lamb. (xix. 36.)[31]

These allusions may appear tenuous, but not if one realises that
St. John is to be read very differently from the Synoptics, and that
we can expect to find some treasure underlying every text we
examine.[32]

---

[28] C H. Dodd, "Le Kérygme apostolique dans le quatrième évangile",
R.H.P R, vol. xxxi (1951), p 272. "In every episode described by John, the
idea of Christ's death, resurrection and exaltation, is associated with all the
events that combine to make up the whole mystery."

[29] The fourth gospel records six miracles: (1) The water changed into wine
(2) The cure of the ruler's son (3) The cure of the paralytic. (4) The multiplication of the loaves. (5) The cure of the man born blind (6) The raising of
Lazarus. Some authors also include Christ's walking on the water But this
was not a work whose effect passed outside himself, and is not, like the
others, called a "sign" or a "work"; it forms part of the episode of the multiplication of the loaves, and cannot really be counted with the other six
miracles

[30] The Pasch (ii. 13), a festival day (v 1); the Pasch (vi. 4); the Feast of the
Tabernacles (vii 2); the Feast of the Dedication (x 22), the Pasch (xi. 55)

[31] It is possible that xix. 14 has some symbolical bearing, suggesting that
on the plane of the Old Testament feasts we are not to go beyond the sixth
hour, nor the sixth day—the parasceve, in other words, the preparation

[32] St. Ambrose, *De Sacramentis*, iii, 11, *P L*, xvi, 435: "Everything said is
a mystery " J Lebreton, *Histoire du dogme de la Trinité*, Paris, 1919, i, p 446:
"Unless we maintain the union of the two elements, fact and mystery, history
and doctrine, we shall find nothing but contradictions in St John's gospel "
Cf O Cullmann, *Early Christian Worship*, p. 56.

iii. EXPLICIT TEXTS

Leaving aside the chiaroscuro of allusion and symbolic suggestion, St. John presents a series of texts stating quite clearly the importance of Christ's death and resurrection.

The Holy Ghost plays a major part in the work of our salvation which does not fit in with a simplified doctrine of the Incarnation as sole cause of our salvation, but is closely linked with our Lord's death and resurrection. Christ declares to Nicodemus that no-one who is not born again of water and the Holy Ghost can enter the Kingdom of God. (iii. 5.) Then, at the Feast of the Tabernacles, our Lord promises that water will flow from his belly, a water which is the Spirit, and that the Spirit will not be given till he himself has been glorified. (vii. 37–9.) He later promises that the Spirit will be sent after his exaltation. (xvi. 7.)

In the parable of the good shepherd, it seems at first as though salvation is effected by his coming to earth. Our Lord and his sheep know one another in a knowledge which is a mutual possession and sharing of life. (x. 14ff.) But it soon becomes clear that Christ will not achieve the purpose of his coming to earth till he has died and risen again. The sheep outside his fold will only hear the shepherd calling them after that. This death and this resurrection are not something being done simply for the purpose of bringing the sheep outside Israel into the true fold; they are the high point of Christ's whole work: "Therefore doth the Father love me, because I lay down my life that I may take it again ... This commandment have I received of my Father." (x. 17–18.) This is one of the most mysterious of all texts: it states positively that the Father loves the Son *because* he is giving up his life for mankind! But it is perfectly clear on the other point: his death and resurrection are the first of our Lord's duties as Messiah.

When the first Gentiles seek to come to the true shepherd, our Lord declares that the grain of wheat must die if it is to bring forth fruit, and not remain alone. (xii. 20–5)

Thus, rather than a soteriology based on the Incarnation alone, we find a richly woven paschal theme developing.

IV. CONCLUSIONS

At first sight, there seems a marked opposition between the intellectualism of salvation by knowledge, and the concrete realism of

salvation by Christ's physical humanity. But in fact the paschal
theme is basically very closely related to the theme of the Incarnation. The body of the risen Christ is the Temple, but this is due to
the fact that, by the Incarnation, the Word has set up his tabernacle
amongst us. His flesh is our food, but this is because it is the manna
come down from heaven. (vi. 49ff.)

Not only at its base, but also at its summit, the theme of the
Incarnation links up with the theme of Easter. The Incarnate Word
cannot fully make use of all his powers until his complete fulfilment
at some future time. While the prologue describes the Incarnation
as God's glory coming down upon mankind for our salvation (i. 14),
we hear our Lord asking the Father to give him back a glory he
had given up during his time on earth. (xvii. 1, 5.) During this time,
he has had lesser glorifications (ii. 11; xi. 4), lightning-flashes of
his glory as Son. But he is waiting for another glorification, in
essence like the first, so new and so magnificent that it will seem
to be the first true manifestation of the eternal glory of the Word,
in comparison with which the earthly phase of the Incarnation must
seem a humiliation. (xvii. 5.) This manifestation of glory is the great
glorification before which "Jesus was not yet glorified." (vii. 39;
xii. 16.)

From the statements which go to make up the so-called Johannine
theme, we may deduce that this ultimate glorification will be the
crowning point of the effectiveness of the Incarnation to redeem
us, for it appears that we only receive the knowledge of faith
whereby we are saved because of the manifestation of Christ's glory:
"So must the Son of Man be lifted up, that whosoever believeth in
him . . . may have life everlasting." (iii. 14ff.; cf. ii. 11; xi. 15.) The
texts which give the impression that the Redemption is fulfilled by
Christ's coming into the world, must be taken as anticipations resulting from Christ's realization that he possessed all the powers necessary for salvation, and perhaps also from the writer's himself
anticipating the moment of glory.[33]

In his sacerdotal prayer, our Lord asks the Father to complete the
Son's work of salvation by glorifying him: "Father, the hour is

[33] There are quite a number of anticipations of the time of glory: xiii. 31,
cf. xiii. 32; xvii. 4; xvii 10ff ; cf xvii. 13; xvii 18; cf. xx. 21; in xvii. 22, Christ
has already passed on his glory to those who believe in the Apostles' preaching; in xvii 24, he is thinking of himself as already seated at the right hand
of God

come, glorify thy Son, that thy Son may glorify thee. As thou hast given him power over all flesh, that he may give eternal life to all whom thou hast given him." (xvii. 1–2.) His prayer looks beyond his own exaltation to the fulfilment of his mission. He offers two reasons for what he asks. First, his Father will be glorified by it. And then he represents to his Father that he must be glorified if he is to exercise his power of giving life to all things. (xvii. 2.) This second reason might be expressed thus: Glorify your son . . . for you have given to him the task and the power of giving life to men, and he can neither perform the task nor make use of the power unless he be glorified. "The full exercise of [Messianic] power is dependent upon Christ's entering into the glory of heaven."[34]

From the next verse (3) onwards we are introduced to the theology of the Redemption on which the fourth gospel is based: The eternal life which Christ in his glory confers upon us is a light; it is the knowledge of the Father and of Christ whom he has sent. The life-light, which came into the world at the moment of the Incarnation, will be diffused in all its fullness over mankind once Christ has passed through his earthly phase and entered into the glory of the Father.

This prayer could hardly express more strongly the salvific nature of the Resurrection. It also shows how the paschal theme in the fourth gospel fits in with its basic conception of salvation as coming through the Incarnation.

What *exactly* does the paschal mystery add to the effectiveness of the Incarnation? This is a question still to be answered. But it is quite clear that Christ's death and resurrection have their place in the soteriology of the fourth gospel.

5. THE THEOLOGY OF ST. PAUL

St. Paul, more than anyone, is the Apostle of the risen Lord; he is supremely the "witness of the Resurrection". He has seen and heard Christ in his heavenly glory, and has seen and heard him only thus. The Christ whom he met transcended the limitations of history; by his resurrection he was established in glory, and this was how the Apostle knew him in that first, blinding experience of salvation. Consequently, his preaching was to be concerned less with recounting the words and deeds of Christ as handed down by tradition,

[34] J Huby, *Le discours de Jésus après la Cène*, Paris, 1932, p 128

than with trying to express his own realization of the risen Christ as the source of redemption. His gospel is primarily this one fact, the resurrection of Christ from the dead; he sees Christ as a source of life, but it is the risen Christ that he sees

1. THE RESURRECTION AS ITS FUNDAMENTAL PRINCIPLE

Whereas with St. John, the Incarnation is always at least in the background of his thought, it almost seems as though to St. Paul the risen Christ is a complete beginning, the first breaking through of the divine into the world of sin.

The principle of salvation is essentially the same for both men. the Son of God, Jesus Christ; but for Paul far more than John this principle is incomplete without the Resurrection. In the discourse he gave at Antioch in Pisidia which the Acts (xiii. 16–41) outlines for us, the coming of the Son of God into the world and the first moment of salvation coincide with the Resurrection: "And we declare unto you, that the promise which was made to our fathers, this same God hath fulfilled to our children, resurrecting Jesus,[35] as in the second psalm also is written: 'Thou art my Son, this day have I begotten thee.' " (xiii. 32–3.) The Father begets Jesus to life as his Son in the Resurrection, and thereby fulfils the messianic promises.

In another discourse later on, St. Paul reiterates that this is where the road to salvation starts. (xxvi. 23)

What is particularly surprising is not so much this statement that salvation begins with the Resurrection, but the other, more fundamental, idea of a Christ whose existence as the Son of God only opens with the Resurrection The Apostle never takes back what he has said—indeed, he says it again in Rom. 1. 4: He "was established Son of God in power, according to the spirit of sanctification, by the resurrection from the dead".[36] These statements are, of course,

---

[35] It would seem as though one cannot, as some renderings do, translate this as "raising Jesus". The translation I give is upheld by very convincing evidence Cf J Dupont, "Filius Meus es Tu", *Rech. Sc. Rel*, xxxv (1948), 529–34

[36] The Greek text may be taken in two ways: "He was defined, thus declared Son of God"; this sense fits the etymology of the Greek verb and was accepted here by the Fathers. Or it may be translated, "He was established, constituted Son of God", and this is the only sense known to the New Testament (cf. Acts x. 42; xvii 31) and the other literature of the time. It also seems to fit this particular text better, coming as it does after the phrase "who was made to him of the seed of David, according to the flesh"

not to be taken quite so bluntly; the Apostle fully believed in the godhead of Christ on earth, who was Son of God before his glorification (cf. Rom. i. 3, ii. 6). But he certainly saw the Resurrection as a beginning both for Christ and for our salvation; it holds a position in his thought equivalent to the position held by the Incarnation in St. John's.

II. ROM. IV. 25

That the death of Christ also plays a leading part in Paul's soteriology, no-one has ever doubted. We find the importance of the two events balanced in a text which contrasts their two roles in the strictest parallelism: "It is not written only for him, that it was reputed to him unto justice, but also for us, to whom it shall be reputed, if we believe in him that raised up Jesus Christ, our Lord, from the dead, who *was delivered up for* [διά] *our sins and rose again for* [διά] *our justification* " (Rom. iv. 23–5.)

The distinction the Apostle makes between two aspects of the one salvation is curious. And many attempts have been made to dispose of the difficulties it creates and restore the monopoly of the Redemption to Christ's death alone

Some think that the text does not really attribute any real effectiveness to the Resurrection. The rhythmic antithesis so natural to Paul's writing demanded a distinction between the effects of death and those of resurrection to bring the long development (23–5) to its close with a harmonious double cadence.[37] Certainly the Apostle was much given to an antithetical parallelism. But this cast of mind would never have led him into merely verbal rhetoric.

The context attributes to the Resurrection a distinct role, at least where the beginnings of faith are concerned, since the object of that faith is the God who has raised Christ from the dead (24). God had promised Abraham that he would raise up life where all possibility of doing so seemed past, in two sterile old people Abraham believed in God's power and, because of his faith, was justified. Christians also believe in the life-giving power of God made manifest in Christ (16–22). Hence the answer seems simple: "Because

[37] J. Weiss, "Beiträge zur paulinischen Rhetorik", *Theologische Studien*, 1897, p. 9, quoted by J M. Vosté, *Studia Paulina*, Rome, 1928, p. 59. See also O Kuss, *Die Briefe an die Romer, Korinther . . Regensburg*, 1940, p 48

he is risen we believe, and therefore we achieve justification."[38] The
Resurrection is the principle of our justification because of the faith
it elicits; it is a motive of credibility.

This connection between Christ's resurrection and our justification is very tenuous, completely external, and greatly at variance
with the realism of St. Paul's thought. In Abraham's case, the vivifying power of God was not the foundation of his faith, but the
object of it. For Christians, according to St. Paul, Christ's resurrection is not merely a motive of credibility, a miracle that elicits faith;
it is the object of their faith: "If thou . . . believe in thy heart that
God hath raised him up from the dead, thou shalt be saved."
(Rom. x. 9.) And if this faith has power to save us, surely that power
must come from its object.

Considering the effectiveness the parallel phrase attributes to
Christ's death, and since the context does not allow of a restrictive
interpretation, we must admit a direct connection between the
Resurrection and our justification. But since the death of Jesus is
of itself sufficient to expiate sin, some exegetes have fixed upon the
one relationship which in no way robs the death of its monopoly,
the lowest form of causality—exemplar causality. The death of
Christ, they say, is an image of our death to sin, the Resurrection is
the exemplar of our justification.[39] Some see only an exemplar
causality in the opening words, "He was delivered up for our sins";
others destroy the balance of the sentence by letting our Lord's
death bear all the weight of our salvation, while allowing his resurrection no more than the value of an example. That Christ in his
glory is an example is frequently stated by the Apostle. (Rom. vi. 4;
1 Cor. xv. 47-9.) But it is a very arbitrary exegesis that sees no
more than that here. Christ's death makes expiation for sin, declares

[38] Cajetan, *Epistolae Pauli et Aliorum Apostolorum*, Venice, 1531, p. 11a
Cf St. Augustine, *Contra Faustum*, xvi 39; *De Trinitate*, ii, 17 (P.L., xlii,
336, 864) This explanation has dominated modern exegesis for some time.
It was particularly commended by Protestant writers. F Prat, *Theology of
St Paul*, vol. ii, p. 209. Cf. R. Bandas, *The Master-Idea of Saint Paul's Epistles*,
Bruges, 1925, p. 315.
[39] St Augustine, *Sermo*, ccxxxi, 2, *P.L.*, xxxviii, 1105. St. Thomas, *In
Epistolam ad Rom.*, iv, 1, 3, *S.T.*, iii, q. 56, a 2.
This interpretation does not exhaust St. Thomas' thought on the matter,
cf T Tschipke, *Die Menschheit Christi als Heilsorgan der Gottheit*, Frei-
burg-i-B, 1940; F Holtz, "La Valeur sotériologique de la résurrection du
Christ", *Eph Theol Lov*, xxix (1953), 609-45; J Lécuyer, "La Causalité
efficiente des mystères du Christ selon S Thomas", *Doctor Communis* (1953),
91-120.

the text; is it not also fully serious in saying that the Resurrection effects our justification? If we are to be faithful to the parallelism of the statement, we must place our Lord's resurrection beside his death as fully effective for our salvation.

Not, of course, in the Socinian manner. The Apostle never ascribes the whole work of salvation to the Resurrection alone. The glorification is not thought of as a meritorious act. Christ's exaltation is the work of the Father ("he was raised"); it is his reward, for only during life on earth can a man merit. (Phil. ii. 8ff.)

But the Father's act of raising up plays a similar role in our justification to that played by Christ's death in the expiation of our sins. Sin is expiated by that death, but justice is only conferred following on the Resurrection [40]

To this major text we may add another, not at first very striking, but most significant: "The charity of Christ presseth us: judging this, that if one died for all, then all were dead. And Christ died for all; that they also, who live, may not now live for themselves, but unto him who died for them, and rose again." (2 Cor. v. 14-15.) The death and resurrection of Jesus are both working towards our salvation. Each plays a different part in it. If Christ is dead, we who are united to Christ are also dead. This death signifies the end of our life according to the flesh. (16ff.) We now have no right to live for ourselves, for this would be to live according to the flesh. Henceforward we shall live for him—and here the Apostle suddenly brings in a new element, Christ's resurrection—who died and rose again for us.

This new life must be linked with the resurrection of Christ, for the Apostle cannot mention one without the other. Our death stands alongside his death; therefore when our new life is spoken of, his resurrection must be, too. Paul leaves it to us to understand his train of thought: "And if one is raised up for all to a new life, we are all raised to that life." Dead to ourselves in his death, brought to

---

[40] Père de Condren expresses St. Paul's thought in a very good formula, though it is perhaps over-simplified: "... far from completing man's justification by his immolation on the Cross, he did not even begin it; by his death and immolation he only removed the hindrance of our sins which made us unworthy to receive justification, which was the first step towards it: later, being risen from the dead ... , he sanctified us by communicating and sharing his new life with us." (*L'Idée du sacerdoce et du sacrifice de Jésus-Christ*, Paris, 1725, p. 122.)

life by his resurrection, we live from now on for him who, for our salvation, died and rose again.

III. THE DEATH SALVIFIC IN THE RISEN CHRIST

But in order to achieve their effects in us, these two causes are, from the first, bound up with each other and working with a single causality. It is by a single act, by the faith affirmed in baptism (Rom. vi. 3ff.; Col. ii. 12), that man comes to share in our Lord's death and resurrection, and the new life which he receives is the result of coming simultaneously into contact with both death and resurrection. (Rom. vi. 9–11; vii. 4.) Our justification consists in a death to sin through our union with the death of our Saviour, and also in a new life through our union with his resurrection; yet the Father does not first of all hand us over to death and *then* bring us back to life, as in the case of Christ (Rom. iv. 25), but justifies us in the simplicity of a single act (cf. iii. 26, 30; viii. 30); and although the resulting state of justification is related to both death and resurrection, it remains a single reality.

St. Paul does in fact elsewhere attribute our justification to Christ's death (Rom v. 9) as well as to his resurrection. Indeed, there seems a striking change of position: in Rom. iv. 25, justification is the effect peculiar to the Resurrection alone; yet it also appears to be the result of both death *and* resurrection.

But the Pauline theory of justification withstands any charge of incoherence, for our contact with Christ's death, as well as our contact with his resurrection, is effected by our union with Christ-in-glory, and only through this union do we receive the benefit of his death, the remission of sins.

St. Paul, in fact, teaches that although the death has expiated our sins, our justification, which consists in the remission of our sins and the new life, is given to us in the risen Christ. Man dies to sin and rises again to life *in Christ* (death, Col. ii. 11ff.; life, Rom. vi. 11; viii 2; I Cor. xv. 22); God's justice, which is implanted in us by this death and this life, is given us *in Christ*. (2 Cor. v. 21; Gal. ii. 17.) Here only are we redeemed (Rom. iii. 24; I Cor. i. 30; Col. i. 14); here only is our salvation. (2 Tim. ii. 10.) Only in this living environment can the justice of God be communicated and grow. And it is the Christ of glory who is meant whenever this phrase is used to express the mystical reality of man's living union with his Saviour. "The Christ of the formula *in Christo Jesu* is always Christ glorified . . . not the historical [earthly] Christ."[41]

In the Apostle's earliest writings, where the phrase is used to express some relationship with Christ not clearly defined (1 Thess. iii. 8; iv. 1; v. 12, 18; 2 Thess. iii. 4), the Christ indicated is the Lord present to the Church through his resurrection. Later, as the phrase grew in depth to mean some mysterious way in which the believer was present in Christ, it does not seem as though Christ was ever thought of except as in his present state of glory; the union it indicated was above all a sharing in the new life into which Christ was born through his resurrection. Such is certainly the sense of the great majority of these texts: "In Christ all shall be made alive" (1 Cor. xv. 22): "Anyone who is in Christ is a new creature" (2 Cor. v. 17): "The law of the spirit of life in Jesus Christ hath delivered me" (Rom. viii. 2): "He . . . hath raised us up together and hath made us sit together in the heavenly places, in Christ Jesus." (Eph. ii. 6.)

We have no reason to interpret the formula in any other way when a text tells us that "in Christ" we shall find death to the flesh, for that death is really no more than another way of describing the new life. In Col. ii. 11[42] it is in the Lord of Glory that we receive the circumcision of Christ—in other words, the stripping away of the body of the flesh. Similarly with the texts which show the Redemption as brought within our reach in Jesus Christ, "who . . . hath transplanted us into the kingdom of the Son of his love, in whom we have redemption through his blood, the remission of sins". (Col. i. 14.) We possess this redemption in a permanent way (ἔχομεν) in the Son, who is none other than our

---

[41] Sanday, quoted by Prat, *Theology*, vol ii, p. 299. Cf. A Wikenhauser, *Die Christusmystik des. hl. Paulus*,[2] Freiburg-i.-B., 1956, pp. 9, 27, 57; L. Cerfaux, *The Church in the Theology of St. Paul*, London, 1959, p 216; L. Malevez, "L'Église corps du Christ", *Rech Sc. Rel.*, 1944, pp. 34–52.

Père Prat (*loc. cit*) denies the exactitude of the interpretation: "It is not precisely the glorified Christ, but Christ the Saviour, the new Adam, that is indicated in the formula, and he is so from the moment from he inaugurates his redemptive mission—that is to say, from the moment of his Passion Thenceforth, we suffer and die with him, and we rise from the dead and reign with him; we share in his form, his life and his glory."

I do not deny that the Apostle saw mankind as linked in solidarity to the earthly Christ; but this link is not defined by the phrase *in Christo*.

[42] Christ, the "head of all principality and power" (ii, 10), in whom we are circumcised, is, in St Paul's mind, the glorified Christ (cf. below, Chapter IV).

Saviour glorified in the kingdom of light to which the context trans-
plants us; our sins are remitted as we are brought into the life of
Christ in glory.[43] The phrase never seems to incorporate us into
Christ in his mortal life.

However, what this phrase does not say seems to be said in full
in the baptismal texts: "Know you not that all we who are baptized in Christ Jesus are baptized in his death? For we are buried
together with him by baptism into death." (Rom. vi. 3.) "Our
old man is crucified with him" (Rom. vi. 6); we are dead with
Christ. (Col. ii. 20; 2 Tim. ii. 11.) These texts certainly seem to
make us one with the dying Christ—he takes our place, he dies to
save us, so we must surely have our part in his death.

We have of course been given a share in Christ's death. But does
our entry into this death have any reality apart from the risen Christ?
The baptismal texts do not say so. We have no grounds for understanding "baptism in [εἰς] Christ Jesus" in any other than the
natural sense of a consecration to Christ as he is now, filling the
Church with his presence. When the Apostle adds that we "are
baptized in his death" he is not contradicting this first idea, but
simply making it clear that this consecration to the living Christ
involves a sharing in his death. "As many of you as have been
baptised in [εἰς] Christ, have put on Christ" (Gal. iii. 27); this
Christ to whom we are consecrated by baptism is not some Christ
of the past—Christ as he is now must be made to stand out in our
minds; and the Christ we put on is the same as the Christ to whom
baptism consecrates us. In the parallel text (Rom. vi 3ff.), the death
we enter by our entry into Christ now exists only in the Christ of
glory.

Hence the question: *How* do we come to our Saviour's death at

[43] Col ii 13, is ambiguous: "He hath quickened you together with Christ,
forgiving [χαρισάμενος] you all offences" The aorist participle could indicate
simultaneous action (Luke ii 16; Acts xiii 33), or an action preceding that
of the main verb. If the first, then the text is saying that our sins are forgiven
in our participation in the Resurrection

L Malevez ("L'Église corps du Christ", p. 47ff) considers that the meaning
of the phrase in Rom iii 24, is doubtful—". . . justified . . through the
redemption that is in Christ Jesus"—because verse 25 goes on to speak of
Christ's blood But even here, Père Lagrange (*Epître aux Romains*, 2nd ed,
Paris, 1922, p. 75) supports the normal rendering, and with good cause:
"The redemption as historical fact certainly belongs to Christ's mortal life,
but it continues to be at the disposal of those who are justified, the merit of
the redemption is in Christ now glorified"

the very heart of his glory? The question is difficult, but the statement it makes that we do so is no less sure.

We now know what the Apostle meant by saying "He rose again for our justification." Christ in glory is the living principle through which redemptive action existing outside us is applied to us; we have no other form of access to the justice of God.

iv. SALVATION GIVEN IN THE RAISING ACTION OF GOD

St. Paul goes even further. The phrase "in Christ' was used to indicate our risen Saviour as the principle of our justification. In another phrase, equally dear to him, he identifies the act whereby we are justified with the actual act by which Christ is glorified; we are divinely brought to life by the Father's act in resurrecting Christ: "Even when we were dead in sins, he hath quickened us together in Christ .. and hath raised us up *with him*." (Eph. ii. 5–6; Col. ii. 12ff.; iii. 1.) The Father has given us life by raising up Christ, we are included in the one life-giving act which was performed for our Lord.

This brings us to another question. How can all men at all times be taken up in the single act of resurrection which brought Christ back to life at a given date in the past? Again the question is difficult, but the statement is perfectly clear.

At the same moment as justice is given to us in the act by which the Father raises up the Son, our sins are also remitted. The texts I have quoted make this clear: while we were dead through our sins, he brought us to life together with Christ. If the Father's raising action confers justice on us, then that same action must also destroy sin in us. For although it is both the end of our sinful life and our entry into the life of God, falling naturally into two divisions because of its similarity to the death and resurrection of Jesus, our justification is in fact a single, unbroken reality. Grace springs up full grown, as it were, in us by the glorifying action of the Father.

Our Saviour in glory thus forms the living sphere in which our justification is worked out; and the phrase "in Christ" defines the causality of the Resurrection. The phrase "with Christ" specifies that this justification is effected by the same act of the Father by which the Son is glorified. Christ's raising up by his Father gives life to Christ and to us in Christ at the same time.

St. Paul states the redemptive value of the Resurrection in a framework of striking magnificence.

In the past God had allowed sin to reign, in the time of his patience and men's ignorance. But at this moment he has decided to manifest his wish for justice, his will to dispense justice and to give justification, to reprimand sinners and refuse to tolerate sin; he will justify some—all those who accept justice according to his will—and mete out justice to the rest. (Rom. iii. 25ff.)

This plan is put into execution with Christ's resurrection. The action whereby the body of the mortal Christ is transformed in-augurates the Father's action of justification; divine life comes to mortal man; the justice of God, which is a living and life-giving holiness, takes possession of him It is the Father who raises up Christ (Rom. viii. 11; 1 Cor. vi. 14; 2 Cor. iv. 15; xiii. 4; Eph. 1. 19; Col. ii. 12) and who justifies us. (Rom. iii. 26, 30; viii 30, Gal. iii. 8.) It is in Christ, and through the act of raising him up, that he justifies us. The resurrection of our Lord is the first of the Father's life-giving works in a new world, the first and the only one, for all the others are accomplished in it. "He hath quickened us together with Christ." (Eph. ii. 5.)

The Epistle to the Hebrews offers us again, in not very Pauline forms, a line of thought already familiar to us. The frame, as it were, is new, but the picture still shows the master's hand. In describing the role of Christ's glorification, the author attributes to it the same work as does St. Paul, but if anything, rather more forcefully. One commentator says of it "In the theology of this epistle, Christ's entry into glory is the capital act of redemption, death being only the condition, the meritorious cause." [14]

The importance of this glorification is made clear from the very beginning of the epistle. To remove the apparent scandal of the death, the author sets Christ's ignominy in the perspective of his glory: "We see Jesus, who was made a little lower than the angels, for the suffering of death crowned with glory and honour: that, through the grace of God, he might taste death for all." (ii. 9) The

---

[14] J Bonsirven, *L'Epître aux Hébreux*, 5th ed , Paris, 1943, p 211 *n*.

phrase "crowned with glory and honour" comes as the summit of the Greek sentence; the death comes before the glory and tends towards it; and the effects of that death flow down from the summit upon us. Christ's death was directed towards his glorification, and because he has been crowned with glory, the value of that death returns to us. In other words, "The death only became a source of salvation and of life because it was followed by the resurrection."[45]

6. THE THEOLOGY OF ST. PETER

St. Peter's sermons in Jerusalem (Acts) made the Cross a thing of the past, and simply offered the risen Christ as the principle of salvation. In his first epistle, he restores our Lord's death to its proper place (i 18ff., iii. 18), but without making the Resurrection any less important.

The epistle opens on this note of praise "Blessed be the God and Father of our Lord Jesus Christ, who according to his great mercy hath regenerated us unto a lively hope, by the resurrection of Jesus Christ from the dead, up to an inheritance incorruptible." (1. 3-4.)

The Father of our Lord Jesus Christ has not *generated* us to any new longing or to a hope as yet unknown; through Christ's resurrection he has *regenerated* the beings we actually are, destining us for an incorruptible heritage which is our "living hope". The newness of the Christ-life is a physical reality, developing from an "incorruptible seed" (1. 23) to its fullness as our final salvation.

St Peter does not enlighten us on the way in which the Resurrection does this, but he lets us see the direction in which his mind is moving. Like St. Paul, he sees the Resurrection as the work of the Father, who, in raising Christ, also regenerates us. Thus it is God's life-giving action in Christ that we receive. Our birth is the result of a seed (i. 23); and one wonders whether this seed is not implanted in mankind by the raising action of the Father, especially since baptism is later related to the Resurrection. (iii. 21.) Despite the inconclusiveness of these statements, we can see that St. Peter's soteriology follows the familiar pattern of a twofold redemption: the death expiating our sins (iii. 18), the life-giving action of God upon Christ being the beginning of our life.

This preliminary study of the sources of our soteriology fixes the

---

[45] A Lemonnyer, *Les Épîtres de saint Paul*, Paris, 1907, vol II, *ad. loc.*

Resurrection at the very centre of the Redemption. The importance of Christ's glorification is so great that it counterbalances that of his death. Hence it would seem that any theory of the Redemption, any evaluation of Christ's death, which does not include a recognition of the essential part played by the Resurrection, can hardly claim to be true—let alone complete.

II

INCARNATION, DEATH, AND RESURRECTION

All that we have seen in the last chapter combines to face us with a somewhat complex problem. According to St. John, the Incarnation is life-giving; according to them all the death of Jesus is redemptive, and his resurrection no less so. If, therefore, we want to understand the part played by the Resurrection in our salvation, we must study its connection in Scripture with these two other mysteries.

The Synoptics were content to put both death and resurrection together as two facts with no other link than God's will in placing them both at the forefront of the Messianic scheme. Yet we can detect a subordination of one to the other. Christ's death is a preliminary condition, a trial to be undergone before the coming in glory and establishment of the Kingdom. (Matt. xx. 20–2; xxi. 42.) In one sentence our Lord links the two as the beginning and end of a single journey: "Ought not Christ to have suffered these things and entered into his glory?" (Luke xxiv. 26.) The actual words declare only the necessity of both death and resurrection into glory. But the Vulgate perceives the underlying intention, and translates this, "... and so enter into his glory". The glorification of Christ is the end to which his death is subordinated.[1]

1. St. John

According to St. John, Christ was accustomed to envisage both events together, as two aspects, dark and light, of his messianic destiny. He saw them as the final point of his life, linked together in the one "hour". At times he quails at the thought of that hour, at others he looks forward to it as his glorification. The harsh side was certainly the one oftenest before his mind (vii. 30; viii. 20; xii.

---

[1] It is probable that Luke saw the mysteries of Christ's death and glorification together in a single movement of ascent towards the Father, saying as he does "the days of his assumption" (Luke ix 51)

27); but this does not necessarily identify it with the Passion, even when the latter is called the hour of glory, nor does it mean that the fourth gospel sees Christ's death as "in no way a humiliation, but an exaltation".[2] The Passion is the hour of the prince of this world (xiv. 30), the hour of humiliation which Christ fears. (xii. 27.) It is only a glorious hour because his resurrection is to come as the conclusion of his death: "The hour is come that the Son of man should be glorified", he cries, when he is told of the Gentile proselytes who have asked to see him. (xii. 20–3.) This enquiry, coming before the time for it is ripe, brings him an assurance that the Gentiles will render homage to him in his glory. And his thoughts instantly turn to the death out of which the glory will be born: "Unless the grain of wheat . . . die . . ." In the great sacerdotal prayer we are left in no doubt as to the meaning of the hour of glory. (xvii. 1.) Elsewhere it includes the death of humiliation, but here it is simply the light of God shining upon the Son of Man: "And now glorify thou me, O Father, with thyself, with the glory which I had, before the world was, with thee." (xvii. 5.)

Thus Christ's unique hour encompasses both his death and his resurrection.

It is not merely that the two aspects are enclosed in a single unit of time. The Hour is not just the time at which Christ fulfils his destiny; it is the fulfilment itself. Death and resurrection are joined together in a single Hour because they are joined together in a single action. At one point our Lord links them together in so many words: "Therefore doth the Father love me: because I lay down my life, that I may take it up again . . . This commandment have I received of my Father." (x. 17–18.) He is going to lay down his life simply in order to take it up again. "Some shortsighted exegetes are almost scandalized by this. Surely it would be more honourable, more heroic to lay down his life with no plan or hope for recovering it."[3] They therefore try to weaken the text. St. Augustine had no such scruples: " 'Therefore doth the Father love me· because I lay down my life that I may take it up again.' What is he saying? 'My Father loves me because I am dying in order to rise again.' "[4] The Resurrection is the goal towards which Christ is working. It could

[2] E. Reuss, *Histoire de la théologie chrétienne au siècle apostolique*, Strasbourg, 1860, vol ii, p 498
[3] F. Prat, *Jésus-Christ*, Paris, 1933, vol ii, p 425
[4] *In Jo Tract.*, xlvii, 7; *P L*, xxxv, 1736.

be merely the objective goal, in that his resurrection is the natural sequel to his death.[5] But in fact our Lord is consciously advancing to his glory, and there is no selfishness in this, for in seeking the glory that is to come through his death, the Good Shepherd is carrying out the command of his Father for the sake of his sheep

This statement of Christ's is part of the paschal theme, that Passover theme which spreads over the whole Gospel like a fine filigree. His death is the way to his resurrection. St. John says that our Lord will "pass out of this world to the Father". (xiii. 1.) Our Lord himself had taught him to link the two mysteries: "I go to him that sent me. You shall seek me and shall not find me." (vii. 33–4.) St. Augustine indicates this as an early prediction of the Resurrection.[6] Our Lord was certainly going to his death; when St. Peter asked to go on this journey with him, he named Peter's own martyrdom as the setting-off point. (xiii. 36; xxi. 19.) But he was also going to a new life. The hour for his passing (xiii. 1) was that solemn hour which, as I have said, was marked by Christ's death but also by his glorification. Our Lord was not so much going *to* his death as *by way of* it: it was a mortal journey whose end was with the Father: "I go to the Father."[7]

Christ's death was not merely one episode of the journey, a necessary preliminary to his glorification; the journey itself was accomplished in his death. For Christ had certainly envisaged his death and glorification in a single ascending movement: "I, if I be lifted up, will draw all things to myself." The Evangelist adds in explanation: "This he said signifying what death he should die." (xii. 32–3.) Thus we can be quite certain that he was speaking of being lifted up on the tree of the Cross. But here, as elsewhere,[8] St. John gives a partial exegesis of something more complex. The victim of the Cross could only draw all things to himself in his glorification, as we know from our Lord himself, for he gave that as a reason for asking for his glory. (xvii. 1–2.) We know how Christ, especially as St. John reveals him, loved to give additional power to the expression of his thought by playing on words, and "lift up" can mean lift up in glory as well as lift up on the Cross. For him everything spoke of some inner meaning. In the upward movement

[5] Cf Rom. viii 17: "...if we suffer with him, that we may be also glorified with him"
[6] *In Jo Tract*, xxxi, 9, *P.L.*, xxxv, 1640.
[7] Cf. xvi 10; vi 63; xiii. 3; xiv 13; xvi 5, 28
[8] Compare xvii 12 and xviii 9.

suggested by the Crucifixion, he could see the exaltation of his humanity. The Cross was the mounting-block by which he was to reach his Father.

The death was so essential a part of that mounting that the Apocalypse puts it in the perspective of Christ's ascension. In Chapter XII, the work of the Redemption is summed up, strikingly foreshortened, as it were, in the birth of the Messiah followed immediately by the Child's being carried up to heaven. But the Apocalypse does not leave our Lord's death out of the work of redemption any more than does the Gospel. Christ, now in glory, still remembers his death (i. 18), still bears the marks of his immolation. (v. 6.) And just as that death is, as it were, inlaid in the life of glory, it is also included in the lifting up into heaven of the Child of the Woman.

Christ's passion, then, is clearly a movement whose conclusion is his glorification, a bridge from this world to the Father whose nature is dictated by its point of arrival.

At what moment does this movement attain its goal? For St. Paul, this glorification is identified with the Resurrection but for St. John it is identified with the Ascension; to him the return to the Father is a rising upwards

Yet this return is not simply a physical change of place, identical with the visible ascension recorded in the Acts. The return is part of Christ's hour, and cannot be isolated from the mystery of his death as the visible ascension was. It completes a rising movement which began in the Passion, and it is simultaneous with the Resurrection—which, according to x. 17, is the end and object of his death. This ascent is a glorification, a change in his very being (xvii. 5) which is above and beyond the level of physical position. Christ receives it without any visible return to his heavenly dwelling; henceforth his existence is a marvel; his relationship with his disciples is on a new level (xx. 17); it is impossible not to believe in him (xx. 28), which is a characteristic of his glorified state (xvii. 2-3); he gives them the Holy Spirit (xx. 22) whom he would not be free to give, according to vii. 39, till after he was glorified, and according to xv. 26, until he had returned to his Father This idea of his return is vital to the fourth gospel; had it been effected by the visible ascension, St. John would hardly have omitted to record it.

There is, then, good reason to say that, for St John, Christ's glorification is identified with his ascension, but that the Ascension is one with the mystery of the Resurrection.[9]

The Evangelist is explicit about the beginning of the movement of ascension and its completion "...knowing that his hour was come, that he should pass out of this world to the Father..." (xiii. 1) His existence in the world was to be followed by his presence with the Father. There is a profound opposition between life in the world and life with the Father, and passing from one to the other involves a transformation in one's way of being. Although a life in the world is not necessarily a life of the world, it must presuppose some adaptation to the world if it is to be a human life perceptible to the senses. Our Lord adopted this way of living,[10] in complete contrast with his life with the Father; and it is to take up that life that he is making his journey from this world to the Father. The prayer after the Last Supper expresses his intention to return to the life he had before he came to earth: "And now glorify thou me, O Father, with the glory which I had, before the world was, with thee." (xvii. 5; cf. xvi. 28.) The Incarnation in its earthly phase obscured the glory which belonged to him as God the Son. This impoverished existence will be followed by the existence in the bosom of his Father due to Christ as God the Son.

However, our Lord was not totally deprived of divine glory during his life on earth; in some way he was already living in the higher place to which the road of his death was leading. (x. 30, 38.) He was going to a place where he already was. "I go to him that sent me. You shall seek me, and shall not find me: for where I am, thither you cannot come." (vii. 34.) He is there, and that is where he is going.

He is therefore not wholly in the world. But neither is he wholly with the Father. He is there in virtue of his holiness as Son; but there remains a distance between God and man which the Incarnation has not annihilated. From this distance he is going by way of

[9] Père Benoit distinguishes two different streams of early tradition on the subject of the Ascension, one related to the visible ascension which gave the Apostles the certainty of their own experience of Christ's exaltation, the other to the essential Ascension which was identical with the glorification whereby Christ was lifted beyond this world into a heavenly existence. ("L'Ascension", R.B, lvi (1949), pp. 161–203.)

[10] In xvii 11ff, our Lord makes it clear that he has been in the world in the ordinary human way.

his death to rejoin his Father. That is why, if they love him, the Apostles must rejoice at his leaving them, for he is entering into a richer existence, into a life shared with the Father who is greater than he. (xiv. 28.) For Christ death is the way leading, in his glorification, to the fulfilment of the Incarnation.

In John's scheme of the redemption-light, this is clearly a redemptive movement since it enlarges the beam of light thrown by the Incarnation. However, one aspect of soteriology, which is important even in St John, remains obscure. What the part is that the death plays in the remission of our sins never appears. St. Paul envisages the Redemption from the point of view of sin to be blotted out, and enlightens us on the relationship between Christ's earthly condition and the sins of mankind; he shows us how the ending of the earthly condition and the union with the Father are stages in a single justification. The fourth gospel does, however, offer us one great light-giving principle: the mystery of the Redemption is accomplished in one movement which bears the Son of God made flesh from his existence on earth to a divine existence with the Father.

Our Lord's death appears in two lights. it is wholly directed towards the Resurrection, but it is also wholly directed towards our redemption. (xi. 51ff.) If we put these two facts together, we can conclude that the redemptive effort Christ made by dying results in the Resurrection; Christ's death is directed towards a salvation which will be made effective in the Resurrection.

The Incarnation is still the central mystery, but to be effective, it must reach its full flowering in glory by way of Christ's death [11] St. John contemplates this threefold mystery summed up in the Father's one great gift to the world: "God so loved the world as to give [12] his only-begotten Son, that whosoever believeth in him . . . may have life everlasting." (iii. 16.)

2. St. Paul

For St. Paul the existence of Christ can be divided into two phases, one marked by his death, the other by his resurrection.

[11] Applying this conclusion to the resurrection of the dead in particular, which is the last stage in our salvation, St Thomas writes. "The immediate condition of our resurrection is not the Word made flesh, but the Word made flesh and rising from the dead." (*III Sent.*, dist xxi, q 2, a. 1 ad 1.)

[12] The word "give" indicates the sending of the Son and the death to which he was to be handed over; the context indicates the glorification.

1. CHRIST'S LIFE ON EARTH

Death is the mark of unredeemed mankind. The Apostle does not look upon it as a purely natural phenomenon, but gives it a religious significance: it is the mark of sin branded, as it were, upon man and upon the universe. "By sin death entered into this world; and so death passed upon all men, in whom all have sinned." (Rom. v. 12.)

God had destined man for a life to which he had no right, but which he could draw from his union with God. Once cut off from God by his evil will, the creature was cut off from the roots of this life and reduced to the resources of his own nature or, as the biblical phrase has it, of his existence in the flesh. And "life in the flesh" is really death.

To St. Paul there is no true life except the imperishable life of God, which he is careful to distinguish from "this life" (1 Cor. xv. 19), "the life that now is" (1 Tim. iv. 8), "life in the flesh". (Gal. ii. 20.)

"This life" is not merely precarious; it is death. Our flesh is drawn towards death by its own weight. (Rom. viii. 6.) Our Lord himself described those not redeemed in his name as dead when he said: "Let the dead bury their dead." (Matt. viii. 22.) "The body indeed is dead because of sin", St. Paul reiterates (Rom. viii. 10), it is "the body of this death". (Rom. vii. 24.)[13]

Scripture recognizes two ways of living, one according to the spirit, the other according to the flesh. The spirit is divine reality, God's transcendence as against man's created and frail being. It is both the power of infinite life and radiating holiness.[14] Any man living under its sway will possess holiness and live with an everlasting life. But man is living in the flesh, which is the antithesis of the spirit and is contrary to it. (Gal. v. 17.)

By the word "flesh" Scripture does not mean to stigmatize the

[13] St Ignatius of Antioch, *Smyrn*, v, 2, describes man cut off from Christ as *necrophoros* ("corpse-bearer") 2 *Clem*, i, 6 says of pagan life, "All our life was no more than a death."
The philosophy of existential despair cannot better the description given in Scripture of this man with death in him as the stone is in the fruit Such philosophy might make use of Scripture if it would be content to be simply the philosophy of condemnation for the man who rejects God. For him who believes in God, Scripture traces a path of light through his earthly life for, as we shall see, it makes death a way of attaining life.

[14] In Scripture holiness is transcendence far more than any moral quality.

material element in man or condemn it as the principle of evil It uses the word to describe man as a whole, cut off from God, with no principle to raise him above himself. "The flesh" takes its stand outside God, just as "the world" does, in a sinful autonomy, desiring only its own wretchedness.

The deepest misery of the man of flesh is the loss of the spirit, and hence the loss of holiness and the power of eternal life. The flesh is struck with an incurable, mortal weakness. "The weakness of the flesh" is proverbial in the Bible But weakness is not all. Withdrawn from the Spirit, who is holiness as well as life, the flesh is in a state of sin. Holiness in the Bible is primarily something that belongs to God simply because of the perfection of his divine being. The man who lives this existence of the flesh, degraded and cut off from God, is, by his own wretchedness, placed outside that holiness; he cannot have the glory of God which, according to Rom. iii. 23, all men need for justification.

It is sin which has brought this way of life according to the flesh into the world; the man of flesh is the son of Adam, who sinned. Born of sin, the flesh remains linked with it; it harbours it and transmits it; it is always struggling against the law of the spirit (cf. Rom. vii. 14-23). It is "the sinful flesh". (Rom. viii. 3.)

Death is the culmination and summing-up of this whole life of weakness, cut off from the life of God. That is why Scripture says of the sinful man that he is dead.

Death is so much the expression of the state of sin that it is almost identified with it. In the Pauline theology of the Redemption death and mortality are set not against natural life, but the life of the Resurrection which is now hidden but will later be manifest in glory, and which is the same thing as the grace of the Spirit (cf. Rom. v. 15, 17, 21; vi. 23; viii. *passim*).

As time went on, a new element was introduced which made the sentence of death heavier still: the Law God-given and good in itself (Rom. vii. 13-14), its effect was to augment sin because of the weakness of the flesh it had to deal with (Rom. viii. 3): it made man conscious of sin where he might have been ignorant (Rom. iii. 20; iv. 15ff.), and introduced a sentence of death (Gal. iii. 10ff.) while giving him no power to avoid it.

Sinful man was in a hopeless position: he had sinned and was therefore in the grip of the weakness of a carnal nature; powerless, he was given up to sinfulness which led him on and increased his weakness. The Law constantly rang a death-knell in his ear. There was no way out of his own damnation: he went by the way of all flesh to sin and to death. The whole world around him shared his sin (Rom. viii. 20) and closed in upon him like a prison (cf. Gal. iii, 23; Rom. xi. 32) whose warders are Hamartia (sin), Thanatos (death) and Nomos (the Law)—cosmic powers which become alive in the dramatic mind of St. Paul. Beyond them we can see other powers, those of the prince of this world of despair. The whole universe is enclosed in sin with no way out into life: "Unhappy man that I am, who shall deliver me from the body of this death?" (Rom. vii. 24.)

If I am to be saved from this world of sin and death is it enough for Christ to pour out the price of his blood for the expiation of sin? Is it enough for him to die for my benefit, or in my place? Surely no-one can die in my place when my sin is part of me and I bear damnation in my very being! St Paul certainly does not see the Redemption as merely a satisfaction made to God's justice. More than any legal reparation or moral conversion, the Redemption is a real transformation, for man's sickness is in the reality of his nature: "All do need the glory of God." (Rom. iii. 23.)

"Who shall deliver me from the body of this death?" he has asked. And he himself replies: "The law of the spirit of life ... hath delivered me from the law of sin and of death." (Rom. viii. 2.) Salvation comes from God by way of a true resurrection of the dead in the Holy Spirit.

Christ starts by himself entering into our misery, he comes to share in our existence according to the flesh.[15]

He makes his entry into the world in a form not at all in accordance with his dignity as Son: "Who, being in the condition of God, did not cleave jealously to his equality of rank with God, but emptied himself, taking the condition of a slave, being made in the likeness of men, and in habit found as a [mere] man. He humbled himself, becoming obedient unto death, even to the death of the Cross." (Phil. ii. 6–8.)

Of what did Christ "empty himself"? Not, of course, of his divine condition, but of the glory (ἴσα θεῷ) to which as God the Son he

___

[15] As the Epistle to the Hebrews was to say: "Therefore because the children are partakers of flesh and blood, he also himself in like manner hath been partaker of the same: that, through death, he might destroy him who had the empire of death.." (ii 14)

was entitled. He accepted the slavery borne by man on earth, a life
at our level—so much so that men recognized him as one of them.
Having made this choice and effected this renunciation, he bore
all the consequences, even to the ultimate consequence of death.

This *kenosis* is not to be identified with the Incarnation as such;[16]
it is only in the earthly Christ,[17] and ends when Christ enters his
glory: the risen Christ bears no marks of slavery but is the Lord
before whom every knee must bow (ii. 8–11). Christ's coming was
a humiliation because the lowliness of this earthly existence went
counter to our Lord's true dignity and was unfitted for expressing
the Godhead. "He ... who was in the condition of God .. emptied
himself." The statement strongly suggests a concession; Christ has
made a concession to his redemptive love at the expense of his
dignity. It is this example of conceding something to charity that
the Apostle is putting before the Philippians, that each may "not
consider the things that are to his own advantage, but those that
are to other men's". (ii. 4.)

Christ's essential self-abasement cannot be simply identified with
the series of humiliations that marked out his life on earth. There is
a basic condition underlying them all, whence they flowed as of
logical necessity, though they were always freely chosen and
accepted. His fundamental renunciation produced a real condition
of life, whereby Christ's existence was patterned on the ordinary
human way of living: "... in habit found as a [mere] man". All
that happened was a normal consequence of this. The acceptance
of every servitude and the final submission were a renewal throughout his life of his initial willing of the *kenosis*. Suffering and death

[16] Scripture never considers the Incarnation in itself as a humiliation The
existence of the Son of God in a human nature in no way prejudices his
glory; it was only so in the conditions in which it took place on earth It
was the Incarnation in its earthly working out which the Fathers considered
a *kenosis* Cf St Cyril of Alexandria, *Glaphyra in Ex*, i, 2, *P.G*, lxix, 476;
M de la Taille, *The Mystery of Faith*, London, 1941–9, vol i, pp 242–3,
n 6.

[17] The subject of this *kenosis* is not the Word of God—St Paul never seems
to be speaking of the Word before the Incarnation—but Christ It is the
Christ of whom the faithful are members, who is put forward as an example
of total self-giving Furthermore, this emptying of himself is meritorious.
Christ's exaltation is contrasted not only with his death, but with his humiliation as a whole, of which it is the reward—humiliation which is proposed to
the faithful for their imitation If this *kenosis* is meritorious then it must
belong to Christ and not to the pre-existing Word. Cf A Feuillet,
"L'Homme-Dieu considéré dans sa condition terrestre", *Vivre et Penser*, ii
(1942), 58–69.

were the logical way of consecrating the physical weaknesses of this impoverished life.[18]

There was a reason for this renunciation: "He became poor for your sakes" (2 Cor. viii. 9), "for sin [to be conquered]". (Rom. viii. 3.) This condition of life was necessary so that Christ could suffer, we explain usually, so that he could put all the weight of the merit of the Passion onto the divine scales. And this is indeed the case. But, to St. Paul, Christ's life on earth is the basis of a far more tremendous redemptive action; because the Son of God lived this life and then left it for a divine life, all mankind passes with him out of a state of sin into the justice of God.

By the fact of living this life, Christ put himself among men, men of flesh, cut off from the power and glory of God, men in need of salvation, of the life-giving holiness of the Spirit.

This Son of God was, on earth, a man according to the flesh. St. Paul speaks of himself as set apart to preach "the gospel of God ... concerning his Son, who was made to him of the seed of David according to the flesh, who was constituted the Son of God in power, according to the Spirit of holiness, by the resurrection from the dead." (Rom. i. 1–4.)[19] Two successive phases in the human

---

[18] Various other texts lead us to this same doctrine, distinguishing two phases in Christ's existence, the first being the result of a freely-willed humiliation. When exhorting the Corinthians to be generous to their brethren in Jerusalem, St Paul reminds them that Christ "being rich, became poor, for your sakes". (2 Cor viii. 9) Again, this poverty only marks the earthly life Christ's existence in a human nature does not of itself constitute any impoverishment of his divinity, and he is now in possession of the treasures of God (Rom. x 12.)

[19] In this text "the flesh" is often taken to mean simply human nature— in the same way as the "condition of a slave" in Phil ii 7 is; "the Spirit of holiness" is then taken to indicate the divine nature; the divine nature makes him Son of God—the human nature, Son of David. But the Apostle is not concerned to analyse the titles Christ has because of the duality of his nature; he is contrasting two successive phases of his existence as man The flesh is indeed the created nature, but it formally designates the earthly existence of our Lord, in his natural life.

W. Schauf translated "according to the flesh" as "dem irdisch-niederen Dasein nach . seiner irdisch-fleischlichen Existenz nach" "Sarx", N T. Abhandlungen, Munster-i.-W., 1924, p. 64, n. H. Bertrams, in "Das Wesen des Geistes", N T Abhandl , 1913, p 107, n 1, has a similar view. F. Prat, Theology, vol. ii, p 403, gives according to "carnal descent". Condren, in 1725, had written "In the Incarnation [God] produced this same Son, but in a new womb, and gave him mortal life and a body which, in the likeness of sinful flesh . would not last forever"; he then quotes Rom i 3 (L'Idée du sacerdoce et du sacrifice de Jésus-Christ, Paris, 1725, pp 86–7)

existence of the Son of God are contrasted: the first opens with his generation according to the flesh, the second with the Resurrection. Son of God though he be, Christ is born Son of David, seeming, because of his flesh, no more than this. He leads the life of weakness that goes with existence in the flesh, subject to the laws of nature; he is descended from a human ancestor and seems to have no father other than this. By the Resurrection, God raises his Son beyond his Davidic inheritance to the power which is his because of his Spirit of holiness.

Having come down from the level of his dignity as Son, Christ sees his liberty curtailed by all the limitations of his flesh; he must submit to physical laws and moral obligations which are not proper to the Son. Despite the dignity of his person (Rom. i. 4; Phil. ii. 6), it was not in appearance only that his outward characteristics were those of a slave; his subjection was rooted in his nature. He was subject to human authorities, to suffering and to death, by the exigency of this fleshly nature, by the law of his *kenosis*.

Because of the *sarx*, the flesh, Christ was in addition subject to the special slavery that went with being an Israelite. For by his flesh he belonged to the Hebrew nation, "of whom is Christ, according to the flesh". (Rom. ix. 5.) This Son of God, who was "of the seed of David according to the flesh" (Rom. i. 3), was a member of the tribe of David of Bethlehem. Having given up the rights that went with his divine condition and taken the status of life according to the flesh in the Jewish people, it followed that Christ submitted to the Jewish law: "Made of a woman, made under the Law". (Gal. iv. 4.) Obedience to the Law became connatural to him Pauline theology is based on what the Gospels record: Jesus was circumcised, went up to Jerusalem as his Jewish nationality required, ate the Pasch. Only from the accretions of the Pharisees did he consider himself dispensed.

Christ's life on earth was not characterized only by weakness. His risen life according to the spirit of holiness stands in contrast to his earthly life according to the flesh (Rom. i. 3–4) and that contrast casts its shadow over it. Such a life according to the flesh must, in one sense, be profane. Rom. viii. 3 even speaks of sin: ". . . sending his own Son, in the likeness of sinful flesh". The word "likeness" applies to "sinful" as much as to "flesh". The Son of God has come in the same flesh that has been propagated since Adam's sin[20] When he says in the same Epistle that Christ has died to sin (vi. 10), St. Paul presupposes some kind of subjection to sin from which Christ is liberated by his death.[21]

The First Epistle to Timothy once again contrasts not the human and divine nature, but two phases in the life of Christ, "which was manifested in the flesh, was justified in the spirit" (iii. 16). Revealed to mankind in a humanity of flesh, he was later justified in the Spirit[22] The Resurrection revealed the true condition of this man which had up till then been hidden beneath the servile aspect of a carnal humanity. Having led an existence which did not express his deepest reality, Christ was justified—was revealed, that is, in the justice and holiness that were his as Son of God. It was precisely because of this need for a justification that the earthly life had to be related to sin. Normally justification means that there has been sin; in this case it means that there is a concealment of holiness

Christ took his place outside the holiness of God not only by belonging to the race of Adam, but also by his Jewish nationality: "As many as are under the works of the Law are under a curse ... Christ hath redeemed us from the curse of the Law, being made a curse for us." (Gal. iii. 10, 13.)

The death Christ underwent was the event that characterized his whole life on earth, its synthesis, the logical goal of his humiliations (Phil. ii. 6–8), and the ultimate effect of his weakness. (2 Cor. xiii. 4.) The moment of death was such a complete recapitulation of the years "of his flesh" that Pauline theology passes over them in silence; it was not that Paul was not aware of them, but they were all summed up in the death.[23] His death proclaimed Christ as son of a sinful race. Thinking of the Cross, the Apostle wrote that "God hath made him sin." (2 Cor. v. 21.)

The words "flesh", "Law", "sin" and "death" mean separation

[20] The word "likeness", however, does limit the range of the statement It cuts Christ off from any of the collusion operating between our flesh and sin, and sees in him only the physical weaknesses brought about by sin, which are in such contrast to divine holiness.

[21] The Apostle says Christ has died *to* sin, not *by* sin—the context makes it clear Cf Lagrange and Huby, as against Prat, vol 1, p 224, *n* 1. Christ died to sin as he now lives to God The dative indicates possession.

[22] I believe that this justification was Christ's glorification. The Spirit is always linked with the Resurrection. His appearing to the angels (1 Tim. iii. 16) reminds us that he is Lord of the angels, which he is as a result of the Resurrection. Cf P Benoit, "L'Ascension", *R.B.*, lvi (1949), p. 182

[23] Rom viii. 3; Phil. ii. 5ff ; Gal. iv. 4–5 as compared with Gal iii 13

from God, deprivation of the life-giving glory of God. Even during
his life on earth Christ's inmost being was caught up in the holiness
of God.[24] But this secret glory was locked in the depths of his being;
his life as Son of God remained isolated in mystery. This Pauline
picture is based on the Gospel story. Not only his body, but all the
faculties—even intellectual—by which our Lord was in contact with
the life of the world, and in which he carried out the Redemption,
were so incompletely possessed by the divine life that he was able
to experience in them the need of being comforted by God.

It was the *sarx*, the flesh, which held back the springs of holiness.
Consisting as it did of the human complexus as it now lives, with
its natural energies and deficiencies, it went counter to the divine
holiness (Gal. v. 17), and rebelled against it. It was not encroached
upon by the life of God, for "flesh and blood"—man, provided only
with his natural faculties—"cannot possess the Kingdom of God".
(1 Cor. xv. 50) The principle is a universal one. St. Paul applies it
to our bodies, which cannot enter into glory unless they are transformed by a higher principle. Christ could have said with his
apostle: While we are in the body, we are in exile from the Lord.
(2 Cor. v. 6.)[25] He had to go back to his Father, and he had to take
a hard road to get there,[26] that of renouncing his earthly existence.

ii. THE PASSAGE TO LIFE IN HEAVEN

The carnal condition brought Christ to death, and, in turn, death
set him free from the flesh.

[24] Rom. i 4 shows that in the Resurrection he appeared as the Son of God
because of a holiness inherent in him because (i. 3) he was always the Son
[25] Later theology was to say, with greater exactitude, that Christ on earth
already rejoiced in glory at the highest point of his intellect
[26] This distance was qualitative in nature; in St. Paul's thought the physical
ascension was not important Because of his flesh, the Son was brought down
to an earthly and servile state; in glory, "he was established Son of God
in power" (Rom. i. 4.)
In the great epistles, Christ's glorification is simply identified with the
Resurrection In the Epistles of the Captivity, the notion of ascension is linked
with that of glorification; but this ascending of Christ's is primarily a personal
exaltation effected by the raising action of the Father (Eph. i 19-23) In
Eph iv. 8-10, the ascension from the Mount of Olives takes on a certain
importance, but judging from Eph i 19-23, it is part of the exaltation of
Christ's person which is the effect of the Resurrection. The liturgical hymn
quoted in 1 Tim iii. 16 separates the Ascension from the Resurrection. But
all the same it is with the Resurrection that it connects the redemptive effects
of our Lord's glorification—his being raised above the angels and being
preached to the Gentiles. It is thus clear that, for St. Paul, the distance separating the earthly Christ from the Father is primarily qualitative

Death was the normal conclusion for our Lord's life on earth, for at the origin of every existence according to the flesh is sin, that sting of death implanted in man's body. Sin, which means being deprived of the undying glory of God, seems in a sense concretized in Christ on the Cross (2 Cor. v. 21.) Obedience even unto death was part of the original acceptance of that flesh whose very name implies weakness and death "... put to death because of the flesh" (1 Pet. iii. 18), says St. Peter; "... crucified through weakness" (2 Cor. xiii. 4), says St. Paul.

The Jewish nationality which Christ had through his flesh also drew him to his death. "We have a law and according to the law he ought to die", declared the Jews. (John xix. 7.) They were interpreting their Law falsely. And yet, in Pauline theology, the Law did condemn Christ. Just as he had become one with sinners by taking their flesh, by taking flesh as a Jew Christ had also become one with a nation that had betrayed its trust. The Apostle seconds the verdict of the Jewish priests: "I am dead through the law" (Gal. ii. 19); in other words, I am dead through the Law in Christ to whom I am united; I share in Christ's death and am therefore dead, with him, through the Law. It placed a curse upon the slightest transgression. And Christ bore in his flesh the curse that weighed upon the whole of Israel (Gal. iii. 10), which led him to his death. The Apostle links these four ideas: born of a woman, subject to the Law, subject to a curse, dead upon the Cross.[27]

Death was therefore the conclusion of Christ's carnal existence; it did not of itself abolish that existence but was its final goal. For every man it is simply the final consequence of the life of the flesh, the declaration of the dominion of sin, the sanction of the Law's rule. Far from abolishing tyranny and servitude, it marks their highest point. In Christ it was the end and object of his will for *kenosis*, it brought his emptying out of himself to its completion. In itself, then, it could not bridge the distance between Christ and the life of God. Had he merely died, far from achieving freedom by his death, Christ would simply have been succumbing to the flesh and to sin.

[27] "Made of a woman, made under the law that he might redeem them who were under the law". "Christ hath redeemed us from the curse of the Law, being made a curse for us: for it is written: 'Cursed is every one that hangeth on a tree'" (Gal iv. 4–5; iii. 13.) Because of his flesh, Christ submitted to the Law and to the curse it contained The result of that submission was death

But it was a redemptive death. For, while the life of the flesh led
Christ to death, death in turn detached him from the flesh. It was
the natural conclusion—but also the end—of the life of the flesh in
its weakness. Christ did not only die *because of* sin, *because of* the
weakness of the flesh, *because of* the requirements of the Law; he
also died *to* all these things. With the collapse of his body all these
slaveries at once fell away from him like so many chains.

Christ died to sin: "God sending his own Son, in the likeness
of sinful flesh and of sin, hath condemned sin in the flesh." (Rom.
viii. 3.) In delivering up Christ's flesh, God was condemning to
death our sin which was imprinted in that flesh. The Apostle says
again, "Our old man is crucified with him, that the body of sin
may be destroyed." (Rom. vi. 6.) Our sinful flesh dies in our union
with Christ; St. Paul assumes that the body of sin has first been
destroyed in Christ. "His death was a death to sin." (Rom. vi. 10.)

Christ died to the weakness of the flesh. He died once for all
(Rom. vi. 10) and is no longer subject to mortality. "The second
time he shall appear without sin" (Heb. ix. 28), he will come in
power.

Christ died to the obligations of the Law The Apostle does not
merely say, "I am dead through the law", but "I, through the
law, am dead to the law." (Gal. ii. 19.) In union with the death
of Christ, that is, I am dead to the Law. He says it more clearly
in Rom. vii. 4: "You also are become dead to the Law by the body
of Christ"—in which the Law is destroyed. The I.O.U. as it were,
of our debts both to the Law and to sin, was nailed to the cross in
the very body of Jesus Christ.[28]

What we see from now on is a resurgence of Christ's divine condition. His glory, which had been hidden by the opacity of the
flesh, shines out as the veils fall away. Henceforth a new existence
begins which is in total contrast with the weaknesses of the earlier
one.

In Rom. i. 3–4, the Resurrection appears as a blossoming out of
the divine sonship in the man Jesus: "Born of the seed of David
according to the flesh, he was established Son of God in power,
according to the spirit of sanctification, by the resurrection . . . from

---

[28] Cf Col. ii 14: "This debt was inscribed in the likeness to sinful flesh,
the corruptibility, the passibility, the mortality assumed by Jesus Christ, which
died with him to give place to the immortality of his resurrection and the
incorruptibility of his glory" See M de la Taille, *Rech. Sc Rel.*, vi (1916),
p. 470, also J Huby, *Épîtres de la captivité*, Paris, 1935, p 73.

the dead." Son only of David in his carnal nature, our Lord has risen in the majesty of the Son of God which was demanded by his own "spirit of sanctification", in other words, his own native holiness.[29]

Phil. ii. 6–11 is a hymn in honour of Christ's exaltation in the divinity, following his freely-chosen *kenosis*. Though his condition was divine, he had given up his equality of rank and honour with God, had accepted the servile condition of sinful man, including its ultimate consequences—death and the horror of the Cross. That is why God has given him his own true divine name, all the power and glory of God, that the whole universe may adore and proclaim that he is "the Lord Jesus Christ".

Thus the mystery of Christ's divinity is fulfilled in glorification.

---

[29] Christ's enthronement in his new state results from the demands of a "spirit of holiness" The phrase is an obscure one, both because this is its only appearance in the New Testament, and because of the complex riches we feel it to contain Some see it as meaning Christ's divine nature, because it is contrasted with "the flesh" (i 3) which they take to mean simply the human nature.

But the flesh is not just the created element in our Lord's person, but his natural humanity as inherited from his ancestors Nowhere else does the divine nature receive from St. Paul the title of Spirit, nor does he generally contrast the flesh with the divine nature, but with either the person or the work of the Holy Ghost.

The person of the Holy Spirit is not in question here, for the principle which requires Christ's resurrection seems to be as much a part of him as the flesh which makes him Son of David. The flesh and the Spirit dwell in the man Christ; one is the basis of his earthly existence, the other the norm of his glorified life. The Spirit affects Christ in his human nature, just as does the "divine condition" (Phil. ii. 6) which never appeared during his life on earth but which, through the Father's intervention, triumphed in the Resurrection. It is clear that this spirit indicates the supereminent holiness with which our Lord is endowed; by his natural being he is of the seed of David, but thanks to this holiness, "he is established Son of God in power". (Cf. H Bertrams, "Das Wesen des Geistes", p. 108; F Prat, *Theology*, vol ii, pp 426–7; W Schauf, "Sarx", pp. 66–7; J. Nélis, "Les Antithèses littéraires dans les épîtres de saint Paul", *Nouv Rev Théol.*, lxx (1948), p. 372.)

The Resurrection in the full majesty of the Son is effected "according to" the spirit of sanctification, that is to say, according to its requirements and following its norm. (Cf. Schauf, "Sarx", p 67.) The glory of the new existence is postulated and specified by that holiness, which is therefore the holiness of the true Son of God, proportioned to the life of the Son, which it requires and which manifests it In theological terminology, we call it the grace of the hypostatic union But in St. Paul's mind this grace does not stand out baldly as a clear-cut idea; it is a fullness, making Christ's being holy in its inmost depths and loading it with innumerable spiritual gifts. (Cf Prat, *Theology*, vol. ii, p. 427.

Stripped of his carnal existence, our Lord has come to the glorious perfection of his union with God which was demanded by his inherent dignity as Son. Even in his body, he now lives divinely.

Thus Christ can be contrasted within himself in the successive phases of his human life, as a man of flesh and a man of glory.

The passage from one phase to the other constitutes a process of justification. The Apostle does not say this in so many words, but clearly suggests it. In Rom. vi. 7–10, he proves that we are dead to sin by means of the truism that "he that is dead is absolved from sin". Justice has no more claim on him and the proceedings against him come to a standstill. "We are surprised that Paul should give this somewhat trivial reason. But he evidently wished to start with a very general principle which could be applied even to Christ, for he goes on to tell us that Christ himself has, in a sense, paid by his death the debt he had contracted through sin."[30] "His death was a death to sin, but his life is life unto God." (vi. 10.) Henceforth he is accountable for sin no longer; the Epistle to the Hebrews says he is "without sin". (ix. 28) This is the idea underlying 2 Cor. v. 21: "Him, who knew no sin, he hath made sin for us, that we might be made the justice of God in him." Christ dies under the insignia, as it were, of sin; but in our exalted Saviour (the phrase "in him" brings us to Christ in heaven), we find our justification; we unite ourselves to him who has become the justice of God for us, having first become sin for us.

Whereas the flesh bore the imprint of sin, the new life is established in holiness. Christ was glorified according to his "Spirit of holiness". Earlier on, the Apostle had declared in the synagogue of Antioch in Pisidia: "To show that he raised him up from the dead, not to return now any more to corruption, he said thus ... 'Thou shalt not suffer thy Holy One to see corruption.'" (Acts xiii. 34–5.) Sin is the sting of death (1 Cor. xv. 56), and holiness is the stimulus towards the new life; it is impossible for God's holy one to see corruption. (Acts ii. 24–7.) This holiness, which is the basis of the risen life, is the characteristic by which that life is marked; it is a life of holiness, "he liveth unto God". (Rom. vi. 10.)

Moreover, the glory of the life of regeneration is coupled with the idea of God's justice. The Apostle says of carnal humanity, of humanity living outside divine justice, that it is without the glory of God, and adds that it has been justified in Christ, thus identifying

[30] Lagrange, *Épître aux Romains*, 3rd ed , Paris, 1922, p. 147

glory with justice. "All have sinned and do need the glory of God, being justified [henceforth] ... through the Redemption." (Rom. iii. 23–4.)

Sinful humanity, humanity made divine: that is the meaning of the earthly way of life and the heavenly way of life; death concludes the one, the Resurrection is the source of the other.

iii. THE CONNECTION BETWEEN THE TWO PHASES

It now remains only to grasp the inner relationship between these two phases of existence: why did Christ's death remove him from the servile condition and bring him to God?

As we have seen, death in itself is simply the conclusion of life according to the flesh, the supreme affirmation of the presence of sin, the ultimate failure of man's weakness. It is not a triumphant liberation or even an escape; death does not do away with death.[31]

Yet, in the same breath as he declares Christ the victim of death, Paul also declares that by his death he was set free from sin, from the flesh and from the mortal weakness of the flesh. What is it that makes this defeat also a victory?

In the past there were theories of a tribute being paid by Christ to sin and death, a tribute which was at the same time a ransom; or it was said that sin could exercise a power of death over all the sons of Adam until that power was, as it were, used up by being exercised upon Christ But these ideas are more the product of imagination than of reason. Theology has merely noted them, and though we find echoes of them in some of the leading exegetes of recent times,[32] they seem justified neither by St. Paul's general principles nor by his actual words.

The paradox of a Christ who triumphs over the flesh in the act of succumbing to it can be simply resolved in the Johannine phrase "I go to the Father", in the idea of passing from the earthly

[31] To say that it did would be to allow sin and the Law, the two principles of death, some causality in our salvation Whereas the Apostle "does not admit of the smallest collaboration from the old régime in the present gift of justice" (P Benoit, "La loi et la croix d'après saint Paul", *Revue Biblique,* 47 (1938), 507.)

[32] Lagrange, *Épître aux Romains*, p. 148: "Sin reigned and had the right of inflicting death on all men. Christ, by taking flesh, submitted to this law, but by inflicting death upon him, sin exhausted its right." Similarly J. Huby, *Épître aux Romains*, 3rd ed., Paris, 1940, p 212. Death then would seem like a bee which uses its sting only to lose it; cf. J Holzner, *Paulus*, Freiburg, 1941, p 316

condition to the divine life by means of death We have left one point by the very fact of having started to move towards another; by his death Christ left the condition of this world and of sin because by it he was moving towards the Resurrection: his death was redemptive because it was the road to his glory.

Though this idea may not seem very Pauline in form, it is in fact essentially Paul's idea as well. For him the death was not a great event standing motionless and apart, but a movement towards the life of glory.

The Apostle sometimes looks at Christ's death as a historical phenomenon, and then it does appear as an event in itself, distinct from the Resurrection—the former being the effect of the weakness of the flesh, the latter of the power of God. (2 Cor. xiii. 4.) But the two events were linked together, for the death merited the Resurrection. We need recall only Phil. ii. 5–11. In return for his humiliation, God raised up Christ in glory. The arc described by our Lord in moving from the right to divine glory which was his down to the annihilation of death, having come to its lowest point, sweeps up again, and demands glory from the Father in proportion to the humiliation that has been accepted. The Resurrection is the conclusion of the *kenosis*, the aim and object of its merit.

Though St. Paul thinks in terms of merit, whereas the Johannine Christ uses the image of movement from place to place, the underlying reality is in fact the same, for supernatural merit is simply man's movement towards the possession of God.[33]

At other times the Apostle leaves aside the historical reality of the death as resultant from the weakness of the flesh, and considers it only in its redemptive value. He does this in the texts which show how the faithful are sharing in the redemptive act through baptism. (Rom vi. 3ff.; Col. ii 11ff) The faithful are united with the historical death of our Lord, but not as a historical phenomenon; they share in it as a mystery of man's salvation.

From this point of view the death of Jesus is welded together with his resurrection in one mystery: "The Crucifixion and the Resurrection are not so much two separate events as one mystery with two facets."[34]

[33] The idea of supernatural merit, apart from purely juridical notions, has its reality on the ontological level. To merit is to place oneself in the moral and physical dispositions suited to the good that God destines one for, is to fit one's being for the possession of God which will crown those dispositions

[34] J Huby, *Mystiques paulinienne et johannique*, Paris, 1946, p. 21.

The justification of the believer is a single reality with two com-plementary aspects, a negative and a positive, death to sinful flesh, and entry into divine life. Now, justification is effected in sharing in and conforming with the death and resurrection of our Lord, which thus appear in the unity of a single mystery in which the death of the flesh is the negative aspect of the Resurrection to the life of God. This merging of the two in St. Paul assumes what St. John says in so many words—that Christ found his glory at the end of his passion, that he found life in the death itself; that the *kenosis* was therefore a movement towards glory, a movement which came to its glorious conclusion at the moment when the *kenosis* reached its ultimate consequence—death.

In itself the *kenosis* did not lead Christ towards life in God, for carnal existence stood for sin as against God, and so went counter to that life. Birth according to the flesh placed man at a distance from God, and death, which was the consummation of life accord-ing to the flesh, did nothing to lessen that distance. However, in Christ, his freely-willed submission to the weaknesses of the flesh, even to their consecration in death, represented the most intense effort to come to God, for it was a submission of obedience, drag-ging man away from the autonomy of his flesh, and carrying him towards God in a renunciation of self which became, in death, a total renunciation. The *kenosis*, while being an acceptance of the flesh, was at the same time a complete negation of it.

For Christ to be borne out of his flesh towards God some stronger driving power than the flesh was needed, for the activity of the flesh could only strengthen man in his opposition to God. (Rom. viii. 7.) To Christ, too, God might well have said, "You would not have sought me, if you had not already found me."[35]

His death, then, was directing Christ towards the Father; though it was the consummation of life according to the flesh, it could also put an end to that life; it could do so, not in itself, but in as much as it was a movement towards life in God. "Christ, rising again from the dead, dieth now no more; death shall no more have dominion over him", declares St. Paul. (Rom. vi. 9.) In other words, Christ is guaranteed the abolition of mortality by his new life: once risen, he will not die again. "Death is swallowed up in victory." (1 Cor. xv. 54.)

We can understand why the Apostle exclaims that "if Christ be

[35] Pascal, *Le Mystère de Jésus*

not risen again . . . you are yet in your sins." (1 Cor. xv. 17) If Christ had merely died, the redemptive movement would not have reached its conclusion, sinful flesh would not have been destroyed, and his death would have no significance for our salvation at all.

iv. THE EPISTLE TO THE HEBREWS

A text I have already quoted from the Epistle to the Hebrews now becomes clearer· "We see Jesus, who was once made a little lower than the angels, for the suffering of death, crowned with glory and honour that, through the grace of God, he might taste death for all." (ii 9)

Our Lord's humiliation and death have the glory as object of their merit. This single object canalizes all the merits of the sufferings so perfectly that his resurrection becomes an adequate result of his death. If Jesus is "crowned with glory and honour that he might taste death for all", his death is redemptive in the Resurrection it has merited; in the resurrection of Jesus there is salvation for all men.[36]

The Resurrection constitutes the basic, prime and total object of the merit of the Passion. Current theology all too often subordinates this first objective to the merits won for mankind; the Resurrection is seen as the end of a side stream flowing out of the mainstream of the Redemption. Yet our Lord had become so completely one with the race of Adam that what he wished to gain for us he first gained for himself.

This text I have quoted is not an aberration of the Epistle to the Hebrews. It is the theological formulation of an idea well-known to the writer, which is generally expressed in the image of Christ's entry into the holy place of heaven by means of his death. This sanctuary of God's life of glory is the goal towards which all Christ's efforts tend. Jesus entered it only "through the veil, that is to say his flesh" (x 20). Death removed the veil, but far from stopping there, it was itself the means by which he passed beyond death. The object of his death was his glorification

The mystery of the Redemption was therefore accomplished in

[36] I prefer not to take Heb xii 2 into account here The translation " because of the joy set before him, he endured the cross" (cf A. Médebielle, J. Bonsirven) is open to question The other rendering, "instead of the joy offered to him", is preferred by many and seems to agree better with Phil ii 6ff

our Lord's humanity before embracing us. One element in his passion illustrates this conception. (Heb. v. 7–9) The author of the epistle recalls the prayer of profound suffering in which the mortal Christ expressed his hope of salvation in God: "Who in the days of his flesh, with a strong cry and tears, offering up prayers and supplications to him that was able to save him from death, was heard for his reverence. And whereas indeed he was the Son of God, he learned obedience by the things which he suffered and being consummated, he became, to all that obey him, the cause of eternal salvation."

The prayer was said in "the days of his flesh", a request from the earthly Christ, springing from his natural being; he presented it in an attitude of "supplication", as the unhappy man asks for grace; the cry and the tears expressed the anguished longing of suffering flesh. He groaned in his own name, and himself addressed the Father "that was able to save him". "It was not platonic or altruistic, this demand to be saved from death "[37] We are astounded, we are shocked by this weakness and longing; it would have been more heroic, we feel, to accept unmoved this death which was to save the world. But this astonishment is born of a lack of understanding. We forget that the drama of mankind in search of salvation was first played out in Christ, and that he himself was the first to be raised by the Father.

There are some who think that Christ was asking to be spared his death, and that his prayer was heard, but in another way, by the Resurrection.[38] This interpretation misses the nuances of the text. The prayer is addressed to the Father, who can save him from death, but it does not express the intention of escaping from death. Whatever the instinctive longing of his flesh might be, our Lord accepted God's will, but in his affliction he turned to his Father, his help and salvation.

Because of his reverence, his deeply religious spirit, he was heard. Not that he was spared death—he had asked for no such exemption. God brought him through suffering to his fulfilment in glory. It was indeed in the Resurrection that his prayer was heard: "He was heard in that [God] raised him up and gave him possession of all the prerogatives of which the Resurrection was the condition and

---

[37] J Bonsirven, *Épître aux Hébreux*, 5th ed., Paris, 1943, p. 58.

[38] e.g , Estius, and D. Buzy in his translation of the New Testament (Paris, 1937).

the origin, and which the author is alluding to when he speaks of
'the cause of our eternal salvation.' "[39]

The episode indicated by this text—which would seem to be that
of Gethsemane—is most moving. The Son of God, in his human
nature, was so much wholly and only man, and the affliction of
sin was so fully embodied in that nature, that the Redemption
became a personal drama of Christ's, to be fully enacted in him.
He did not, of course, need to be justified from any personal sin;
but he had brought himself down to our state of wretchedness to
such a point that he became "the mouth of our nature"[40] whereby
we cried out our need of God, to such a point that he had to beseech
for himself "that the power of death be brought to nothing, and
that that life which had once been given to our nature might come
into force".[41]

"Because the children are partakers of flesh and blood, he also
himself in like manner hath been partaker of the same. that, through
death, he might destroy him who had the empire of death, that is
to say, the devil." (ii. 14.) He shared in our wretchedness that we
might triumph over it in him. God "perfected, by his passion, the
leader who brought many children into glory" (ii. 10), and "being
consummated, he became, to all that obey him, the cause of eternal
salvation". (v. 9.)

From the preceding pages, we may draw these conclusions:
(1) The redemption of human nature is a drama unfolding first
of all in Christ. It takes place in him as a sanctifying transformation
from the state of sinful flesh to the holiness of divine life which is
its direct opposite.
(2) This transformation was worked out in our Lord's death and
glorification as in a single mystery, for death was the end of sinful
flesh only in so far as it resulted in glorification, the principle of
divine life.

We may say further that the death and resurrection of Jesus are
bound up with the fundamental mystery of the Incarnation. His
death is the fulfilment of the initial will to *kenosis*, the dedication
of Christ's human weakness and his loss of glory; but at the same

[39] A. Lemonnyer, *Le Épîtres de saint Paul*, Paris, 1907, vol. ii, p. 218.
[40] Theodoret, in his commentaries on 1 Cor. xv. 27ff. and Heb. ii 5–8
(*P G*, lxxxii, 360, 692.)
[41] St Cyril of Alexandria, *Ad Reginas de Recta Fide Oratio Altera*, 40,
P G, lxxvi, 1392

time it removes the state of *kenosis* by bringing about his resurrection. The Resurrection is the divine life of the Son of God, shining forth in a humanity for which he has renounced all life not of God; it is the glorious fulfilment of the mystery of the Incarnation.

Now we shall have to consider how the Redemption, which took place in Christ alone, extends to us. But first it will be useful to look once more at the drama of the Redemption, placing it in a framework—a framework adequate to contain its rich reality which God himself had prepared throughout the history of mankind: Sacrifice.

3. THE DEATH AND RESURRECTION IN THE FRAMEWORK OF SACRIFICE

Our Lord himself summed up his redemptive act in the notion of sacrifice. At the Last Supper, he set beside his own death the memory of the sacrifice that sealed the old covenant: "This is my blood of the new testament, shed for many." Christ's blood flows in sacrifice like the blood of the victims at the foot of Sinai, to establish a new covenant. St. Paul, in his turn, places the Redemption in this ritual framework: "Christ, our pasch, is sacrificed." (1 Cor. v. 7.) Most of the theological statements about Christ's death are based on this idea.[42]

But once we try to fit Christ's redemptive act to the sacrificial ideas we get from religious history, we realize how narrow the mould is How can we compare the immolation of an animal with the gift of self made by a man who is God, who is priest as well as victim, who offers himself without any ritual trappings, and who immolates in himself the whole mass of his followers?

However, if Christ declares that the redemptive act took the form of a sacrifice, it is up to us to try and see in that act all the great outlines of the sacrifice of the past.

The study of the history of religions has found, in the multiplicity of sacrificial forms, one very deep stream into which all the rest flow, and which gives them a kind of unity.

In man's eyes sacrifice is a means of recognizing the rights of the divinity and fulfilling his own inborn desire to be united with his god. Man is moved to offer sacrifice by a twofold wish (though

[42] Cf Rom iii. 24-5, Eph v 2, Heb vii 27; ix 14, 28; x 12-24; 1 Pet i. 2, 18-19; 1 John i. 7; Apoc. vii 14

often a distorted one): to honour the sovereign power of his divinity (a power that may be either benevolent or angry and vengeful), and a desire, which is rather more self-seeking, but is still basically a homage, to unite himself to that power.

This sacrificial act takes place in two stages. In the first, man is the actor, and it is by his own initiative that he makes a gift to God. The second stage takes place in the mystery of the Divinity: if the offering is worthy of acceptance, God takes it; and since he only accepts one gift to give another in return, he grants the creature a share in his divinity.

1. THE RESURRECTION, ACCEPTANCE OF THE SACRIFICE

(a) *Acceptance in the Old Testament*

In its essence, a sacrifice is a gift. The giving of something that is one's own to another, which is the definition of any genuine gift, is the most real way in which we can express our desire to recognize the sovereignty of God. Man singles out the material good dearest to him, the one most necessary to life: some article of food, or a living creature which is also precious and useful to him—such as a domestic animal—and offers it to God. This, to restrict ourselves to the sphere of the Bible, was the worship of the Hebrew and other Semitic religions: it was a gift [43]

The will of the offerer is that his gift be taken by God and pass into divine ownership. This will is clearly expressed when the offering is food. [44] The idea of offering a banquet to the gods is very much emphasized in the Assyro-Babylonian religions, extending

[43] For the Assyro-Babylonians, sacrifice was a gift, a present, and one of the phrases oftenest found on their ritual tablets was this: "Before such-and-such a divinity thou shalt give a present." A Vincent, *La Religion des judéo-araméens d'Éléphantine*, Paris, 1937, p 182. To the Hebrews, the idea that fitted all forms of sacrifice was that of the *qorban*, offering, or the *minhah*, gift. The name of *qorban* was given to: the holocaust (Lev i. 2-3, 10), the *minhah* (ii. 1), peace offerings (iii 1) and sin offerings (iv 32) See W Moeller, *Biblische Theologie des A.T*, Zwickau, 1937, p. 223, P Heinisch, *Theologie des A.T.*, Bonn, 1940, p. 190; F. Noetscher, *Biblische Altertumskunde*, Bonn, 1940, p. 327: "The essential of sacrifice is thus the gift, the handing over of one's possession of something to the divinity."

[44] In Semitic as in other religions, particularly in the Assyro-Babylonian religions, "sacrifice always bore a strongly marked relation to nourishment"· P Dhorme, *La Religion assyro-babylonienne*, Paris, 1910, p 265: Lagrange, *Études sur les religions sémitiques*, 2nd ed., Paris, 1905, p. 266: "The matter of the sacrifices was always something that could be eaten or drunk." (Lagrange, *Études*, p. 267)

even to bloody sacrifices. The same is true of the Hebrews. The altar was "the table of the Lord" (Ezek. xli. 22; Mal. i. 7, 12), and even the bloody victim laid upon it was "the food of the Lord". (Lev. iii. 11; xxi. 6, 8, 17ff.)[45]

Therefore, when man made his gesture of oblation, he did not merely expect God to answer: "All is well; I accept this lifting up of your heart." He longed to see his gift received into God's hands, accepted by him as a possession, in an acceptance whereby God did not merely indicate his approval, but actually took hold of the gift That was the object of every offering, and without an actual acceptance no sacrifice was complete.

In making ready for this changeover to divine ownership, man accompanied his act of offering with a rite which set the oblation apart from all profane use. He immolated the victim and put an end to the form its existence had hitherto taken, so that it might become something sacred to God. The study that has been made of ancient religions makes it impossible to see the immolation as a destruction; it was for the purpose of the oblation, forming the negative element in the transfer of a profane thing to divine owner-ship. There were often the most minute preparations and cleansings to try and make the victim capable of passing into God.[46]

Man had conceived the idea of an altar, and hoped in this symbol-ism to lay hold of the intangible Divinity. Did the altar represent God himself, or simply his table? Sometimes one, sometimes the other.[47] The priest laid the victim on the altar as upon God's table and in his bosom. The blood, the supremely sacrificial element, "in which is life", was spread on the horns of the altar (Exod. xxix. 12; Lev iv. 25, 30), which were the part that most particularly repre-sented the Divinity.[48]

[45] Every offering was sprinkled with salt (Lev. ii. 13; Ezek. xliii 24); for the Lord's table must not be lacking "the salt of the covenant" which must always be part of a meal between friends. To eat salt with a man was to be his guest. (1 Esd iv 14.)
[46] "The cleansing the victim underwent .. shows that they were trying to make it divine " (Lagrange, Études, p. 268.)
[47] The idea of the altar as representing the Divinity is as well attested as that of the altar as God's table Cf. Lagrange, Études, p 191.
[48] There was a custom among the Semitic religions of putting four horns at the four corners of the altar. It is suggested by Gressmann (Die Ausgra-bungen in Palästina und das. A T., Tübingen, 1908, p 27ff.) that these horns were simply masseboth put on the altar—the steles which were supposed to incorporate the divinity and which were venerated in the high places; in them the presence of the divinity was realized.

This consecration of the victim was finally completed by burning [49] This was what changed it from an oblation into something
possessed by God. (Lev. ii. 16; iii. 11, 16.) "Sacrifice with an odour
of sweetness" is an expression we often find in the Bible to describe
it. Indeed, in its living non-materiality, it seemed an emanation
from God: "The Lord thy God is a consuming fire " (Deut iv. 24)
By taking hold of the offering, it fulfilled man's wish that "the
Divinity might penetrate [the victim] and take possession of it".[50]

All these rites were attempting with their symbolism to transfer
the victim from the profane sphere to the sacred enclosure of things
transcendent. To the primitive mind, the effect of these rites went
beyond mere representation; it imbued the signs with the power
to realize what they signified The victim was thus consecrated a
thing divine; the word "sacrifice" was interchangeable with the
phrase "to sanctify a victim". (Deut. xv. 19.) It had become so impregnated with divinity that in its turn the holiness of God flowed
into whoever touched it (Lev. vi 27), and whoever ate it entered into
communion with him.[51]

A sacrifice was thus a transfer and a transformation. When, on
solemn occasions, fire "came forth from the Lord" (Lev. ix. 24;
2 Chron. vii. 1–3) and consumed the victim, it did not destroy the
gift men had given, but sanctified and divinized it.

(b) Acceptance in the New Testament

This interpretation of the sacrifice of the past had passed into the
New Testament. For our Lord, the altar sanctified the victim (Mat.
xxiii. 19), and, according to St. Paul, this occurred in other religions
too, the victim being handed over to the power of the divinity.
"Behold Israel according to the flesh: are not they, that eat of the
sacrifices, partakers of the altar? . . . The things which the heathen
sacrifice, they sacrifice to devils, and not to God. And I would not
that you should be made partakers with devils. You cannot drink
the chalice of the Lord and the chalice of devils: you cannot be

---

[49] In the Assyro-Babylonian cults "fire was the intermediary between men
and the gods " (P Dhorme, *Le Religion assyro-babylonienne*, p. 269)

[50] Lagrange, *Études*, p. 268

[51] Then, too, one had to be pure to taste an object once it was sacrificed
(Lev xxii 4–7); and because it was a holy thing and must not be touched
for any profane use, the victim must be burnt if it was not wholly consumed
in the sacred meal. (Exod. xxix. 34)

partakers of the table of the Lord, and of the table of devils." (1 Cor. x 18, 20–21.) To eat of a victim sacrificed on an altar was as much a communication with the divinity for the Greeks and Jews as for believers in Christ. The oblation had penetrated the divinity and been penetrated by it in turn.[52]

If Christ's redemption unfolded along the lines indicated by the old sacrificial pattern, we must take it that our Lord's death consisted in a transforming offering, whereby the victim's profane being was destroyed and he was taken up into God.

The New Testament authors certainly did not develop the sacrificial theology of the Redemption so consistently as to bring them to such an explicit definition. They seized upon the essential aspect of the redemptive act, and saw it as Christ passing from his earthly existence into the possession of God; but though putting it in the framework of a ritual sacrifice, they did not make any methodical use of the full wealth of the analogy. The theologians must have the patience to make a sort of mosaic, to join fragments of ideas into the coherence of a synthesis whose broad outline exists in the idea of sacrifice common to the authors of both Old and New Testaments.

As with the sacrifices of old, the death of our Lord was a free gift. Our Lord himself saw it so: "The Son of Man is come ... to minister, and to give his life a redemption for many." (Matt. xx. 28.) When he instituted a rite for communicating in his death, adding an element of figure to the reality of his sacrifice, he took bread and wine, two foods which primitive religions used to offer to God and share in communion as soon as they had been made God's property. In the language of sacrifice, then, our Lord's death must be taken as a sign of giving He explained further: "This is my body which is given for you." (Luke xxii. 19.) The Apostles re-echoed this· "He gave himself", "He delivereth himself." (Gal. i. 4; ii. 20; Eph. v. 25; Tit. ii. 14.) To whom did he give himself? To God, to men, or to his executioners? To all three, of course, but we may formulate it like this: For love of men, he gave himself to God, by the hand of his executioners. The redemptive act was a gift of love "He hath delivered himself for us, an oblation and a sacrifice to God for an odour of sweetness." (Eph. v. 2; Heb. ix. 14.)

---

[52] There are inscriptions to show that, according to an even more material notion, the god himself actually entered the victim. (Cf. A. Médebielle, "Expiation", *D B. Suppl.*, col. 149ff)

By his death, Christ was moving and rising towards God's taking possession of him, just as other sacrifices rose up to God in smoke.

What had he to give that the Father did not already possess? We see what this must be. He was in God with all the roots of his being. But while he was immersed in God in these depths of his substance, and was conscious of the fact, his existence was adapted to a world which did not belong to the divine transcendence; to all appearances it was a profane existence, tarrying on the threshold of the temple. In the redemptive scheme there remained in Christ a self that *was* still on the threshold, simply in order that he might thus make an entry into the sanctuary in spite of being essentially present there already.

To complete God's possession of him, our Lord gave himself to the Father in the immolation of that more distant self. He tells us so: 'Ἁγιάζω' ἐμαυτόν "I sanctify myself" (John xvii. 19); in other words, "I consecrate myself to God in sacrifice."[53] The corresponding Hebrew word is normally used to mean consecration to God, transfer to the divine sphere. God's holiness was in the divine nature itself, it was synonymous with the transcendence of his being (1 Sam. ii. 2; Ps. xcix. 1-5; Isa. lvii. 15.) A creature is sanctified not simply by being what he is but by the fact of leaving the profane world and penetrating the sphere of the divine being. Sanctification called for separation from the profane world, immolation—in so far as that was possible—and oblation; it was the same as sacrifice. (Exod. xiii. 2; Deut. xv. 19.)[54]

Our Lord was, then, defining his passion as a sacrifice by which he vowed himself to God's holiness in the oblation of his earthly being.[55]

The sacrificial giving is incomplete without the divine acceptance. Will God accept Christ's gift of himself, will he receive it and

[53] Interpreters ancient and modern have seen this expression as a term of sacrifice St. John Chrysostom paraphrases it: "I offer thee a sacrifice " (*In Jo*, xvii, 19, *P.G*, lix, 443) Most of them, however, are thinking of only one aspect of the sacrifice, the immolation; this must of course have been present on the horizon of Christ's mind, but did not fill it wholly

[54] St Augustine (*De Civ. Dei*, x, 6, *P L.*, xli, 283) wrote in this sense: "Every man who was consecrated through God's name and vowed to God was a sacrifice in that he died to the world in order to live to God."

[55] R. Asting, *Die Heiligkeit im Urchristentum*, Gottingen, 1930, p. 314-5: Ἁγιάζειν means separation from the profane world and entry into the divine sphere He who was sent from God cut his bonds with the profane world and returned to his Father "

impregnate it with holiness? If he ever accepts any sacrifice, he will accept this one; for Christ "hath delivered himself a sacrifice . . with an odour of sweetness" (Eph. v. 2), a lamb without spot, undefiled. (1 Pet. i. 19.) If he does accept it, there must be more than merely a sign of consent. The sacrificial mentality demands that the holiness of God should really take possession of the victim. The sacrifices of old were efficacious only on the level of signs, but in Christ's sacrifice, where there is no apparatus of ritual, where all is reality, the acceptance must be real, too: the Divinity must open out to the victim and close upon it.

In his sacerdotal prayer that the sacrifice may be accepted and may achieve its redemptive purpose, our Lord's first intention is his glorification. One commentator[56] paraphrases the "Father, glorify thy Son" of John xvii. 1 like this: "Exalt him to a state of glory by accepting this great sacrifice " The glorification is the divine acceptance of the victim without which the offering would not attain its proper end, and which sets it apart as something holy, as a sacrifice. "I sanctify myself", said our Lord: through the immolation and oblation of myself, I pass into the holiness of God.

The Epistle to the Hebrews, which is the great priestly epistle, sets out very clearly the role played by the life of Christ in glory in completing the redemptive sacrifice.

A disciple of Paul's is showing Judaeo-Christians—inclined to be lukewarm and tempted to compare the Christian religion with the pomp of Jewish ceremonial—the superiority of Christianity. A religion's excellence is to be measured by the relationship it establishes between God and man; in both Jewish and Christian religion this relationship is formed through the mediation of the priest, a mediation which takes place primarily in sacrifice. Therefore the doctrinal object of this epistle is to establish the superiority of Christ's priesthood over the priesthood of old, and in working out this comparison, the exposition of Christ's sacrifice is "the pith of our argument". (viii. 1.)

The sacrifice of the Son of God shows its superiority over all others by its once-for-all efficaciousness: it alone expiates sin and effects union with God, for it alone enters the true sanctuary, the Godhead, and in it every man can come to God. The inferiority of the Levitical sacrifice is shown by the fact that its victims could

[56] P. W. Von Keppler, *Unseres Herrn Trost*, 2nd ed., Freiburg-i-B , 1914, p. 342

never get beyond a figurative sanctuary; it was a sacrifice that only sanctified in figure.

In the Epistle to the Hebrews, the sacrifice which began on the Cross is completed only in God. Accustomed as he was to tracing the pattern of Christ's oblation in the sacrifices of old, the author describes that oblation in the terms of Old Testament ritual. For this he chooses the most solemn and significant ritual of all, the Sacrifice of Atonement. Once a year the High Priest, having immolated a bull and a goat outside the sanctuary, took their blood and went into the Holy of Holies. He thus bore his victim, for its life was in its blood, into God's dwelling-place, and sprinkled it over the covering of the Ark, where Iahweh dwelt. He was placing his victim in God's bosom, as far as it was possible for a man to do so.[57]

Against this backcloth, the author sets out the account of the sacrifice of the Redemption. Our Lord immolates himself outside the tabernacle, on earth; there he pays the ransom for sin. (ix. 12.) But "the sacrifice (its earthly phase, that is) is mentioned only indirectly as the means of gaining entry to the sanctuary"[58]; for it is not completed simply by the outpouring of blood. In the old rite they immolated the victim in order to take its blood through the first sanctuary into God's dwelling; similarly, Christ offers himself in order to go by way of his immolation into the Holy of Holies of the Godhead. "Christ...by a greater and more perfect tabernacle not made with hands, that is, not of this creation. neither by the blood of goats, or of calves, but by his own blood entered once for all into the Holies." (ix. 11–12.)

The exegetes are not in agreement as to the exact way Christ took to come to the inmost sanctuary. What is this tabernacle which is the anteroom of the sanctuary of heaven? Some moderns think it was heaven itself or the lower heavens: "The expression 'passing through' and the analogy with the tabernacle of Moses rather suggest that this tabernacle was heaven."[59]

---

[57] The *kapporeth* (covering of the Ark) expressed the meaning of the altar most fully, for it was there, between the two cherubim, that Iahweh appeared (Lev. xvi. 2) and was permanently enthroned among the people. (1 Sam. iv 4, 2 Sam vi 2; 2 Kings xix 14–15; 1 Chron xiii 6, xxviii. 2)

[58] J. Bonsirven, *Épître aux Hébreux*, p. 384

[59] A. Médebielle, *La sainte Bible L'épître aux Hébreux*, Paris, 1938, p. 333. This interpretation is based on Heb iv 14 and ix 24, but is incorrect According to ix 24, Christ does not enter *through* heaven, but *into* heaven, which is the true sanctuary. In iv 14, the lower heavens might be meant; but these were thought, of old, to belong to the order of creation; iv. 14 would then

To the early Christians, and especially the Greeks, the tabernacle was Christ's body, which our Lord, in a sense, passed through by his immolation. For this passing constitutes a means of our redemption; Christ enters the sanctuary by it[60] as well as by means of his blood (ix. 12), and by stripping the veil from his flesh he is preparing the way. (x. 20.)[61] This context would lead us to this interpretation. The Holy of Holies was virtually inaccessible, for God wanted to teach us that the true sanctuary, where union with God takes place, would remain closed so long as the Old Covenant stood as an anteroom of salvation which the rites of every day could not get beyond. (ix. 8–9.) By the sacrifice of his body, Christ went beyond this compartment of history, did away with it, and gave us access to God. In this context it is natural to liken the immolation of the flesh to the passing of the High Priest through the first tabernacle into the sanctuary; this passing was a rite of sacrificial oblation, and so prefigured Christ's immolation, but it did not achieve its object. Further on the author makes his meaning clear: it was through the veil of his flesh that our Lord penetrated to enter the inmost tabernacle of God, and through that same veil we penetrate with him. (x. 20.)[62]

This final sanctuary is clothed in mystery; the author's thought is far beyond any material, local interpretation of it. Faithful to the old idea of a heaven partitioned into compartments one above the other, some commentators consider that the author is following a strict parallel between Christ's entry into heaven and the High Priest's entry into the Jewish tabernacle; having passed through the lower heaven, Christ penetrates into the empyrean, the dwelling of the Godhead. But this is too strict a parallelism, and makes far too material a relationship between type and antitype. Our Lord passes through the immolation to reach the end of his journey in

leave ix. 11 unexplained It is possible, too, that the Vulgate may give the true meaning translating iv. 14 as "hath passed into heaven". Here again, heaven is the sanctuary of the Divinity, not a place in the sky.

[60] διά suggests cause as well as locality, as in x 20

[61] Cf B F. Westcott, *The Epistle to the Hebrews*, 2nd ed., London, 1892, pp. 256ff.; J. Bonsirven, *Épître aux Hébreux*, p. 382.
The epistle might be saying that Christ is passing through a tabernacle not of this creation, because this tabernacle and this passing are a heavenly reality

[62] Cf C Spicq, *L'Épître aux Hébreux*, Paris, 1953, vol. ii, p. 315–6 This idea grows out of the Pauline doctrine that man can escape inclusion in the world of sin by uniting himself to the immolated body of Christ The opening through which we can pass has been made in the body of Christ.

God. The divine sanctuary is not a reality in the order of place; we should not perhaps separate it entirely from all notion of place, but the emphasis is on God's presence. Entry into the sanctuary is synonymous with entry into glory (ii. 9ff.), being in the presence of God (ix. 24), and sitting at the right hand of God (i. 3, 13; viii. 1; x 12; xii 2), which means the consubstantial possession of the Godhead. Though expressed in ritual terms in this epistle, the effect of Christ's death remains the same: a close communion with God.[63]

This entry into the sanctuary is actually an element of the sacrifice —its concluding phase; the immolation and the offering bear Christ towards God, in whose bosom the sacrificial movement will reach its completion.

This is clear from the juxtaposition of Christ's entry into glory with the rite of Yom Kippur. By this parallel, the entry into glory appears as the final phase of a sacrifice. For the sprinkling of blood on the Propitiatory (Lev. xvi.) was both the last and most significant act of offering whereby the victim was placed close beside God, and the mark of God's accepting it.[64] The epistle understood it so; the High Priest of Israel offered the blood, bearing it into the Holy of Holies. (ix. 7.) Similarly, our Lord bore his sacrifice into the Godhead. The contrast made between Christ's sacrifice and the sacrifices of every day suggests the same conclusion. During the days of prefigurement, the priests, standing in the tabernacle, were occupied with the daily repetition of their sacrifices (x. 11), because access to the Holy of Holies where these would be consummated, the image of the true sanctuary of God, was forbidden to them. (ix. 6–8.) "But this man having offered one sacrifice for sins, forever sitteth on the right hand of God." (x. 12.) His sacrifice was decisive, for it had attained its goal in God.

In the light of the liturgy that prefigured it, then, the glorification of Christ appears as the completion of his sacrifice, its acceptance

---

[63] "As Père de Condren understood it, the heavenly Temple . was none other than the bosom of God." (J Bonsirven, *Épître aux Hébreux*, p. 19.)

[64] It is true that in Lev xvi 16–19 the rite of aspersion seems less a rite of offering than a rite for making use of the expiatory power of the blood: the sprinkling purifies the Propitiatory of any uncleanness it may have contracted during the year by being in the midst of a sinful people. But this chapter stands out as something of a compilation and is generally recognized as such (Cf P. Heinisch, *Das Buch Leviticus*, Bonn, 1935, pp. 77–80) The explanation given in these verses is adventitious It is also surprising that the sprinkling of the horns of the altar (xvi 18) was originally intended to purify the altar, although this rite always symbolized offering

by God.[65] And so it also appears when the author dispenses with the help of this rather uncertain light, and takes up Christ's sacrifice in its reality, looking upon it as a consummation in God through suffering.

"Consummation (τελείωσις) is perhaps the word most characteristic of the epistle."[66] "To consummate (τελειοῦν) is to make perfect (τέλειος), to bring something to the ideal goal (τέλος) which is that thing's point of perfection."[67] The Old Law could never consummate anything. (vii. 19; ix. 9; x. 1.) Generations had gone forward by prolonged efforts, but had never come to the "repose of God"; torrents of blood had been poured out in an attempt to appease the Divinity, each outpouring calling for another, for none could get beyond the veil, either in the sanctuary of the Divinity or the understanding of the sinner. The saints of the Old Law died still on the threshold of consummation. (xi. 40.) But the way is opened to us in Jesus Christ, who was the first to enter by his own sacrifice: "It became him ... wishing to bring many children into glory, to perfect the author of their salvation by his passion." (ii. 10.)

The perfection of Christ on earth was therefore still in a state of evolution. In what did its perfecting consist? Suffering worked upon his soul, drawing out its deepest reserves of heroism; it inscribed on it an experimental knowledge of our sufferings and our shrinking from the demands of God: "Whereas indeed he was the Son of God, he learned obedience by the things which he suffered, and was consummated." (v. 8–9.)

But the word τελείωσις goes much further than this purely moral interpretation; it signifies a consummation in the whole being. It is a tremendous word which is synonymous with the crown of glory

[65] Yet we are brought up short by the very text that leads to this conclusion. It was as "high priest of the good things to come" that Christ "entered once for all into the Holies". (ix 11–12) As high priest, by the merits of his sacrifice, not as victim. But we must look closer. The high priest of the New Testament enters the glory of heaven because he is both victim and priest. "By his own blood he entered." (ix. 12.) The veil was drawn away by the immolation of the body, the victim was first to go in, and with him the priest, because he was the victim Sacrifice and priesthood are bound up with one another in the thought of the epistle, both in Christ and in the Sons of Levi.

[66] F. Prat, *Theology*, vol. 1, pp. 394–5. Cf. C Spicq, *Épître aux Hébreux*, vol ii, p 224.

[67] Cremer, *Wörterbuch*, Gotha, 1902.

and honour granted to Christ after his humiliations (cf. ii. 9 and 10), and which characterizes the state of the souls united to God in glory (xii. 23); and, since saviour and saved must take the same road, and Christ's final perfection must be no less than that of the saved, it must also mean the raising up of the state of flesh and blood to life in glory. (ii. 10–15.)[68]

This consummation in glory crowns the act of sacrificial offering. The author here gives a more conceptual formula for the reality he has elsewhere expressed by an image, the image of the entry into the Holy of Holies.[69]

For the ancients, sacrifice offered and consecrated simultaneously; once offered, the victim was at the same time stripped of its profane being and consummated in the transcendent perfection of God[70]

The epistle remains faithful to this conception of sacrifice; consummation in God is the shining reverse side of oblation. τελείωσις however, characterizes more directly the effect of the sacrifice upon the offerer than upon the victim. "For the law, having a shadow of the good things to come ... by the sacrifices which they offer can never consummate those who seek to come [to God]." (x. 1.) But the two effects are closely linked the victim did not consummate the offerer in the past because it did not attain its own consummation; it was offered only as a sign, and never penetrated within the sanctuary But Christ did come to this completion in the perfection of God, because his sacrifice was consummated in God. Consummation can be identified with access to God,[71] or, more exactly,

[68] C. Spicq, *Épître aux Hébreux*, vol. i, p. 282: "Perfection" is not the result of a course of virtue, but of a consecration Often the terms "holiness" and "consummation" are used interchangeably with no appreciable difference of meaning. But they are not interchangeable It is well known that the effect of the rites of old on men's souls was superficial, yet the epistle says that they sanctified, qualifying this by "to the cleansing of the flesh" (ix 13.) But consummation has too much real significance to bear such qualification; it means a perfecting of the whole being, and for Christ the perfection of his glory

[69] The idea comes close to the phrase "I sanctify myself" from the sacerdotal prayer, but with this difference, that "sanctification" implies an immolation, although its emphasis is on consecration to God, whereas "consummation" envisages only the latter

[70] Père Prat writes· "Expiation and purification were, as it were, the reverse side of sanctification and consummation: the former wiped out sin, the latter put a positive perfection in its place To sanctify was to consecrate a thing to God, setting it apart from profane use " (*Theology*, vol. i, p 394)

[71] In Christ's consummation we find our access to glory (ii 10) The Law does not consummate, for it does not give access to God. (vii 19) The Law

it expresses the perfection man attains through his access to God.

Thus both death and the glorification are complementary aspects of the one sacrificial action, in which they represent immolation and consummation respectively.

In this sacrifice we are saved, simultaneously in its beginning, Christ's death, and in its end, his resurrection. His death is redemptive in as much as it results in his resurrection; we find expiation for our sins in our salvation, and that salvation is in the Resurrection.

The sacrifice of the past could not cleanse "the conscience of dead works" because it did not have its conclusion in God; Christ could abolish sin because in his sacrifice he had access to God; he wiped away sin because he had offered a sacrifice which enabled him to sit at the right hand of God. (x. 11–14.)

The expiation was not so much a debt to pay as a gulf to bridge, by the painful abandonment of a profane state of life in order to achieve union with God. The expiation was effected by a movement towards God, with a love which encompassed all justice.

Here again, then, the drama of the Redemption was wholly enacted in Christ. In spite of the groanings of his flesh, everything in him that shrank from the suffering involved was drawn inwards by this sacrifice.[72] The redemptive sacrifice consisted in Christ's personal return to God. But if it was to be redemptive, this return must not remain merely an individual one; sin was not so much a debt as an estrangement, and could only be destroyed in us if we became one with the sacrifice which carried Christ to God. Our salvation must also be seen in terms of going to God; for us, as for him who saved us, access to God is attained by the journey through the immolated body of Christ: "Having, therefore, brethren, a confidence in the entering into the Holies by the blood of Christ; a new and living way which he hath dedicated for us through the veil, that is to say,

does not consummate, for the sanctuary is still closed to its sacrifices. (ix 8) Christ consummates us because he is sitting at the right hand of God (x. 12–14) The ancients were not consummated, that is to say, they did not have access to God (xi 40.) The just in glory are consummated (xii. 23.)

[72] It is still true that Christ offered his oblation only for us. We read in the *Anathematizations* of St. Cyril of Alexandria: "If any one says that he offered his oblation for himself and not solely for us (for he who knew no sin had no need of oblation): let him be anathema" (Denzinger-Bannwart, 122) According to the Epistle to the Hebrews, his death primarily profited our Saviour himself. But there is no contradiction here The Passion had the resurrection of Christ as its goal, but the Resurrection, and therefore his whole sacrifice, had only our salvation as its goal Had it not been for our sin, Christ would have had no reason for dying and rising again.

his flesh . . ." (x. 19–20.) The believer advances to salvation by a new and living way—the immolated and risen body of Christ.[73] By uniting himself to that body, he follows his Saviour through his immolation to his new life.

But now we must go on to look at Christ's resurrection under a new sacrificial aspect—not now as the consummation of his offering, but as communion in his sacrifice.

ii. THE RESURRECTION, COMMUNION IN THE SACRIFICE

(a) Communion in the Old Testament

The sacrifice of the past included a communion In order to honour and appease his divinity, man cherished the ambition of coming into contact with it. "The idea of union with God was certainly one of the elements constituting a sacrifice" in the Semitic religions [74]

In primitive society, whether of clans or tribes, social relationships flowed from the sharing of bodily life, from community of blood, "wherein is life", or community of food. Therefore, to create a bond between himself and God, man tried to establish a similar community of blood or food.

Though in the sacrificial offering of blood the symbolism of communion is less significant, we can still perceive an intention of union alongside the rite of offering.[75]

[73] "The way is called living, not only in the past because it was traced through a living being by the shedding of blood, but in the present too. Our only access to God is through Jesus Christ. . and this presupposes a very close communion between us and him It was something like this that Theodoret meant when he wrote: 'Just as, following the Law, the High Priest went into the Holy of Holies through the veil, so those who believe in the Lord enter into the joys of the heavenly city by the reception of his most holy body.'" (J Bonsirven, *Épître aux Hébreux*, pp. 437–8) The body laid open by the Passion is the way we take and the blood is what bears us into the sanctuary, but they are a body and blood to which we are united now in a living union, the glorified humanity of Christ.

[74] Lagrange, *Études sur les religions sémitiques*, p 268

[75] Cf. Lagrange, *Études*, p. 260 The blood was borne upon the sacred stone, that the Divinity might receive it and thus there might be one blood between him and man. It would clearly be a "blood of covenant" if God, having accepted it, sprinkled the offerers with it; one blood brought by man and brought by God, in which both parties to the covenant communicate and fraternize. (Exod. xxiv. 6, 8.) Besides creating a bond of relationship, it was the supreme instrument of cleansing and consecration; for once it had entered God's possession, this blood of sacrifice washed every impurity with the holiness of God, and extended its own consecration upon every man or object sprinkled with it (Lev. xiv 6–7)

It was primarily through the sacrificial meal that man entered into the intimacy of God. Having covered God's table with gifts, the offerers were invited to sit down at it. God receives only to give in return. This victim which has, through the rites of immolation and offering, become the property of God, is now given back to man, but sanctified, consecrated to his divinity. Man sat at God's table, in his presence; man was his guest, nourishing his life with sacred food, and as the feasters made merry, God's joy was joined with men's.

The symbolism of offering required a sacred meal as its natural conclusion. The sacrifice of communion seems to have been the earliest form of worship, and later on at least the most widespread rite, constituting the type of sacrifice.[76]

It may seem that in Israel the idea of God's sovereignty, a livelier sense of sin and fear of the Lord, prevented man from assuming the familiar attitude of a fellow-feaster with God. In Hebrew ritual the communion sacrifice is somewhat overshadowed by the holocaust and sin-offering in which the meal is either foregone altogether, or reserved for the priest. But apart from certain cases which stand out particularly in biblical writings, sacrifice normally included a meal.[77]

Israel was a nation united within itself and welded to Iahweh, because it sat at the table of its God. "Behold Israel according to the flesh: are not they, that eat of the sacrifices, partakers of the altar [of Iahweh]?" (1 Cor. x. 18.) The Hebrews were brothers among themselves, and while some of them might bear the name Abia, "God is my father", there were others with the name of Achia, "God is my brother". The flesh of the victims, sprinkled with salt, had established a contact: "there was salt" henceforward between them and God, "a covenant of salt".[78] A victim consecrated to God drew all who fed from it into the orbit of divine holiness. Israel was to be a holy nation, set apart from all other peoples,

---

[76] Cf. Lagrange, *Études*, p 273.

[77] The sacrificial instinct spontaneously takes this form (1 Kings xix. 21); the offering of the first-born of the flock, the first-fruits of the earth, of tithes, all ended with a meal. "In the place which the Lord your God will choose . . . thither shall you bring all the things that I command you . . . There shall you feast before the Lord your God." (Deut. xii. 11 and *passim*) "Sacrifice in their vocabulary was almost a synonym for eating and drinking before Iahweh. All sacrifices . . other than holocausts, seem to have included a meal" (J. Coppens, "Eucharistie," *D B Suppl*, col 1157

[78] Lev 11 13; Num xviii 19; 2 Chron xiii 5

because it was a nation of priests who offered victims to Iahweh and were nourished by them.

In the sacrificial scheme of things, these bonds took effect *ex opere operato*. The eating of the paschal lamb constituted a sacrificial meal,[79] and for that reason, created a union. Anyone not circumcised was therefore excluded (Exod. xii. 44–48); but any Hebrew who refused to eat his share cut himself off from the Covenant. (Num. ix. 13.)

(b) Communion in the New Testament

This communion was not lacking in the sacrifice of Christ. The New Testament writers were bound by the idea of sacrifice they had inherited from the past to see a communion as completing our Lord's oblation, and their own concept of the work of redemption would also lead them to do so. They could not have thought of any real communion with the immolated Christ had the redemption merely been accomplished on the juridical level, by the payment of our ransom. But the drama of redemption was enacted in the person of Christ, in the sacrifice which transformed and divinized his humanity through its immolation. And the action of Christ would simply close in upon itself without touching us at all if man could not communicate in the victim of the Cross now consummated in glory.

When Scripture seeks to define the character of the new sacrifice by giving an example from the past, the choice does not fall upon a holocaust, but upon a communion sacrifice: the Pasch. St. John recalls it at the moment when Christ's immolation is complete. (John xix. 36.) St. Paul declares that "Christ our pasch is sacrificed." (1 Cor. vi 7.) St. Peter's allusion is less explicit: "You were redeemed with the precious blood of a lamb unspotted and undefiled." (1 Pet. i. 18–19) Before his death our Lord prepared a table and offered his immolated body in an actual meal. This last supper has two facets—one looking towards the typical feast of the Pasch which our Lord has just celebrated, the other looking towards the Cross;

---

[79] The immolation of the lamb was a true sacrifice; such was the primitive conception of it. (Exod. xii. 27; xxxiv. 25.) This character later became blurred, though the blood of the lamb was still poured out at the foot of the altar in the Temple According to the Book of Jubilees (xlix. 20), even the fat was burned on the altar St. Paul spoke of the paschal lamb as a sacrificial rite (1 Cor. v 7)

thus it sets the offering of the Cross among the sacrifices of communion and likens it to the sacrifice of the lamb . . . The communion of his disciples is the final end of our Saviour's offering: "Take and eat, this is my body [Matt., Mark] given for you." (Luke, 1 Cor.) The sacrificial offering of his body is made for the disciples, and as the body has been delivered up for them, let them take and eat it.

Christ says that he himself sits at the table of his sacrifice. This present Mosaic Pasch is the last he will celebrate on earth, but he will soon eat the new Pasch in the Kingdom: "With desire I have desired to eat this pasch with you before I suffer. For I say to you, that from this time I will not eat it till it be fulfilled in the kingdom of God." (Luke xxii. 15–16.) At the end of the paschal meal, Christ says again: "I say to you, I will not drink from henceforth of the fruit of the vine, until that day when I shall drink it with you, new, in the kingdom of my Father." (Matt. xxvi. 29; Mark xiv. 25.)

These words herald the great messianic banquet;[80] at the same time they introduce the institution of the Eucharist, and by setting them side by side, the nature of both is made clearer. The Eucharist appears as the earthly anticipation of the feast to be celebrated in the joy of the new wine in the Kingdom. The banquet in the Kingdom is, in its turn, seen as a prolongation of the Eucharist, and is none other than the total fulfilment of the eucharistic supper; a "perfected" Pasch at which we communicate in the true sacrifice of the Lamb.

Our Lord himself will eat this Pasch with the Apostles and drink new wine with them.

It will be on "that day", at the end of time, that the feast will be eaten, and in the Kingdom of the Father. Now, for Christ the final day is the day of his glorification, and the Kingdom begins with his entry into glory.[81] That is the moment when Christ sits down at the table of his sacrifice.

The disciples will then take their places in turn. They will gather round their risen Master in a mysterious feast.[82] They will communicate in the Redemption, united to Christ in glory, and receiving, in him, the glorifying action of God.

[80] Though Matthew and Mark put them after the supper, they were in fact pronounced before the institution of the Eucharist. Cf. P. Benoit, "Le Récit de la cène dans Luc xxii, 15–20", *R B.*, xlviii (1939), pp. 357–93.

[81] See below, chapters v and vii.

[82] See below, pp. 319–25.

All this combines to identify the inauguration of the messianic banquet with the resurrection of our Lord, and to define his glory as a paschal meal, a communion in the Cross.

The glorification is God's acceptance of Christ as victim, and the communion of Christ as priest. Communion and acceptance come together because victim and priest are one. In the Epistle to the Hebrews, the acceptance of Christ the victim gives Christ the priest access to God, and the consecration of the victim is one with the consummation of the priest: the acceptance of the victim *is* the communion of the priest.

Having so wholly communicated himself, Christ is communicated by God to those who unite themselves with his sacrifice.[83] His glorified bodily being is offered to us as food for our salvation. The believer communicates in the blood and eats the body (1 Cor. x. 16); he has a share in the altar (Heb. xiii. 10) and is sprinkled with blood as in the past (Heb ix. 14, 20; xii. 24; xiii. 12; 1 Pet. i. 2). Judging from the effects of the communion in the sacrifices of old, all those at table are drawn into the same sanctification as the victim and formed a sacrificial community, receiving divine life from the victim of Calvary transformed in God.

In the light of sacrificial theory, the glorification of Christ appears as a necessary phase of his oblation. It is the completion without which his sacrifice is essentially mutilated and is therefore no sacrifice—just as there can be no movement which does not arrive anywhere, and no gift where there is no-one to accept it.[84] His glorification not only completes his sacrifice in itself, but also makes it beneficial: in the divinized victim God communicates himself to the offerer and to all who eat at the altar.

In all the writings of the various Apostles, the Redemption always appears as a divinization of man in Christ, by way of the death of all in man that is not yet in God

The Godhead stands, as it were, at both ends. Christ's divine

---

[83] J J Olier, *La Vie intérieure de la très-sainte Vierge* (ed. Faillon), Paris, 1866, vol. ii, p. 236· "After his resurrection he existed wholly to be communicated and given to men."

[84] St Bonaventure found an excellent formula: "Justification was merited by the Passion alone, and not the Resurrection—but in the Resurrection alone, and not the Passion, do we find its purpose and goal" *Sancti Bonaventurae Opera Omnia*, vol. iii, p. 401, Quarrachi, 1887

condition (Phil. ii. 6), the Incarnation (fourth gospel). is its beginning; God concludes the work with his glorification. Man's effort is
not enough either to start or to consummate; the economy of the
Redemption shows grace at its most magnificent.

Christ's work was to travel from one end to the other, to prepare
himself for the Resurrection. He took the opposite way from that
taken by the first Adam, and came to glory in God by renouncing
the glory that was his own

It is by the perfecting of what was incomplete in Christ's earthly
existence that we are saved. Christ's glorification is the mystery
whereby the treasures of his divinity flow to us, through the opening
of his mortal life.

This doctrine of salvation through the Resurrection is the great
factor which synthesizes the theology of the Redemption It throws
light on the part played by the Incarnation, establishes the need for
our Lord's death, keeps a true balance between the two mysteries,
and unites them in harmony.

III

THE RESURRECTION AS OUTPOURING OF
THE HOLY SPIRIT

What is the nature of this new existence which Christ's death
has merited for him, in which salvation is to be found? And what is
the gift that union with his glorified Saviour assures the believer?
These preliminary questions must be answered before we can reach
a deeper understanding of the Resurrection and its significance for
our salvation.

Scripture is remarkably consistent in setting together in opposition
the two ideas of flesh and spirit. Since his death marked the end of
Christ's existence according to the flesh, one line of research seems
opened to us: surely our Lord's new existence must be characterized
by the Holy Spirit, and the gift it makes possible for us must be
that same Spirit.

I. THE SYNOPTICS AND THE ACTS

According to the Synoptics, our Lord lived even during his time
on earth under the guidance of the Spirit; the descent of the Spirit
was the rite that conferred upon him the Messiahship (Matt. iii. 16;
Luke iv. 18; cf. i, 35). But our Lord gave the disciples no share
of this moving principle of his;[1] not until after the Resurrection
did he call down the outpouring of the Spirit upon them. (Luke
xxiv. 49.) Luke, with his two books, becomes, as it were, the Evangelist of the Holy Ghost; he presents us with a diptych, whose
hinge is Christ's death and resurrection, showing the activity of the
Holy Spirit, first in Christ alone, then in the followers of the glorified
Christ. From the moment of Christ's glorification, the activity of
the Spirit, which had been limited to our Lord himself, spread out
among all the faithful and was borne to the ends of the earth
"Being exalted therefore by the right hand of God, and having

[1] Except in so far as the power to work miracles contained the gift of the
Spirit.

received of the Father the promise of the Holy Ghost, he hath poured forth this which you see and hear." (Acts ii. 33.)

The giving of the Spirit is the essentially messianic grace, the fulfilment of the promise made by the Father (Luke xxiv. 49) for "the last days" (Acts ii. 17), and it crowns our Lord's work of salvation.

2. St. John

In the fourth gospel, our Lord, on the eve of his death, declares that his going will result in the coming of the Spirit: "If I go not, the Paraclete will not come to you; but if I go, I will send him to you." (xvi. 7.) We have seen that this going is not local, not a passing from the world into some upper space, but a movement of ascent marked by the raising up on the Cross and concluding in glory. The visible ascension will be merely the outward sign of the essential raising up of Christ into the glory of the Father. (xiii. 32.)

On the evening of Easter Day, Christ appeared to his Apostles and breathed upon them: "Receive ye the Holy Ghost." (xx. 22.)[2]

These episodes in St John bring us very close to the mystery of the giving of the Spirit According to the Acts, it would seem as though the outpourings of the Spirit were the result only of the ascension in space; the fourth gospel connects them with the glorification of our Lord itself: Christ sets in motion the economy of the Spirit simply by having risen.

St. John assures us of this in connection with a phrase our Lord spoke in the Temple, during the Feast of the Tabernacles.

This feast of the month of Tishri marked the close of harvest time, of fruit- and olive-picking. It commemorated the coming out of Egypt and the wandering in the desert. Like the Hebrews in the

[2] Those authors who see our Lord's going only as the visible ascension find it surprising that he should give the Holy Spirit so soon Hence they try to minimize the importance of this Easter giving. Some early writers took this first sending as a psychological preparation for the outpouring of Pentecost Cf. Theophylactus, *En. in Ev. Jo.*, xx, 22, *P.G*, cxxiv, 297. Others saw it as simply a simulacrum of the sending of the Spirit: Theodore of Mopsuestia, cf the condemnation of the Three Chapters, Denzinger-Bannwart, 224, and R Devreesse, *Essai sur Théodore de Mopsueste*, Vatican City, 1948, p. 417.

But the return to the Father was in fact essentially effected by the glorification, and our Lord was faithful to his promise by sending the Holy Spirit on Easter Day itself.

desert, everyone lived for a week in tents of leafy branches set up
on the flat roofs of their houses, in public squares and in the out-
skirts of the city. Remembering their tremendous past, the people
were moved to enthusiasm, and their hearts opened to the hope of
a more splendid liberation whereby God should lead them through
other deserts to their messianic destiny as foretold by the Prophets.

It was the most joyful of the Jewish feasts as well as the most
spectacular, "the most holy and the greatest".[3] Each morning, the
populace assisted at the sacrifice, everyone holding in his right hand
a palm entwined with myrtle and willow (*lulab*), and in his left a
citron (*ethrog*). The Levites chanted the great Hallel (Ps. CXIII–
CXVIII), and the multitude sang the last psalm, beating time with
their palms. A priest attended by Levites went down to the Pool
of Siloam and took some water from it in a golden jug. The procession returned to the Temple through the Water Gate and the
trumpets sounded three times to recall the messianic promise: "You
shall draw waters with joy out of the fountains of salvation." (Isa.
xii. 3.)

In the East, in lands of drought, water is the symbol of life.
Wherever a spring appears, life appears, the desert becomes fertile,
man washes in the living water, quenches his thirst and goes on his
way with renewed strength. The Prophets promised an abundance
of miraculous water at the end of the world. (Isa. xliv. 3–4; xlix. 10;
Ezek. xxxvi. 25.) The miraculous water which sprang up on the
roads of Sinai, which saved the people from death, will spring up
again, living and life-giving, when the Messiah comes (Isa. xlviii.
21), on the road to deliverance.

These waters—springing up, or poured out—were an image of
the Holy Ghost in the eyes of the Prophets. "I will pour out waters
upon the thirsty ground...I will pour out my spirit upon thy
seed." (Isa. xliv. 3.) The phrase "to pour out the Spirit" was coined
by the Scripture. (Isa. xxxii. 15; xliv. 3; Zech. xii. 10; Joel ii. 28.)

Tabernacles was originally an agricultural feast, and the cere-
mony with the water was to beg for the gift of autumn rain. But
by our Lord's time attention was focused on the rock in the desert,
and still more on the rock of the future from which the messianic
waters were to spring. The feast looked forward to the day when
the people would drink with joy at the springs of salvation.

On the seventh and last day the morning ritual of the water took

[3] Josephus, *Antiquities*, viii, iv, 1.

on an even greater solemnity; it was the "Day of the Hosanna", and rejoicings went on through the night in the illuminated Temple. According to the Mishna, anyone who has never seen "the joy of the water" has never really seen joy in his life.[4]

"On the last, and great day of the festivity" (John vii. 37), while the priest brought the water, amid the hosannas and rustling of palms, a cry was heard: "If any man thirst, let him come to me and let him that believeth in me drink! As the Scripture saith, 'Out of his belly shall flow rivers of living water.'" (vii. 38.)

While the attention of the multitude was held by the festival of the water, this voice made itself heard, producing silence, and turning all eyes upon our Lord. Water springing from a rock, gift of life and refreshment, symbol of messianic abundance—the multitude were shouting and waving in its honour, but they did not know that the rock was in their midst and the spring ready to gush forth.

St. John explains that the water our Lord was speaking of was the Spirit: "This he said of the Spirit which they should receive, who believed in him." They "should receive" in the future—for "as yet the Spirit was not given". (vii. 39.)

The Evangelist indicates the reason for this delay: "...because Jesus was not yet glorified". (vii. 39.) Only Christ in glory can bestow the Spirit.

We might do no more than take this declaration as it stands. But a further analysis of the text brings us suddenly to the very heart of the Easter mystery.

The exact sense of our Lord's words depends on the punctuation we give them. Until recently, most editions gave us the text like this: "If any man thirst, let him come to me and drink. He that believeth in me, as the Scripture saith, 'Out of his belly shall flow rivers of living water.'"

Christ is thus the supreme source of the Spirit, but the believer who drinks of him becomes in turn a fountain springing up, and from him flow "rivers of living water".

Origen seems to have been the first to make the believer a source of the Spirit in this way The text, thus interpreted, gave him scriptural support for his doctrine of the *gnosis*. The water the Gospel refers to is the divine *gnosis* springing up out of the Trinity.

[4] For a detailed description of the feast, see Strack and Billerbeck, *Kommentar des N.T. aus Talmud und Midrasch*, vol ii, pp 774–812

From its source in the Father it comes down upon mankind by way of the Logos who communicates the Spirit. Man drinks in that *gnosis* by drinking in the teaching of the Word from the four rivers of Paradise in the Gospels. Living water is thus identified with "the water of teaching"; it is drunk by faith, and is once again transformed into *gnosis* in the believer, into a knowledge perfect as it is in God, "springing up into life everlasting". (John iv. 14.) As this *gnosis* is stored up in the understanding of the believer—the belly, as Scripture calls it—the waters overflow and spread wide. And thus the Christian gnostic himself becomes a mystagogue for others, a mediator of the *gnosis*, a source of the Spirit.[5]

So great was Origen's authority that this exegesis was accepted throughout the East. In the West we find it first of all in Origen's disciple, St. Ambrose,[6] then in St. Jerome.[7] It held uncontested sway from that time onwards.

Origen, however, knew of another interpretation which must have come spontaneously to his mind as a traditional one. By it the source of the Spirit is not the immaterial Logos or the soul of Christ, but his bodily humanity; his body is the rock in the desert which, when struck by the rod of the Cross, lets flow rivers of living water.[8]

This exegesis, which is less philosophical and more Christian, becomes the right one if we punctuate the text of St. John differently· "If any man thirst let him come to me. And let him that believeth in me drink; as the Scripture saith, 'Out of his [the Messiah's] belly will flow rivers of living water.' "

Christ is thus the only source of the Spirit, and it is from his belly that the believer must quench his thirst.[9]

---

[5] *In Gen.*, hom. vii, 5, 6; xi, 3; xiii, 3–4. (*P.G.*, xii, 202, 223, 234–6.) Also *In Num.*, hom. xii, 1–2, *P.G.*, xii, 656–61 Also *In Ezech.*, hom. xiii, 4, *P G.*, xiii, 764ff.

[6] *Expl. Ps* xxxix, 22; *P L.*, xiv, 1067, *Epist.* LXIII, 78, *P.L.*, xvi, 1210.

[7] *Praef. in Paralip.*, *P.L.*, xxviii, 1326

[8] *In Exod.*, hom xi, 2, *P.G.*, xii, 375ff.; *Com. in Cant Cant.*, ii, *P.G.*, xiii, 141

[9] This punctuation and this interpretation have been reinstated by Père Lagrange, *Évangile selon saint Jean*, 3rd ed, Paris, 1927, pp 214–7. Cf earlier, T Calmes, *L'Évangile selon saint Jean*, 2nd ed., Paris, 1906, pp 73–4 Père Lagrange bases his exegesis upon the study of patristic tradition made by J. Armitage Robinson in "The Passion of Saint Perpetua. The Letter of the Churches of Vienna and Lyons", *Texts and Studies*, i, 2, Cambridge, 1891, p 98, and C. H. Turner, "On the Punctuation of Saint John vii, 37 and 38", *Journal of Theological Studies*, xxiv (1923), pp 66–70 The material collected for these studies was methodically arranged and considerably enriched in a

This interpretation is clearly indicated by the context. John explains our Lord's words (vii. 39) The water, he says, means the Spirit, which those who believe are to receive. The believer is therefore not himself a source, but comes to Christ to quench his thirst (Lagrange). Thus we read, "Let him drink, he that believeth in me." Then, too, grouped like this, the words correspond to the first phrase of the sentence: "If any man thirst, let him come to me"; in John's style, this means that whoever believes in Christ comes to him. (cf. vi. 35.) The sentence contains two parallel phrases in the Semitic fashion:

> If any man thirst, let him come to me,
> and let him that believeth in me drink.

To encourage his believers to drink from his belly, Christ quotes Scripture, with its assurance that rivers will flow from the belly of the Messiah.[10] But the believer will not find this source open to him as yet, for the springing up of the Spirit is conditional upon the bodily glorification of Christ: "As yet the Spirit was not given, because Jesus was not yet glorified." (vii. 39.) This last makes it quite conclusive: the belly from which the rivers of the Spirit are to flow is that of the Messiah. The idea of a believer becoming a source of the Spirit is foreign to the context.[11]

This exegesis was widely held in the West till the Alexandrian influence came to do away with it. Even then it remained strong enough to influence the very men who taught Origen's interpretation. St. Jerome, for instance, and Rufinus and St. Ambrose, could not help seeing a symbolic fulfilment of John vii. 37 in the water flowing from Christ's side as it once flowed from the rock that became a fountain." "Drink ye Christ, for he is the rock spurting

remarkable article by H. Rahner, "Flumina de Ventre Christi", *Bib.*, xxii (1941), pp. 269–302, 367–403

[10] The only contrary indication to this interpretation of any importance is that the scriptural quotation does not seem to apply to Christ: "From *his* belly shall flow rivers .." Would he not have said, "From *my* belly.. "? But, as Père Lagrange points out, "In a quotation, one generally expects the text to be given as it stands."

[11] We cannot take iv. 14 as indicating a different meaning ("The water that I will give him, shall become in him a fountain of water, springing up into life everlasting"). This water is a source of eternal life only for the believer who possesses it, as with "the meat which endureth unto life everlasting". (vi. 27.)

water, drink ye Christ, for he is the fountain of life . . Drink ye Christ, for from his belly shall flow rivers of living water."[12]

This tradition of exegesis goes back to the oldest and most authentic sources of Johannine exegesis; we find it in the second- and third-century authors who expressed the ideas of St. Irenaeus, inherited in their turn from the Church at Ephesus which was taught by St. John.

St. Hippolytus was the first in the West to quote the text; this is the form he gave for it "Rivers will flow from his body."[13] In his scheme of thought, this *logion* was part of a compact system of scriptural texts, forming together a synthesis on the importance of our Lord's bodily humanity in our salvation. "The sacred flesh of Christ" was the spiritual rock (1 Cor. x. 4)[14] which, once the Passion had struck it open, flowed with the rivers of the Spirit.

For Hippolytus and all the West, St. Irenaeus was the master of this theology of living water.[15] All the elements of a synthesis can be found spread among his writings. Wherever his influence was felt[16] we find a belief in the realist conception that the source of the Spirit was in Christ's bodily humanity, and the flowing of blood and water were the symbolic realization of the promise he gave on the Feast of the Tabernacles. The Church of the martyrs looked with love upon the pierced Christ in their midst, from whose side they drank the waters of the Spirit which sustained their heroism.[17]

---

[12] St Ambrose, *Expl. Ps*, i, 33, *PL*, xiv, 940 For other witnesses see H. Rahner's article, pp. 390–400

[13] *In Dan.*, i, 17

[14] *Com Fragm. in Prov*, xxiv, 61.

[15] H Rahner, "Flumina de Ventre Christi", pp 371–4
By placing the Gospel text beside the definition of the Church as the body of Christ, Irenaeus drew the conclusion that the Church also was a source of the Spirit, and from her side too the faithful might drink from the clear spring flowing from the body of Christ Cf *Adv Haeres.*, III, xxiv, 1. *P G*, vii, 966

[16] It took hold in Africa, as Tertullian shows in *De Baptismo*, ix, *P.L.*, i, 1210. St Cyprian encompassed the whole idea with his explicit quotation of the text from John. "The Lord cries that whoever thirsts should come and drink of the rivers of living water that flow from his belly" (*Epist. ad Jubaianum*, *P L*, iii, 1116; *Epist. LXXIII*, *P.L*, iv, 379 Africa offers many similar indications, cf H. Rahner, "Flumina", pp. 382–7.

[17] Of the deacon Sanctus, of Vienna in Gaul, it was said, "He stood upright, neither bending nor yielding, firm in bearing witness, bathed and fortified by the heavenly spring of life-giving water which flowed from Christ's side. Cf Eusebius, *Hist Eccl*, v, 1, *P.G*, xx, 417

With Rahner, one can follow this tradition right back to Ephesus itself, for all its elements can be found in the argument St Justin had there with the Jew Trypho, around the year 135 Christ pierced is "the good rock" where we drink the water of life[18] and Justin is evidently relating the spiritual rock (1 Cor. x. 4) to the belly of Christ in St. John, for he declares that "we are hewn (as from a quarry) from the belly of Christ".[19]

To explain the scriptural text (John vii. 38) which forms an insuperable difficulty for the supporters of Origen's interpretation,[20] Irenaeus and Cyprian easily found not perhaps the quotation word for word, but at least equivalent expressions which harmonized with their interpretation. Irenaeus quoted Isaiah xliii. 19–21; Cyprian quoted the more topical text:

> "They thirsted not in the desert, when he led them out; he brought forth water out of the rock for them; he clove the rock, and the waters gushed out". (Isa. xlviii. 21.)

Their whole theology of the living water seemed to them to be summed up in this prophetic text: Christ was the rock which, struck by the Passion, let flow the water of salvation. It is clear that this quotation must be sought for in this and similar texts. Having applied to himself the figure of the Temple (ii. 19–21), of the brazen serpent (iii. 14), of the Manna (vi. 32ff.), our Lord offers himself as the fulfilment of Moses' rock, foretold by Scripture, and celebrated by the Jews in the festival of the water. These Fathers added to these texts from Isaiah one from Zechariah, for to them it was

[18] *Dial. adv Tryph* , cxiv, *P G.*, vi, 740
[19] *Dial. adv Tryph.*, cxxxv, *P.G* , vi, 788
[20] "The doctors laboured most anxiously to find evidence of this in Scripture " Toledo, *Com in S. Jo. Ev.*, Coloniae Agrippinae, 1589, p 706. St Cyril of Jerusalem, *Catech* , xvi, 11, *P G.*, xxxiii, 932, altered it to read: "He that believeth in me as Scripture demands." Early writers thought they had found the reference in a mistranslated text from Proverbs (v. 16) Moderns quote Isaiah lviii. 11; but it is clear that the fountain that springs up in the believer according to this text waters his own garden alone A M Dubarle, in *Vivre et Penser*, 3rd series, 1943–4, pp 238–41, suggests Prov. iv 23 But the life-giving water that springs, according to this text, from the heart of the wise man spreads out only over his own existence. To make it say more, this verse must be taken in conjunction with the Proverbs (x. 11; xiii. 14; xviii 4) drawn from a collection by a different man at a different time—not a very commendable procedure And in any case, Christ is quoting a messianic and prophetic text, and these proverbs are neither. We must conclude with Père Lagrange· "The doctrine of the disciple as a source of living water seems foreign to the Old Testament."

"the pierced [Christ]" who was the source of the Spirit, as this
text says: "And I will pour out upon the house of David, and upon
the inhabitants of Jerusalem, the spirit of grace, and of prayers:
and they shall look upon him whom they have pierced .. In that
day there shall be a fountain open to the house of David." (Zech.
xii. 10; xiii. 1; cf John xix. 37.)

Hence we know that it is from Christ's body that the faithful
drink of the Spirit. Our Lord used a thoroughly physical word
which we may translate as "from his belly", "from his side", or
"from his heart". The part played by Christ's body in our salvation
keeps appearing. Our Lord in his glorified body will be the
messianic temple as opposed to the former temple of stone (ii. 19).
It is a remarkable coincidence that it is said of that temple (Ezek.
xlvii.) that a torrent will flow out from under its gates to fertilize
the desert.[21] When he promised the Eucharist, Christ declared that
eternal life would be received from contact with his flesh (vi 51-9);
and this life, assimilated in faith by eating the body of Christ, was
at the same time a thirst-quenching water: "I am the Bread of Life;
he that cometh to me shall not hunger, and he that believeth in me
shall never thirst." (vi. 35.)[22] When the Jews showed their stupefac-
tion at the realism of what he was asking of them ("unless you eat
my flesh"), our Lord refers them to his glorification (vi. 63), and
to the Spirit by whom alone can his flesh sanctify: "It is the Spirit
that quickeneth; the flesh profiteth nothing." (vi. 64.)

The outpouring of the Spirit is thus seen to have a necessary connexion with the bodily glorification of Christ It is presented in the
Acts as an effect of the exaltation into heaven, and in the promise
given after the Last Supper as a consequence of the return to the
Father, but there no essential link seems to exist between it and the
glorification of Christ. Our Lord's words on the Feast of Tabernacles and the interpretation given them by the Evangelist place the
source of the Spirit in the glorified body of Christ, and link the outpouring of the Spirit with the bodily glorification of our Saviour.

---

[21] More than one author has made this link between John vii 38 and
Ezek. xlvii. Cf A. Schweitzer, *Die Mystik des Apostels Paulus*, Tübingen,
1930, p 347, A M. Dubarle, "Le Signe du Temple", *R.B.*, xlviii, 1939, p 37.
[22] The two promises (vii 37, and vi. 35) are related even in the way in
which they are expressed. in both "to believe in Christ" corresponds with
"to come to him".

Before seeing the promise fulfilled in reality, St. John assisted at its anticipation in symbol on Calvary.

In his eyes the blood and water flowing from Christ's side constituted the most significant of the events that accompanied the death of his Master. So outstanding was it that he thought it necessary to call Christ as witness to his words: "And he that saw it hath given testimony, and his testimony is true. And he [Christ][23] knoweth that he saith true; that you also may believe." (xix. 35.) For him, the flowing of the blood and water was proof of the truth upon which everything else rested· "... that you also may have faith."[24]

There have been many explanations suggested of the symbolism of the two elements. In the mind of St. John, they conjure up two principles of salvation. In his gospel, whenever water is giving a symbolic significance, it always indicates the principle of salvation that is twice called "Spirit". Sometimes it is a metaphor to describe grace (iv. 14), a grace which is a communication of the Spirit of Christ (vii. 37–9);[25] elsewhere real water is made the principle of salvation, acting in the power of the Spirit: "Unless a man be born again of water and the Holy Ghost" (iii. 5), and finally, it was for Christ an instrument of healing in as much as it symbolized this baptism in the Spirit.[26]

[23] The ἐκεῖνος indicates Christ (cf. 1 John ii. 6; iii. 3, 5, 7, 16; iv. 17)

[24] "Literally, 'in order that you may believe'. But since πιστεύητε is not qualified, it must be understood as faith in general." Lagrange, Évangile selon saint Jean, p 501

[25] In the Apocalypse, the paradisal river (xxii. 1–2) is an image of the person of the Spirit, who proceeds from the Father and the Lamb, and of the totality of the gifts he gives

[26] The cure of the man born blind holds more of a lesson than any other miracle recorded by John. Our Lord declared that he was the light of the world (ix. 5), and then prepared to heal the blind man. He spat on the ground, made clay of the spittle and placed it upon the man's eyes A strange action. However variously it may be explained, this clay is not of a nature to herald a cure and cannot, in our Lord's intention, be the agent of the cure. It must have been meant to make the blindness more evident. "It would have prevented his seeing, had he not been blind: it added blindness to blindness" (Lagrange, Évangile selon saint Jean, p 260ff.) Christ's action suggests to us that the water of Siloam was to remove the clay to give back the vision It was symbolic water "The name Siloam ... was a proper name which first of all meant [a] canal . and thus indicated some sort of sending, or transmission of water From this popular name, John made a symbolic name meaning sent—'Siloam, which is interpreted, Sent' (John ix. 7)—turning it into the passive, he who was supremely 'the sent' . . Christ himself .. Christ

As for the blood flowing from Christ's side, its essential symbolism can be none other than the humanity of our Lord bleeding in his passion. This blood, in running out, brought with it through the wound in the flesh the water of the Spirit which lay in its depths.

Such was the interpretation of the Irenaean school, summed up in this sentence of one of the Fathers: "By the blood which was poured out, we receive the Holy Ghost; for the blood and the Spirit are linked together since, by the blood which is of our nature, we can receive the Spirit who is not of our nature."[27]

The theology of the living water develops further if we add what St. John tells us in his first epistle to what he says in his gospel. Once again we find the two symbolic elements, but the overtones are more varied.

The Apostle defines the object of the Christian faith as Jesus, Son of God, who came by water and by blood (v. 5–6).[28] This "coming", as the word is used by John, means the incarnation of the Word of God.[29] The water and blood by which it took place signify "not the means but the distinctive nature"[30] of the Son of God's coming to earth, the nature of his coming and hence of his being. John understood the two elements, water and blood, as metaphors for the two aspects of Christ's being: his divinely spiritual, and humanly corporeal, constitution.

From the beginning of Chapter IV, the Apostle is arguing against

sent the blind man to the pool which bore his own name, where his action would be felt by baptism " (Lagrange, *Évangile selon saint Jean*, p 261)

The blind man found "illumination" in the water of Siloam; the water recalled baptism in the Spirit (iii. 5), the name Siloam suggested the name of Christ

"Illumination" is effected in the Spirit whom we find in Christ

[27] *In Pascha*, sermo ii, *P.G*, lix, 726ff. C Martin, "Un περι τοῦ πάσχα de S Hippolyte retrouvé?", *Rech Sc. Rel*, xvi, 1926, 162–5, suspects this of being a sermon of St Hippolytus But this attribution has been contested Cf. R H. Connolly, "New Attributions to Hippolytus", *Jour Theol Stud.*, xlvi, 1944–5, 192–200

[28] Some manuscripts add "and by the Spirit". But this must be rejected as being insufficiently attested, as an attempted harmonization (cf. verse 8) which does not make proper sense

[29] J. Chaine, *Les Épîtres catholiques*, Paris, 1939, p 213, thinks that the participle ἐλθών, because it is in the aorist, indicates a given event in the life of Christ (his baptism, for instance) But John x 10, also uses the aorist for our Lord's coming in general

[30] J Chaine, *Les Épîtres catholiques*, p 213.

the Docetist heresy, which refused to accept that our Lord had truly
come in the flesh. (iv 2ff)[31]

Faced with these "Antichrists", the Apostle reaffirms his statement: He is come "not by water only, but by water and blood"
(v 6), not simply as a spiritual being, but in a human body. The
Spirit bears witness to the coming in this twofold reality: "And
the Spirit is witness of this, for the Spirit is truth" (v. 6 in the Greek
text); he speaks to the heart of the Church (John xv. 26) and,
because he is truth, it is this faith which he proposes to the faithful
But to have irrefutable proof according to the Law, God demanded
that two or three witnesses should agree (Deut. xvii. 6; xix. 15;
John viii. 17–18). So the Apostle produces two more witnesses: "For
there are three that give testimony: the spirit, the water and the
blood· and these three are unanimous." (v. 8.)[32] Now, the water
and blood are more than mere metaphors, for only realities can
give evidence. The real water and blood spoke for the truth of our
faith when they flowed from Christ's side, "that you may have
faith". The danger from Docetism explains the solemnity of the
Gospel account and John's insistence on guaranteeing its truth: the
water and blood flowing forth revealed the mystery of the divine
and human nature of Christ—the object of our faith.[33]

---

[31] Towards the end of the first century and at the beginning of the second,
the Docetist heresy was at its height in Asia Minor As well as John, other
Church leaders, St Ignatius and later St. Polycarp, were very much alive to
the danger it constituted to the faith. This heresy denied Christ's true bodily
humanity, and declared that he had suffered in appearance only. Hence the
equal insistence with which the Apostle and the two bishops declare their
faith in the body and their faith in the blood of Christ.

St Ignatius writes: "For myself, I know and I believe that even after his
resurrection Christ had a body. Make no mistake, even the inhabitants of
heaven, the angels, glorious as they are .. if they do not believe in the blood
of Christ, they cannot escape judgement." (*Smyrn*, iii 1; cf. vi 1, *Trall*,
ix 1)

Starting, almost word for word, with the text of 1 John iv. 2–3, St. Polycarp
shows in his turn that the blood of the Cross is proof that Jesus Christ truly
came in the flesh· "Any man, indeed, who refuses to recognize that Jesus
Christ came in the flesh, is an anti-Christ; any man who rejects the witness
of the Cross is a devil." (*Phil.*, vii 1.)

[32] We know that our Sixto-Clementine Vulgate text (giving three witnesses
in heaven which are contrasted with three witnesses on earth) is not attested
by Greek textual tradition, nor even by the oldest Latin manuscripts

[33] The next verse (9) does not mean that the witness of the spirit, the water
and the blood is human, as is often thought (by J Bonsirven, and perhaps
also by J Chaine), but rather, "If we are accustomed to accepting a threefold

The water coming from Christ's side thus reveals a mysterious complexity. It is an image of the Spirit (iii. 5; vii. 37-8) and it also represents the nature from on high that is in Christ (1 John v. 6), so that the Spirit and the heavenly element in Christ are intimately linked.[34]

The spiritual water which quenches the thirst of the believer comes down, then, from the eminence of the Word, and springs from the body of Christ, his glorified body which has passed through death. Its source is high up in the bosom of God and in the Word who proceeds from him, and it gushes out close to our human mouths, from the open wound in a man's body. The two great Johannine themes come together in the giving of the Spirit at Easter: salvation by the coming of the Word, and salvation through the immolated body of Christ.

We know now why the sending of the Spirit was dependent on Christ's going (xvi. 7). Père Lagrange's answer to the question was, "It is God's secret."[35]

Generally we frame the question wrongly, wondering "Why could the glorified Son not have remained on earth and still given his Spirit?"[36] It seems inexplicable that the whole sanctifying work of Christ should depend on a change of place[37]

The return to the Father upon which the sending of the Spirit depends is more than merely a change of place, it is a divinizing transformation (xvii. 5) effected in Christ's death and resurrection. The sending of the Spirit demanded this exaltation first. For, first

human witness, then *a fortiori* must we accept this witness given by God."

The interpretation of 1 John v 6-8 offered here does not agree with the usual exegesis whereby the water is the water of Christ's baptism. But in its favour are its own coherence, its harmony with Johannine doctrine as a whole, and the fact that the fourth gospel does not record Christ's baptism Also, several modern writers relate this text to John xix 34. Cf. A Schweitzer, *Die Mystik des Apostels Paulus*, Tubingen, 1930, p. 347; O. Culmann, *Christian Worship*, pp. 115-16, A. Tricot, *L'Église naissante*, Paris, 1946, p. 426.

[34] To be born from on high is to be born of the Spirit (John iii. 3, 5)

[35] *Évangile selon saint Jean*, p 418.

[36] Lagrange, *Évangile selon saint Jean*, p. 418.

[37] Reasons are then sought simply from the point of view of the faithful, to explain the delays in the sending of the Spirit: according to St. Augustine, the sensible presence of Christ made the Apostles unable to rise to the spiritual dispositions necessary for receiving the gift of God (*Sermo CCLXX, In Die Pentecostes, P.L*, xxxviii, 1238). Père Lagrange (*Évangile selon saint Jean*) argues that Christian life in the Spirit is a life of faith, and "Christ glorified would have put evidence in place of faith". These are rather extrinsic reasons.

of all, the Spirit could only be sent from beside the Father in the high places of heaven (xv 26); the original source of the Spirit is there. And then, it is from the belly of Christ, by the contact of faith with the flesh of the Saviour, that the believer can drink of the waters of life; man has no other point of contact with the reality of heaven, the life of the Spirit springs up for him nowhere but in the body of this man. Christ must be exalted in his flesh into the glory of the Father in order for the rivers to flow from his belly.

The evening of Easter Day, Christ breathed on the Apostles and said to them, "Receive ye the Holy Ghost." (xx. 22.) It was Christ in the whole of his being, bodily and divine, who breathed the Spirit upon the Apostles, wholly raised as he then was to the height whence the Spirit proceeded.[38]

3. St. Paul

In the thought of St. John, dominated by Christ in glory, our Lord, even on earth, primarily appears as divine; he is therefore not subject to the action of the Spirit, but himself sends the Paraclete as soon as he has, by dying, rejoined the Father. St. Paul is more conscious of the reality of the deficiencies our Lord accepted during his life on earth, and shows him submitting himself to the glorifying action of the Spirit. Filled from the beginning with the Spirit, Christ becomes in the Resurrection a source of the Spirit for all those who are "in him".

1. CHRIST RAISED BY THE SPIRIT

(a) By the Spirit

The Spirit is the principle of Christ's glorification: "And if the Spirit of him that raised up Jesus from the dead dwell in you; he that raised up Jesus Christ from the dead shall quicken also your mortal bodies by the power of the Spirit that dwelleth in you." (Rom. viii. 11.)[39] The Holy Spirit appears as an agent of the

[38] This enables theology to explain why the risen Christ is not only a living being, but a life-giving spirit, a source of life because he is life, because he is a being wholly communicated For he is totally raised to the eminence of the Son, and the Son, as Son, is source of the Spirit.

[39] The textual tradition for this verse, however, is not unanimous. One variant, equally well-attested reads "because of [or, "with regard to"] his spirit" But this is thought by critics to be unimportant (Tischendorf, Von Soden, Westcott and Hort, Nestle, Vogels, Merk)

Resurrection; the glorification of the faithful is explicitly attributed to him and that of Christ indirectly. The Father is behind the action of resurrecting, but it becomes effective by means of the Spirit. Each of the two causes has its part; the Spirit, here and in many other places, appears as the active person, the executive principle; he exercises a quasi-instrumental activity that is proper to him.[40]

There is an unbroken tradition in both Old and New Testaments that the Holy Spirit personifies the holiness in the Divinity which is what makes God transcendent over the flesh; he is, further, the life-giving principle and irresistible force of divine action. If we are to penetrate the nature and redemptive significance of the Resurrection, it is necessary to realize that it was the Spirit who raised Christ to glory. Every suggestion indicative of the part played by that Spirit is worthy of our consideration

(b) By the Power which is the Spirit

Such a suggestion is to be found in the constant attribution of the Saviour's glorification to the power of God. To St. Paul the Resurrection was a work of such power that he can only express his wonder at it by heaping up all the words that suggest force: "That you may know ... what is the exceeding greatness of his power towards us, who believe, according to the energy of the might of his power which he wrought in the person of Christ, raising him up from the dead." (Eph. i. 18–20.) Though Christ on the Cross had succumbed to the weaknesses of his flesh, he rose up in a new life by the *dynamis* ("power") of God: "Although he was crucified through weakness, yet he liveth by the power of God." (2 Cor. xiii. 4.) We ourselves shall rise by the power of God; for so it was

[40] Looking at the subtly differentiated relationships established among the persons of the Trinity by the preposition διά here, and ἐκ and ἐν elsewhere, exegetes seek to differentiate the doctrine of appropriation. While works *ad extra* belong to the activity common to the three Persons, this is certainly not the case with the divinizing action of grace whereby the creature is drawn into the divine life (Cf G. Thils, *L'Enseignement de saint Pierre*, 2nd ed., Paris, 1943, p 66) The attributing to the Holy Ghost of a special and quasi-instrumental causality in the Resurrection is explained, if the grace of Christ is the principle of his glorified life, and if, also, there exists a special relationship between that grace and the person of the Spirit Grace is certainly the principle of the glorified life—we call it the formal cause—and grace, also called "spirit", is, according to St Paul, to be considered as a participation in the Holy Spirit

with Christ: "God hath raised up the Lord, and will raise us up also by his power." (1 Cor. vi. 14.)

Now the power is indissolubly bound up with the Spirit. Even in the Old Testament, the Spirit of God acted with an irresistible power. It was God's creative power in the world (Gen. i. 2; Ps. ciii. 29-30; cxxxviii. 7); it seizes hold of man, dominates him, and imparts to him a dynamism, either physical (Judges xiii. 25; xiv 6; xv. 14), intellectual or moral. (Num. xxiv. 2; 2 Sam. xxiii. 2; Isa. xi. 2.) The New Testament is invariably faithful to this traditional notion. In St. Luke, the evangelist of the Spirit and the power, it is in the Holy Ghost that Christ was promised by the power of the Most High. (Luke i. 35.) To enable him to wield the messianic power given by that first anointing Christ received a further descent of the Spirit in the Jordan. (iii. 22) Full of the Spirit (iv. 1, 18) and his power (iv. 14), he entered upon his public life; the power he possessed was communicated by contact with him (vi. 19) and worked miracles; the Spirit was the finger of God by which our Lord cast out devils. (cf. Luke xi. 20 and Matt xii. 28.) St. Peter explained this life of miracles by Christ's having been anointed with the Holy Ghost and with power. (Acts x. 38.)

The consistency with which the power accompanied the Spirit in Christ remained unchanged for his followers. Our Lord had promised his disciples that "power from above" would be sent down upon them, and this power was personified in the giving of the Spirit. (Acts i. 8; Luke xxiv. 49.) The whole Christian life develops as it were on top of human weaknesses, and is therefore both a life according to the Spirit, and a demonstration of the power of God Every work of power indicates the presence of the Spirit, and wherever the Spirit is present he shows himself in works of power. "The close connection between these two concepts of spirit and power is one of the characteristics of Pauline theology",[41] and indeed of all biblical theology.

We must then conclude that if Christ was raised up by the power, it was by the Holy Ghost that he came back to life.

This conclusion is confirmed by the fact that his death is attributed to the weakness of Christ, whereas his new life is related to the

[41] J. Lebreton, Les Origines du dogme de la Trinité, 4th ed, Paris, 1919, vol. i, p 398. St. Cyril of Alexandria continues along the lines of Scripture when he writes, "The Spirit is the natural action and power of the divine substance. He carries out all the works of God " Thesaurus, Assert., xxxiv, P G., lxxv, 580, 608; lxxii, 908

power. Weakness is as much a characteristic of the flesh as power is of the spirit, and besides, the two notions of flesh and spirit are also inseparably linked, this time by association of opposites. "The flesh" means the created, upheld in its being and its activity by its own principles alone; "the spirit" means the transcendence of God and his action, and all sharing in that transcendence. In the history of salvation, flesh and spirit are bound together like the two sides of a balance-scale, always moving in opposition and contradiction to each other. The mention of either concept almost always draws the other with it on the horizon of the mind, even when it is not explicitly spoken of. In all New Testament literature no parallelism of ideas remains so constant, and none stands out more in Paul's epistles.

Whereas the spirit is endued with power, the flesh appears as devoid of any power for salvation. "The weakness of the flesh" is as much part of Biblical vocabulary as "the power of the spirit". Our Lord had formulated the law that "the flesh is weak" (Matt xxvi. 41): "The spirit quickeneth; the flesh profiteth nothing." (John vi. 64.) These two opposing pairs of ideas—spirit and power, flesh and weakness—are so closely related that either word of a pair can be used indifferently: "The weapons of our warfare are not carnal, but mighty." (2 Cor. x. 4.) A proper balancing of sentence and thought ought to demand " ... but spiritual", but in fact a perfect synonym has been used.

When the Apostle writes: "He was crucified through weakness, yet he liveth by the power of God" (2 Cor. xiii. 4), we can express his thought thus: "He died because of his flesh, yet he liveth by the spirit." St. Peter repeats this statement almost word for word: "Christ died once for our sins ... being put to death indeed in the flesh, but enlivened by the spirit." (1 Pet. iii. 18.)

(c) By the Glory which is the Spirit

Because it is a work of power, therefore, we feel the action of the Holy Spirit in the Resurrection. His action is also suggested when Paul declares that Christ "is risen from the dead by the glory of the Father". (Rom. vi. 4.)

The glory (*doxa*) and the Spirit are closely connected in Paul's mind.

In the Old Testament, there are hints of a relationship between the glory of God and the Spirit The two realities come together in the ideas of power and holiness that they respectively imply The glory of God (*kabod*) is concretized in the fiery and luminous cloud in which the Lord came down and showed himself in his temple.[42] In rabbinical thought this cloud was God's dwelling, the place of his presence; it was called the Shekina, the Dwelling. The Spirit sometimes took the place of this cloud. In Isa. lxiii. 10–14, he takes on the role of guide to the people as in the desert; it was he who rested upon the Messiah-King in the same way as the cloud. (Isa. xi. 2.)

At the beginning of the New Testament, the Spirit, who is the Power of God, came down like that cloud of glory, upon Mary, and surrounded her with the mystery of God as with a luminous shadow: "The Holy Ghost shall come upon thee, and the power of the Most High shall overshadow thee." (Luke i. 35.) It is generally agreed that this means the divine *kabod* coming down upon our Lady and surrounding her with the luminous mystery of the presence of God, and this glory is identified with the Spirit and the power of his action.

While our Lord was conversing upon Tabor with Elijah and Moses, a cloud appeared, "the excellent glory of God" (2 Pet. 1. 17); it covered Christ and his interlocutors. A voice came from it saying, "This is my beloved son. Hear ye him " This theophany recalls the one that took place on the banks of the Jordan. Both revealed our Lord's divine sonship. A great many authors think the cloud on Tabor can be interpreted as John the Baptist interpreted the dove (John 1. 33), that is, as being of the Holy Ghost.[43] God declared of the man upon whom the dove descended. "Thou art my beloved Son", for there is a connection between the Spirit and sonship. (John i. 34.) Surely this cloud is also an image of the Spirit, this bright cloud from the midst of which God declared: "This is my Son", after it had "overshadowed" Christ. (Mark ix. 6.)

St. Paul was soaked in the Old Testament, and the glory (*kabod*) in which God dwelt was familiar to him. When he speaks of the

[42] Exod xxiv 16–17; xl 32; Num x. 34, 1 Kings viii. 11; Ezek x 4; xliii. 2–5; xliv 4; 2 Chron vii. 1–3
[43] Origen, St Albert the Great, St Thomas, Cornelius a Lapide, Jansenius of Ghent and Suarez are quoted by U Holzmeister, *Bib*, xxi (1940), 205ff St. Ambrose relates this episode to the text "The power of the Most High shall overshadow thee." (*In Luc*, i, vii, *P L*, xv, 1704 See also J. Daniélou, "Le Christ prophète," *Vie Spir.*, lxxviii (1940), p 161.)

Israelites having possessed the Glory, the Covenant and the Law,
he is certainly referring to this biblical glory. For him the Glory was
a concrete reality, and he seldom uses it to mean the subjective glory
that our worship gives God. (2 Cor. viii. 19.) He maintains the
established bond between the ideas of glory and of the Spirit. But
his thought takes a new turn; it moves quite considerably away
from that visual representation of glory so dear to the Bible and
Judaism, and in spiritualizing the concept, brings it closer to the
Spirit.

In the Old Testament, the glory of Iahweh is the revelation of
God's majesty, of his holiness and his power.[44] In St. Paul, that
glory is similarly characterized by holiness and power.

The two concepts of glory and power interpenetrate to such an
extent that the Apostle can speak quite simply of "the glory of his
power" (2 Thess. i 9), and "the power of his glory" (Col. i. 11;
Eph. iii. 16.) When Christ comes, he will transform our body of
lowliness into the likeness of his body of glory by the power of God
working in the Resurrection. (Phil. iii. 21.) Earlier on the Synoptics
had linked the two terms: the coming in glory was to be a coming
in power (Mark viii. 38; ix. 1; xiii. 26.) It is therefore no falsifica-
tion of its meaning to translate Rom. vi. 4, as "He is risen by the
power of God."

This must mean that the Spirit is linked with the glory, for both
are united in the power. On the last day we shall live again in a
body of glory, which is a body full of power, which is a spiritual
body (1 Cor. xv. 43–5.) Glory, power and spirit—the three are
linked like a chain.[45]

This divine glory is God's holiness as well as his power. What is
called carnal humanity, which is closed to holiness, is the same that
is deprived of glory: "All have sinned and do need the glory of
God." (Rom iii. 23.) It has been said that "the glory [for St. Paul]
is the attribute peculiar to the state of justification."[46] The glory of

[44] B Stein (*Der Begriff Kebod Jahweh und seine Bedeutung für die atl
Gotteserkenntnis,* Emdstetten, 1939), concludes his study of this on p 299:
"The glory is the revelation of the divine transcendence (holiness), recognized in the lofty actions of God " Cf H Kittel, *Die Herrlichkeit Gottes,*
Giessen, 1934
[45] In the Annunciation story we find them similarly placed together: the
cloud of glory, the Spirit and the power of God
[46] H Kittel, *Herrlichkeit Gottes,* pp. 208, 235. Cf R Kittel, *Th. W. N. T.,*
vol. ii, p. 254.

God present in us is none other than the gift of his justice, and that gift is the outpouring of the Spirit.

Even in this life that Spirit transforms us and, as at the Resurrection, he is in us simultaneously as holiness, power and glory. (2 Cor. iii. 18–iv. 6.) When Moses turned towards the Lord, his face shone with the reflection of God; when the believer turns towards the Lord Jesus and contemplates his glorious face, he is transformed into an ever brighter image of that same glory. And the irradiating power which transforms us into beings of light (2 Cor. iii. 18; iv. 6) only comes out from Christ because he himself is wholly penetrated by the Spirit: "We are transformed into the same image from glory to glory, as by the Lord who is the Spirit." The Spirit is the glory of God in Christ, and the power that sanctifies us.

This invasion, as it were, of divine holiness is marked by a parallel advance of glory and of the Spirit; the Christian experiences the possession of the Spirit from the first giving to the complete gift, just as he experiences a glory born and growing within him. We bear within us the first fruits of the Spirit (Rom. viii. 23); these encourage us to hope for a full harvest, which we shall receive when God raises us from the dead by his Spirit. (Rom viii. 11.) We therefore possess glory, but are still waiting for its full flowering, and we possess the Spirit, but are still waiting for his full outpouring.

This oneness of action of the Spirit and the glory, this balanced rhythm of their developing, is to be explained by St. Paul's identification of the glory with the Spirit, at least in so far as the two things affect man [47]

Thus the statements that Christ was raised by the creative power of the Father, and by the glory of the Father, stand alongside the other statement that he was brought to life by the Spirit of the Father. It was important to prove this, not only to confirm the part played by the Spirit, but also to illustrate it If we are to know the properties of this new life produced by the Spirit, it is by no means immaterial to realize that it is through that Spirit that the creative power of God takes effect, and this glorious holiness is diffused.

[47] Rom viii and 2 Cor iii follow a parallel course In the first the Apostle calls "glory" what in the second he calls "Spirit"; the glory and the Spirit are the shining out of the holiness and power of God We find this same identification in St Peter. "The Spirit of glory (and of power), the Spirit of God, resteth upon you " (1 Pet. iv. 14) To him "the terms 'glory' and 'power' are parallel " (G. Thils, *L'enseignement de saint Pierre*, Paris, 1943, p. 42)

ii. CHRIST TRANSFORMED BY THE SPIRIT

(a) *According to the Demands of the Spirit in Him*

The Spirit, before actually effecting the Resurrection, had implanted in Christ characteristics which demanded the new life: "He was constituted Son of God in power, according to the Spirit of holiness, by the resurrection from the dead " (Rom. i 4.) Christ's enthronement in his status of filial power was called for by "the spirit of holiness"; it took place "according to" the norm and the exigencies of that spirit.

Though distinct from the person of the Spirit,[48] this "spirit of holiness" is related to him; it indicates that principle in Christ which stands in contrast to the flesh (Rom. 1. 3–4), and it is primarily the Spirit of God who resists the flesh, so that any holiness that raises man above his carnal nature has some part in him. One can compare the Pauline text with the Annunciation story[49] and draw this parallel: the angel speaks of a work of the Spirit, of the power of the Most High, of the birth of a Son of God; the Apostle proclaims the resurrection of Christ as Son of God, in power, according to a spirit of holiness.[50] There is a continuity between the initial sanctification and the Resurrection; the glorifying action accomplished by the Father through his Spirit (Rom. viii. 11) corresponds to the holiness with which Christ was marked by the Spirit from the beginning.

(b) *According to the Nature of the Spirit*

Raised up by the Spirit, and according to the demands of the initial sanctity imparted by him, Christ's new life bears the mark of the Spirit in its essence; it is none other than the life of the Spirit himself, the infinite power of divine life which shone out in the

[48] I have not identified this "spirit of holiness" with either the divine nature, or the person of the Holy Spirit; I have interpreted it as the divine holiness which characterized the man Jesus, and demanded for him a resurrection into an existence suited to that holiness, the existence of a true Son of God (cf *infra*, p 51, n 29)

[49] A. Resch, *Das Kindheitsevangelium nach Lukas u Matthäus. Texte u. Untersuchungen X B*, Leipzig, 1897, pp 264–9, shows a strong connection between St Luke's account of the childhood and the teaching of St Paul

[50] Herveus Burgidolensis, *P L*, clxxxi, 601ff. gives this commentary on Rom. 1 4: ". .according to the Holy Spirit who sanctified the womb whence [Christ] was to be born "

man Christ Jesus Hence, in the formulae of St. Paul, we may say that the principle of life in Christ is no longer the soul in its weakness, but the Spirit and its power.[51]

The soul (*psyche*) is the principle of life in earthly man, his weak soul with only its own natural powers. It is the life of the flesh and is of the same order as the flesh, in contrast to the Spirit. The Spirit is the glorious holiness of God and his power of life: in God it is a personal entity, in man a communication of holiness and everlasting life. The adjective "spiritual" indicates for St. Paul a relationship with the Holy Spirit, whereas the adjective "psychic" applies to anyone without that relationship. The "psychic" man is indistinguishable from the carnal man; Scripture says he is closed to the things of the Spirit of God. (1 Cor. ii. 14.)[52]

Of Christ, who had lived on earth according to the soul, Paul says that he became a spiritual being in the Resurrection. (1 Cor. xv. 45.)

When God breathed the breath of life into Adam's nostrils, "man became a living soul" (Gen. ii. 7.) This text simply means that man became a living being. But in Paul's mind the Genesis story grows in detail from contrasting the life bequeathed to us by the first Adam with that communicated by the second. The first man became a living being endowed with a principle of carnal life, the soul. (1 Cor. xv. 45.) But besides this body that comes from Adam, there is a spiritual body whose prototype is the risen Christ (xv 44): "As it is written · The first man, Adam, was made into a living soul. The last Adam [Christ], into a quickening spirit." (xv. 45.)

The two humanities stand side by side, one belonging to our life on earth, the other to resurrection in glory The first stems from the creation of Adam; he became a "living soul", a man vivified by the soul with all its weakness. But one day men will know another existence in a spiritual body, for Christ, principle and prototype of

[51] In theological terms, we should say that the person of the Spirit is the quasi-formal cause, and grace, the communicated spirit, the formal cause The soul is no longer the principle of life by its natural power, but in as much as it is vivified by grace There must exist between grace and the Holy Spirit a special relationship of a formal order, hence the possibility of attributing one particular causality in the Resurrection to the person of the Spirit, and another to that of the Father who works through the Spirit. (Rom viii 11.)

[52] The Epistle of St Jude (verse 19) defines psychic men as "having not the Spirit". St James (iii 15) stresses the pejorative sense and describes "earthly, 'psychic', devilish [wisdom]"

the new race of mankind, is a spirit, a heavenly being living by the life of the Spirit.

Christ was not always this life-giving spirit, but "became" so. He was the son of our common ancestor and moulded into his image, before becoming the principle of spiritual humanity. To him also applied the law that "that was not first which is spiritual, but that which is psychic". (xv. 46.) The life-giving spirit, the "heavenly man", as the Apostle also calls him, can be identified with the God-man only in as much as the divinity of Christ is fulfilled in the Resurrection. Ambrosiaster comments, "The second Adam became a living spirit through the Resurrection."[53]

The soul, principle of natural animation in Christ, yielded in its struggle with death. The bodily humanity of our Saviour was thenceforward filled with the overflowing vitality of the Spirit of God. Transposed from psychic existence into the life of the Spirit, Christ's body became "spiritual", and, as such, heavenly (xv. 40), belonging to the transcendent order of things—whereas flesh and blood cannot enter heaven (xv. 50); it is a body of glory and of power (Phil. iii. 21; 1 Cor. xv. 43), wholly penetrated by the spirit of glory. (1 Pet. iv. 14.) The opposition between Christ's carnal life and inner holiness is done away with; the laws of matter no longer hamper him; time and place no longer bind him, for the power and eternity of the Spirit have taken the place of weakness. This spiritualization "is in his very substance to such a point that we cannot merely say that Christ has become spiritual, but simply spirit".[54]

With a failure of understanding undreamed of in Pauline theology, liberal exegetes go on from this fact to conceive the Apostle's glorious Christ as an ethereal substance dissolved in God; our Lord's humanity is thus in some way sublimated by the Resurrection into some impersonal power or fluid that is sprinkled about for the Christian to bathe in, breathe and live by.[55]

The texts upon which this interpretation is based are the verse

[53] P L., xvii, 269. Most Catholic exegetes agree with this (cf F. Prat, Theology, vol ii, p. 174) and also Protestant (cf. B. Weiss, Lehrbuch der biblischen Theologie des N T, 7th ed., Berlin-Stuttgart, 1903, p. 294, A. Schweitzer, Die Mystik des Apostels Paulus, Tübingen, 1930, p 163).
[54] L Malevez, "L'Église corps du Christ", Rech Sc. Rel, xxxii (1944), 50
[55] A. Deissmann, Die neutestamentliche Formel "in Christo Jesu", Marburg, 1892; W Bousset, Kyrios Christos, 4th ed, Göttingen, 1935; A Schweitzer, Mystik, E Käsemann, Leib und Leib Christi, Tübingen, 1933.

we have just analysed (I Cor. xv. 45), and still more this other: "Now, the Lord is a spirit " (2 Cor. iii. 17.)

This text does, it is true, identify Christ with the Spirit. But this Christ-Spirit remains a personal being. There is the same relationship between him and the Apostle as there was between Christ on earth and the Twelve: it was he who called Paul and gave him a mission and special powers. (I Cor. ix. 1; Gal. i. 15–16; 2 Cor. xiii. 10.) It is he who will judge him (I Cor. iv. 4); it is to him, who having been dead rose again, that the Apostle dedicates himself, for him that he lives and dies. (Rom. xiv. 8ff.) This Christ is certainly no impersonal fluid. Even when St. Paul is considering Christ or his body as the sphere of life in which the believer is born and grows, he does not think of that body as an immaterial substance; it always remains, in his thought, the physical body of the Saviour. The Resurrection is called ἀνάστασις; it was produced by a divine action indicated by the verb ἐγείρειν (to rouse from sleep). He who "rises up" (ἀνίστασθαι), he who is woken up, is the same as he who lay down in the sleep of death: "He was buried and he rose again the third day." (I Cor. xv. 4.)

"The Lord is a spirit"—this statement can only be understood by analysing its context. There are two key words for understanding it, "letter" and "spirit"; one kills and the other quickens. (2 Cor. iii. 6.)

In these two concepts we have two institutions contrasted, that of the letter and that of the Spirit (iii. 6; Rom. vii. 6), the covenant of the prefiguration and that of the fulfilment. The first is dominated by a law of death (2 Cor. iii. 7; Rom. viii. 2)[56] engraved upon tables of stone. (2 Cor. iii. 3, 7.) A thing of shadow, devoid of substance, it gives rise only to condemnation and death (2 Cor. iii. 6–9), its evanescent glory can be compared with the fleeting reflections on the face of Moses. (2 Cor. iii. 14) It was the "old dispensation" (2 Cor. iii. 6, 14), now outworn.

As against the letter, the Spirit, the total and final reality, puts an end (iii. 14) to the prefigurative testament, and its glory spreads out beyond it and will never cease. (iii. 10–11.)

Letter and Spirit are contrasted like death and life (iii. 6–7), the

---

[56] Rom vii. 6 gives the same antithesis, " . . in newness of spirit, not in the oldness of the letter " Taking this in the whole context of Rom vi–viii, it is most illuminating. The Apostle constantly contrasts the Law and grace (vi. 14), the law of the spirit of life and that of death (viii. 2), the flesh and the spirit (viii 4.) Cf K. Prümm, *Bib.*, xxxi (1950), 183–7

Law and grace (Rom. vi. 14), condemnation and justification (Rom.
vi. 10–11; cf. viii. 1–2); like the shadow and the body of Christ in
glory (Col. ii. 17), like flesh and Spirit.[57]

"The Lord is a spirit"; he is the whole life-giving reality of
heaven; in him resides the fullness of everything that puts an end
to the rule of the Law, by "accomplishing it".[58]

There is, therefore, no question of an identification of Christ with
the Holy Spirit, no negation of the materiality of the risen body,
but it is affirmed that Christ in glory is the total and life-giving
reality in which all things are fulfilled.

St Paul does go on to say, "where the Spirit of the Lord is, there
is liberty". (2 Cor. iii. 17.) His intuitive line of thought passes unbroken from Christ-as-spirit to the person of the Holy Ghost, for
to him Christ is the full and final reality, "the life-giving Spirit",
simply because he is filled with all the living power of the Holy
Ghost

In common with the whole of the New Testament, St. Paul
declares that the spirit is the full, life-giving reality, the reality from
above (John iii 6), of the world to come, as opposed to the realities
of earth which are simply his shadow. In him is revealed the being
of God, his glory and his power, and in him everything finds its
fulfilment.[59]

[57] Cf P. van Imschoot, "L'Esprit de Yahvé et l'alliance nouvelle", *Eph
Theol. Lov*, xiii (1936), 220, *n* 141; K Prumm, "Die katholische Auslegung
von II Cor iii, 17a", *Bib*, xxxi (1950), 469· "Spirit" and "letter" indicate the
two economies of salvation
[58] Since F. Prat's *Theology* (vol ii, pp 435–41), and E B Allo's *La Seconde
Épître aux Corinthiens*, Paris, 1937 (pp. 103–11), the letter-spirit antithesis has
been explained as the opposition between the superficial and deep senses of
the Old Testament This exegesis is only legitimate if one goes no further
than the notional level; for what are in fact being contrasted are the figurative
shadow and the life-giving reality, the Law in its weakness, and the saving
person of Christ
[59] We are touching here upon a vital point in the theology of the spirit
which should be developed more fully The spirit, as opposed to the flesh,
is the reality from above, from the world to come, the only true reality.
John links the two ideas "spirit and truth" (iv. 23; xiv 17; xv 26; xvi 13),
and with him "truth" means full and divine reality as well as what is revealed
by that reality, as opposed to earthly reality Cf. R. Bultmann, *T.W.N.T.*,
vol i, pp 245–51 The spirit is the full reality compared with which all
others are merely shadows, for he is the expression of the reality of God;
cf. P Volz, *Der Geist Gottes*, Tübingen, 1910, pp 169ff. It is indeed noteworthy that all the definitions of God given in Scripture apply particularly
to the spirit God is Spirit, he is transcendent holiness, omnipotence (and he
is called "the Power", Matt xxvi 64), he is love, and the glory is the expres-

Christ is spirit, reality, truth, it is he who gives history its meaning and its fulfilment (2 Cor. iii. 14–16), because he himself is wholly saturated by the Holy Spirit.

He is so filled by him that he is transformed into his shining glory and his power of life, and becomes in his turn a principle of life and of glory: "We all reflect upon our face the glory of the Lord and are transformed into the same image from glory to glory, by the working of the Lord, who is spirit " (2 Cor. iii. 18.)

Christ is so completely transformed by the Holy Spirit that everything in him is changed into spiritual reality.[60] It ceases to matter whether we say "in Christ Jesus" or "in the Spirit". One is sanctified in Christ (1 Cor. i. 2) and in the Spirit (1 Cor. vi. 11); one is justified in Christ (Gal. ii. 17) as well as in the Spirit. (1 Cor. vi. 11.) For the life of Christ is the life of the Spirit himself; who lives by one lives in the other as well· "He who is joined to the Lord becomes one spirit with him." (1 Cor. vi. 17.)

We have found in our text nothing that denies the materiality of the body of the risen Christ, but a confirmation of 1 Cor. xv. 45: "The new Adam was made into a quickening spirit." The Spirit of glory, God's power and life-giving holiness, has become the vital principle in Christ, and has transformed the man of weakness, made in the likeness of sinners, by the holy and sanctifying power of God, into the fullness of God.

III. THE RISEN CHRIST, SOURCE OF THE SPIRIT

It was for us that Christ was raised from the dead (2 Cor. v. 15); the Spirit of God took possession of him, so that all those later to be in Christ should also be raised. The Spirit of the Resurrection is intended for us; he will act simultaneously upon Christ and upon us. "He rose again for our justification" (Rom. iv. 25), and we shall

sion of his being The Spirit is the personification of all this: he is Spirit, the Spirit of Holiness, the Power of God, the divine Love poured out into our hearts; he is identified with the divine glory

Christ, who died to give us the Holy Spirit, gives us in him the reality of heaven, God himself

[60] According to St. Cyril of Alexandria, Christ in glory forms so perfect a unity with the Spirit that he may even be given the name of Holy Spirit. Cf. S. Lyonnet, "S. Cyrille d'Alexandrie et II Cor iii 17", *Bib* , xxxi (1951), 25-31. St Ambrose (*De Mysteriis*, ix, 58, *P.L* , xvi, 409) uses a bold phrase that demands intelligent interpretation: "The body of Christ is the body of the Spirit of God, for Christ is spirit."

rise again in him who "was justified in the spirit" (1 Tim. iii. 16) for us.

Whereas the first Adam was simply a "living soul", the new Adam became a "quickening spirit". (1 Cor. xv 45.) The first man had a life whereby he lived for himself alone, a soul whose power to animate was in proportion to the size of his body and limited by it. While the letter kills, the Christ-Spirit is a fire that spreads outwards, a life which blossoms out by being lived. Transformed in the Spirit who is the outpouring of life and communication, he himself has become the outpouring and gift of himself. he is a life-giving spirit.

The Spirit is a power of animation acting simultaneously upon our Saviour and upon us Christ rose up in the spirit, on the one hand, and for us, on the other; his new life is the life of the Spirit, directed towards us.

We may be surprised that so important a fact is not more often explicitly affirmed. But it is presupposed throughout the Pauline theology of salvation, which is wholly centred upon the Holy Spirit, whom man finds in his union with the glorified Christ. His glorified body is spiritual food (1 Cor. x. 3); and whoever is united to Christ in his body forms one spirit with him. (1 Cor. vi. 17.)

Thus the Spirit is, according to St. Paul, the vivifying principle by which the Saviour returned to life, in which he lives divinely, and which spreads out to the faithful from the glorified body of Christ.

The Spirit must not take hold of Christ till after his death. In calling for Christ to live first in the flesh, the scheme of redemption was *ipso facto* making it necessary for him to be deprived, in his body, of that radiance of the Spirit, for flesh and spirit were at war. (Gal. v. 17.) Our redemption had to be completely accomplished in Christ first, by his passing from carnal existence, the sphere of Adam's sin, to divine life in the holiness of the Spirit. He had to be the first man in whom mortal humanity was vivified by the power and the glory; those that believed were to come and unite themselves to him in order to benefit from the redemption that was in him. (Rom. iii. 24.)

Endowed with the gift of the Spirit himself, Christ has become the dispenser of it. He gives it to the Church, which is one with his bodily humanity vivified by the Spirit. Could the Church have received the Spirit before the body of Christ had been vivified by him? No indeed, for the Church is the body of Christ

The Church is Christ's body by being grafted into the Saviour, in his death and his resurrection (Rom. vi. 3; Col. ii. 12.) Having become the body of Christ in his death and resurrection, she dies to the flesh with her Saviour and rises in the Spirit through the single act of raising by the Father, the same act which vivifies Christ. Thus the outpouring of the Spirit is one in the Church, though its manifestations are endlessly varied, for it is none other than the Father's act in raising Christ, unique in itself, and giving life to all that believe. This outpouring of the Spirit is equally directed towards the body of Christ and the faithful—who are the body of Christ. The gift of the Spirit which raises up the faithful is not given in addition to that which raised the Saviour, for the faithful find their justification, their gradual sanctification and their final resurrection in participating in the resurrection of Christ. There is only one outpouring of the Spirit, the one whereby Christ is glorified.

Several elements in this synthesis still need supporting. But I have anticipated somewhat because it was necessary in order to indicate the importance of the Spirit's glorifying action upon Christ in our redemption.[61]

IV. SUMMING UP

St. John and St. Paul, therefore, differ upon this point: for John, Christ sends the Spirit from the Father's side, having passed over

---

[61] The mystery of the outpouring of the Spirit in the risen Christ is seen in an altogether fresh light when the redemptive act is placed in the framework of sacrifice The Resurrection then appears as the acceptance and the communion. Liturgical documents expressing the Christian conception of sacrifice often attribute the acceptance of the sacrifice of Jesus, God's taking possession of it, to the consuming action of the Spirit (Cf the Secret for the Friday after Pentecost)

This conception is linked with Scripture by real, though tenuous, threads In the sacerdotal prayer (John xvii) our Lord asks that his offering be taken into God, and that by being thus accepted it may be fruitful for himself and those who believe in him. To this end he asks that the glory of God should descend on his sacrifice and impregnate it. This was how God took possession of a victim or of the Temple in the past, by his luminous glory, the *kabod* In the New Testament there is an unquestionable relationship between the glory of God and his Spirit. The sacerdotal prayer can be taken as an *epiclesis*, and the outpouring of the Spirit in Christ as an element of his sacrifice

into the new life by his own power (John x. 17–18); for Paul, he lives in God because the Father has raised him from the dead in the Spirit, and he can bestow the gift of the Spirit because he himself is saturated in it by him. John, however, recognizes the fact that the Spirit is the source of the life from above and its formal prin ciple: "Unless a man be born ... of the Holy Ghost ... what is born of the Spirit is spirit " (John iii. 5ff.) But he does not extend this axiom to Christ. Johannine theology does not allow for the distinction between a Christ according to the flesh and a Christ according to the spirit, for it does not pursue its analysis of the state of Christ on earth right back to its roots in the sin of Adam. The whole gospel is dominated by a picture of Christ penetrated by the glory of the Word, Christ as the Apostle had known him in his mystical life for over half a century, a picture corresponding only to the total reality revealed by the Resurrection [62]

But the two Apostles agree in making the bodily humanity of the Saviour the point from which the divinizing spirit gushes out for us. Our life takes a path through the heights, traced as it is in the Christ-Word, as St. John says, in the Christ-Spirit, as St. Paul says, but a path quite accessible to man, since it is in the body of a man.

To the thinkers of Greece this must have seemed madness, for their ideal was quite outside bodily life, and those of them who became Christians, tainted by this philosophy, tried to pass beyond the body of Christ to drink of the Word in the loftier regions of God, although in fact the bodily humanity is the necessary channel reaching up into those regions. The Christian God is certainly not Pascal's "God of philosophers and scholars". In Christ he has chosen what is lowest and furthest from the substance of God to be, through the workings of the Spirit, the principle of all redemption.

The Resurrection is the final triumph of the spirit, "not at the expense of the flesh, but to its eternal advantage".[63] In the

[62] John does, however, come very close to Pauline thought with his concept of the divine glory The earthly Christ was not possessed of the fullest glory, but must get it from the Father before he could save the world. (xvii 1–5.) And the Johannine glory comes close to the concept of the spirit Like the Spirit, it holds the graces of salvation (i 14); it constitutes the bond of union among believers (xvii 22); it is revealed by the power of the miracles (ii 11); it bears witness to the divinity of our Lord. (i. 14; cf. xv. 26.) St. John's thought also touches St Paul's in its affirmation that Christ is the source of the Spirit in his bodily being, and that he is so only in his glory

[63] L de Grandmaison, *Jesus Christ*, London, 1930–34, vol. iii, p 237.

Saviour our flesh is lifted from where it had fallen: from Adam onwards it was the bearer of sin throughout the world, and now in
Christ its cargo has become instead the Holy Spirit.

In the previous chapter I showed how in Christ's glorification we
find man's divinization in Christ. This chapter has shown that the
Spirit is the principle of this new life. It now remains to analyse
the effects produced by the outpouring of that Spirit.

IV

THE EFFECTS OF THE RESURRECTION
IN CHRIST

When our Lord died, the centurion bore witness that "indeed this man was a son of God". (Matt. xxvii. 54; Mark xv. 39.) Throughout the day he had heard the Son of God talked of; the expression seemed to him well fitted to express his admiration, but it did not hold for him the depths of meaning it came to have later. St. Luke suggests the sort of meaning the legionary must have intended, when he attributes to him the comment: "Indeed this was a just man." (xxiii. 47.) When Thomas the Apostle saw Christ again after his resurrection, he fell upon his knees: "My Lord and my God!" (John xx. 28) These were two characteristic reactions to Christ, the one before the Resurrection, the other after it. A change had taken place in Christ which called for a deepening of the evaluation made of him before.

Henceforth two titles were to stand out in the minds of those who believed in Christ, "Lord" (*Kyrios*), and "True Son of God". The Epistle to the Hebrews drew from its study of the resurrection a third title to add to these· "Eternal Priest".

1. CHRIST THE LORD

The word *kyrios* ("lord") and its Semitic equivalents, *mar* and *adon*, indicate legitimate domination and power, and originally meant "Master", or, more strongly, "Sovereign".[1]

The Septuagint uses it for God in place of the ineffable name Iahweh, for Iahweh is the legitimate master, lord and absolute sovereign of Israel and of the universe. The title thus gains a sense of transcendence, though its application is never restricted to the

---

[1] Foerster and Quell, *Th W N.T*, vol iii, pp. 1038–94

Divinity as such, for it continues primarily to express power and domination.

In the ancient East, the Semitic term had long had two possible evocations. On the one hand, it had become the formal title for kings,[2] and on the other, it was used for sovereign gods. The late Hellenistic period inherited this, and bestowed the title of "lord" upon its kings and some of its gods. Thus the commonly accepted meaning of the word was not unlike that given it by the Septuagint, but lacked its solemn majesty.

As a royal title, the name was fitting for the Messiah, the supreme king; and in him it also rose to its religious significance, because of the transcendence prophesied for the hero of Israel.

The Septuagint gave him this title, speaking of "the Lord, [Iahweh] Father of my Lord [the Messiah]". (Ecclus. li. 14.) In so doing, it took its inspiration from Psalm cx. 1: "The Lord said to my Lord: Sit thou at my right hand." Our Lord was later to give this same interpretation of the psalm, and the fact that his enemies did not contradict him suggests that this was the accepted exegesis, and that the Palestinian Jew also called the Messiah his "Lord".[3]

For Christians Christ was this divine King-Messiah. The earliest Palestinian communities called him "Maran" ("our Lord")[4] and the Greek communities proclaimed him "Kyrios".

In the first public profession of faith in Christ we read: "Let all the house of Israel know most certainly that God hath made both Lord and Christ this same Jesus whom you have crucified." (Acts ii. 36.) In St. Peter's mind the two terms are even more closely joined: God has made Jesus the Lord-Messiah.

Following what must have been a recognized proceeding among the Hellenic communities, St. Paul applies to our Lord those texts of the Old Testament in which "Kyrios" takes the place of the name of Iahweh. This title is not equivalent to the name of God

---

[2] L. Cerfaux, "Le Titre Kyrios et la dignité royale de Jésus", *Rev Sc. Phil Theol*, xi (1922), 40–71; xii (1923), 125–53.

[3] The fact that the epithet "lord" is not found applying to the Messiah in primitive rabbinical literature is surely because of the way Christians used it, for it was a literature polemic in character Cf. Strack and Billerbeck, *Kommentar zum N T. aus Talmud und Midrasch*, vol iv, pp. 458–60, L. Cerfaux, "Le Titre Kyrios", p 128

[4] We have proof of this in the prayer "Maran atha" which the liturgy has preserved for us by transmitting it to the Greek communities. (1 Cor xvi. 22, *Did.*, x 6.)

here any more than it is in the Septuagint; it only indicates lord-ship, but in this case it is the lordship of God.[5]

The words "Christ" and "Lord" suggest each other. The lordly title affirms his transcendence, his equality with Iahweh, but in the sense of a messianic transcendence; it conjures up the royal exercise of divine lieutenancy in the world.

1. CHRIST THE LORD IN THE SYNOPTICS AND THE ACTS

If this is the case, the royal and sacred title must have been applied to our Lord from the first moment when his disciples recognized the messianism of their rabbi The evidence for this was slow to win their minds and was at first sporadic and without great display. Peter's messianic profession (Matt. xvi. 16) was the result of a special enlightenment of his own. To many people the claim to messiahship appeared ridiculous. "Prophesy unto us, O Christ!" (Matt. xxvi. 68); "Hail, king!" (Matt. xxvii. 29.) Christ did not claim the title of Lord[6] and those around him only used it in a weakened sense, rather the same as "Rabbi" or "Master".[7]

However, Christ did give himself this title on one occasion, claim-ing also the glory of lordship and sovereignty over all things. He told two of the disciples to go and get him a mount: "And if any man shall say to you, What are you doing? say ye that the Lord hath need of him." (Mark xi. 3.) He entered into the Holy City, the city of King David, amid messianic acclamation. "Hosanna, blessed is he that cometh in the name of the Lord!" It was a day when all things bowed to the will of God, and if men were silent the very stones would cry out. (Luke xix. 40.) It was a Sunday, and God was anticipating by exactly a week the glory of Christ's coming.

From Easter onwards, "Kyrios" became the characteristic title

---

[5] Paul is also very discerning in transferring to Christ the ancient texts proper to Iahweh, applying to him all those which are applicable to the Messiah while still belonging to God. Cf. L Cerfaux, "Kyrios dans les cita-tions pauliniennes de l'Ancien Testament", *Eph Theol Lov.*, xx (1943), 17

[6] Except perhaps implicitly in Matt. xxii. 43–5, and in the perspective of the *parousia*. (Matt. xxiv. 42; xxv 11)

[7] In Mark, Christ is called "Lord" only by a pagan woman. (vii. 28) In Matthew the title is used more often, but never goes beyond the sense of a term of courtesy or veneration; we must also remember that our Matthew is a relatively late translation As for Luke and John, though they themselves may depart in their gospels from the reserve of the other Evangelists, they leave us with the same impression of the outlook of Christ's contemporaries

of Christ. His glorification revealed the sovereign lordship of this man—a revelation which, true to God's way of doing things, came not so much by verbal affirmation as by realization. "This statement that Christ is Lord because of the Resurrection is a thread running throughout the New Testament."[8] The preaching of the Apostles, from the beginning, consistently linked the exercise of lordly power with the exaltation of the Saviour "For the Apostle [St. Paul] as for the first community of Christians, it is invariably the Resurrection that has established Christ in his power as Kyrios."[9]

Christ had himself announced that his kingdom would be inaugurated that day. Welding his death and forthcoming glorification into a single moment, he had said to his judges: "Hereafter you shall see the Son of Man sitting on the right hand of the Power and coming upon the clouds of heaven." (Matt. xxvi. 64.) Caiaphas had asked: "Art thou the Messiah, Son of God?" and our Lord replied that he was, and that henceforward they themselves should see he was. For from then on the Son of Man was to be seated at the right hand of the Power, invested with God's lieutenancy; he was to come into the world in the majesty of heavenly kingship.[10]

After the Resurrection, our Lord declared: "All power is given to me in heaven and on earth." (Matt. xxviii. 18.)

When St. Peter was expounding Christ's messiahship to the multitude gathered outside the upper room (Acts ii. 22–36), he began by reminding them of the miracles which were, as it were, Christ's credentials during his life on earth. Death was able to vanquish him, for such was God's plan; now God had raised him up again. David seemed only to be prophesying of himself when he said: "Thou wilt not leave my soul in Sheol, nor suffer thy Holy One to see corruption." (Ps. xv. 10.) But in fact he was foretelling the Messiah: "He was a prophet, and knew that God had sworn an oath, that of his seed one should sit upon his throne. Foreseeing this, he spoke of the resurrection of Christ." (ii. 30–1.) As early as this the Apostles' argument was already permeated by the conviction that the assurance given to David would be fulfilled in the glorification of Christ: the Resurrection reminds the Apostle of the throne of David. The Ascension and sending of the Spirit completed the

[8] Foerster, *Th W.N T*, vol iii, p 1088.
[9] L. Cerfaux, "Kyrios dans les citations pauliniennes", p. 12
[10] This sitting at the right hand of God which marks his communion in life and power is always held to be the effect of the Resurrection (Acts ii 32–3; v. 31; Rom viii. 34; Eph. 1 20ff.; Col. iii. 1, Heb 1. 3; 1 Pet iii 21–2.)

exposition: Christ mounted once again the throne that had long
been empty, but which stood thenceforth in heaven. (ii. 33-5) And
he concludes, "Therefore let all the House of Israel know most certainly, God hath made both Lord and Christ this same Jesus whom
you have crucified." (ii. 36.)

The Sanhedrin forbade the Apostle "to speak in this name". But
he disobeyed and declared before the council "The God of our
fathers hath raised up Jesus, whom you put to death, hanging him
upon a gibbet. Him hath God exalted with his right hand, to be
Head and Saviour, to give repentance to Israel and remission of
sins." (v. 30-1.)

What does he mean by this? Has Peter forgotten that even before
the Passion he had confessed to his Master: "Thou art the Christ"?
No indeed, but now the lordship of Jesus of Nazareth is revealed;
the era of the Messiah is begun. Christ is endowed with messianic
powers and placed officially at the head of God's people to lead
them to the source of repentance and forgiveness. Rejected in the
Passion, the stone has become the head of the corner and from
henceforth there is no salvation in any other name. (iv. 11-12.)

In the synagogue of Antioch in Pisidia, St. Paul develops his argument for Christ's messiahship along similar lines. (Acts xiii. 23-39.)
He unfolds the history of Israel, recalls the promise of a Saviour
given to David, and preaches Christ, to whom the Baptist bore
witness, and whom the inhabitants of Jerusalem failed to recognize.
This Christ, God raised from the dead; that is the most important
fact, the final point in the history of Israel, and the conclusion of
the exposition of Christ's messiahship. (xiii. 23-39.)

The Resurrection is not a proof; it is the fulfilment of the
messianic promise. "And we declare unto you [the realization of]
that promise which was made to our fathers God hath fulfilled it
to us, their children, by raising up Jesus, as in the second psalm also
is written, 'Thou art my son; this day have I begotten thee.' " In
Psalm II, the Messiah-King publishes amid the nations that are in
revolt the decree constituting him King: "The Lord hath said to
me: Thou art my son, this day have I begotten thee." The kings of
the ancient East claimed to be sons of their national gods, and based
their authority on that origin. Christ's kingship dates from the
"this day" of his divine generation, and that day blazed out in the
Resurrection. For the Jews of Antioch, St. Paul does not unfold all

the meaning of this filiation; he simply declares the enthronement of the Messiah and leaves it at that.

He does, however, bring a further prophetic text to the support of his statement (xiii. 34). "And to show that he raised him up from the dead, not to return now any more to corruption, he said thus: I will give you the holy things [promised to] David, the assured things." (The text is from Isa. lv. 3.) It is in the resurrection of David's son that the messianic benefits promised to David the father are given, and in the incorruptibility of his life they are assured forever.[11]

Later, when he is defending himself to King Agrippa, he says again that the hope of the Twelve Tribes has been fulfilled in the resurrection of Christ. (Acts xxvi. 6–8.) Through this Son of David's entry into the majesty of incorruptible life, Israel's triumph has begun, and the good things of the "latter days" are theirs.

ii. CHRIST THE LORD IN PAUL'S EPISTLES

In proportion as the preaching of the Apostles moved away from the Jewish centre of interest, the formal title of the risen Christ lost its primitive complexion. "Christos" ("Messiah") became a proper name to be used without any article, suggesting the Redemption but not recalling the Hebrew messianism "Kyrios" came more explicitly than before to indicate the divine being revealed in the Resurrection and the universality of his dominion. But the bond between Christ's enthronement as Lord and his resurrection remained firm: "If thou confess with thy mouth that Jesus is Lord, and believe in thy heart that God hath raised him up from the dead, thou shalt be saved." (Rom x. 9.)[12]

During his first captivities, the Apostle had time to consider the scope of Christ's exaltation, and follow its repercussions throughout the whole cosmos.

(a) Universal Dominion

The Epistle to the Philippians, which gives the best account of

---

[11] Cf J Dupont, "Filius Meus Es Tu", *Rech Sc Rel.*, xxxv (1948), 529
[12] Cf A. Lemonnyer, *Théologie du Nouveau Testament*, Paris, 1928, p 160; H Sasse, "Jesus Christus der Herr", in *Mysterium Christi*, Berlin, 1931, p. 120

the humiliations of the Son of God in the flesh, gives a parallel account of their repercussions in glory: "He emptied himself . . . he humbled himself unto death . . . For which cause God also hath exalted him, and hath given him a name which is above all names: that in the name of Jesus every knee should bow, of those that are in heaven, on earth, and under the earth· and that every tongue should confess that Jesus Christ is Lord in the glory of God the Father." (ii. 7–11.) God has exalted Christ, giving him a name above all others, the only sovereign name, the name proper to Iahweh himself, the "Lord-God". From the beginning Christ possessed "the condition of God": the giving of the name is no mere title of honour for the Semites, the name and the being described by the name are one. This name, superior to all others, which compels the adoration of all creatures, can indicate none other than the sovereign majesty of God and his dominion over all things. The divine power is conferred upon this Jesus who once hung on a gibbet, and forces from us the acclaim, "Lord Jesus Christ!"

Every creature on the "three levels" of the world[13] bends the knee at this name, paying to it the homage given only to God,[14] in heaven, on earth, and in the depths below the earth. (ii. 10.) Who are these vassals? The angels, certainly, men, and since all must be included, the demons, for these are the three categories of being who inhabit these dwellings So say most interpreters. It may be pointed out that evil spirits also dwell in the air and the high places (Eph. ii. 2; vi. 12), and that those who dwell under the earth seem more properly identified with the dead in Sheol, as Paul says: "To this end Christ died and rose again, that he might be Lord both of the dead and of the living." (Rom. xiv. 9.) But did he intend any such literal interpretation? Surely we must believe that he "meant by this triple designation to affirm the submission to Christ of all beings, animate and inanimate, in short, of the whole universe."[15] The man who accepted humiliation of his own free will, is established at the very summit of creation, in the power and glory of God.

[13] C Guignebert, "Exégèse sur Phil. ii, 6–11", *Actes du congrès international d'histoire des religions tenu à Paris en 1923*, Paris, 1925, vol ii, p 297, *n* 1.

[14] St. Paul repeats word for word the text of Isa. xlv. 24, and applies it to Christ

[15] J Huby, *Les Épîtres de la Captivité*, 3rd ed , Paris, 1935, p 314, *n.* 4, based on Apoc v 13.

(b) Lord of the World to Come

The Epistles to the Ephesians and the Colossians are concerned with defending Christ's absolute primacy in the world and with defining its nature, for them Christ constitutes the actual principle of the cosmos· "Who is the image of the invisible God, the first-born of every creature· for in him were all things created in heaven and on earth, visible and invisible ... All things were created by him and for him; and he is before all, and by him all things subsist." (Col. i. 15-17.)

This Christ as principle of the cosmos is not the pre-existing Word —this would fit neither Paul's perspective nor that of John's pro-logue—but Christ "in whom we have redemption" (i. 14), the visible image of God (i. 15), head of the Church (i. 18.) But he is a Christ who has passed beyond the weakness of his earthly existence: he holds the primacy over all things, "the first-born from the dead ... in whom it hath well pleased God that all fullness should dwell". (i. 18-19)

Christ is "the first-born of every creature". (i. 15.) He holds priority both of cause and of duration over the rest of creation. The reason given by the Apostle—"for in him were all things created"—presupposes both priorities. St. Paul insists on that of duration "He is [exists] before all." (i. 17.) This is, of course, a prerogative of divinity, but then the Christ of the Resurrection is wholly divine. Lifted up into the life of God, in the fullness of time (which, in the mind of St. Paul, is the fullness of reality), Christ is set before all things. While on earth, his age was measured as the world measures age, but henceforward he is wholly seen in God, at the summit and origin of creation.[16]

The title "first-born of every creature", while placing Christ above the rest of creation, does not separate him wholly from it; he becomes its principle, because of the fullness of being God has

[16] Christ's priority of duration is not thought to be in the nature of succes-sive time Whatever may have been said on that score, St. Paul never seems to allow of any pre-existence of the man Christ in successive time

Whereas Plato grants a heavenly pre-existence to the ideas of this world's realities, Judaism accorded a similar pre-existence to sacred things, to the Temple, the Torah, the Sabbath.

The Messiah was given a heavenly prehistory (cf Micah v 2, Dan vii. 13-14, and the apocalyptic writings about the Son of Man) According to the New Testament, it was at the end of his life on earth that the Man Christ was lifted to the heights of God whence he dominates history

implanted in him: "He is indeed principle of them all . . . because in him it hath well pleased the Father that all fullness should dwell." (Col. i. 19.) The *pleroma* ("fullness") which, in biblical thought and the philosophy of the time, meant "the universe filled by the creative presence of God",[17] is primarily present, in all its being and power, in him

It is "in him" that God calls everything into being (ἐκτίσθη) and maintains it (ἔκτισται) (i 16). The world is based on him as "upon its focal point, where all the threads, all the generating lines of the universe are knotted together and co-ordinated".[18]

As principle, Christ is the centre of cohesion and harmony; everything starts from him and returns to him (i. 16–18). The world, as it were, pulls itself together in him and becomes a cosmos, an ordered universe. "In him all things stand and stand fast [συνέσιηκεν]." They are centred upon him, and depend on him for their existence; for in him dwells the whole power of God. "If anyone could have an instantaneous vision of the whole universe, past, present and future, he would see all things ontologically depending from Christ, and wholly intelligible only through him."[19]

Though he had always been Son of God, Christ did not become the centre and universal bond of the cosmos until after he had saved and reunited the shattered world in his sacrifice· "It pleased the Father . . . through him to reconcile all things [by directing them] to himself, making peace through the blood of his cross, through him (I say) both the things that are on earth, and the things that are in heaven." (i. 20.) In Christ God does not reconcile the universe with himself, but re-establishes the harmony among things, making them all converge towards Christ.[20] All the powers of heaven and all the creatures of earth have their culmination in him and are reunited at this pinnacle of the world's architecture, for once risen he holds the fullness of all things.

There was a time during our Lord's human existence when the various planes and lines of the universe had not yet come to cul-

[17] P Benoit, *Bible de Jérusalem, Épîtres de la Captivité*, ad. i. St. Paul borrowed the word *pleroma* from biblical writings, in which it indicates the universe filled with the creative presence of God, and from Stoicism as popularized throughout the Graeco-Roman world, in which it had a similar significance in pantheistic form. It seems clear that in Col. i. 19, the *pleroma* indicates not simply the divine nature, but the total fullness of being.

[18] J. Huby, *Épîtres*, p. 40.

[19] J Huby, *Épîtres*, p 40.

[20] F Prat, *Theology*, vol. ii, p. 97

mınate ın hım The world remaıned broken apart, wıth a crack across the universe at the poınt where the upper and lower creatıons joıned ın man, untıl the sın that caused the crack was wıped out by the blood of the Cross. Standıng ın thıs centre of the unıverse, because of hıs carnal beıng, Chrıst bore that fıssure ın hımself durıng hıs lıfe on earth. But by hıs death and resurrectıon he wıped out the contrasts and, lıfted to the pınnacle of all thıngs, joıned the shattered pıeces together agaın ın hımself. Henceforth he was to be a magnet drawing all creatıon, and reunıtıng it in hımself. "He that descended ıs the same also that ascended above all the heavens, that he mıght fıll all thıngs." (Eph. ıv. 10.)[21]

Clearly, these declaratıons are somethıng of an antıcıpatıon. The world we lıve ın ıs stıll torn apart, the submıssıon of the angels ıs not yet complete, the rule of death has not been abolıshed. The world of harmony and peace, centred wholly upon Chrıst, belongs to the end of tıme. In the Epıstles of the Captıvıty, the Apostle ıs brıngıng the eye of prophecy to bear on the world, he ıs judgıng ıt by a prıncıple, by the death and resurrectıon of Jesus, by that cosmıc revolutıon whıch took place ın ıts entırety ın Chrıst, but whose effects have not yet spread out over the world.[22] The great epıstles, more conscıous of the delays of hıstory, only look forward to the submıssıon of all thıngs to Chrıst and unıversal peace at the end. (1 Cor. xv. 24–8)

The lordshıp of the unıverse ıs an eschatologıcal attrıbute of Chrıst's, but ıt ıs a realıty from the Resurrectıon onwards. The Lord of the next world is none other than the Chrıst of Easter; ın hıs glory he is the end and fullness ın whıch all thıngs subsıst and are consummated: "It hath well pleased the Father that all fullness should dwell in hım." (Col. ı. 19.)

Because he is the end and pınnacle of all thıngs, the actıon of Chrıst ın glory goes back to the begınnıngs of the world; he ıs the fırst because he ıs the last, the goal, the *pleroma* contaınıng all realıty. One day the world wıll receıve ıts perfect form from hım,

---

[21] Heb. ıı. 9. "He was crowned wıth glory and honour: that through the grace of God it mıght be ὑπὲρ παντός that he tasted death " Should thıs be taken as masculıne or neuter? Generally one would assume neuter. If thıs is so ın thıs case, the effects of the Redemptıon extend to the whole of creatıon Theodoret (*In Hebr.*, ıi, 9, *P G.*, lxxxii, 692ff), understands ıt in thıs sense

[22] In the same epıstles, the Apostle envısages the belıever already seated ın heaven wıth Chrıst (Eph ıı 6.)

and will live only by him and his redemption. But the beginning is also dependent upon this goal; the whole world and the whole of time is suspended from him. "All things were created by him and for him." (Col. 1. 16.)

That is why carnal realities herald the spiritual ones which must of necessity follow, for they depend upon them. "If there is a psychic body, there is also a spiritual body . . . that which is psychic first, then that which is spiritual." (1 Cor. xv. 44, 46.) The Old Testament heralded the coming of the later era as a shadow falls in front of a body: "All was a shadow of things to come, but the body [that this shadow outlined] is of Christ" (Col. 11. 17.) The dead letter was the notification of the heavenly and complete reality, of the Lord who is life-giving Spirit (cf. 2 Cor. iii.) The Christ of glory is the prince of the past and of all lower realities, because he is lord of the world to come, possessor of all fullness, having primacy over all things by God's will. (Col. i. 18–19.)

(c) *Lord of the Angels*

There can therefore have been little understanding of the Christian mystery in those Judaizers who lessened the absolute lordship of Christ by setting angels (Col. ii. 18), thrones, dominations and principalities (i. 16; ii. 10, 15) between God and men.

Certainly, when the world was left to itself, those creatures who were the most powerful must have ruled it. Christ himself became lower than they (Heb. ii. 7), an evil spirit several times confronted him (Luke iv. 2–13; xxii. 31; John xiv. 30), and a good angel came to strengthen him (Luke xxii. 43)

But by his resurrection, Christ "was made better than the angels' (Heb. 1. 4); "the almighty power wrought in his resurrection" lifted him "above all principality and power, and virtue, and dominion and every name that is named". (Eph. i. 19, 21.) Their dominion over the world was snatched from them. The whole angelic host was drawn into the Saviour's exaltation and fastened to his triumphal chariot: "And [God] despoiling the principalities and powers, he hath exposed them confidently in open show, dragging them in triumph in Christ." (Col. ii. 15)

Who are these angels? Good angels or bad? St. Paul does dis

tinguish between the two (2 Cor. xi. 14; 1 Tim. v. 21), but he is not concerned with the distinction here.[23]

The angels made subject to Christ by the Father are heavenly beings appointed to govern the world, who direct the stars, who preside over the fates of nations by means of the civil authority (1 Cor. ii. 8; and perhaps Rom. xiii. 1),[24] who were mediators between God and Israel, and promulgated the Law. The Apostle shares this conception with the whole of Jewish apocalyptic writing.

Before Christ took the reins of the world, these powers held dominion over the universe; men were subject to them (Gal. iv. 3) and paid homage to them by obeying the laws promulgated by them. The Galatians and Colossians still thought they were subject to them, as also to Mosaic practices. "The Colossians had been told that the Law had been given by angels, because they had lent their aid to promulgating it, and did not look with indifference upon disrespect to the Torah."[25] But in Christ's death "the certificate of the debt" for which we were responsible and which placed us at the mercy of the powers' vengeance was wiped out by God; he stripped them of all hostile power by binding them to Christ's triumph. (Col. ii. 14-15.)

The Apostle is not concerned here with the goodness or badness of these angels, but with their function. His tone of hostility towards them was due to the attempts of innovators to continue to allot to them the part they had played. They were the rulers of a world which did not move in the orbit of Christ, principles of a way of life belonging to the past. They are contrasted with Christ in the same way as the Law, and the whole carnal order. Just as the flesh contradicted the spiritual economy by its weakness and often by its wickedness, so also did these powers, because they were of the order of "weak elements of the world", and because there were malevolent beings among their number. The latter, stripped of the autonomy of their power, represent disarmed adversaries in the triumph of Christ.

Christ's supremacy over the angelic powers is not, in the Apostle's

[23] E. Tobac, *Le Problème de la justification dans saint Paul*, Louvain, 1908, p. 201, *n* 11 St. Paul "uses, it seems, the same title of powers and dominations to indicate beings belonging among the good angels and others who belong among the evil" Cf. Col. i. 16; Gal iii. 19; Eph vi. 12.

[24] Cf. O. Cullman, *Christ and Time*, London, 1951, pp. 191–210

[25] Theodore of Mopsuestia, *In Epistolas B Pauli*, ed Sweete, Cambridge, 1880, vol i, p. 294

mind, any mere marginal effect of the exaltation of the risen Christ;
it is of its essence. Christ is the only Mediator and even the Church,
since she works amid the world, can profess faith in Christ alone
only if the powers that rule the world are also subject to this same
head. Later in life the Apostle was to find it necessary to cleanse the
atmosphere of the Asiatic communities from pre-gnostic influences,
and to insist that "there is one Mediator between God and men, the
man Christ Jesus". (1 Tim. ii. 5.) There are now no intermediaries
acting between God and man save Christ, or in Christ.[26]

Christ's relationships with inanimate creation and with the angelic
world do not follow the same pattern as his relationship with his
Church. Some writers, carried away by their passion for synthesis,
have thought that the whole of creation could be comprehended in
the one concept of the Church with Christ at its head. "The body
of Christ" would then take on fantastic dimensions, "becoming
cosmic, and embracing spiritual and material creation in a vast
whole".[27] The universe of the angels, mankind rising up from the
pedestal of the material creation, the whole cosmos, would thus constitute the multiform body over which Christ, as head, presides.

Several texts seem to place the angels, the Church and the world
alongside each other in the same subordination to Christ. God re-
establishes the whole universe under the one head (Eph. i. 10);
Christ is the head of the powers (Col. ii 10), as of the Church Col 1.18);
he fills all things (Eph. iv. 10), as well as the Church. (Col. ii. 10.)

The recapitulation of all things is certainly not limited to the
establishment of the Church, but embraces the whole cosmos. But
loftier than Christ's cosmic role is his role as "head of the body":
"He raised him up from the dead, and set him on his right hand
in the heavenly places, above all principality ... He hath subjected
all things under his feet, and above all hath made him head over the
Church, which is his body." (Eph. i. 20–23.) To be head is a function
of lordship; but in Christ's sphere of influence, one area is marked
off from the rest—the Church This role lifts him a degree above
mere sovereignty over the angels; it is the highest rung in Christ's
elevation. The Apostle surveys the honours of the risen Saviour

[26] The subjection of the angels to Christ must have held great importance
in primitive teaching, for we find an allusion to it in the liturgical hymn
quoted by St Paul (1 Tim. iii 16); it is also affirmed in 1 Pet. iii. 22, by
St Ignatius of Antioch (*Trall.*, ix 1), and in the *Epistle of Polycarp* (ii 1)
[27] E. B Allo, "L'Évolution de l'Évangile de Paul", *Vivre et Penser*, 1st
series, 1941, p 166

(Eph. 1 19–23); his seat at the right hand of God, his being lifted above the spirits, the subjection of all creatures beneath his feet—all these are, as it were, a staircase leading up to his function as head. Lordship of the cosmos is directed towards the dignity of being head of the Church.

The power of head of the faithful and the dominion over the angels derive from the same fullness of power, and the former rests upon the latter: "In him dwelleth all the fullness of the Godhead corporeally, and in him you are filled [function of the head of the Church], who is the head of all principality and power." (Col. 11. 9–10.) But the two titles, though most closely related, are not the same. The title of head, given to Christ, master of the powers, expresses supreme dignity and dominion; but the Church alone is the body to which Christ communicates his personality and his life.

Because the Church is identified with the Saviour's physical body (cf. chapters v and vi), the relationship between it and its head are unique and cannot extend to the world of the angels. The point of identification between Christ and the Church lies in bodily human nature. In it the Saviour carried out his work of salvation, having accepted it in its carnal state that he might be numbered among a sinful race, and then having drawn it into the life of God. We are in turn made part of it and gain for our bodily being death to the flesh and divine life. Everything in St. Paul goes to show that salvation in Christ is prepared only for human nature, and fitted to it alone. The purely spiritual creature may bathe in the influence of Christ, but cannot penetrate into the focal point where the divine transformation takes place, Christ's bodily humanity.

Dominion over the powers and power over the faithful are thus on quite different levels, and this inequality is expressed in the way each is stated. "The powers are subjected, put down by force, and are placed under Christ's feet by his victory. On the other hand, the Church is one with him, even if she is subjected to him."[28] All proclaim that "Jesus Christ is Lord" (Phil. ii. 11), but the faithful call him familiarly and lovingly "our Lord"; they belong to him in a special sense, for he belongs to them.

iii. CHRIST THE LORD IN THE APOCALYPSE

Christ's lordship, as set out in the Apocalypse, would need a long study.

[28] L. Cerfaux, *The Church*, pp 338–9

In his glorification, Christ underwent a profound transformation. We know how the Semites attached the importance of the reality to the name. "To him that overcometh I will give the hidden manna, and I will give him a white stone, and in the stone a new name written, which no man knoweth but he that receiveth it." (Apoc. ii. 17.) The image of the stone suggests the analogy of several uses: the precious stone in a ring with a name carved on it, or the *tessera*, the entrance fee to the theatres. The important thing is that it is white, the colour of those who possess the life of Christ (cf. iii. 5), and that it bears the new name which indicates a renewal of nature such as can be understood only by those who have experienced it.

And to the Church of Philadelphia Christ declares: "He that shall overcome, I will make him a pillar in the house of my God; and he shall go out no more; and I will write upon him the name of my God, and the name of the city of my God, the new Jerusalem, which cometh down out of heaven from my God, and my new name." (iii. 12.)

The believer has three names inscribed upon him, which express his new being and where he belongs: he is the Church's, he is Christ's, he is God's. Christ has inscribed his new name upon the believer. The Apocalypse, being "the gospel of the risen Christ"[29] does not know the old one. The new is known only to him who bears it: "His eyes were as a flame of fire, and on his head were many diadems, and he had a name written which no man knoweth but himself. He was clothed with a garment saturated with blood; and his name is called, The Word of God." (xix. 12–13.)

The new name to replace the old means a transformation similar to that which occurs in the believer, and defines the new mode of existence of the glorified Christ: the existence of the Word of God.

Although the Apocalypse lacks the Pauline notion of all things being reconciled and recapitulated in the risen Lord, it does bring one new element to enrich Christ's Lordship: the Resurrection places the reins of history in the hands of the Saviour. Providence becomes Christian; events are presided over by Christ, Saviour of all who believe.

To Christians who had already been persecuted and were to be persecuted more and more violently, St. John unfolds the synthesis of the supernatural history of the Church. The drama takes place

[29] Bossuet, *L'Apocalypse*, preface.

on two stages at once, heaven and earth; Christ in heaven is the producer. The leitmotiv is given in the introductory vision. (i. 9–20.) In the midst of the seven golden candlesticks, the Apostle perceives the features of Christ in the glory of his divinized humanity: "I was dead, and behold I am living forever and ever." The light of divinity, at once bright and soft, illuminates his face; his look pierces like a fire, his voice has the majesty of great waters. The bronze feet suggest stability of power; the sword coming from his mouth the power of his words. In his right hand he holds seven stars. The golden candlesticks represent seven Churches, the whole Christian Church. The stars are the angels, their mysterious representatives; Christ holds them in his mighty but gentle right hand. The whole book sets out to affirm that the risen Christ is present among the golden candlesticks, and to record the history of the stars in his hand.[30]

In Chapter IV the curtain rises on the scene of heaven. Seated on his throne, God holds in his hand a scroll sealed with seven seals and containing the fate of the world. The whole court waits for him who is to carry out this decree, when Christ appears, risen from the dead. He is the Lamb and the Lion, both victim and the victorious hero; he has seven horns and seven eyes "which are the seven spirits of God", the fullness of the Spirit's vision and might. God gives him the plan for the new history of the world and charges him to carry it out. And immediately the whole universe offers homage to Christ and also to God, "every creature, which is in heaven, and on the earth, and under the earth and in the sea". (v. 13.)

This exalting of the Lamb brings the salvation of God into the world ruled by the Dragon, and brings about that crisis in the universe whose development forms the new history. With solemn deliberation, he breaks the seven seals and unfolds the designs whereby God will bring the crisis to its solution. Isaiah foretold of the Servant that after his death "the will of the Lord shall be prosperous in his hand". (liii. 10.) His will that the faithful be saved governs all that happens so that even the victories of the infernal dragon are turned to their good. Presided over by the Lamb,

[30] This object is defined in i 19–20, at least in one possible translation: "Write therefore .. the mystery of the seven stars, which thou sawest in my right hand " (It is thus translated by Calmes, Moulton, and Buzy)

history steadily directs some towards "the pool of fire and brim-
stone" (xx. 9), and others towards the heavenly Jerusalem.

2. MIGHTY SON OF GOD

Related to the title of Christ the Lord is the name "Son of God".
It even seems as though at the time of our Lord the two titles
were one. "Thou art the Son of God, thou art the King of Israel!"
cried Nathaniel (John i. 49)· "Thou art the Christ, the Son of the
living God!" declared St Peter (Matt xvi. 16): "Art thou the
Christ, the Son of God?" asked Caiaphas. (Matt. xxvi. 63.)

Scripture attributed to the Son of David this title and the prerogative of God's paternal love: "I will be to him a father, and he
will be to me a son." (2 Kings vii. 14; cf. Ps. lxxxviii. 28.) The
mysterious seventh verse of Ps. II, "Thou art my son; this day have
I begotten thee", was given a simple messianic interpretation which
St. Paul was content to adopt in talking to the Jews of Antioch.
(Acts xiii. 33.) Various Jewish apocryphas used the terms "Messiah"
and "Son of God" synonymously (Enoch cv. 2; 4 Esd. vii. 28
(probable text); xiii. 32, 52.)[31]

The Jews had no idea of a Messiah who would really be God's
Son. Caiaphas' question must be interpreted as a messianic one,[32]
similar to the first disciples' professions of faith. (John i. 49; Matt.
xiv. 33.) In the first part of the Angel Gabriel's message, the context
does not demand any more literal interpretation for the phrase "Son
of the Most High". Mark, and, even more, Luke, realized that in
the mouth of his contemporaries the title "Son of God" was
primarily messianic, for they make it interchangeable with that of
Christ. Luke iv. 41 is a typical example: "Devils went out from
many, crying out and saying: Thou art the Son of God. And rebuk-

[31] The fact that later rabbinical writings were more sparing in giving
the title of Son of God to the Messiah, doing so only when forced to by such
an explicit text as Ps ii 7, must clearly have been the result of reaction
against Christian teaching. Cf Strack and Billerbeck, *Kommentar*, vol iii,
pp 15–20

[32] The High Priest condemned Christ's answer as blasphemy because it
was a claim to be the Messiah, Son of God in the fullest sense that title
suggests, in a sense which seemed to infringe the majesty of God himself
St. Luke shows his mind moving step by step: Caiaphas first asks, "Art thou
the Christ?" Then, after our Lord has said that he will sit at the right hand
of God, he asks, "Art thou then the Son of God?" (xxii 66–70)

ing them he suffered them not to speak, for they knew that he was the Christ."[33]

Certainly the title takes on a profound religious significance when the Father inspires its use (Matt. xvi. 16), and the Apostles clearly felt God's presence in Christ (Matt. xiv. 33; Luke v. 8); but not until after the Resurrection was their faith formulated in an invocation reserved to Iahweh himself: "My Lord and my God!" (John xx. 28.)

1. BIRTH AS SON

If their eyes were wholly opened to the mystery of Christ from then on, it was because the mystery had broken through the cover that concealed it. Before, Christ had been born Son of David in the weakness of the flesh, but in the Resurrection he was established Son of God in the glory of power, according to the spirit of holiness. (Rom. 1. 4.)[34]

It was not that Christ underwent any substantial transformation. St. Paul writes that he has been set apart for the Gospel of God . . . concerning his Son, of the race of David according to the flesh and constituted Son of God in power by the Resurrection. Christ, therefore, is Son quite beyond and before any event of history. The humiliations of his time on earth covered his dignity as Son but did not efface it. They did, however, make it suffer a real eclipse, for the weakness of the flesh was a servile livery, a disguise put on over the sonship which made him appear as simply a son of David. The Resurrection was not simply a declaration like the one that guaranteed Jesus of Nazareth to the Jews after his baptism; it produced a complete change in his existence. Christ reaped the benefits of the sonship in his bodily humanity. In short, he was established

[33] Compare Matt. xvi. 16 with Mark viii. 29 and Luke ix. 20; Matt. xxvi 63 with Luke xxii 66, Matt xxvii. 40 with Luke xxiii 35; Matt. xxvii 54 with Luke xxiii 47

We see that Matthew retains the title "Son of God" where Luke often keeps only that of Christ; clearly the first gospel is bent upon affirming the divine character of the Messiah to the Jews But even here the title of Son of God is first and foremost a messianic description (Cf xvi. 16 and 20)

[34] "For the Acts as for St. Paul, the title 'Son of God' does not fully belong to Christ until the time of the Resurrection." J Dupont, "Filius meus es tu", *Rech. Sc Rel.*, xxxv (1948), 535 For a study of the psychological genesis of faith in the divine sonship of Christ cf. J. Schmitt, *Jésus ressuscité dans la prédication apostolique*, Paris, 1949, pp. 213–6.

Son of God; he was so already, but now he was established "Son of God in the glory of power", established in the existence proper to the Son of God.

The Resurrection was not merely a coming back to life, but a birth into a new life which Christ did not have in his bodily humanity.[35] Before the Christian can have a regeneration, Christ must have one. Born of the Virgin into the life of a son of man, on Easter day he was reborn into the life of the Son of God. St. Paul is not afraid of the notion of Christ's having a second birth. At Easter he interprets the Father as making that solemn statement, "Thou art my Son; this day have I begotten thee." (Acts xiii. 33.)[36] "This day" starts at the first instant of Christ's existence (Rom. i. 3; Phil. ii. 6), but its high noon is at Easter. Following his birth into the world in Bethlehem, comes a new Christmas in a blaze of light.[37]

The prophecy of the Old Testament had linked the titles "Messiah" and "Son of God" (2 Sam vii. 14; Ps. ii. 7), though with no idea how close to God that sonship would be. The union of the two remained constant in the person of Christ and in the mind of his disciples (Matt. xvi. 16 and Mark viii. 29; Matt. xvi. 20, Acts ix. 20, 22) and the effects of both were parallel in their unfolding. Our Lord was the Christ who "is to come" because he was the Son of David yet begotten by God. To St. John the coming was synony-

[35] Christ by his resurrection did not return to life as we all know it, but took up a kind of life that was immortal and belonged to the divine order—St Paul, in Romans (vi. 10), uses the phrase "his life is a life in God". (St Thomas, iii, q lv, a 2)

[36] St Peter seems to be expressing a similar idea in Acts ii 24: "God hath raised him up, snatching him from the birth-pangs [ὠδῖνες] of death . " Christ's death seems to represent the birth-pangs of his new life; or perhaps it is Sheol, the depths of the death, that is in labour with Christ in its womb These are splendid images, but do not belong to Scripture. The rebirth is from the Holy Spirit—not from death or the earth Besides, St Peter is using a biblical phrase (Ps. xvii 6; cxiv. 3) which may be translated as "the bonds of death", and which the Septuagint renders as "sorrows of death, of Sheol". St Luke is quoting the Septuagint usage, but St Peter did not speak Greek. Thus we may read, "snatching him from the bonds of death"

[37] The Resurrection is identified with the birth as Son elsewhere in Christian literature Cf Appolinarius in Cramer, Catenae Graecorum Patrum, Rom i 4, St Hilary of Poitiers, Tract. in Ps., ii, nos. 27–9, P.L., ix, 277–9; St. Ambrose, De Sacramentis, iii, i, 2, P.L, xvi, 431; Rufinus of Aquileia, Com. in Bened. Joseph, P L., xxi, 329; St Maximus of Turin, Sermo XXXVI de Paschate, P L, lvii, 606; Herveus Burgidolensis, In Rom., 1, 4, P.L, clxxxi, 601; Salmeron, Comm. in N.T, Cologne, 1614, vol. xiii, p. 294; Condren, L'Idée du sacerdoce et du sacrifice de Jésus Christ, Paris, 1725, pp. 86–91.

mous with divine generation. The sonship was stated with reserve at first, and the Messiahship was certainly not thrust forward; but at Easter both appeared in their full power.

ii. BIRTH IN THE SPIRIT

The new life in the believer is the effect of the Spirit (1 Cor. vi. 11), as is the sonship. (Rom. viii. 14–17.) One can only be a son in the Spirit of the Son. (Gal. iv. 6.) One must be born again of the Spirit, declares the fourth gospel (iii. 5), and St. Paul speaks of "the regeneration and renovation of the Holy Ghost". (Tit. iii. 5.) Christ's new birth springs from the same principle, as St. Paul tells us implicitly; according to him, the Father raises Christ by the Spirit (Rom. viii. 11), and the Spirit forms the life-principle in the glorified Christ (1 Cor. xv. 45), Christ in his existence as Son.

The Apostle stands in the same doctrinal line as the gospel of his disciple St. Luke. The angel had said: "The Holy Ghost shall come upon thee and the power of the Most High shall overshadow thee, and therefore also he who shall be born of thee shall be called holy, the Son of God." (Luke i. 35.) The angel does not attribute the divine effect to the virginal conception as such, but to the intervention of the Holy Ghost In the Old Testament every child born miraculously is marked by holiness—as with Isaac, born according to the Spirit (Gal. iv. 29), and Samson the Nazarite and Samuel. Born of a unique intervention of the Spirit, who is the holiness and power of the Most High, the Child of the Virgin Mary was to be holy with a unique holiness, the Son of God. This was not because of the Virgin Birth as such,[38] but because of the working of the Spirit which, in effecting that virgin birth, consecrated a human being to holiness and to divine sonship.[39]

[38] Exegetes arbitrarily introduce a theological difficulty into the text by asking the question, How could the angel declare that the Infant was to be holy and the Son of God because of the miracle of virginal conception? The angel in no sense attributes the holiness of the child to the miracle produced by the action of the Holy Ghost, but to that most holy action itself

[39] The Spirit here reveals an aspect of his mysterious nature. People have written of the maternal part played by the Spirit in bringing up the children of God (e g , A. Lemonnyer, "Le rôle maternel du Saint-Esprit dans notre vie surnaturelle", *Vie Spir.*, iii (1921), 241–51 It works first when they are born. They are washed, sanctified by God, in the name of Jesus Christ, in the Holy Spirit. (1 Cor. vi. 11.) Titus iii 5, speaks of the "laver of regeneration of the Holy Ghost" We are "born of water and the Holy Ghost" (John iii 5), of whom water is the symbol The Church exalts the material role of the

III. IMAGE OF THE FATHER

According to St. Luke, the Spirit had divinized the man Christ from the beginning, and now, according to St. Paul, he was bringing that divinization to its conclusion. By the action of the outpouring of the Spirit that raised him, the Father begets Christ more completely like himself; our Lord is changed into a perfect image of the Father. When St. Paul speaks of Christ as "the image of the invisible God" (Col. i. 15; 2 Cor iv. 4), he is not thinking of the Word in his pre-existence, but of Christ whom he sees in the light of the Resurrection. He recognizes the Father in the features of that shining face, in "the glory of Christ who is the image of God". (2 Cor. iv. 4.) The Apostle is quite aware that the Saviour was divine when he was on earth; but here he only sees Christ come into that life of glory which alone corresponds to the full reality of his being; "in him dwelleth all the fullness of the Godhead corporeally" —in other words, his corporeal being is filled with the divine plenitude [40] In his resurrection Christ showed himself in his true condition, revealing the divine traits that had been blurred by the humiliation he had chosen to undergo. (Phil. ii. 5-9.)

For St. John too, Christ is the image of the Father, his revelation in the world. His mission is to make known the name of the Father (John xvii. 11, Greek text); to spread the knowledge of that name. He gave it to the world by his preaching, but even more by his own being as Son, which revealed the most intimate and most essential thing about God, his quality of being Jesus' Father [41]

baptismal font Cf. Bédard, *The Symbolism of the Baptismal Font in Early Christian Thought*, Washington, 1951

Christ himself was born Son of God in the power of the Holy Spirit, in his earthly conception as well as in his resurrection When he was baptized, the Father acknowledged as his Son him on whom the Spirit rested *The Gospel of the Hebrews*, quoted with approval by St Jerome, speaks of the maternal role of the Spirit on that occasion. (*In Isa*, iv, *P L.*, xxiv, 145; *In Mich*, ii, *P L*, xxv, 1221.)

Since the mystery of God is revealed in Christ, we may even allow that the Spirit plays this role in the divine life The Father begets "the Son of his love" (Col i. 13) in the Spirit

[40] L Cerfaux, *The Church*, pp 322–3: " σωματικῶς; that is to say, in the glorified σῶμα of Christ". Other authors quite rightly stress the idea of the Incarnation (Prat and Huby). But what this is is the Incarnation in its glorious fullness.

[41] St. Augustine, *In Jo Tract.*, cvi, iv, *P L.*, xxxv, 1909· "Not that name by which thou art called God, but that by which thou art called my Father; which name cannot be made manifest without the manifestation of the Son Himself "

Even during his life on earth Christ declared, "Who seeth me seeth my Father" (John xiv. 9; xii 45); this was a partial anticipation of the future, for it was to be "in that day [of the glorification] you shall know, that I am in my Father." (xiv. 20.) If the Father was to be known in the Son, the Son had to be revealed in his sonship, in the glory that he possessed with the Father and with which he was again to be wholly filled in his exaltation. (xvii. 5.) Thus he asks for his glorification in order that both the Father and he whom he has sent may be known. (xvii. 1-4.)

John's thought, though very different from Paul's in its expression, remains parallel with it in substance. in the Resurrection Christ's sonship is affirmed and the image of the Father is revealed. "We might say that in the Incarnation the Son of God was born Son of Man, and that in the Resurrection the Son of Man was born Son of God."[42] The birth is a unique one· Christ is born into the life of the Son by entering the bosom of the Father.

In order that the features of his Father's beauty may be seen, the Spirit must wipe out "the likeness of sinful flesh". (Rom. viii. 3.) The flesh, as such, stands in contrast to God; it indicates being, but only being that is not affected by the holiness of God, that remains in the isolation of a creature. To speak of a life of the flesh is to recall the framework of death that surrounds it. Christ was Son even in his carnal state, but only because he was not to remain in it.

No part of his flesh resisted the action of the Spirit. Christ became spirit even in his body, and it is in the life of the Spirit that the essential feature of likeness to God resides, for "God is Spirit"— that is why the heavenly spirits are called the sons of God (cf. Luke xx. 36)—and the Holy Spirit, like the glory which belongs to him, is an expression of the divine nature.[43]

Before the Resurrection the mystery of Christ had been hidden by his body; now it was expressed by it. Being a Man-Spirit, Christ now declared himself Man-God.[44]

---

[42] Condren, *L'Idée du sacerdoce*, pp. 86ff. Cf. Salmeron, *Comm. in N.T.*, p. 294.

[43] Cf below, p. 102 I am not saying that the Spirit designates the nature of God, which would be extremely controvertible, but that he is the personal expression of the attributes of the Godhead (power, spirituality, holiness, glory, love)

[44] St. Ambrose, *De Excessu Fratris sui Satyri*, xci, *P.L*, xvi, 1341: "Then man in the flesh, now God in all things" The context makes it clear that this refers to a total elevation in the power of God

IV. A LIFE FOREVER NEW

The coming of the Spirit has swept away the ruin left by Adam (Rom. vii. 6); it renovates (Tit. iii. 5) and creates not merely a renewed being, but *a new being* (καινή κτίσις). It has not simply introduced a new sort of man to the world, but places man at the starting-point of this whole new life, at birth (Tit. iii. 5); and all that the power of the sacrament has not yet succeeded in re-creating will gradually yield to this baptismal youthfulness. (2 Cor. iv. 16; Col. iii. 10.) The Spirit is youth, for he is life (Rom. viii. 11; 1 Cor. xv. 45; 2 Cor. iii. 6); a life that will never fail, for it is the life of God.

Since the believer finds his newness of life by conforming himself to the risen Christ, and this newness is constantly renewed as he conforms to him more closely (Col. iii. 10), we must take it that Christ will never grow any older than he was at the Resurrection, that his life remains new, that his body, new-born in the Spirit, never grows beyond the moment of his Easter birth and therefore that the Father's action in raising Christ continues eternally in its single moment.[45]

It is true that, using as we must the past tense of the verbs by which we express it, the raising action of the Father is part of past history as far as we are concerned.[46] But though it belongs to our time, to one precise moment of it, yet it has an eternal actuality. When the believer meets Christ's resurrection, it is as the astonishing and new thing it first was. Every man who shares in the new life in Christ, no matter when in history he does so, is said by St. Paul

Herveus Burgidolensis, *In Rom.*, i, 4, *P.L.*, clxxxi, 601. "Since he himself says of the elect that they are the children of God because they are of the resurrection, surely we may say even more forcefully that he who is by nature God's Son according to his divinity, is made Son of God according to his humanity in the resurrection"

[45] St Ambrose (*De Sacramentis*, V, xxvi, *P.L.*, xvi, 453) seems to base himself on this notion "If Christ be thine today, thou raisest him for thyself today How? 'Thou art my Son, this day have I begotten thee.' Today is the moment of Christ's resurrection."

[46] The raising action of the Father is expressed in the aorist: the tense of an incident that has happened (Rom. iv 24–5 and *passim*); considered in Christ, the Resurrection is put in the perfect tense: a past action whose effect remains. (1 Cor. xv 4, 12–20) A. Vitti, *La Resurrezione di Gesù e la soteriologia di S. Paolo*, Civiltà Cattolica, 1930, vol ii, p. 307), thinks that the use of the perfect allows us to conclude that the Resurrection itself is permanent I think not The perfect indicates the permanence of the act in its effect, but of itself it only affirms here the state of resurrection.

to rise with him, to be taken up in the very act of the Saviour's resurrection.

Earlier on, when he attributed the phrase: "Thou art my son, this day have I begotten thee" to the Father in raising Christ (Acts xiii. 33), he made no attempt to unfold its theological depths to the Jews. But saying it again—"He was constituted Son of God... by the Resurrection" (Rom. i. 4)—he explains further. The Resurrection brought Christ wholly to birth in the life of the Son, extending to his whole being the glory of his eternal generation. And in that birth there is no "tomorrow". Alongside our ancestor Adam, the old man, who continues to decay within us (2 Cor. iv. 16), here is the young Adam, the new man, Son of God, in the everlasting newness of his sonship.

We thus have a number of elements to fit together. The Resurrection is a divine birth; the life of the glorified Christ never grows older than the date of his birth; believers at any time in history can profit in Christ from the same raising action which profits their Saviour. We might conclude that the Resurrection remains forever in act, thus giving Paul's thought a philosophical expression foreign to it. But we should be mutilating that thought if we retained only those statements that place the Resurrection in the past and ignored those which presuppose that God's act of raising is a permanent lasting reality We must accept ideas which seem mutually exclusive, and see the Resurrection as both an event preceded and followed by others and a divine action outside history.[47]

The eschatological nature of the Resurrection gives a biblical formula for this philosophical concept of a permanent actuality in the Resurrection. Christ has left "this present time", he has come to the end of time. The Epistle to the Hebrews was to explain that the immolation took him through the antechamber of heaven, the Holies, image of changing and imperfect things, and brought him into the full reality, the Holy of Holies. He has come to fulfilment, to his goal and perfection. The history of the world is virtually accomplished, for death and resurrection, in Christ, have brought

[47] W. Künneth speaks of "the actuality of the Resurrection", of its "presence". (*Theologie der Auferstehung*, Munich, 1933, pp. 166–92.)
Once again, I do not say that in St Paul's mind Christ's glorification was a permanent divine action The Apostle looks on it as something that happened in our history at the time of Pontius Pilate, and therefore as something belonging to the past But considered in its reality as he describes it, it is in fact a divine action remaining actual

the final fullness of time which, in Scripture, is not merely the norm, but the reality of history. The Church is moving towards that fullness which she will one day attain, when she has come to "the stature of Christ" in glory, but Christ already possesses it himself alone and fully. Thus he has advanced no further than the first moment of his glorification, for that is his fullness and his goal.

Rom. i. 4 sets the power alongside the dignity of the Son: "He was established Son of God in power." Christ is established in power; power is a mark of the new life.[48] The Apostle contrasts the two phases of Christ's existence: that of Son of David in the weakness of the flesh (1. 3), and that of Son of God, which, to stand in antithesis to the first, calls for a mention of the power of God. To be fully elevated as Son of God, Christ must be enthroned in the power of God.

Power was the attribute the Jews were most constant in giving God. The phrase "the power of Iahweh" indicated God himself, and so did simply "the Power".[49] The angel announced that the Child would be the Son of God because his conception was to be the result of "the power of the Most High" (Luke i. 35), and Christ foretold his coming in power as the manifestation of his divine sonship: "Hereafter you shall see the Son of Man sitting at the right hand of the Power" (Matt. xxvi. 64), associated with God in his most essential quality. Christ's enthronement in the dignity of the Son called for a communication and demonstration of infinite power.

And indeed, after the Resurrection Christ was to say to his Apostles, "All power is given to me." (Matt xxviii. 18.)[50]

The bestowal of power was implied in the very action whereby God raised him up. The Resurrection inspires boundless wonder in

[48] There is much discussion among exegetes· some make the phrase "in power" qualify the verb, and translate "he was powerfully declared"; others make it qualify the Son. The context shows that the latter is the correct interpretation

[49] Dalman, *Die Worte Jesu*, Leipzig, 1898, vol i, 164ff.

[50] Herveus Burgidolensis relates this text to the Pauline one. "He was predestined to be Son of God in the might of immortality and power, of whom it was said after his resurrection· All power is given to me in heaven and on earth." (*Comm. in Rom*, *P L*, clxxxi, 601)

St Paul, and he exhausts his entire vocabulary in attempting to describe the infinite might of God (Eph. i. 19ff.) Any return from death to life is to him a revelation of God's power (Rom. iv. 17), but does not astound him. At Troas he performed that very miracle with no special *éclat*. (Acts xx. 10.) His marvelling at the "operation of the might of God" in Christ was because it was a manifestation of the whole of God's power. The Pauline theology of justification yields this general law: the nature of the cause is carried on in the effect. God raises up the Saviour and those that believe in him by the Spirit, and therefore Christ and they that are his become spirit (1 Cor. xv. 44ff.); he raises them by his glory (Rom. vi. 4) and they live in glory. (1 Cor. xv. 43; 2 Cor. iii. 18; Phil. iii. 21.) He gives life by his power (2 Cor. xiii. 4), by an extraordinary working of power, and Christ rises up clothed in infinite power, and our bodies once "sown in weakness, shall rise in power". (1 Cor. xv. 43.) That power is none other than the working of the Spirit; and the power of the risen Christ is infinite, because there is no limit to the interpenetration of Christ by the Spirit.

vi. THE FATHER'S HEIR

If he is Son, then he is heir, heir of God (Gal. iv. 7; Rom. viii. 17). Christ on earth, in his saving humanity, had not yet received the inheritance. The glory, power, and universal dominion stood, as it were, empty, awaiting Christ's coming of age. St. Paul suggests this in the Epistle to the Galatians. (iv. 1–7.) Though men were heirs in virtue of the promise, they had not yet come into the enjoyment of the goods brought by the Messiah, for the time was not yet ripe. Meanwhile, they were living as children, under the tutelage of the Law and "the elements of the world". Christ, born in the flesh, lived among them subject to the same regime of childhood and servitude, that he might bring them in him to the sonship and its inheritance. In his glorification, our Lord has inherited the whole Divinity, the life of God, in so far as bodily humanity can live that life, his attributes of power and holiness, and all that belongs to the Father, Creator of the world. Redeemed mankind, coming into this inheritance, are co-heirs with Christ.[51]

[51] At the moment of Christ's entering into the fullness of divine life, according to several of the Fathers, he ceased to be ignorant about the day and hour of the Judgement which, judging from Mark xiii. 32, he had been during his

vii. FULLY FREE

Constituted in the fullest dignity of his sonship, Christ has done with servitude. The flesh, that mark of slavery imprinted upon Christ on earth which made it possible for his divine liberty to be fettered, has been destroyed.

For the Spirit has established his sway over him unchecked, "and where the Spirit of the Lord is, there is liberty." (2 Cor. iii. 17.) The Spirit of God knows no coercion; his activity and his charismatic manifestations scorn the laws of nature and even of reason (1 Cor. xiv.) He comes and goes in mystery, baffling all our calculations (cf. John iii. 8); he is God's spontaneity breaking out into the world. Henceforth all the restrictions inherent in Christ's carnal nature are done away with: gone is all subjection to any law other than that which belongs to his own new life—the Law of Moses has no more hold over him—gone all limitations of time and space. He came out of the tomb before the angel rolled away the stone, he stood amid the Apostles when they were behind shuttered doors.

---

time on earth In the economy of the flesh, Christ declared: "Of that day or hour no man knoweth, neither the angels of heaven, nor the Son, but the Father." But when asked after his resurrection he simply replied, "It is not for you to know the time or moment" (Acts i. 7) He himself knew it from then onwards See Origen, *In Matth* , lv, *P G.*, xiii, 1686, St. Athanasius, *Or III Contra Arianos*, xlviii, *P.G.*, xxvi, 425; St. Cyril of Alexandria, *Thesaurus*, *P G.*, lxxv, 376ff

For them the ignorance was in one sense real, and not merely, as for St Augustine (*En. in Ps* , xxxvi, 1, *P L* , xxxvi, 355), the reticence of the Master who would not teach us anything that was not useful for us

This teaching is in perfect harmony with the present position of Catholic theology about our Lord's knowledge. This distinguishes three types of knowledge in Christ on earth· the knowledge of vision, which could not be expressed because it was not conceptual; messianic or prophetic knowledge, which was divine in origin, but conceptual, and enabled Christ to reveal those divine truths necessary for our salvation; and lastly, the knowledge from experience, human in origin The first dwelt at the summit of the human soul, beyond the point where our redemption took place; the other two belong to the humanity which, in order to redeem us, passed from the condition of weakness to that of Son of God. Christ could know what was incommunicable while having a real ignorance of what was communicable.

While the scriptural evidence adduced by these Fathers does not prove that Christ's knowledge progressed in the matter, at least their statement tallies with the doctrine of the Redemption as the divinization of man accomplished first of all in Christ, through his death and resurrection The knowledge that dwelt in this redemptive humanity, as well as the humanity itself, would have received a new perfection, a perfection fitting to Christ's function as judge which he began to exercise from the Resurrection on

Did he pass through solid stone, through the walls of the upper room? Where did he stay before his ascension when he was not appearing to anyone? He stayed with the Father in the Holy Spirit, which makes these questions meaningless, for the laws of our space no longer bound him.[52]

viii. THE UNIVERSAL MAN

In laying aside the flesh whereby he belonged to the Jewish nation, Christ set himself above all the national differences of men. St. Paul makes an antithesis, as type and antitype, of circumcision on the one hand, and on the other, of the death and resurrection of Christ. He distinguishes the circumcision of the Jews from the immaterial circumcision of Christ, which we receive in our union with the Saviour's burial and new life. (Col. ii. 11-12.) Although when he was eight days old he was marked as belonging to one nation, the circumcision of his death and resurrection, which is "a despoiling of the body of the flesh" (Col. ii. 11), has unfastened him from the Jewish structure, and this universal Man can now become the foundation for the world-wide Church, whose members will henceforth be neither Greeks nor Jews nor barbarians.[53]

The unfettered liberty Christ enjoys, the entry into his inheritance, the universality, the exaltation in power, and the sonship which sums them all up—all this, we must remember, is the work of the Holy Spirit.

The Old Testament has already made us familiar with the ways of God's Spirit; though his working in Christ goes far beyond anything he has done before, it still continues along a line we recognize. By him God opens out upon the world, and in him man opens upon the infinity of God. The Spirit as it were breaks into limited beings, opens them wide and unfolds them. Thanks to him Israel, breaking off from the rest of mankind, had made an approach to the holiness of God, had become a miracle in the history of the ancient world; its prophets had broken the bonds of time and space. Thanks also to him, Christ received a communication of the Godhead in his human nature, and was in contact with the infinity of God's attributes; he overcame the laws of his material nature and all the

[52] It was his care for the nascent Church that made him still present and accessible to the senses, even to the point of eating with his disciples.

[53] F. Prat, *Theology*, vol ii, p 117. in St. Paul's mind "Christ visibly broke all the bonds linking him to Judaism, whose memory is almost forgotten".

restrictions they laid upon him, and as we shall see, his very individuality in some sense opened out to embrace all believers within itself.

3. THE PRIESTHOOD OF THE RISEN CHRIST

When we come to the Epistle to the Hebrews, Christ's domination appears in a new light, his lordship over the world becomes a priestly one "Having offered one sacrifice for sins, [Christ] forever sitteth on the right hand of God, from henceforth expecting, until his enemies be made his footstool." (x. 12-13.) As the offerer of sacrifice, Christ has taken his place at the right hand of God's power, and it is in virtue of that offering that his adversaries will be made subject to him. The Apocalypse also draws our attention to this, when it calls the master of human destinies "Lamb" and "Lord" As long as one looks only at Christ's universal power, one can, strictly speaking, leave aside the Cross, and see the Lord only as the Son of God in the glorious fullness of his incarnation. But Christ's lordship is first and foremost exercised in redemptive activity, and henceforth it will always bear the imprint of his five wounds.

1. THE EPISTLE TO THE HEBREWS

(a) The Glory as the Decisive Phase of Christ's Priesthood

No-one who takes the texts of this epistle in their full force and daring will deny that the glorification of Jesus Christ was the beginning of a decisive phase of his priesthood. The author is persuaded that "the consummation", that is the glorifying transformation Christ has undergone by virtue of his death, has inaugurated Christ into the function of "High Priest according to the order of Melchisedech.": "And being consummated, he became, to all that obey him, the cause of eternal salvation, called by God a high priest according to the order of Melchisedech." (v. 9-10.)[54]

---

[54] Several of the Fathers stress the change in Christ's priesthood brought about by the Resurrection: Tertullian, St Athanasius, St Cyril of Alexandria, Theodore of Mopsuestia. Cf. C. Spicq, *L'Épître aux Hébreux*, vol. 1, p. 300, n 1; J. Lécuyer, "Le Sacerdoce chrétien et le sacrifice eucharistique selon Théodore de Mopsueste", *Rech Sc Rel.*, xxxvi (1949), 481-516 The new nature of Christ's heavenly sacrifice comes out clearly in C Spicq, *L'Épître aux Hébreux*, pp 297-300

As long as we do not forget the modifications imposed by the doctrinal framework of the Epistle, we may say that his entry into glory was for Christ a priestly anointing, a true investiture. "For the Law indeed maketh men high priests who have infirmity; but the word of the oath, which was since the Law, the Son who has come to perfection for evermore." (vii. 28.) Following upon the Law, which established priests full of mortal weakness, there has come a word which establishes a priest who has come to the perfection of divine life, the word said over Christ consummated in sacrifice: "Thou art a priest forever, according to the order of Melchisedech " (vii. 17)

(b) The Glory as a Priestly Consecration

Christ's exaltation is part of the very definition of his priesthood: "It was necessary that we should have such a high priest, holy, innocent, undefiled, separated from sinners, and made higher than the heavens." (vii. 26.) This last quality might be due simply to his initial raising to the dignity of the Son. But this would be a very incomplete exegesis; our Lord's entry into the divine sanctuary by the sacrifice of the Cross preoccupies the author too much to be absent from his mind here

The epistle takes up this definition elsewhere, and states it more clearly and more weightily: "Of the things which we have spoken this is the sum: We have such a high priest, who is set on the right hand of the throne of majesty in the heavens, a minister of the Holies, and of the true tabernacle, which the Lord hath pitched and not man." (viii. 1-2.) Unlike the people of old, we have a high priest "that hath passed into the heavens" (iv. 14), who "entereth in even within the veil . . . made a high priest forever according to the order of Melchisedech". (vi. 19-20.) The passing into heaven is of the essence of Christ's priesthood, and it is that which makes it different from the levitical priesthood.

If we deny Christ that consummation, we reduce him to the level of the old covenant, we take away the whole meaning of his priesthood: "If he were on earth, he would not be a priest: seeing that there would be others to offer gifts according to the law." (viii. 4) God already had priests on earth; our Lord could have had no part in their function, for he did not belong to the tribe they sprang from; and his suffering would have gone for nothing, for it would no more have brought him into the true tabernacle than anyone else's suffering did. Here again an explanation is needed· Christ's priesthood and sacrificial actions are heavenly in their effects; his saving death reverberated in heaven, into which it forced an entry in the same way as Aaron's sacrifice thrust the veil aside from the tabernacle. But Christ's ministry is heavenly in itself and not only in its effects As the liturgy of Moses is called earthly, because it took place in a tabernacle made by the hand of man, Christ's liturgy is heavenly because it takes place in the sanctuary of God. (viii. 1–5.)

The statement could hardly be clearer: the entry into glory is a consecration, and the activity of the risen Christ is a priestly ministry. It does not, however, justify us in considering the Resurrection as Christ's vocation to the priesthood, his first anointing and the commencement of his sacrificial action. This Socinian thesis goes beyond the facts the epistle gives us and even contradicts some of them. So does the similar, mitigated Socinianism which would divide Christ's sacrifice into two phases, the first, opening phase taking place on earth, and the second, more important one, consisting in Christ's offering of himself in heaven; the epistle does not support this either. We might perhaps maintain the integrity of the sacrifice of the Cross while postulating a heavenly sacrifice, distinct from the bloody sacrifice, which would consist in the offering made by Christ of his work on earth and of his death, but though this would be quite orthodox, the exegesis would suffer.[55]

The epistle in fact recognizes only one sacrifice, the sacrifice on the Cross. The sacrificial character of the Cross and the uniqueness of that offering need no proving. (cf. vii. 27; ix. 12, 14, 27–8; x. 10–12.) Christ was, then, a priest. His vocation to be a priest was contained in his generation as Son (v. 5), and he was already Son, though the fact was veiled by his humiliations.

We come up against statements that appear contrary: the entry into glory is the consecration of the priest, and yet the priesthood is included in the sonship he already possessed. The strictly Pauline epistles face us with a similar paradox, when they make the resurrection the origin of the sonship Christ already possessed. This paradox also occurs in Hebrews. "The titles of Son of God and

---

[55] You will find these various hypotheses and their supporters in A. Michel, "Jésus Christ", *Dict. Théol cath* , col 1339.

High Priest are closely connected [there]."[56] For the Son, as for the Priest, the Resurrection was a beginning; both achieved their consummation at that moment (v. 9–10; vi. 20); it is the "Son who is made perfect for evermore" who is established as high priest by God's oath, and evidently the "This day have I begotten thee" (v. 5) was spoken in the same breath as "Thou art a priest forever" (v. 6) —that is to say, at the Resurrection.

(c) Eternal Priest

Among the new aspects of Christ's priesthood, the light of eternity on his face particularly interests the author. Christ's glorification places his priestly activity in the "eternal now" of God; this is affirmed over and over again (v. 6; vi. 20; vii. 3, 8, 16–17, 20–28) and is the essential point of comparison between Christ and the King of Salem, his type, "without father, without mother, without genealogy, having neither beginning of days nor end of life; truly a figure of the Son of God, he continueth a priest forever." (vii. 3.) The text of Psalm cx. 4—"The Lord hath sworn, and he will not repent: Thou art a priest forever"—forms a leitmotiv whose reiteration impresses upon the reader the idea that eternity is the characteristic trait of Christ's priesthood. To be a priest in the manner of Melchisedech means primarily to have the endless priesthood which that mysterious king gave the impression of having, since there is no historical indication to attach him to any human genealogy.

This eternity of glory is not simply an endless duration of time, but an exaltation of this priesthood into the divine order of things, into the duration, and hence the life, of God himself.[57] By the rite of Easter, man was wholly assumed into God and into the fullness of his life. That is why Christ's priesthood is bound up with his sonship: the glorification consecrates the Priest because it is the flowering of his nature as Son: a richer priesthood in the fullness of sonship.

The eternity of the priesthood merges with its character of heavenly perfection. "Eternal Priest" and "Heavenly Priest" are identical titles, both expressing a key-idea of the theology of history,

[56] J Dupont, "Filius Meus Es Tu", *Rech Sc. Rel*, xxxv, 1948, 538ff

[57] C Spicq, *L'Épître aux Hébreux*, vol i, p. 267, *n* 5. The term *eternal* "evokes a spiritual perspective whenever it appears, and one might often translate it as *divine*."

particular to this epistle. After the fragmentary and therefore manifold revelation (i. 1), after the testaments of this world, with their priests, who were many, because weak and mortal (vii. 23), and their rites, which were constantly repeated because they effected nothing—after all these earthly and ephemeral shadows of the reality, Christ has come, the heavenly priest, who consummates all things in the fullness of his eternal priesthood.[58]

What does his glory add to Christ's priesthood? Even during his ephemeral and earthly life, Christ was already the eternal and heavenly priest. "The power of an indissoluble life" (vii. 16) animated him even then, and the death on Calvary could not essentially damage it. The sacrifice of Jesus was offered "in the eternal spirit" (ix. 14), and though the Cross was fixed to the earth, he was thenceforward "on earth" no longer (viii. 4), for his death opened out into the life of heaven. The Resurrection was a public and solemn ratification of the first vocation, once hidden, contained in his sonship. Though it gave a heavenly character to the sacrificial action of Christ dying, it did not modify that action, but only specified it, as every action is specified by the goal it is to attain. But while the entry into glory gives the priestly action its specification, this is because it is essential to it; priesthood and sacrifice are inconceivable without it.

Christ's priesthood and sacrifice draw their decisive efficacy from their heavenly character. Because a true priest has entered the true sanctuary by means of a sacrifice offered in the eternal Spirit, a true redemption has been effected. (ix. 11-14.)

The priesthood is without succession (vii. 23-4), the sacrifice perfect and sufficient, never repeated, indeed unrepeatable (x. 10-14) for both are eternal.

By virtue of the immortality of his life, Christ can apply to men the salvation he has won for them in his own consummation: "Being consummated, he became the cause of eternal salvation . . ." (v. 9); "He is able to save forever them that come to God by him; always living to make intercession for them." (vii. 25.)

Thus his glory gives Christ's sacrifice both its specification and its efficacy.

[58] The notion of eternity special to this epistle comes close to the Johannine concept of truth, that truth which is the transcendent reality of heaven, known only through the revelation of the Word in the Incarnation

(d) Our Mediator in Heaven

A priesthood is a mediation, the active presence of one man between God and other men Christ was already bound intimately to God by his initial grace, but only in the divinizing Resurrection could his closeness to God be fully realized, for before that Christ's humanity was separated from God by a journey of blood. The author makes the most felicitous use of Psalm CIX, in which he finds all the three elements which are to him the basis for the transcendence of Christ's priestly mediation: sonship, eternity according to the order of Melchisedech, and being seated by the Father. His being present with God in such intimate familiarity is what gives Christ's mediation its special character, and it is only in his glorification that Christ comes thus to take his place by the Father with his whole being, and more particularly, with that part of his being in which our contact with God in Christ takes place.

This direct proximity to God raises his mediating action to supreme efficacy: "Being consummated, he became to all that obey him, the cause of eternal salvation, called by God a high priest according to the order of Melchisedech " (v. 9–10.) Henceforth he exercises jurisdiction over "the good things to come" (ix. 11), those "marvels of the world to come" (vi. 5), of the world above. There is no reason why a mediation of grace should not have been exercised even during his life on earth, but it did not achieve its fullness of saving power and universality until Christ had drawn his body, which had been held back in the world of sin, into the glory of God. "In his perfection he became the cause of eternal salvation." We find God and salvation in Christ, who has attained consummation, for God's grace is henceforth open to the world in this man who in all things belonged to our world.

Because of this closeness to God, a new way of intercession is possible to our Mediator. Christ "becomes . . our paraclete, the advocate taking up our cause, rather as a man of importance might present his client's case to a prince".[59] This intercession is not now the supplication he once made prostrate and weeping. (v 7) Christ is seated (i. 3, 13; viii. 1; x 12; xii. 2) beside the Father, and he intercedes for us simply by being there "He is entered . . . into heaven itself, that he may appear now in the presence of God for us." (ix. 24.) From Christ's prayers on earth we did not learn that the mere

[59] J. Bonsirven, *Épître aux Hébreux*, p 412.

showing of our human nature, that nature which still bore the marks of sin, was an intercession for us. Now this humanity which is ours, which is of our sinful race, has returned to God in the risen Christ, and its presence in the bosom of the Father, showing the seal imprinted upon it in five places, in witness of its death to sin and possession by God, exercises for us a coercion of love on God's heart. It is as if Christ said: "Father, in thy Son, behold prodigal man returned." He is now truly present before the face of God for our benefit.[60]

Into this close union with God there also gathers an assembly of believers round the Mediator On earth he had offered sacrifice to convoke the assembly: now in his glory, he honours God in its midst. For God has set him as "the apostle and high priest of our confession . . . at the head of his own house which house are we". (iii. 1, 6.) Whereas his sacrifice on the Cross traced but one sign in heaven, Christ now presides in the midst of a great people: "I will declare thy name to my brethren; in the midst of the assembly will I praise thee . . . Behold I, and my children, whom God hath given me." (ii. 12–13.)[61]

(e) High Priest in Heaven

The mediating activity of the priest reaches its high point in that exchange of gifts between God and men which constitutes sacrifice. Hence the question: Does the priesthood of glory include a sacrifice as the priesthood of blood did before? The epistle certainly seems to deny this categorically, recognizing only one oblation, consummated once and for all. Yet the problem of a sacrifice in heaven has

[60] This is how St Cyril of Alexandria explains the eloquence of this presence "This, indeed, is how we say that he now stands for our advantage, to the eyes of his God and Father, he is, in a sense, introducing humanity, that humanity which had been turned away by the sin of Adam " (*In Ep ad Hebr.*, ix, 24, *P.G* , lxxiv, 985)

[61] If we turn to strictly Pauline literature, we find even more clearly expressed this idea that the glorified Christ remains embedded in humanity, even in his deepest union with God. The glory that raises him above the world brings him closer to us, though it sets him apart from our mode of being. Whereas, while he remained as one among other men, his own humanity was his alone, he can now penetrate them and unfold himself among them Then our Saviour lived among us, present beside us in a closed individuality Now that humanity enters even our most secret hiding places; while remaining himself, he becomes us He has become the perfect Mediator between God and men

worried all the commentators; whatever their answer, the very fact
that they are so preoccupied with it proves that it is a problem that
must be faced.

There is a *liturgy* in heaven whose celebrant is Christ:

> Of the things which we have spoken, this is the sum: We have
> a high priest, who is set on the right hand of the throne of majesty
> in the heavens, a minister of the Holies, and of the true tabernacle
> which the Lord hath pitched, and not man. For every high priest
> is appointed to offer gifts and sacrifices: wherefore it is necessary
> that he also should have something to offer. If then he were on
> earth, he would not be a priest: seeing that there would be others
> to offer gifts according to the Law. Who serve unto the example
> and shadow of heavenly things. As it was answered to Moses,
> when he was to finish the tabernacle: See (saith he) that thou
> make all things according to the pattern which was shewn thee
> on the mount.
>
> (viii. 1–5.)

We cannot shut our eyes to the mysterious brightness of this
text: a complete liturgy takes place in heaven, of which the old
earthly liturgy of Sinai was a copy. The worship of the heavenly
sanctuary is centred upon sacrifice; Christ could not be a priest if he
had nothing to offer; the Mosaic rites were only a stammering, flat
and commonplace translation of that heavenly model On the altar
of the Cross a priest who came from heaven was celebrant, and a
victim was offered for whom the tabernacle of God was opened;
but this is not the reason for Christ's sacrifice being called heavenly:
the sacrificial liturgy there unfolds simply from our Lord's existence
in glory. Indeed, the progress of verses 3 to 5 goes to strengthen the
affirmation that Christ performs the ministry of the heavenly
sanctuary; thus it is in heaven, while sitting beside the Father (1–2)
that Christ "has something to offer", and it was of an eternal liturgy
that the rites of the Mosaic sacrifice were a shadow, an earthly and
inadequate frame.

If we are to make this text fit in with the absolute uniqueness of
Christ's sacrifice in both number and kind, which we believe, we
must allow that the mystery of the Cross is prolonged in eternity.
In the thought of this epistle, the Christian sacrifice was not a deed
which took place and was wholly completed in time, so that only
the merit remains. In the author's mind, the act of offering is eternal

and heavenly, because it becomes eternal in itself, and is prolonged in Christ's existence in glory. Though the text is not explicit, it is certainly suggestive; how else can we explain how the heavenly priest has "something to offer"?

There are other texts which assume, if not the perpetuation of the offering, at least the permanence of the victim state: "By his own blood, he entered once into the Holies, having obtained eternal redemption " (ix. 12) Whereas the priest of the order of Aaron entered once a year into the sanctuary by virtue of blood not his own, Christ opened the way to God by the blood of his own immolation. He did not bear the blood of victims upon his hand; he was the victim for whom the veil was opened, and since he entered once for all through the veil of his immolated flesh (x. 20), we may believe that the state of victim in virtue of which the sanctuary opened for him, continues forever. Once again, the epistle does not actually say so, but suggests it.

If man, in his turn, wants to penetrate the sanctuary of God, he can find Christ in his victim state, and join himself to him in the very act, it would seem, of his entry into God: "Having therefore, brethren, a confidence in the entering into the Holies in the blood of Christ, a new and living way which he hath dedicated for us through the veil, that is to say, his flesh." (x. 19-20.) One should not weaken a word without good cause; it does not say that the way of entry is opened thanks to the blood of Christ—thanks, that is, to the merit won forever through its being poured out—but *in* that blood [62] With this key we can enter into God, sprinkled with the same blood as Christ himself. Christ must still be the victim; by that victim we enter just as he did The way is living, marked out in the living flesh which, before its immolation, was a veil spread over the tabernacle, but which is now a veil forever torn aside. Christ remains the victim, and for us, as for Christ since his sacrifice, this victim is always in the act of opening the tabernacle. We penetrate into the tabernacle through Christ's immolation, and therefore, it would seem, together with him.

We must take literally those texts which speak of the Saviour's blood as an instrument of salvation. "The sprinkling of blood which speaketh better than that of Abel", to which we are come (xii. 24),

---

[62] The ἐν τῷ αἵματι of x. 19 means the same as the διὰ αἵματος of ix 12 Cf ix 12 and ix 25 This instrumentality of the blood, and therefore of Christ in his victim state is stated again in ix. 14; xii 24, and xiii 12.

is not merely a visionary image, while only the merit of this sacrifice has a real part in God's acceptance. The blood of Christ "cleanses our conscience from dead works". (ix. 14.) It is the blood itself, Christ actually being pierced, that cleanses our souls. The victim, cause of our purification, is always present, and not merely in the pardon he has won for us. St. Peter also speaks of "the sprinkling of the blood" we receive (1 Pet. i. 2.)

The epistle certainly knows no new sacrifice, nor any perpetuation of the offering in a later state, for the sacrificial passing from this world to the tabernacle of the Father has been completed once for all. Yet we have to reconcile the need for a unique sacrifice with the need for continuity; this can only be met by the eternal permanence of the victim in the ever-actual acceptance of God. The Saviour's glorification, which took place in his soul at the moment of his death and was completed in the resurrection of his body, was the realization of that acceptance; if that glorification remains forever actual, then the victim remains forever in the first moment of God's welcoming embrace; the offering remains in the moment of fullness in which it was accepted by the Father Though the sacrificial act took place in the past, its conclusion is something ever actual in the everlasting glorifying welcome of God. The act of passing from this world to the Father took place once for all, but the meeting with the Father continues forever: the victim is fixed eternally at the high point of the offering.[63]

His glory inaugurates a new phase in Christ's priesthood: its final phase of fullness. His activity on earth was an effort towards God in the pain of renunciation. It began when Christ came into the world: "When he cometh into the world he saith: Sacrifice and oblation thou wouldest not: but a body thou hast fitted to me ... Then said I: Behold I come ..I come to do thy will, O God." (x. 5–9.) The final phase begins and remains at the exact moment of the sacrifice's being consummated. Christ stays at the high point of his priestly function, the offering of his death becomes eternal in the divinizing acceptance which crowns it. Henceforth Christ's priesthood is "accomplished". No longer does Christ stand, striving upwards; he is seated, for he has reached his goal. This sitting beside the Father is the characteristic attitude of the heavenly priest. In

[63] St. Athanasius, *Or. II contra Arianos*, P.G., xxvi, 165: "He offers a true sacrifice which remains and does not pass away."

spite of its overflowing activity, that priesthood is at rest; it is the
serene dynamism of perfection

ii. THE APOCALYPSE

Like this last epistle coming from St. Paul, the book which concludes the Christian revelation presents the sacrifice of the Cross
in its eternal phase. The Apocalypse shows us Christ in glory as
priest and victim. The two are presented to our eyes, now in turn,
now simultaneously, but here, in contrast to the epistle, it is the
victim that holds our attention most strongly.

We have seen how St. John's gospel appears to be a gospel of
Christ's priesthood. We noted (Chapter I) its preoccupation with
worship, and the central place it gives the Temple. It is noteworthy
that it differs from the Synoptics in its account of the Precursor, for
here he presents Christ to the world not as its judge, but as its
expiating victim. (i. 29) Later, our Lord declares that he "sanctifies
himself" for the Apostles, and his death recalls the sacrificing of
the lamb. (xix. 36.) He foretold a worship in spirit and in truth
(iv. 23); he drove the sellers out of the Temple in the name of the
Resurrection, prophesying that it was there that the new worship
was to start.

In the vision with which the Apocalypse opens, Christ appears in
priestly garb, "clothed with a tunic down to the feet and a golden
girdle about his breast". (i. 13.) The long tunic and golden girdle
round the breast were a priest's dress. But that vision passes; in the
centre of the Apocalypse's imagery we find the Lamb, Christ
the victim of Calvary,[64] whom the author calls with tenderness, "the
little Lamb".

Christ is received into heaven in this guise, and enthroned in
glory. One of the ancients announces that a conqueror is coming,
the Lion of Judah, who will break the seals on the book, and there
appears, soft and white, a lamb. Christ has triumphed as a victim,
and as such he inaugurates his reign and takes the government of
the world into his hands.

On his throne in heaven he remains what he was made on

[64] All thoughts of the priesthood do not, however, disappear The sacrifice
of the Lamb gains priesthood and kingship for the faithful. If the faithful
are priests and kings through Christ, then he himself must be so in a higher
degree The two concepts of priest and victim can no more be separated in
the Apocalpse than they can in the Epistle to the Hebrews

the altar on earth: "And I saw in the midst of the throne . . . and the four ancients, a lamb standing as it were immolated." (v. 6.) "The preposition ὡς (as) is not used here to indicate an appearance at variance with reality; rather it affirms a reality at variance with the appearances. The Lamb is actually standing, an attitude which symbolizes life",[65] yet he is immolated.

St. John's gospel tells us that our Lord's five wounds remained open on his risen body, a finger or hand could be placed in them. Are these marks upon the Lamb a mere memorial of his immolation—as it were a receipt inscribed upon Christ's members for the price he gave to redeem us? Or are they the outward marks of a deeper imprint left by his sacrifice, the expression of an everlasting state of victimhood? The more one studies the Redemption in Scripture, the more literal one becomes in interpreting it. Christ penetrates to the Father's side as the paschal lamb, with none of his bones broken, but marked with the stigmata of his immolation. He remains a man pierced. Until the end of time men will contemplate him in his wounds as well as in his majesty. (John xix. 37; Apoc. 1. 7.)

The faithful are the first to know that the Lamb is forever immolated; they come and wash their clothes in the crimson of his blood and draw them out dazzlingly white. (vii 14.) They are not content merely to apply to themselves the pardon that blood won for them in the past; they immerse themselves in the victim of Calvary now present, and become impregnated with his cleansing power.

Christ will never heal these mortal wounds; the imprint of his ever-actual immolation will never disappear from his body. In situations where one would least expect it, when he comes in terrible power, it is as a lamb that he comes, bearing the mark of the lance for all to see upon his breast. All Christ's lordship bears the marks of his passion. It is the Lamb who is the "Lion of Judah," the conqueror who holds the destiny of the world in his hand. The warrior who "doth judge and fight with justice, whose eyes are as a flame of fire", wears a garment sprinkled with blood, probably his own. (xix. 11–13.) The Lamb fights the Beast and defeats him (xvii. 14); the author speaks of "the wrath of the Lamb" (vi. 16), and the torments to which he condemns his enemies. (xiv. 10.) Alongside violent, un-lamblike images we find others which seem more in

[65] A. Médebielle, "Expiation," *D B. Suppl*, col. 237.

keeping in their gentleness. "The little Lamb" is the shepherd, he walks ahead (vii 17) and his faithful flock follow in his steps (xiv. 4) to the fountains of the waters of life (vii 17) The bride in her exile longs for him, and prepares herself "for the marriage of the Lamb". (xix. 7–9; xxi 9.) In the heavenly city, he is the temple where believers mysteriously come together, and the soft and bright lamp which lights the everlasting day (xxi. 22–3.)

These are not mere poetic images, but stand in their own right as theology. The lordship of the risen Christ is as priest and as victim; universal power and the right of judgement are the attributes of a life which has attained maturity in immolation, and all that he is to those who believe in him—head, shepherd, purity, eternal life—he is in virtue of being the immolated Lamb.

III. SUMMING-UP

These ideas are not the monopoly either of the Epistle to the Hebrews or the Apocalypse; the thought in all Paul's epistles need only be placed in a framework of sacrifice to show how similar it is. And since so many minds seem to find an insoluble enigma in this permanence of an ever-actual immolation in the midst of a life of glory, it may be useful to return to the Pauline conception of the act of redemption, to find its justification and explanation.

Christ had accepted human nature in its carnal state to make himself totally one with sinful man. Hence the imputation that he had sin to expiate was no mere legal fiction, existing because of a divine decree; it was founded upon his flesh which convicted him of belonging to a sinful race. In a state of glory, he would not have been able to offer himself in sacrifice, since he would have had nothing to give which did not already belong to God. But having this nature inherited from Adam, he had a flesh to sacrifice, well fitted to be immolated and offered, in it Christ could give himself, could cross the distance by which it separated him from the Father; and in order that the offering might be a real one, the sinful flesh must be immolated so that it might cease to hold Christ outside the full radiance of the Godhead

In the immolation of Calvary, the flesh died and with it sin. This death was never undone, the flesh never returned to life in Christ, there was no resurrection for the flesh in the Pauline sense of the word. The glory did not reawaken the old life; the power of the

"psyche" was never again to function in frailty; the new life in its
spirituality spells forever the end of the flesh. God would have been
going against his word, revoking his acceptance of Christ's sacrifice,
had he merely raised him to the earthly life he had before; he would
have been annulling the sacrifice, which was a passing over, would
have been putting Christ once again at a distance from him. That
is why he consecrates, in his Son, death to earthly life. "Christ died
once for all; but in that he liveth, he liveth unto God." (Rom. vi.
10.) He stands in his own death, living by the Spirit in the death
of the flesh.

That the immolation is permanent in no way prejudices the full
vitality of the new life. The absence of carnal life is the negative side
of life in the Spirit, all that this destroys in human life is its carnal
weakness. The Spirit exalts all man's vital powers at the cost only
of their limitations. Nothing of the richness of his human life is
lost to Christ. As in the sphere of knowledge "the spiritual man
judgeth all things; and he himself is judged of no ["psychic"]
man" (I Cor. ii. 15), since spiritual knowledge eminently includes
natural, so in the sphere of being, life according to the Spirit perfectly includes the life of the "psyche"

It is not as being a separation of body and soul that the death
remains actual. This separation, as such, belongs to the order of
carnal weakness, has no salutary value, and is not worthy of preser-
vation. It is consecrated by the glory in as much as that is redemptive, and in as much as it brings the earthly life to an end by
terminating it in the life of the Son. Christ's death becomes eternal
in the goal which gives it the power to save; in other words, in the
divine life

But Christ is not fixed in death as in a state following an act; the
sacrifice remains actual.[66] Not in the act of happening, of course, but
in its final point, the moment of its consummation. Indeed, as
Scripture describes it, Christ's glorification can be defined as a permanent act beyond which Christ's existence never passes. Our Lord's
redemptive death is also ordered towards the glory in which it is
fulfilled, and with which it coincides, as in any change the end of
one way of being coincides with the beginning of another. In the
ever-actual permanence of his glorification, Christ's death itself thus

[66] I hope I may be allowed to define the liturgy of heaven in terms that
are not scriptural

remains eternal in its actuality, fixed at its final point, at the moment
of its perfection.

Thus the death and resurrection are intertwined in their dynamism, and Christ can not only claim salvation for those who believe
in him by reason of his merits; he need only communicate himself
to extend to them his death, in which is life.

His glory has, therefore, conferred upon Christ as priest a fullness
which he did not have during his life on earth. It has brought his
priesthood and sacrifice to perfection, and maintains them there. It
does not alter their meaning—it gives them all the meaning they
have   priesthood and sacrifice are "eternal" and "heavenly" in
nature

"Our Lord", "Son of God", "perfect Priest"—these titles given
to Christ at Easter evoke a new messianic reality; the first supposes
a kingdom to be governed by Christ the Lord, the second, many
children of whom this Son is the eldest, and the third, believers
gathered round their High Priest.

V

THE RESURRECTION OF CHRIST, BIRTH
OF THE CHURCH

In the prophecy of the Old Testament, as well as in Christ's teaching and the preaching of the Apostles, Christ's person is bound up
with a reality which projects beyond it and yet forms one body with
it. Scripture tries to define this entity and express the richness of it
with magnificent phrases: "the People of God", the "Kingdom",
"Temple", or "Church" of God, "the Body of Christ", "the Bride
of Christ". In this chapter I am presupposing the basic unity of this
entity, despite its many varying titles and facets. This is simply an
attempt to fix the date of its birth, and to mark the stages by which
the Israel of old passed into this new People of God

I. THE DATE OF THE CHURCH'S BIRTH

1. THE SYNOPTICS

Preserving the inheritance from the Prophets that Christ's message contained, the Synoptics present the reality of the Messiah's
coming in the framework of the Kingdom of God.

The teaching of the three Evangelists about the coming of that
kingdom needs to be examined closely. Some parables, comparing
the Kingdom to a seed, date the coming of the Kingdom from
Christ's preaching. The entry of the Kingdom into the world
follows upon the work of John the Baptist. He is the Precursor, the
last of the Prophets sent to announce the Kingdom; from then on,
the Kingdom makes its way into the world in power (Matt. xi
12ff); the coming into action of the Spirit of God and the flight
of the devils are proof that it has come in triumph. (Luke xi. 20.)

Yet even at that moment the Kingdom appears to be a reality of
the future. Our Lord declares that it is near, not that it is present:
"The time is accomplished, and the Kingdom of God is at hand

repent and believe the good news." (Mark 1. 15)[1] This was to be the theme of his preaching for some time When Christ gives the Twelve a share in his ministry, he tells them to preach this message: "The Kingdom of God is at hand." (Matt. x. 7) Much later in his public life, he entrusts the same message to the seventy-two disciples. (Luke x. 9) The Kingdom, then, is not established, on the eve of the Passion it is still awaited. (Luke xxii. 18.)

Our Lord had certainly told those who were to preach the Kingdom something about its coming, and they remained in expectation up till the end. They tried in advance to assure themselves places at the right and left hand of the King, when he came to the throne (Matt xx. 21) For them the Kingdom was not yet inaugurated, for our Lord himself had not yet entered it Their state of mind might well have been expressed in the words of the Good Thief· "Lord, remember me when thou shalt come into thy kingdom." (Luke xxiii. 42; cf Luke xix. 11.)

One must not therefore give too wide an interpretation to those texts which affirm the arrival of the Kingdom during Christ's life on earth. It would be surprising if John, in his prison, had remained a splendid lonely figure from the Old Testament, left outside the Kingdom (Matt. xi. 11) which publicans and harlots were able to enter. (Matt. xxi. 31.) The Kingdom of God was present in Israel by its tangible, and already effective, proximity. "The Kingdom of Heaven is in your midst", declared our Lord. (Luke xvii. 21) But this presence was to be followed by the real coming. The Pharisees had asked when it would come. Our Lord's reply was that the Kingdom was coming—was a reality of the future—but that one could not therefore say, "Behold here, or behold there" it is; its coming would not be observable at all, for it was already there in the midst of them. This context suggests that it was certainly present but present so far simply as a principle and a hope. The messianic

---

[1] People often prefer to translate this, "The Kingdom has come" because of the use of the perfect (ἤγγικεν) which indicates that the movement of approaching is already a thing of the past Cf Lagrange, Évangile selon Saint Marc, Paris, 1920, p. 16, P Jouon, L'Évangile de Jésus-Christ, Paris, 1930, p 10. Certainly the movement of approach is already complete; but the coming of the Kingdom is only at the stage of closeness defined by the words ἐγγύς and ἐγγίζειν. The Kingdom is palpably near, but has not arrived (Cf. Rom xiii. 12; Phil. iv 5.) The two words "characterize the immediate proximity of the miracle" of the coming, they "belong to the family of sacred words" indicating messianic hope See Preisker, Th W N.T , vol. ii, pp. 330, 332

climax that was to bring it into the world was still in the future.
Thus the Kingdom would suddenly appear without it having been
possible to foresee and watch its coming.[2]

It was in Christ's person that that fundamental presence and that
hope were contained, and in him that the Kingdom was suddenly
to be revealed. The Spirit, by whom the Kingdom of God was to
be imposed on the world, was already operative in Christ. (Luke
xi. 20.) The Kingdom was, as it were, incarnate in Christ, and its
lot was linked with his. It came with Christ (Mark xi. 10); to see the
Son of Man coming was to assist at the arrival of the Kingdom (cf.
Matt. xvi. 28 and Mark x 39, Greek text); the words "Christ"
and "Kingdom" seem interchangeable (cf. Matt. xix. 29 and Luke
xviii. 29); by following the one one enters the other,[3] and anyone
rejected by Christ is by that very fact expelled from the Kingdom.
(Matt xxv. 34ff) "The least" in the Kingdom are identified with
Christ, for he is the whole Kingdom.[4]

Our Lord's coming on earth was not as yet a royal coming, and
therefore the Kingdom remained a seed and a hope. In the mind of
the Apostles, the inauguration of the Kingdom required the glorification of their Master: "Grant to us that we may sit one on thy
right hand and the other on thy left hand, in thy glory", St. Mark
quotes them as saying (Mark x. 37), while in Matthew, it is "in thy
kingdom". (xx. 21) To them the Kingdom of God was that age

---

[2] There are two possible translations of this much-argued text (cf A Feuillet,
"La Venue du règne de Dieu et du Fils de l'homme", *Rech. Sc. Rel*, xxxv
(1948), 545-8)· "The Kingdom is in your midst", and, "The Kingdom will
be [suddenly] in your midst." The first is closer to the Greek text (ἐστίν);
the second departs from it, preferring a possible interpretation of the original
Aramaic, in which the auxiliary verb did not have to be expressed.
The first translation alone allows of several explanations Either the presence
of the Kingdom is immanent in the people of Israel, who form the basis
of the messianic kingdom (Lagrange, Knabenbauer, L Marchal), or that
presence is contained within the person of our Lord (J. Weiss, W G. Kummel,
as quoted by Feuillet, p. 547, n. 2, E. Stauffer, *Die Theologie des N.T*, Stuttgart, 1941, p 103) This second explanation is the one I prefer However,
unlike those writers who favour it, I believe that this presence, though
already effective (Luke xi 20), was not yet revealed, for the context speaks
of a kingdom yet to come

[3] Cf. K L Schmidt, *Th. W. N.T*, vol i, p. 590ff ; A Feuillet, "La Venue
du règne de Dieu", p 549

[4] Origen says truly that Christ is himself the Kingdom (αὐτοβασιλεία),
In Matth. Tract., xiv, *P G*, xiii, 1197. Earlier, Marcion had written, ". of
the gospel in which Christ himself is the kingdom of God" Cf. Tertullian,
Adv. Marcionem, iv, 33. ᴰ *L*, ii, 441

of glory promised by the Prophets, which obsessed them as it obsessed the rest of the Jews. And those who, on the "holy mount", were privileged to contemplate Christ transfigured in "the excellent glory" (2 Pet. 1. 17), thought that the time had come. Their only doubt was how to reconcile this immediate establishment of the Kingdom with the teaching of the scribes that Elijah must first return. But our Lord broke into this circle of ideas to talk of his death: the inauguration of the kingdom which they are expecting soon and in splendour is to be preceded by the deepest humiliation; the entry into glory is to take place in a resurrection from the dead. (Matt. xvii. 9–13)

Though Christ was not in accord with his disciples about the way in which it would come, he did at least share their expectancy. When setting out for the last time on the journey up to Jerusalem, while those around him were talking of the coming of the Kingdom, he compared himself to a nobleman going to take possession of a king-dom (Luke xix 11ff) The kingdom which he ruled was, then, not yet founded When later on, he said, "Ought not Christ to have suffered these things and so to enter into his glory?" (Luke xxiv. 26), we seem to catch an echo of that phrase so often used, that he must enter into his kingdom, an echo, and the fulfilment of an expecta-tion.

The setting up of the Kingdom presupposes a display of power. That is why the driving out of demons "by the finger of God" was evidence that the Kingdom had, in a sense, come. (Luke xi. 20.) But its true coming in power was to be later: "There are some of them that stand here, who shall not taste death, till they see the Kingdom of God coming in power." (Mark viii. 39.) It is not that the Kingdom will in itself be more powerful than at present, but simply that it will come, in the glory and power which characterize "the coming".

Christ told his judges that the prophecy of Daniel (vii.) was about to be realized. Hereafter they were to see the Son of Man coming on the clouds of heaven. (Matt. xxvi. 64.) Daniel had described both the foundation of a kingdom and the consecration of a king. After the world had seen the passing of the four earthly empires, whose characteristic features and ephemeral nature were symbolized by the four beasts, "one like the Son of Man came with the clouds of heaven". In this heavenly being the kingdom from above was inaugurated; at his coming "power and dominion and the glory of the kingdoms" were given "to the people of the saints". In the writer's mind, the messianic leader and his community were so closely linked and benefited so inseparably from the one kingship, that when the symbolism is explained (verses 18–27) we cannot distinguish between the king and his people—indeed, it is only the community of saints that is mentioned.

When our Lord unfolded this vision before his judges, he announced, as well as his own glorification, the inauguration of the Kingdom. Certainly the Gospel context specially emphasizes the individual significance of the Son of Man; yet this coming must be interpreted as the arrival of the Kingdom as well as of its king. The text does nothing to modify the meaning of the reference to Daniel which it suggests. They had asked our Lord if he were the Messiah. Yes, was his answer, and my kingdom is now beginning.[5]

All these texts presuppose the idea of a kingdom incarnate in the person of our Lord, a kingdom revealed in Christ's own coming in triumph. Messianic kingdom and messiahship go together; the Kingdom is inaugurated at the moment when Christ enters upon the exercise of his messianic power.

A sombre parable coming only a few days before his death, the parable of the wicked husbandmen, leading into that of the cornerstone, also brackets the coming of the Kingdom with the glorification of our Lord

Having said what the husbandmen did to their master's son, he asked: "What therefore will the lord of the vineyard do to them?" And his hearers replied, "He will destroy those husbandmen and will give the vineyard to others." And our Lord concluded, "Therefore I say to you, that the Kingdom of God shall be taken from you, and shall be given to a nation yielding the fruits thereof." At the time of our Lord's speaking, the Kingdom of Heaven set up on earth was still the theocracy of Israel, administered by the priests and scribes.

To let his opponents know what happened to the son who had

---

[5] To understand the full ecclesiological bearing of Dan vii, read F Kattenbusch, "Der Quellort der Kirchenidee" in *Festgabe fur A Harnack*, Tubingen, 1921, pp 143–72; Y Congar, *Esquisses du mystère de l'Église*, 2nd ed , Paris, 1953, pp 13ff.; O Cullmann, *Konigsherrschaft Christi und Kirche im N T.*, Zurich, 1941, pp 37ff ; K L Schmidt, *Th. W N T* , vol. iii, p 525 The ecclesiological significance of Christ's answer comes out clearly in A. Feuillet, "Le Triomphe eschatologique de Jésus d'après quelques textes des évangiles", *Nouv. Rev. Théol* , lxxi (1949), 818

been put to death, Christ left the parable of the vineyard and went on to another, that of the cornerstone. Then, "fixing his eyes upon them, Jesus said. What is this then that is written, The stone which the builders rejected, the same is become the head of the corner?"

The second image resumes where the first had left off, with the rejection of the son. The builders of the house, selecting their materials, had rejected a stone as unsuitable. God picked it up, and made it the "head of the corner" of his house.

This is more than just a symbol of the Resurrection. Christ was announcing the Kingdom founded upon his death, and inaugurated in his resurrection. The image of the house indicates a community of nations, and the stone the place the Son occupies in it, rejected by man and then chosen by God. In the first parable the husbandmen had plotted "This is the heir, let us kill him, that the inheritance may be ours." The second parable, in contrast with the first, tells us how the son returns to his place as heir of the kingdom denied him by the Jews.[6]

On the eve of his death, our Lord "sat down at table and the twelve Apostles with him. And he said to them· With desire I have desired to eat this pasch with you, before I suffer. For I say to you, that from this time I will not eat it, till it be fulfilled in the Kingdom of God. And having taken the chalice, he gave thanks, and said. Take and divide it among you; For I say to you, that I will not drink of the fruit of the vine till the Kingdom of God come." (Luke xxii. 14–18.)[7]

Even as late as this, then, the Kingdom of God was still a reality of the future; our Lord said it was to come (Luke xxii 18), and the old institutions which prefigured it were still in force.

[6] Cf J. Pirot, *Allégories et paraboles dans la vie et l'enseignement de Jésus-Christ*, Marseille, 1943, p 238
[7] These words which, in St Luke, come before the Eucharist, are placed by the other Synoptics after the account of the institution, and given in a different form· "Amen, I say to you, that I will drink no more of the fruit of the vine, until that day when I shall drink it new in the kingdom of God." (Mark xiv. 25)
It is Luke who gives them their natural framework, putting them at the end of the eating of the paschal lamb, before the institution of the Eucharist Cf P. Benoit, "Le Récit de la cène dans Luc xxii, 15–20", *R.B.*, xlviii (1939), pp. 357–93 Mark and Matthew summarize the Cenacle story and make it follow the tradition of primitive liturgy. And since there is only one chalice in the liturgy, they place after that the words which were actually said after drinking the last chalice of the paschal meal and before the institution of the Eucharist

(xxii 16.) But from thenceforward, our Lord would not eat that Pasch again until its fulfilment in the Kingdom; he would not again taste wine till the Kingdom was come. The Kingdom was in sight; never before had Christ spoken of it as so close. He took leave of the ancient paschal rite which was to be "fulfilled" by a new reality in the coming Kingdom.

Matthew (xxvi. 29) and Mark (xiv. 25) place the Kingdom of God in the far-off eschatological future; the "new wine" to be drunk there suggests a drink that will elate the feasters at a mysterious table. But in St. Luke, the kingdom is close and of this world; its coming is linked with that of the Eucharist, and in the Evangelist's mind, the institution of the Eucharist inaugurates the true pasch of the Kingdom. "From now on, we get in Luke a suggestion of something other than a purely eschatological banquet in this Kingdom of God … It instantly suggests that sphere into which the new paschal rite opens out, the Church."[8] The birth of that Church was very near.

The words Christ said when he passed the chalice round at the supper, according to St. Luke, make it quite clear that the Church was to be born between this meal and Christ's appearances after the Resurrection: "I will not drink of the fruit of the vine till the Kingdom of God come " (xxii. 18.) Luke does not speak of any sublime fulfilment of the pasch in the world to come; he purposely changes the text given by St. Mark and leaves out the mysterious new wine. He was declaring simply that this is the last time Christ would taste wine on earth before his messianic consummation. "In allowing us to understand that Christ will eat and drink again in the Kingdom, he was no doubt simply thinking of the meals that were to take place after the Resurrection."[9] Christ would once again eat with his disciples on earth in his new life (Luke xxiv. 30, 42–3; Acts i. 4), and drink with them (Acts x. 41), and St. Luke is alone in emphasizing these meals. In his mind the inauguration of the Kingdom was to be placed between the paschal supper and the appearances of the risen Christ. Luke thus teaches us that the Kingdom had not yet come, but that it was very close and was to be inaugurated before Christ returned to his Apostles.

The image Christ used to announce the Kingdom explains both the delay and the nearness. Isaiah (xxv. 6–7) had foretold for "that

[8] P Benoit, "Le Récit de la Cène", p. 388
[9] P. Benoit, "Le Récit de la Cène", p. 389

day" an abundant feast for the nations on Mount Zion. The favourite symbol in rabbinical literature to describe the Kingdom was that of a banquet Our Lord had used it in many different forms,[10] and now, in this supreme moment, he returned to it. "I will drink no more of the fruit of the vine until that day when I shall drink it new in the Kingdom of God." (Matt. Mark.)[11]

Christ certainly did not identify the Kingdom with this joyful banquet in so many words. But a meal taken in the Kingdom must in fact be the one he had so often spoken of, and which was the Kingdom itself.

Though the words open up an eschatological perspective, the banquet was not relegated to some distance in the future; placed by Christ in the framework of the mystery, it could begin at once. Thus Luke has taken it upon himself to interpret this Kingdom of the Church on earth, and he places here the commands given to those whom Christ put at the head of his Church, which close with the words: "I dispose to you as my father has disposed to me a kingdom, that you may eat and drink at my table in my kingdom." (Luke xxii. 25–30.)

But Christ gave an unexpected deepening to the image· the messianic banquet was a paschal meal. "I will not eat this pasch again till it be fulfilled in the Kingdom of God." (Luke xxii. 16.)

In the Old Testament, the whole nation gathered in the sacrificial sharing of the paschal lamb, symbol of the national community, bond of its unity and expression of its sacred character (cf. Exod. xii. 43–9.) The new Kingdom in its turn was to consist of feasters at a sacred table, of the totality of those who communicate with Christ in the true sacrifice of the Lamb.

To his hearers, already imbued with the mystical doctrine of a meal shared round God's table, the image was a striking one; it suggested intimacy with God and an indestructible brotherhood, sealed by the sacred food, among the banqueters; as a paschal meal, it spoke of a joyful deliverance and a land flowing with milk and honey

The paschal meal involved the immolation of the lamb. In Luke, with the promise of the Pasch's being "fulfilled", followed by the

[10] Matt v. 6, viii 11; xxii 1ff , xxv 10, xxvi 29; Luke xii 37; xv 23; xxii. 15–18; xxii. 29–30
[11] This was the original phrasing of our Lord's words We realize why Luke altered it. Cf P Benoit, "Le Récit de la Cène", pp 388ff

institution of the Eucharist, Christ was indicating that he himself
was the victim "delivered for us". Our food at the meal, he was yet
also to be our fellow-banqueter in the fulfilment of the Pasch (xxii.
16), he was to eat and drink in joy at the table of his own sacrifice.
The disciples would eat and drink with him, in the joy of their
paschal deliverance, being nourished by him. The people of the
Kingdom would be all those who communicate in the true Pasch.

In the former series of texts, the Kingdom was to be born as soon
as Christ was glorified, his death being the condition of his glorification. But here, the death itself comes into the mystery of the
Kingdom, and yet it is in glory that the Kingdom unfolds, for the
feast of the immolated lamb is celebrated in the joy of the new wine,
and the Saviour, having passed through death, takes part in it. Here,
more than anywhere, the Kingdom is identified with Christ; the
disciples enter it by taking part in a meal in which Christ gives himself to them, in his immolation and in his glory.

The texts which date the inauguration of the Kingdom from the
glorification of Christ present that kingdom as an other-worldly
reality, belonging to the divine sphere, in the clouds of heaven. But
the Kingdom's history includes a previous, earthly phase, when it is
subject to human organization, and governed by the Master's
stewards, by Peter and the rest of the Twelve, who are set over the
household to give them their measure of wheat in due season. (Luke
xii. 42.) Though it is earthly in a human sense, it is already the
Kingdom of heaven, a reality of the other world introduced into the
existence of this one.[12] Matthew's gospel applies the term "Church"
to the Kingdom in this phase. (Cf. xvi. 18 and 19.)

But the Kingdom did not exist even in this earthly form before
Christ's death. At Caesarea Philippi, our Lord promised Peter that
he would build his Church upon him and give him its keys. It was
a declaration and a promise, the building and the giving were to
come later. Matthew notes (xvi. 21ff.) that from then on our Lord
began to speak of the necessity of his dying and rising again. It is
indeed a noteworthy fact that the two prophecies come together.

Thus the inauguration of the Kingdom did not precede Christ's
death, but was identified with his entering into glory. The

[12] Many modern Protestant theologians refuse to identify the kingdom with
the Church on earth See F M. Braun, *Aspects nouveaux du problème de
l'Eglise*, Fribourg, 1942, pp 161–70 But for Christ they are two distinct phases
of the one heavenly reality This is proved by the parables of the cockle, of
the net, of the seed that springs up without the sower's knowledge

messianic explosion, so to say, from which the Kingdom had to rise, took place in Christ himself; the Kingdom opened in him.

II. THE ACTS

After the Resurrection, Christ appeared to the Apostles for forty days, "speaking of the Kingdom of God". (Acts i. 3.) The time had come, thought the disciples: "Wilt thou at this time restore again the Kingdom to Israel?" (i. 6.) Our Lord rectified their ideas, directing their thoughts to a spiritual kingdom, marked by the presence of the Spirit. "You shall receive the power of the Holy Ghost coming upon you."

From Pentecost on, the Apostles had seen, before St. Paul, and more keenly than he, "in the resurrection of Christ and the descent of the Holy Spirit, the beginnings of the Kingdom of God."[13]

St. Peter was the first to give the great news. He proclaimed the arrival of Christ at the throne of David, his father, at the right hand of God (Acts ii. 31–6). He told Christ's enemies that the prophecy made long ago about them was now fulfilled. "Jesus Christ of Nazareth, whom you crucified, whom God had raised from the dead . . This is the stone which was rejected by you the builders, which is become the head of the corner." (iv. 10–11.) The leaders of the house of Israel had tossed Christ aside as a stone that was unusable, but God had taken that stone up again and made it the corner-stone, the principle of strength and cohesion for the whole building.[14]

---

[13] L Cerfaux, *The Church*, p 208.

[14] In ancient literature, the "corner-stone" put at the top of the wall was supposed to be a source of strength for the whole house In this text, this high stone shows a tendency to turn into a foundation stone "And in none other is salvation found "
St Peter was much struck by this image of the rejected stone becoming the stone chosen by God He was to return to it years later (1 Pet ii. 4–8.) The corner-stone, once the top of the column, has now definitely become a foundation stone upon which the faithful are built up. Peter incorporates into this image his declaration, made much earlier, that Christ is the prince and author of life (Acts v 31; iii. 15) The faithful form a "spiritual house", a living building whose spiritual life is drawn from its foundation stone This image from the Synoptics attains its complete development: Christ dead and risen again has become the organic foundation of a building living in the Spirit

The outpouring of the Spirit was the proof that Christ was thus exalted (ii. 33) and that the Kingdom of God had begun.[15]

iii. ST. JOHN

In the Synoptics Christ sums up prophetic tradition about the Kingdom and brings it to its conclusion.

St. John gives us a saying of Christ's more in line with the liturgical nature of the fourth gospel, which completes a different tradition.

Prophecy had foretold the building of a temple with perfect proportions (Ezek. xl–xlii), on a Mount Zion raised up higher than all other mountains (Isa. ii 2), to be most holy (Ezek. xliii. 12; xlv. 3–4), forever enveloped in Iahweh's cloud of glory (Isa. iv. 5), for God was to dwell in it forever (Ezek. xxxvii. 26–8); a receptable of mysterious riches, a river was to flow out from under its gate to irrigate the desert and bring life to the Dead Sea. (Ezek. xlvii. 1–12; Joel iv. 18.) The Temple will stand in the midst of the people forever, to sanctify them and show that they are holy. (Ezek. xxxvii. 28.)

This expectation is easily understandable in the light of the tremendous importance, both as symbol and as reality, which the Temple held in national and religious life. It was inconceivable that the messianic kingdom, crowning the ancient theocracy, should not have a Temple in Jerusalem whose glory should be proportionate to that of the Kingdom itself. Their hope was based on the firm foundation of God's word. Nathan had promised David that a Messiah should spring from his seed, and should build a house to Iahweh. (2 Kings vii. 13.) When the prophecies about God's kingdom received their first hint of fulfilment with the return from exile, Zerubbabel, who raised the Temple from its ruins, saw some of the messianic praises applied to him. (Zech. iii. 8; vi. 12.)

Daniel had rather hazily foreseen a new institution in the messianic future which he tried to express by the image of the sanctuary, having first represented it by the symbol of the Son of Man: "Seventy weeks are counted . . . that vision and prophecy may be fulfilled, and the saint of saints may be anointed." (ix. 24.)[16]

---

[15] Cf R Koch, *Geist und Messias*, Vienna, 1950

[16] Cf Lagrange, "La Prophétie des soixante-dix semaines de Daniel", *R B*, xxxix (1930), 183, 196; A Feuillet, "Le Fils de l'homme de Daniel et la tradition biblique", *R B.*, lx (1953), 197.

When Christ, with some cords knotted into a scourge, drove out
the merchants, the priests in charge of the Temple arrangements,
who benefited from the business carried on there, asked him "What
sign dost thou show unto us, seeing thou dost these things?" And
our Lord replied: "Destroy this temple, and in three days I will
raise it up." The Jews then said, "Six and forty years was this
temple in building; and wilt thou raise it up in three days?" But
he was talking of his body. (John ii. 18–21.)

When ordered by the Jews to show the evidence of his power, our
Lord answered: "Destroy this temple and I will rebuild it." That
was his proof. The sanctuary the Jews were going to destroy was
their temple of stone, the one the argument logically suggested [17]
They were angry that this layman should assume power over the
House of God. Unless there was a gesture to indicate that he meant
his body, which seems unlikely, the answer remains a total enigma
if "this temple" was not the temple under discussion The
Evangelist's reflexion, "he spoke of the temple of his body", explains the second part of the answer, which seems to make nonsense
—"In three days I will raise it up"—and which was what the Jews
objected to: "Six and forty years ... and wilt thou raise it up in
three days?"

This was brought up as a charge against Christ at his trial. "We
heard him say, I will destroy this temple made with hands, and
within three days I will build another not made with hands." (Mark
xiv. 58.) The Evangelist points out that it was a false witness, but
he does not therefore mean to contest "the authenticity of the saying
—its very strangeness puts it beyond any possible doubt. The false
witness turned on to the revolutionary and anarchistic construction
put upon a very mysterious utterance." [18]

"It would seem that the witnesses were not wrong in contrasting
a temple built by hands and a temple not built by hands." [19] Unless
we are to look on Mark's text as a later Christian development, [20]
the contrast between a material and a spiritual temple must come
from Christ.

---

[17] The first verb λύσατε, "bring down", "destroy", applies more to the
Temple, the second, ἐγερῶ, "I will raise", more to the body.
[18] L de Grandmaison, *Jesus Christ*, vol iii, p. 234
[19] J Huby, *Évangile selon saint Marc*, 13th ed , Paris, 1929, p 394.
[20] So thinks M Fraeyman, in "La Spiritualisation de l'idée du Temple dans
les épîtres pauliniennes", *Eph Theol. Lov.*, xxiii (1947), 406. In this case we
are left with the primitive interpretation of our Lord's words.

A similar charge was brought against the deacon Stephen: "This man ceaseth not to speak words against the Holy Place and the Law. We have heard him say, that this Jesus of Nazareth shall destroy this place, and shall change the traditions which Moses delivered unto us." (Acts vi. 13–14.) The accusation was not without foundation. His discourse before the Sanhedrin closed with the declaration that God does not dwell in temples made by the hand of man. (Acts vii. 48.) The Spirit had given this Hellenistic Christian the work of cutting a path out of the Mosaic system for the Christian community. He had the soul of a Paul, but a younger Paul than the one we know in the Epistles. He had no fear of proclaiming the abolition of the Mosaic institutions and the forthcoming destruction of the Temple, and so interpreting our Lord's prophecy.

The Jews were taking it upon themselves to destroy their temple. The Christ of flesh was the keystone of the old order.[21] Take away the keystone and the house will collapse. At the moment of Christ's death, the veil of the Temple was rent from top to bottom. The material destruction bore witness in the eyes of the world to the spiritual.

To take the place of the temple of stone, the body of Christ was built up in the Resurrection.[22] Up till then the Lord God had dwelt amid his people in that temple of stone There he held court, "sitting upon the cherubims" (1 Sam. iv. 4), surrounded by angelic hymns of praise. (Isa. vi. 1–3.) There on the holy hill was the point of contact at which the prayers and sacrifices of the people came to

[21] The second part of the chapter makes this clear.

[22] This interpretation is given by Le Hir, *Études bibliques*, vol. 1, Paris, 1869, pp. 77ff; T Zahn, *Das Evangelium des Johannes*, Leipzig, 1912, pp. 170–2; M de la Taille, *The Mystery of Faith*, vol 1, pp 216–17, A. Durand, *Évangile selon saint Jean*, 3rd ed, Paris, 1927, pp. 72–4; A. M Dubarle, "Le Signe du Temple", *R B*, xlviii (1939), 21–44; O. Cullmann, *Christian Worship*, pp 71–4 It is the one generally accepted today.

There is one difficulty about this exegesis. Our Lord's words link in a single pronoun and therefore a single concept the two realities, the temple to be destroyed and the temple of the Resurrection: "Destroy this temple and I will raise it up" One might therefore conclude that the two are identical But other examples show that in Christ's way of thinking one concept could contain two realities, one belonging to the prefigurative order of things, the other to the era of fulfilment. In the parable of the wicked husbandmen, the same vineyard indicates God's kingdom in the Old and the New Testaments; in Luke xxii 15–16 it is the *Jewish* pasch which is "fulfilled" in the Kingdom; in Mark xiv. 25, Christ says, "I will drink no more of this fruit of the vine, until that day when I shall drink *it* new in the Kingdom . "

the Lord, where Iahweh was revealed to those who believed in him, and invited them to communicate at his table

The Temple was the source and guarantee of the people's unity. When Israel gathered before the tabernacle of reunion, or in the court of the Temple, they were conscious that the bond linking them to Iahweh made them one, and whenever they sat down to table with God at the sacrificial meal, the bonds uniting them became closer.

Three days after his death, Christ became, in his body, the new Temple, the dwelling place of the glory, the place of the divine revelation, the point of contact between God and his people, and the bond uniting the people together. He was to be the house of prayer and praise where the people would gather, where they would worship together in the odour of sacrifice and sit down to table with God. But in this temple not made with hands, worship would be offered in spirit and in truth.[23]

Alongside the idea of the messianic temple St. John also mentions the Kingdom of God. Our Lord declared to Nicodemus that "unless a man be born again of water and the Holy Ghost he cannot enter the Kingdom of God". (John iii. 5.) Exegetes no longer believe that baptism with water and the Holy Ghost came before the Resurrection. It was Christ in glory who set in motion the economy of the Spirit. (vii. 39.) Man's birth as a citizen of the Kingdom cannot be separated from Christ's entry into glory, and until that entry, the Kingdom was not established on earth.

For this evangelist of Christ the Lamb (i. 29; xix. 36; Apoc. *passim*), the mystery of the Kingdom can be expressed in terms of a flock. (x.) Christ is its leader. It seems as though this flock existed before the Passion, with Christ on earth walking at its head, awaiting only the reunion in the fold of Israel of the "other sheep". It is usual with the Christ of John's gospel, conscious of the riches of salvation he possesses, to anticipate his life of glory. Certainly the sheep are beginning to gather round their shepherd: the parable

---

[23] In his discourse about the end of the world, Christ returned to this same notion, but expressed in the form common to the Synoptics whereby the idea of the Kingdom replaced that of the new temple. The destruction of the Temple marks the end of the old dispensation and coincides with the coming in glory of Christ and of the Kingdom Cf A Feuillet, "Le discours de Jésus sur la ruine du Temple", *R B.*, lvi (1949), 61–92 But only the Johannine account affirms the correspondence between the destruction and rebuilding of the temple and the death and resurrection of Christ.

came on the occasion of the Jewish leaders casting out a sheep of the flock of Israel, the man born blind, whom Christ took among his own sheep, declaring that he did not lead his flock astray. Yet his gaze was going beyond the reality of the present. The flock he described was already, without prejudice to his own unique leadership, led by other shepherds who came and went in Christ.[24] But the Apostles had not yet received their shepherds' crooks (John xxi. 15–17) Our Lord was in fact speaking of a reality of the future. The thought of his death and resurrection hovers over the whole allegory (x. 15, 17). The flock was still in an imperfect state, penned within the enclosure of the old economy; other sheep were wandering outside that enclosure (x. 16); our Lord must die and rise again to bring them into the unity of a flock which has no barriers of nationality.

On Palm Sunday, while the multitude crowded round Christ, some pagan proselytes tried to come to him. (John xii. 20–33.) They said to Philip: "Sir. we would see Jesus." This was something unprecedented, and the Apostles deliberated together and laid the matter before their Master. Like the question put by the priests after he had driven out the merchants from the Temple, this overture from the Greeks suddenly opened a great vista to our Lord's mind. He saw the Gentiles crowding round him, and a wave of joy broke over him· "The hour is come, that the Son of Man should be glorified." But the thought of his triumph brought with it that of his death, which came so powerfully upon him that he was filled with an anguish of agony. He remembered that for his work to bear fruit he must first die: "Unless the grain of wheat falling into the ground die, itself remaineth alone. But if it die, it bringeth forth much fruit." In the Church's symbolism, beside the true vine stands this humbler image of the ear of wheat laden to bending point. It is a simple parable, but the essential teaching is the same as if it were an allegory. Christ is like the seed dying that it may be multiplied; when he is born again out of the tomb, he will no longer be one, but many, a laden ear born out of the sacrificed seed.[25]

[24] These are the shepherds who come in, go out, seek and find the rich pasture. Cf. Num. xxvii. 17; Deut xxxi 2 This is supported by Knabenbauer, Tillmann, Lagrange, and Prat.
[25] According to St Maximus of Turin, Christ's flesh flowers again in the Resurrection, and bears fruit. (*Hom. LX De Ascensione Domini, P.L.*, lvii, 369 Cf too *Sermo XXX De Paschate, P.L* , lxii, 595)

IV. THE SYMBOLISM OF EVENTS

As we study the Gospels more deeply, we come to perceive the word of God not only in what Christ said, but in everything he did and in all the circumstances of his life. By failing to advert to this, one is letting part of the priceless seed fall upon stones. A great many of the miracles are a kind of mime of what is taught by his words. Our Lord multiplies the loaves, and announces that he will give the bread of heaven; the walking on the water demonstrates the marvellous nature of his body, which is going to be given as food; he declares that he is the Light, and heals a blind man; he says he is the Resurrection and brings Lazarus back to life. The story of the Passion, above all, is rich in happenings which seem so arranged by God as to be a commentary upon it. John more than any of the others, is aware of this symbolism. When Judas left the upper room, "it was night". The innocent Christ was condemned, while Barabbas was acquitted. He was taken out of the gate; Simon was made to carry the cross behind our Lord. On either side of him criminals were crucified; one of the robbers goes into the Kingdom the other is determined to remain outside. The bones of the Lamb are not broken; a stroke of the lance causes blood and water to flow from his side, and, in the Jews' temple, the veil is rent. Each of these facts conceals a mystery, and the New Testament writers show more than once how struck they are by their symbolism. (Luke xx. 15; Heb. xiii. 12; John xix. 35ff.; 1 John v. 8; Heb. x. 20; Matt. xvi. 24.)

Even coincidences in time can sometimes be significant. It is noteworthy that according to the Synoptics Christ ate the Pasch before his passion, whereas in St. John the priests did not immolate the paschal lamb until the evening of Good Friday. Strange though this double piece of information may seem, it can hardly be called in question, for upon so essential a point neither the information of the Synoptics, nor the accuracy of John's memory could be at fault. The fact that Christ and the Jewish priests celebrated the paschal meal at two different dates is best explained by a difference in reckoning which divided the nation; similar cases found in rabbinical writings support this suggestion. This unlikely fact fitted in well with Christ's design. The eating of the lamb with his Apostles marked out the Eucharist and the whole messianic banquet as a sacrificial and paschal meal.[26] By coinciding with the immolation of the lambs in the Temple, Christ's immolation stands out as that of the true Lamb.

This placing of the acts of our redemption in the chronological pattern of the rites which typified them suggests that there must be a reason for the three days between Christ's death and resurrection. No doubt God's plan here was primarily an apologetic one: the genuineness of the death, duly recorded on Calvary, could be open to no doubt after three days in the tomb. But the choice of the third day seems also directed towards illustrating the mystery of the Resurrection as redeeming us, just as the coincidence with the immolation of the lamb expressed the mystery of the death.

The barley ripened about the time of the pasch After the feast, "the next day after the sabbath", the children of Israel had to bring the first sheaf to Iahweh for a holocaust. (Lev. xxiii. 10-14.) The harvest then began. Thus, early in the morning the first Sunday after Christ's death, the priests would be offering to God the first-fruits collected from the other side of the Cedron. That same morning, Christ rose, the first sheaf of a different harvest. St. Paul seems to hint at this. (1 Cor. xv. 20.)[27] The parable of the grain changing into the ear is now fulfilled and the harvest has begun. The first sheaf is consecrated by fire, and the whole harvest will be holy (Rom. xi. 16);[28] the new people is now a religious reality, consecrated in the fire of the Spirit.

The fact that the Resurrection took place on the first day of the week is not without its mystery, if we read the Apocalypse. Christian history as a separate entity began on a Sunday (Apoc. i. 10) with the appearance of the risen Christ, and will develop in a sevenfold cycle until it is completed in an endless sabbatical rest. The history of the new creation started on this first day of the week.[29]

[26] Our Lord may have held the sacrificial meal of the Eucharist before the sacrifice itself simply to place the Eucharist in line, as it were, with the Pasch of old, which he could not have done after the Resurrection.

[27] J. Lebreton, *Vie et enseignement de Jésus-Christ notre Seigneur*, 3rd ed, Paris, 1931, vol. 1, p. 27: "The same Paschal day, the fourteenth day of Nisan, is assumed by St. Paul: he died on the day of the Pasch (1 Cor. v. 7) and rose on the sixteenth day of Nisan, day of the first-fruits (*ibid*, xv 20)."

[28] This symbolism developed to its fullest long ago. Cf M de la Taille, *The Mystery of Faith*, vol. 1, pp. 188-9, n. 5, referring to Epiphanius, John Chrysostom, Cyril of Alexandria, Eutychius, Procopius of Gaza, and Rupert of Deutz.

[29] St. Thomas writes: "The Sabbath, which signified the first creation, is changed to the Lord's day, on which is commemorated the new creation

V. ST. PAUL

The idea of the Church attains the dimensions proper to it in the theology of St. Paul. The development of his thought and terminology continued up to the Epistles of the Captivity where it reached its highest point. Here his definition of the Church and her relationship with Christ receives its perfect formulation: "He [God] hath given him [Christ] as head over all the Church, which is his body." (Eph. i. 22–3.)

The two halves of this statement give the framework for our examination into the date of the Church's birth. Two questions present themselves: At what moment did Christ become head of the Church? And is the body of Christ with which the Church is identified the body of the risen Saviour?

(a) The Christ of Easter, Head of the Church

The first chapter of the Epistle to the Ephesians enumerates the effects of the omnipotent force at work in the Resurrection, "that you may know ... what is the exceeding greatness of his power towards us ... which he wrought in Christ, raising him up from the dead ... And he hath subjected all things under his feet, and hath given him as head over all the Church, which is his body ..." (i. 19–23.) The first effect of this raising power is the establishment of Christ as lord over all things. This first exaltation is completed in another. When everything is placed under the feet of the risen Christ, he is given to the Church as her head. All his glorification is directed towards this headship; in it the power of the Resurrection receives its crown.

The intimate union between the Church and Christ in his corporeal humanity makes it possible for Paul, later in the epistle, to exhort husbands and wives to take that relationship as their model: "Women, be subject to your husbands, as to the Lord; because the husband is the head of the wife, as Christ is the head of the Church, the saviour of his body." (Eph. v. 22–3.) Before becoming head of the Church, he had to win her for himself by saving her: he who is her Saviour is her Head. "It is to this saving and redeeming action

born in Christ's resurrection " (*Summa Theologica*, 1a iiae, q 103, a. 3 ad 4. Cf. Y Congar, "La Théologie du dimanche", in *Le Jour du Seigneur*, Paris, 1948, pp 147–55.

that he owes his headship of the Church."[30] His function as head crowns his function as redeemer.

But the very next verse seems to go against this conclusion: "Husbands, love your wives, as Christ also loved the Church, and delivered himself up for it; that he might sanctify it, cleansing it by the laver of water in the word of life." (v. 25–6.) It was, then, his love as husband which impelled Christ to die for his Church, and being husband is equivalent to being head. The bride already existed, therefore, and Christ died for her.

It is not a valid objection. The metaphor of the bride conjures up a Church which existed before her espousals, and in this it is an imperfect metaphor. Christ's love of the Church was a love directed towards a future reality, a bride created by his love. He delivered himself for her, so as to make ready "a laver of water" from which she was to emerge spotless and glorious, and at that moment he would unite himself to her. "We might think that St. Paul, instead of using the original word, 'baptism', had chosen this expression, 'laver of water', to allude to the Greek marriage ceremonies, with special reference to the most important prenuptial religious rite— the bathing of the betrothed girl."[31] Having purified her, Christ has presented himself to his bride (v. 27) and united himself to her in her flawless beauty. The heroic sacrifice of love came before Christ's real and living union with his Church, and before that union, the Church as such did not exist at all. His bride's life began as the act of the Redemption was completed, in the Resurrection (cf. Eph. i. 20ff.), when the "laver of water in the word of life" came to receive its complete symbolism and effectiveness.

The Epistle to the Colossians is concerned to establish Christ's primacy over all things; it makes the Saviour's lordship a thing of cosmic dimensions. St. Paul does this only to make clear the width of Christ's redemptive mission. Having indicated Christ's place as keystone of the universe, he considers him in his primacy over the Church: "And he is the head of the body, [that is] the Church." His right to be head stems from his being the principle, the first-born from the dead, that in all things he may hold the primacy"; and finally, the reason for this primacy over the cosmos and the

[30] J. Huby, *Les Épîtres de la Captivité*, p. 228; M. Meinertz, *Die Gefangenschaftsbriefe des hl Paulus*, 4th ed, Bonn, 1931, p 97.
[31] J Huby, *Les Épîtres de la Captivité*, pp. 229ff.

Church . . . "because in him it hath well pleased the Father that all fullness should dwell." (Col. 1. 18–19.)

His role as head of the Church stems from the fact that he is the principle. What does this mean? From the fact that he is the first, heading the procession of all who are to be raised from the dead.[32] Better still, because the totality of the divine power of life is concentrated in him, "for in him it hath pleased the Father that all fullness should dwell." All the fullness of life and of God's sanctifying power is gathered up in the body of Christ. (Col. 1. 19; ii. 9.)[33] In Pauline theology this dynamic Christ can only be the risen Saviour.

St. Paul works out his thought for us: this Christ-principle is the firstborn from the dead. He is the head because he is the first in the victory, first in time (1 Cor. xv. 23), but also in rank; in him life wins its supreme triumph; above all, he is first by the supremacy of his purpose: his resurrection opens the way to life for mankind. (1 Cor. xv. 45.) The word "first-born" of itself carries no such wealth of meaning, but the Apostle confers it. The first-born is the source and fullness of the life of the Church: "He hath given him as head over the Church, he . . . the firstborn from the dead."

According to this same epistle, Christian life in all its stages, even on earth, is a resurrection; the Church is an assembly of those who were dead and have risen again. (Col. ii. 12; iii. 1–3.) The phrase "first-born from the dead" expresses "under a slightly different aspect the same concept of Christ as head of the body of the Church".[34]

The Christ of glory, head of the Church, also appears as the eldest brother of a great family whose Father is God (Rom. viii. 29), or the founder of a new race quite different from the race of Adam, the Christian people. This humanity is rooted "in Christ" as in its native soil. We may therefore say that it is born in the Christ of glory, for the phrase *in Christo* is reserved to the risen Saviour.

As the father of mankind reborn, Christ receives the title of the new Adam. This honour is due both to his obedience, and to his life-giving action.

In the Epistle to the Romans (v. 12–21), the second Adam is con-

---

[32] Theodoret, *In Col XVIII, P.G*, lxxxii, 600

[33] L. Cerfaux, *The Church*, pp. 322–3, *Christ in the Theology of St Paul*, London, 1959, pp 426–7

[34] A. Durand, "Le Christ 'Premier-Né' ", *Rech Sc. Rel.*, 1 (1910), 64.

trasted with the first because of his obedience. Whereas mankind, in
the past, was condemned by pride to sin and death, Christ by his
death of obedience has brought them new life in justice: "As by the
disobedience of one man, many were made sinners, so by the
obedience of one, many shall be made just." (v. 19.) Yet even in this
epistle, the merit of submission is not the only reason for calling
Christ the new Adam. The new life, before being given to men, is
in Christ himself; it is "a gift [of God] in the grace of one man".
(v. 15.) Because of his death, our Lord was able to give a life of
grace, just as disobedience had first polluted the whole of human
nature at its source. For the first man to become the father of a sinful humanity, he had not only to sin, but to beget; and Christ had
not only to be obedient, but to communicate the life which his
obedience had won.

The parallel between the two heads of the human race is completed, in this, by the First Epistle to the Corinthians: "Thus it is
written· The first man Adam was made into a living soul; the last
Adam into a quickening spirit... The first man was of the earth,
earthly, the second came from heaven. Such as is the earthly, such
also are the earthly; and such as is the heavenly, such also are they
that are heavenly. Therefore, as we have borne the image of the
earthly, let us bear also the image of the heavenly." (xv. 45–9.)

To the question. "How do the dead rise again? or with what
manner of body shall they come?", the Apostle replies that there
are two principles of life: our common ancestor, and Christ; and
that there are two ways of life corresponding to them. From the first
Adam we get our earthly and mortal life, from the second, a
heavenly way of living in a spiritualized humanity.

It is not an antithesis between two moral acts whereby the first
man deserved to transmit mortality, and the second a divine life;
it is simply a question of the principle animating them and enabling
each to beget—the one to death, the other to immortality. Here the
second Adam is not Christ dying in the weakness of the flesh, but
the Man of Heaven, who has reached the peak of his divine life in
the Resurrection, and who, unlike our ancestor in the flesh, begets
us to the life of glory.

On the Cross the submission which atones and merits was completed; in the Resurrection Christ gives new life in the Holy Spirit.
The first man and woman, by their disobedience, were reduced to
the "carnal" state in which they could pass on to us only a life

marked out for death; similarly, his obedience has established the second Adam in the "spiritual" state in which he can pass on to us the life of justification. Once our brother in Adam because of his carnal humanity, Christ has now become our father in the newness of his life of glory.[35]

Henceforth, Christ appears with "the children whom God has given him". (Heb. ii. 13.) But his fatherhood is closer than that of our ancestor in the flesh. Adam, man of dust, was only the first link in the chain of generations leading to us; he lived only his own life, being simply "a living soul"; the "heavenly man" is a "living spirit" who begets us directly by animating us with his own life.

Out of the old humanity, God chose a holy people, to be an out-line of the Church, but remaining, in its make-up, still in the sphere of Adam, an earthly and carnal reality. Membership of that people was guaranteed by a mark of the same nature in the flesh. To his new people God applies a circumcision too, but Christian rather than Mosaic: "It is in him too that you have been circumcised with a circumcision not made by the hand of man; by the despoiling of the body of flesh, by the circumcision of Christ, having been buried with him in baptism, you are risen in him and with him by faith in the power of God who has raised him from the dead. And whereas you were dead by your sins and the uncircumcision of your flesh, God has made you live again with Christ, forgiving you all your sins." (Col. ii. 11-13.)[36]

The expression "in him" makes it clear from the beginning that the seal of membership in the new people is imprinted upon the believer by a sharing in the risen life of Christ.[37] This circumcision

[35] In this text St Paul explicitly attributes to Christ in glory the fatherhood only of the Church in glory. But we are right to recognize in him the fatherhood of the Church pure and simple, since, according to St. Paul, it is an assembly of those risen from the dead even with those of its members whose development is not complete.

Only a narrow and arbitrary literalness would refuse to see the Church on earth in the image of the heavenly man. According to one textual tradi-tion, held by most critics to be the best (Tischendorf, Westcott and Hort, Soden, Nestle, Vogels), St. Paul himself passes from the perfect image which the believer will bear when he rises from the dead, to the imperfect image he bears at present: "As we have borne [at the beginning] the image of him who was earthly, let us bear [from now on] the image of him who is heavenly." (Verse 49)

[36] Translation based on Huby's rendering.

[37] Then, too, what has just gone before places us in the atmosphere of that life of glory; verse 9 speaks of the fullness of the Godhead dwelling cor-

is not just a small excision made in the flesh, but "the despoiling of the body of flesh". The operation is performed in baptism, which brings us into the death and resurrection of our Saviour. By this despoiling of the flesh, we share in the death of Christ, yet this putting to death of the carnal being is the result of our union with our Saviour's life: "Whereas you were dead ... by the uncircumcision of your flesh [this symbolizes the carnal state] God has made you live again in Christ." Before being raised with Christ, they were in the uncircumcision of flesh, and therefore dead; "the circumcision of Christ", imprinted upon us by sharing in the resurrection of Christ, has come to put an end to the flesh.

This contrast between the two Adams places the risen Christ at the head of a new race of men. The contrast between the two circumcisions makes a parallel between this Christian humanity and the people of God gathered round their tabernacle, thus pinpointing the ecclesiastical nature of the new people. From both points of view, the Church depends upon the Resurrection, for it was then that Christ, first man of the new creation, received the life of heaven in the death of his flesh, the circumcision of the Holy Ghost, and became both father of a new race, and head of the new People of God.

(b) The Glorified Body of Christ, Principle of the Church

It is not only as her Head that Christ is related to the Church. Even in the Synoptics there are the beginnings of an identification between our Lord and his kingdom. St. Paul accentuates this identification and declares that the Church is actually the body of Christ. What body is it? Is it our Saviour's own body? If so, the mystery of Easter must have an influence upon the Church, for it affects Christ in his "bodiliness".

The identification between the Church and the body of Christ is not made equally strictly everywhere. The Church is first of all described as one describes a body, rather than actually defined as the body of Christ, and it is a description dominated by the metaphor of the head and members making up a single body with varying functions. In Hellenistic times, the comparison of civil society with

poreally in Christ and being handed on to us, and verse 10 recalls the universal sovereignty of Christ It is in this Christ of the fullness of life that "you are circumcised".

the human body had become a commonplace. We might be hearing
the fable of Aesop, as Menenius Agrippa recounted it to the Roman
populace, when Paul uses it to show the usefulness of the varying
charismata in the Church: "The body also is not one member, but is
made up of many . . . If they all were one member, where would be the
body? There are many members indeed, yet one body . . . The eye
cannot say to the hand: I need not thy help; nor again the head to
the feet: I have no need of you." (1 Cor xii. 14–21; cf. Rom. xii. 3–8.)

But whereas the Greek metaphor supposes a simple moral union
among the members of a society, St. Paul bases his exhortation on
the real identification of Christians with the body of Christ, and
puts forward the fable because of that identification. "As the body
is one, and hath many members, and all the members of the body,
whereas they are many, yet are one body, so also is Christ [one,
and possesses many members]." The faithful are thus united to
Christ as the members to the body. He continues: "For in one Spirit
were we all baptized into one body [that of Christ], whether Jews
or Gentiles, whether bond or free." (1 Cor. xii. 12–13.)[38] All you
who are baptized are consecrated to the body of Christ, and hence
Christ is one body possessing many members. "You are the body
of Christ [united and identified with him in his body], and, individually, his members." (1 Cor. xii 27.) Hence this definition:
"The Church, which is his body." (Eph. 1. 22–3; Col. 1. 18, 24)

Nowadays we call the Church the mystical body of Christ, and
to many people, the expression means no more than a social group,
organized and united like a body, with Christ as its head. St. Paul's
meaning is more literal. He is not comparing the Church with a
body, nor does he merely say that it is *a* body; it is the body of
Christ, identified, not the least metaphorically, with the physical
body of our Lord.[39] The Church is the body of Christ because she
is united, in all her believers, to the risen body of her Saviour.[40]

---

[38] For a justification of this rendering, cf L Cerfaux, *The Church*. pp. 267–
76; *Christ*, pp. 337–9 J Havet, "Christ collectif ou Christ individuel en I Cor.
xii, 12?" *Eph Theol. Lov* , xxiii (1947), 499–520 W Goossens, *L'Église corps
du Christ*, Paris, 1949, pp 42, 67

[39] E Percy, *Der Leib Christi in den paulinischen Homologoumena und
Antilegomena*, Lund, 1942, p. 5· "If we speak of anyone's body, whether in
Greek or in a modern language, we can only mean his own body " Disagree-
ing with this, as far as Greek is concerned, cf. J Dupont, *Gnosis*, Louvain,
1949, p 450. According to him, the Pauline *soma* ("body") must be understood in the light of Stoicism, where the *soma* means either the universe or
human society, taken as a whole, and considered as forming a single entity

The Pauline idea is not precisely the same as our conception of the body. The Semitic mind has a more comprehensive intuition of human nature, and does not separate the body from the principle that gives it life and is expressed through it. Hence St. Paul can use a personal pronoun for the body,[41] because it is extended to mean the whole human person. "So also ought men to love their wives as their own bodies. He that loveth his wife, loveth himself." (Eph. v. 28.) Belonging to the body of Christ is therefore synonymous with belonging to Christ himself.[42] However, the accent remains on the material element; the field of vision only extends beyond the body in its material nature in the body's own perspective. The body may designate the whole man, but only because the human being is present and expresses himself in his "bodiliness". "The Church is the body of Christ, meaning Christ's corporeal being, Christ himself as existing corporeally."[43] To be the body of Christ means, therefore, to be "in Christ", but in a bodily Christ.[44] And conversely, to be in Christ is to belong to his body.

The Church's union with Christ's body gives Paul a motive for

(p 431) St Paul thus speaks of the Church being the body of Christ as Seneca wrote to Nero (*Clem*, i, v, 1): "You are the soul of the Republic, and it is your body " (P 442)

The Apostle may have expressed his thought in Stoic terminology, but that thought is certainly based on a Christian teaching, older than Paul, which was revealed to him on the road to Damascus—the communion of the faithful with their Saviour. For the first Christians the experience of unity derived not from the social organization of the Church, but Christ's presence in it, primarily perceptible in "the breaking of bread and prayers". (Acts ii. 42)

St. Paul remains in this tradition, basing Christian unity upon the singleness of the bread of the Eucharist (1 Cor. x. 17) Texts like 1 Cor. vi 15-17, x 7, and Eph ii. 16, must be taken in a literal sense for which no analogy exists in Stoic literature.

[40] P. Benoit, *Bible de Jérusalem, Épître aux Colossiens*, 2nd ed., p. 52: "There is no question of either a metaphor, or an entity existing only in the mind, a social group whose members use Christ's name, the Church is the body of Christ because it is made up of all Christians whose bodies are united, by baptism, to the physical body of the risen Christ." Cf. also L Cerfaux, *Christ*, p. 351.

[41] 1 Cor. vi. 13-14; 2 Cor. iv 10-11; cf 1 Cor. vi 15 and 1 Cor. xii 27 In Rom vi. 6 and Col ii. 11, the "body of sin" and the "body of flesh" apply to our whole bodily nature, the soul included, since it is infected by sin and reduced to a carnal state

[42] 1 Cor xii 13: "We are all baptized into one body [that of Christ] " Gal. iii. 27: "We are baptized into Christ."

[43] L. Malevez, *L'Église, corps du Christ*, p 33.

[44] I am thus completely opposed to the conception which has recently become popular whereby the Church is Christ's body because she is a body

exhorting us to respect our own bodies "Know you not that your bodies are the members of Christ? Shall I then take the members of Christ and make them the members of a harlot? God forbid. Or know you not that he who is joined to a harlot is made one body with her? For it is said: They two shall be in one flesh. But he who is joined to the Lord is one spirit." (1 Cor. vi. 15–17.)

Because he always sees man as a unity, the Apostle can say not merely that the faithful are members of Christ, but that their bodies are members of Christ. Even in his material being, the Christian is a member of Christ, and it is of Christ in his physical being that we are members in our bodies. Furthermore, the parallel he puts forward between the two unions—with Christ and with the harlot—demands that we be quite literal in understanding the body of Christ to which we are united. "It is the union of a physical body with another physical body which is in question in the mention of intercourse with a prostitute, and to this Paul opposes union with the body of Christ as an antithesis."[45] The union is an absolutely real one, and Christ is thought of as a corporeal being. Paul concludes: "He who is joined to the Lord is one spirit." One would have expected him to say, "He who is joined to the Lord becomes one body with him." They are two ways of expressing the same thought. The body of Christ is "spiritual", our union with it is in the order of the spirit, and the faithful are one spirit by being that body. (Eph. iv. 4.) The change to "one spirit" suggested itself to the apostle as opposed to the union in "one flesh".[46]

In the Epistle to the Ephesians (v. 22–33),[47] the apostle once again works out these same ideas of the union in a single body of man and woman, of Christ and the Church. This time they are not placed

animated by Christ Cf. T. Schmidt, *Der Leib Christi*, Leipzig, 1919, pp 142ff ; A Wikenhauser, *Die Kirche als mystischer Leib Christi nach dem Apostel Paulus*, Munster-i -W., 1940, pp. 87ff.

[45] L Cerfaux, *The Church*, p 280

[46] It is hardly necessary to point out that, to St. Paul, union with Christ's personal body is not of the order of the flesh, is not a natural union. It is not the same as the union between the members of a body in which the members have no separate personality; it is not the same as the union in marriage, which is physically no more than a contact. It is of a different order; the union is more real, and it does not suppress the individual personality; it is of the order of "spirit"

[47] The union identifying the Church with the body of Christ is the basis for the ecclesiology of Colossians and Ephesians Cf. A Schlier, V Warnach, *Die Kirche im Epheserbrief*, Münster, 1949; P. Benoit, "Corps, tête et plérôme dans les épîtres de la captivité", *R.B.*, lxiii, 1956, 7–72.

in antithesis, but provide a comparison on which to base an exhortation on the relationship between Christian husbands and wives:
"Women", he urges, "be subject to your husbands as to the Lord:
because the husband is the head of the wife as Christ is the head
of the Church, the saviour of the body." (v. 22.) The image of the
head suggests pre-eminence and the right to command; it would fit
in with a purely moral union connecting the Church to Christ by
social bonds. But from this starting-point, the Apostle's thought
takes a very definite line; the union of marriage seems to him more
than a moral one, and the relationship between Christ and the
Church is formed in a single physical body: " . . Christ is the head
of the Church, who is the saviour of the body". The argument implies the idea that, parallel with the Church as Christ's body, the
wife is the husband's body. The role of "head" adds to this idea
of one body the further note of an authority vested in Christ and
in the husband.

He does not suggest to husbands that they make use of their right
to command, but recommends their special duty of love and
devotion. He returns to the example of Christ and the Church,
recalling that Christ's devotion extended to dying for her (v. 25) and
that his love makes him assimilate the Church into his own body;
"Men ought to love their wives as [being] their own bodies. He
that loveth his wife, loveth himself. For no man ever hateth his
own flesh, but nourisheth and cherisheth it, as also Christ does the
Church: because we are members of his body. For this cause shall
a man leave his father and mother, and shall cleave to his wife, and
they shall be two in one flesh. This is a great mystery, but I say it
relates to Christ and the Church." (v. 28–32.)

A man's love for his wife springs from the fusion of two beings
into a single body. Husbands should give full vent to this natural
tendency, for such love is a holy thing, and though born out of a
union of the flesh, its model is the highest heavenly one, Christ
himself. Just as the identification of the Church with his own body
makes Christ love his spouse, so does the identification of the wife
with the husband's body give him a duty to love her. Everything
points to the analogy between the duties resulting from the mystical
union and the carnal union being founded on an identification of
two beings in one flesh. Mystical union calls to mind the Genesis
text "They shall be two in one flesh" as much as does the union
between man and wife.

When we discourse about the union of Christ and the Church we take the union of man and wife as a starting-point. St. Paul does the reverse: the reality of the union of the faithful with the body of Christ, and the moral relationships resulting from it, help him to show how real are the union of marriage and the duties it brings. The union of Christ and his Church is much deeper than the union of marriage, and the identification in a single body more absolute. Union in the flesh is only a reflection and a sign, an earthly shadow, cast back over the beginnings of mankind, of the final and heavenly reality. The promise of Genesis—"They two shall be in one flesh" —is understood in a divine sense: Christ and the Church are wedded together for ever, and are united in a single body. "The body of Christ is the bridal chamber of the Church."[48]

The Christian community has one rite which both manifests and effects its union with Christ in a single body, the Eucharist: "The chalice of benediction which we bless, is it not the communion of the blood of Christ? And the bread which we break, is it not the communion of the body of the Lord?" (1 Cor. x 16.) "Communion of the body and blood"—a phrase rich in meaning[49]; it indicates participation in the body and blood, communion in Christ through his body and blood; there is added the unspoken idea that in that body and blood there is a community among ourselves; the presence of the next verse, which seems added over and above the central development, becomes clear only if we give the thought this nuance: "Because the bread is one, we in our multitude are but one body, because we all partake of this single bread." (Verse 17.) We are but one body, because we all eat the bread which is the one body of Christ and enter in communion with it.[50] "One can see no reason

---

[48] "Cubiculum Ecclesiae corpus est Christi." St. Ambrose, *In Ps. CXVIII Sermo I*, 16, *P L*, xv, 1271. This body, says St Ambrose, is the body that suffered, died, was pierced and rose again. The union of the Church-bride in a single body, the body of Christ, is described in its fullest realism.

[49] Cf. E B Allo, *Première Épître aux Corinthiens*, Paris, 1934, *ad loc.*

[50] O Kuss, *Die Briefe an die Römer, Korinther und Galater*, Regensburg, 1940, p 160, points out: "Because all Christians eat one bread, the bread which is the body of the glorified Christ .. they are joined into one unity, one body; this body is the body of Christ (cf. Rom. xii 5) into which we have already been plunged initially by baptism (1 Cor xii. 13)."

Y Congar, in *Esquisses du mystère de l'Eglise*, p 32-3, writes that "it is in the strongest sense of these realities that modern critics have seen the institution of the Eucharist as the origin of the Church (cf. F. Kattenbusch, *Der Quellort der Kirchenidee*), and the eucharistic body as the reality from which the mystical body derives its name" It has also been said that "the

why the Church should be named the body of Christ, and should in fact be so, except that by giving her his body, Christ transforms her into himself so that she may become his body and all may become his members."[51]

This identifying of the Church with the individual body of Christ present in the Eucharist is simply St. Paul's way of explaining the words of institution. He had "received" the eucharistic formula in this way: "This is my body which [is delivered] for you. This do for the commemoration of me ... This chalice is the new testament [ἡ καινὴ διαθήκη] in my blood. This do ye, as often as you shall drink, for the commemoration of me." (1 Cor. xi. 24-5.) It is generally recognized that Paul is closer to the letter in reporting the words of consecration of the chalice than Matthew or Mark.[52] Our Lord declares that the chalice, because of the blood it holds, constitutes the new *diatheke*.

The biblical use of *diatheke* is different from its normal profane use. In the language of the time, the word was a juridical term meaning a testamentary disposition. St Paul uses it twice in this sense: once in Gal. iii. 15, and again in Heb. ix. 16-17; but in the latter case the surrounding verses use the word in its biblical sense. In the twenty-three other cases of the word being used in the Pauline epistles (including Hebrews), it does not mean a will, but, as in the

institution of the Eucharist may be considered as an action which founded the Church." (K L Schmidt, *Th. W. N T*, vol iii, p. 525) Cf also A E. J. Rawlinson, "Corpus Christi" in *Mysterium Christi*, Berlin, 1931, pp. 277–87, 294ff.; L Cerfaux, *The Church*, p. 265; W Goossens, *L'Église corps du Christ*, p 87 (with reservations)

[51] St. Albert the Great, *De Eucharistia*, dist. iii, tract. I, ch v, 5, (ed. Borgnet, xxxviii, 257). This doctrine is a traditional one in the Church. I need only select a few among many patristic texts: St John Chrysostom: "He unites himself to us and makes us his body, not only by faith, but in reality": "We are nourished by him, we unite ourselves to him, we become one body of Christ and one flesh" (*In Matt , hom.* lxxxii, *P G.*, lviii, 743ff., *In Jo , P.G.*, lix, 260–2; *In I Cor , P G ,* lxi, 199–201

St Augustine, *Tract. de Sacramentis Fidelium*: "For we are made the body of him, and by the mercy of him whom we receive, we exist." (*S. Augustini Sermones post Maurinos reperti*, Rome, 1930, p. 30)

St. John Damascene, *De Fide Orth.*, iv, 13, *P.G* , xciv, 1153: "Because we partake of a single bread, we all become a single body of Christ, a single blood, and members one of another, being made of one body with Christ " For the Middle Ages cf H. de Lubac, *Corpus Mysticum*, Paris, 1944.

[52] Cf. H. Schürmann, "Die Semitismen beim Einsetzungsbericht bei Markus und Lukas", *Zeit. f. Kath. Theol.*, lxxiii (1951), 72–7. The text of Matthew and Mark seems the result of liturgical change The statement that the blood is present has become more concise, but the sentence is not so clear.

Bible, a divine dispensation, a scheme of relationship between God and his people brought about because God so wills.[53]

God had declared a new *diatheke*, a new economy (Rom. xi. 27; Isa. lix. 21; Jer. xxxi. 31ff.) from which sin was to be excluded, in which the law was to be written on men's hearts. St. Paul defines this "new dispensation" by the presence of the Spirit, and contrasts it with the economy of the letter. (2 Cor. iii. 6; Jer. xxxi. 31ff.) The Apostle is the minister of this new religious form, in the service of the spiritual dispensation. Hence he gives the "two Testaments" approximately the same sense as we do (Gal. iv. 24-6)

In the formula handed on by St. Paul, Christ declares that the eucharistic chalice, because it holds his blood, constitutes the new *diatheke*. There is nothing to suggest the juridical interpretation of the term; the Last Supper has nothing in common with the making of a will. Besides, Christ does not say that the chalice is *his* testament, but the new testament, thus recalling Jer. xxxi. 31ff.; he is contrasting the "new testament" with the old dispensation, which was also sealed in blood.[54] Christ's work was to introduce a new economy by his death. Though at this moment he joins Jeremiah in calling it a *diatheke*, he generally speaks of it as the "Kingdom of

[53] The idea of a covenant or pact is, in itself, quite foreign to *diatheke*, but it is in fact suggested because of the meaning of the Hebrew word of which *diatheke* is a translation. But in fact, the idea was very little in evidence, for even the Hebrew word came, in the Bible, to indicate a disposition of God's will in Israel's favour.

"Testament" is a better rendering of the idea contained in *diatheke* than "covenant", in as much as "testament" expresses a disposition of the sovereign will of God. "Covenant" does, however, have the advantage of reminding us that the divine *diatheke* created a special relationship between God and his people

Concluding his study, J. Behm (*Th. W. N.T*, vol ii, p 137), declares: "Neither 'pact' nor 'testament' gives the true meaning of the idea of *diatheke* in the Greek Bible. The *diatheke* is generally the disposition of God, the powerful manifestation of God's sovereign will in history, whereby he governs the relations between himself and mankind according to his plans for their salvation; it is the ordering [*Verordnung, Stiftung*] of the divine will which brings with it a corresponding order of things."

L Cerfaux, "Le Privilège d'Israël selon saint Paul", *Eph. Theol. Lov*, xvii (1940), 16: "In any case, the term "covenant" in no way corresponds to *diatheke*" This is certainly so if "covenant" is given only its ordinary meaning J Bonsirven, *Le Judaisme palestinien*, Paris, 1934, vol. i, pp. 79ff, wants to give it at least a new shade of meaning; he defines the Covenant as "the act which founds and defines the order and nature of the relationship between God and Israel" Cf. C. Spicq, "La Théologie des deux alliances dans l'épître aux Hébreux", *R.S.P.T.*, xxxiii (1949), 15-30

[54] Cf. L. Cerfaux, "Le Privilège d'Israël", pp. 14ff

God". The two ideas are closely related[55]; the Kingdom of God is established at the same moment as God's plan comes into force, and the new relationship between God and man is formed. For St. Paul, the "new *diatheke*" means the Christian institution in its concrete reality (2 Cor. iii. 6); everything abstract that might be contained in the idea is stripped away when he identifies it with "that Jerusalem which is above ... which is the mother of us all". (Gal. iv. 26.)

While the first part of the eucharistic formula is merely a statement of the real presence of the immolated body, the second stresses the new economy that is introduced by that immolated humanity and only indirectly mentions the presence of the blood; this chalice is the new testament because of the blood it contains.[56] We cannot explain this relationship between Christ's blood and the *diatheke* by saying that the shedding of his blood opened the Christian era. It is not a question of the shedding of the blood, but of the chalice and the blood which it contains; this chalice *is* the new testament. Given the concrete meaning of the *diatheke* in St. Paul, the version of the eucharistic formula preserved by him is a most forceful expression of the ecclesiastical sense of the Eucharist. The body and blood of the immolated Christ are at the centre of the Church, and she is contained in them as in her principle.

What these texts teach us about the relation between the Church and the body of Christ is also suggested by others. There are statements in St. Paul which can be explained by no other supposition. Thus when he writes, "As many of you as have been baptized in Christ, have put on Christ. There is neither Jew nor Greek ... you are all one in Christ Jesus. And if you be Christ's, then are you the seed of Abraham, heirs according to the promise." (Gal. iii. 27-9.) Those Gentiles who have come to believe have entered the race of Abraham, because they have put on Christ. This is a legitimate reasoning only if it be true that the Christian is united to the bodily humanity of his Saviour: inclusion in Christ only makes us

[55] J. Behm, *Th W N T*, pp. 136-7; L Cerfaux, *The Church*, p 238: "The words 'New Covenant' conjure up the picture of a people who ... receive this new arrangement from God." E. Käsemann, *Leib und Leib Christi*, Tubingen, 1933, p 177, also links the body of Christ, the Church, and the new *diatheke*.
[56] That this significance does not extend to the body is because Christ's thought was dominated by the memory of the blood with which the old institution was sealed on Sinai (Exod. xxiv. 8).

descendants of Abraham if it unites us to Christ's bodily being, for
that bodily being is the only link between him and the patriarch.

It is true that the Apostle seems to recognize a descent from
Abraham by faith alone, unconnected with his flesh: "It is written:
Abraham believed God, and it was reputed to him unto justice.
Know ye therefore that they who are of faith, the same are of the
children of Abraham." (Gal. iii. 6; cf. Rom. iv 11.) If the Apostle's
mind were entirely expressed in this text we should have cause for
astonishment. That undoubtedly carnal seed of Abraham to whom
the promises were given, would, by a somewhat arbitrary exegesis,
be identified with all who copy Abraham in his faith.

But St. Paul realizes that it was to Israel that the promises were
made: "To whom belongeth the glory ... the testaments . . the
promises." (Rom. ix. 4; iii. 1–2.) By making faith the sole heir of
those promises, he means to exclude the Law. It is faith that makes
us like Abraham in the act which won justification for him, not
the Law (Rom. iv. 13ff.), for the faith of the Father of Israel was
already reputed to him unto justice (Rom. iv. 10–12), before he carried out the essential act of the Law upon himself. It was still under
the rule of faith that the promise was given to him, and no condition
attached to its fulfilment but faith alone. (Rom. iv. 13–16.) Justice
could, therefore, come to us, and sons, heirs of the promise, could
be born to Abraham quite outside the framework of the Law; only
faith was necessary.

But this still gives us no principle whereby we can reduce the
title "descendant of Abraham" to a merely moral relationship. The
dispute between faith and the Law resolves itself in the moral
sphere; faith is not set against a physical relationship with the
patriarch. The question whether it is necessary to belong to the
messianic race to benefit from the promises is still unresolved.

For St. Paul this belonging certainly demands a moral condition,
but one built upon a physical basis. This was, after all, the case with
the first members of the race. Abraham had more than one son, yet
"In Isaac alone shall thy seed be called. That is to say, not they that
are the children of the flesh, are the children of God; but they that
are the children of the promise, are accounted for the seed." (Rom.
ix. 7–8.) There must be not only birth, but a divine choice too. This
law, which was valid for Isaac, remains valid for his descendants·
"For all are not Israelites that are of Israel " (Rom. ix. 6.) The
Apostle distinguishes a sonship according to the flesh, and a sonship

according to the promise, and he anticipates the reality of the New Testament by calling this latter sonship according to the Spirit. (Gal. iv. 22ff.) Thus one can discern in the true descendant of Abraham a twofold parentage—the racial relationship, what is given by the flesh, and what is given from above, the promise or vocation to which man responds by faith

Does it follow that when Abraham's seed multiply in Christ, one of these two links is broken? Are we left with only that faith which places us in the line of Abraham by likeness of soul but does not actually make us his sons? If so, the promise made to Abraham grows poorer as it grows wider. Though the beneficiaries of the promise are multiplying, Abraham would recognize them not as his seed but simply as his imitators. This would not seem to be St. Paul's notion.

He has spiritualized the concept of the seed of Abraham, by applying it to the Church rather than to the race of old, but he has not impoverished it. This Jew who had grown up in the knowledge of messianic promises bound up with the race of Abraham did not conceive of there being a people of God without Abraham for their true father. In Rom. iv, his faith seems to make the believer no more than an imitator of the patriarch, for that is the reasoning demanded by the context; but in fact, for St Paul, faith produces not merely assent of the mind, but a total adherence which transforms the believer into Christ. In Romans, the complexity of his thought is simplified; he stresses only faith, and a faith which seems to be merely an assent. But in Galatians (iii. 26-8), he synthesizes his whole doctrine: "You are all the children of God by faith, in Christ Jesus. For as many of you as have been baptized in Christ, have put on Christ. There is neither Jew nor Greek ... You are all one in Christ Jesus." By the faith expressed in baptism, the believer has clothed himself in the dead and risen Christ, and is therefore, even in his body, lifted up to a kind of life in which all the differences resulting from carnal bodiliness are done away with; he takes his place in a new race, the race of Christ, in his spiritual body. "And if you be Christ's, then are you the seed of Abraham, heirs according to the promise." (Gal. iii. 29.) Even more than was the birth of Isaac, this birth in Christ is wholly according to the Spirit. And it is at the same time a birth into Abraham, for it is the effect of being joined to and identified with the physical being of Christ, which was received from Abraham. The patriarch becomes the father of all who believe; he brings forth children in Christ, not now by generation according to the flesh, but through faith; we are his children in the body of Christ.[57]

The consistency with which the body of Christ is put at the foundation of the messianic edifice is a striking manifestation of the doctrinal unity of the New Testament. The rejected stone becoming the head of the corner, the body rebuilt as the new Temple, the eating of the lamb becoming, in its fulfilment, the messianic banquet· all these images link the Church with the body of her Saviour, and some of them suggest the two as identified. St. Paul's differs only in laying aside the language of figure, to unite the two literally.

VI. SUMMING-UP

Let us remember that the new people is made up of all those who are joined to the body of Christ by the Spirit and by faith.[58] God does things with greater reality than we would dare to believe. In his Son, who became one with our sinful race by being born in fallen flesh, he reunites us all, saves us and divinizes us, by making us to be reborn in that body in which sin was killed, in which all principles of division were destroyed, and in which the holiness of the Spirit blazes forth.

The Church had to wait for Easter to be born. The body of Christ is, as it were, her native soil, the root of her existence: it contains the Church and gives her life. But that body is the one that was immolated and glorified: the stone taken up again with honour, the paschal lamb, the Temple rebuilt in three days.

Before his exaltation, Christ in his physical nature was no more than a living being, a living soul, like his father Adam. (1 Cor. xv. 45.) To transform our flesh into himself, he had accepted a humanity descended from Adam, made up of the weight of the flesh, and an animating principle to match, the soul. This soul, and the compound being it animated, formed a living reality, but one

---

[57] One is reminded of the splendid phrase of St. Justin which I quoted earlier· "It is we who form the true race of Israel, we who are hewn from the bosom of Christ as from a quarry." (*Dial. cum Tryph.*, cxxxv, 3, *P G.*, vi, 788) Similarly, Israel was hewn from Abraham (Isa li. 1.)

[58] St Hilary, *In Ps*, cxxv, 6, *P L*, ix, 688. "For he himself [Christ] is the Church, through the sacrament [that is to say, the mystery] of his body which contains the whole Church in itself."

See also St. Cyril of Alexandria, *In Jo*, xi, 11, *P.G.*, lxxiv, 560: We are one body, "because he has incorporated us into one body, clearly his own, as members".

which could not communicate life outside itself. St. Paul makes this quite clear in the contrast he makes between the two Adams. (1 Cor. xv. 45.) The limits of the soul's power of life are the limits of the one body it informs. The physical life of Adam does not overflow to other beings, nor contain them in itself.

As with his life, so with his radius of action, natural man is circumscribed by the limits of the flesh. His action cannot, of itself, work at a distance; it can only affect the surroundings with which it actually comes into contact. And the contact of the flesh has no power to save. Christ declared, "It is the Spirit that quickeneth: the flesh profiteth nothing." (John vi. 64.) He had just been teaching that his flesh was to give life to the world. But he was not speaking of the flesh in its natural state, to be assimilated by digestion. Such flesh, thus eaten, would profit nothing towards eternal life.

It did not matter that Christ's bodily humanity, in its carnal phase, could not communicate its life to us, for every man already had that life by birth.

In his death and resurrection, Christ was changed from a living soul into a life-giving Spirit. The physical Christ became spirit, even his material nature being divinized. He was no longer a "flesh that profiteth nothing", but a "spirit that quickeneth".[59] The spirit is an overflowing principle, a soul wide open, endowed with limitless power, with a universal power of giving life. Matter, which limits and divides, which is weak, henceforward borrows the qualities of spirit; it loses its narrowness and lays aside its weakness. Christ in his bodily humanity becomes capable of giving life to the world, and containing it within himself. He does not multiply himself in the ordinary way of nature, lighting new fires of life from his own, he becomes many while remaining one. The very life of this human nature communicates itself, or rather, Christ communicates himself, assimilating us to him in the life of his bodily humanity, and clothing us in his being (Gal. iii. 27), in such a way as to make us into his body, into his actual bodily human nature.

It is a life filled with mystery, of which the only possible principle can be the Spirit of God who baffles all our experience. No bodily life lived according to the flesh could claim such power.

Since the Church is the body of Christ, in whom the Saviour

---

[59] According to Prudentius (*Hymnus de Novo Lumine Pascalis Sabbati, P.L.,* lix, 819), the sparks, which are the Christians, are struck from the solid rock of the body of Christ

lives the life of his embodied glory, it was necessary that her birth should await Easter. But on that day she was born, at the same moment as the glorified body with which she is identified, but to which she adds nothing.[60] We may say that the body of Christ rose as a mystical body.[61]

2. THE PASSAGE FROM THE OLD TESTAMENT TO THE NEW IN THE DEATH AND RESURRECTION OF CHRIST

When the Christian Church was born on the first day of the week, what became of those who had been God's people? The Jewish nation continued to exist, but were they still the Israel of God, a people who held a mystery of divine predilection hidden behind the events of their history?

It is a question about which we are right to be curious. We can still seek to find the bridge that formed a passage from the Old Testament to the New. But one may also ask whether in fact there

---

[60] This presupposes the idea of the *pleroma*, which will come in the next chapter

[61] There is a fairly widespread opinion that the Church was founded at Pentecost Cf P Bonnetain, "La Pentecôte", *Rev. Apol.*, xlii, 1926, 193; G de Broglie, "L'Église, nouvelle Ève, née du Sacré Coeur", *Nouv Rev. Théol.*, lxviii, 1946, 11. But this is not the meaning of the coming of the Holy Ghost at Pentecost; it was, rather, the confirmation of the Church, by the fullness of the spiritual gift it gave, and the power to expand. The Church had already come into existence her head already exercised his powers, the Spirit had begun to be given, the primacy of power was given to Peter. But God's works develop gradually. The Church did not receive the gift of the Spirit in its fullness, nor enter fully into the use of her powers, nor as it were appear in the light of day until Pentecost Cf U Holzmeister, "Quid S Scriptura Doceat de Mysterio Festi Pentecostes", *Verb. Dom.*, vii, 1927, 164, N. Adler, "Das erste christliche Pfingstfest", *Ntl. Abhand.*, xviii, 1, Münster-i.-W., 1938, pp. 138–40.

The encyclical *Mystici Corporis* of Pius XII declares that the Church founded in Christ's death became manifest at Pentecost. This encyclical is often quoted in opposition to those who date the birth of the Church from the Resurrection. (J. Van der Ploeg, *R B*, lv, 1948, 109 a summarising of W. Grossouw's book *In Christus*, Utrecht-Brussels, 1946) But there is in fact no opposition Christ's death and resurrection make up a whole, and to date the Church from his resurrection is to make it due to his death, since the Resurrection is the result of that death. St. Maximus of Turin writes: "The resurrection of Christ was prefigured first of all in Adam, for just as he is rising from sleep took to himself Eve who had been fashioned from his side, so Christ rising from the dead established the Church from the wound in his own side." (*Sermo XXX, De Paschate, P.L.*, lvii, 596.)

This also explains how the Church can be dated from the Incarnation, for the Resurrection is simply the Incarnation come to full flowering

was a bridge uniting the two peoples, whether there was not a complete break between them.

It is important to keep a real connexion between the two. In New Testament thought, the Christian people was related to the old institution by an organic bond. The Kingdom's roots were in the Israel of old (cf. the parable of the wicked husbandmen); our Lord was fulfilling promises made to Israel (Acts ii. 30–36); he was restoring the throne of David (Luke i. 32; Acts xv. 15–16); the new Israel was wholly made up of true children of Abraham. (Gal. iii. 29.)

The nature of the Church's relationship to Christ makes it clear why her origin must be fixed at the Resurrection. The Church is made up of the totality of those who are united by the Spirit to the "spiritual" body of Christ, so that she could not be born before he was glorified. Surely then, we must look to their relationship with Christ's body on earth for the reason and the date of the ending of that older people; it will also show the bond that unites them to the new people.

1. THE RELATION BETWEEN GOD'S PEOPLE OF OLD AND THE BODY OF CHRIST

Scripture recognizes Christ as present in the midst of the people of Israel. It does not simply recognize that they had the seeds of Christ's teaching, and rites prefiguring him, but actually relates them to the person of Christ.

St. Paul looked at the Old Testament with the prophet's eye, which sees beyond the appearances to grasp the true significance of history.[62] At the time of the Exodus from Egypt, the people were granted miracles which prefigured the institutions of the future. Just as Christians are baptized at the body of Christ, eat him in a spiritual manna, drink from him the waters of the Spirit, so the Hebrews received a baptism, ate a spiritual food, and drank from a rock which always went with them. "And the rock was Christ" (1 Cor. x. 1–4.) The rabbinical legends spoke of a rock which never left the people. St. Paul explains: "The true rock which went with Israel was no material stone, as the legend you may have heard

[62] Prophetic knowledge does not merely bear upon future events, but is a theological understanding of things. Proof of this is to be found in Zechariah, chs i–viii (cf. A. van Hoonacker, *Les Douze Petits Prophètes,* Paris, 1908, p. 579), in Daniel and in the Apocalypse For what the Fathers had to say on the matter cf. M. Pontet, *L'Exégèse de saint Augustin prédicateur,* Paris, n d , p. 329, *n.* 73

describes, but Christ himself." (Allo.) Paul is making no merely typological exegesis. He does not say, "The rock means Christ, is to be interpreted as Christ", but, "The rock was Christ"; Christ was actually present, not merely in type; he dwelt among the people by a mysterious presence. And the Apostle continues "Neither let us tempt Christ as some of them tempted [him]." (Verse 9.) To him the Lord was Christ; he says so explicitly, in a well-supported and possibly original reading.[63]

The Apostle reminds the Gentiles of Asia Minor· "Be mindful that you were at that time without Christ, being outside the society of Israel." (Eph. ii. 12.) That was before Christ had, in his own flesh, abolished the wall (Eph. ii. 14) which kept the promises inside the Jewish nation. Israel, on the other hand, already possessed Christ.

It is hard to define precisely the nature of Christ's presence in the history of his people Paul never envisages it as being a presence in his divinity alone. If he is asked how Christ is related to Israel, he answers, "According to the flesh." (Rom. ix. 5; i. 3.) Christ is rooted in Israel by his flesh, and Israel in turn implants its roots in Christ, its descendant according to the flesh, from whom the people draw all their substance. This is the Apostle's conception of history, at least if we extend his thought to cover conclusions that come from juxtaposing scattered texts. According to him, Israel consists solely of the children of the promise made to Abraham (Rom. ix. 6–13); elsewhere it appears that only Christ was promised to him. (Gal. iii. 19.) The promise covered the whole seed of Abraham (cf Gen. xxii. 17–18) and St. Paul was well aware of the collective nature of those declarations (Gal. iii. 29; Rom. iv. 16; ix. 7; xi. 1); yet he assures us that the seed of Abraham is Christ alone (Gal. iii. 16.) Unless he is in this case just indulging in rabbinical subtlety of exegesis, this interpretation assumes that the people of Israel can, in our mind, be concentrated in Christ as their constitutive principle, *the* seed of the promise *par excellence.*

In St. John, the phrase about the Temple being destroyed and rebuilt (ii. 19) shows the close connexion between Christ's body and both testaments, it being taken first in its earthly phase, then as risen.

[63] "Neither let us tempt Christ, as   ." The reading is admitted by several scholars (Bachmann, Gutjahr) Cerfaux, in "Kyrios dans les citations pauliniennes de l'A. T ", *Eph Theol. Lov* , xx, 1943, 13, seems to allow it It certainly shows what the first Christians thought, as we find from *1 Clem.*, xxii; *Barn* , v, 6; Ignatius, *Magn* , viii, 2, and from one variant of Jude, 5

In the second part of the sentence, the Temple is none other than the risen body; it is the dwelling-place of God, and the hub of the new economy. In the first part, the Temple is the House of Iahweh, built of stone, which expresses the whole of the old economy. But these meanings are not mutually exclusive; the house of the new worship, which is the risen body, will be a carrying forward of the earthly temple ("I will rebuild"); and the earthly temple to be destroyed is linked with Christ's body—but his earthly body—for it is destroyed in the death of the earthly Christ.

The new temple consists in the risen body of Christ, and the old temple is involved with his earthly body; both economies are linked to the body of Christ, each under a different aspect of it.

The Apocalypse (xii), embracing the peoples of both testaments in a single vision, presents them in the image of one woman, who bears Christ in her womb, and after giving birth to him, brings brethren into the world for the Saviour. In her earlier form, the Church is the mother of Christ, her flesh bearing the seed of the Saviour; she bears him "hidden and rooted" in her loins since the day when, in Paradise, God promised her a messianic seed.[64] Whereas the new people is related in the Spirit to the glorified body of Christ, the people of the Old Testament was related to the Christ of flesh by the bond of generation; it was a people made up of the totality of those who were related in their flesh to the flesh of Christ: it was a Church, Christian according to the flesh.

By this the Apocalypse crystallizes a conception essential to Hebrew messianic teaching. To the mind of Israel, the people of God are a *messianic race*. At the first moment of their existence, they were contained in a single pair who were promised by God a messianic progeny (Gen. iii. 15); and the stages whereby God's people were finally marked out from among Eve's descendants were a racial selection. The messianic stream, meant at first for the whole of mankind, gradually narrowed to flow into ever smaller ethnic groups; first Seth (Gen. v, 1–5), then Shem (Gen. ix. 26), then Abraham (Gen. xii. 1–3) was its head, and after further eliminations

[64] The presence of the "ancient serpent" before the woman shows that John dates the Church back to the promise of a Messiah made to our first ancestors. Pontet (*L'Exégèse*, pp. 310–11) defines the old testament: "It is a racial movement, a series of choices made by Providence towards producing a Man-God The patriarchs and kings were the sowers of Christ, in the strict and Hebraic sense of the word ... The old testament is Christ hidden and rooted."

(Gen. xxi 12; xxv. 23; xxviii. 13–14), it was finally limited to the seed of Jacob, upon whom the promise rested. Yet it still became progressively more concentrated. The Bible makes it clear that one of Jacob's sons was to be bound by closer bonds to the Messiah than the rest (Gen. xlix. 8–12); Judah thus was to form the political and religious centre of the nation. The messianic power of Judah came to culminate in one family, that of David, to which the Messiah was to belong. The tribes of the north who cut themselves off from this messianic root died out, and after the Exile, God's people were more or less reduced to the tribe of Judah, from whom they took their name—Jews.

The People of God in the Old Testament were thus made up of a race, and their election was bound up with the thread of human generation; for them genealogies were of prime importance. From the prophecy made to Eve right down to the Annunciation to the daughter of David in Nazareth, the promise was always directed to "him who shall proceed out of thy bowels". (Cf. 2 Sam. vii. 10.)

That race is the race of Christ, that is what characterizes it. Thanks to the bond of flesh relating him to his ancestors, their descendant of the distant future moved back over the generations and was present to them. Israel at all times bore Christ in its flesh; prophecy often had a clear recognition of this thousand-year pregnancy. When Judah seemed lost, Isaiah indicated the promise of divine protection as a virgin conceiving and bearing a son. Judah bore a promise in his flesh, Judah could not perish. In the midst of the Assyrian invasions there arose the light of a great deliverance, for "a child is born to us, a son is given to us". (Isa vii.–xi.)

Owing to this seed it bore, Israel benefited from the power of the future Messiah,[65] and before becoming Christ's personal property, his messianic titles were shared by that people whose flesh was the very flesh of Christ.[66]

---

[65] Judah's pre-eminence, for instance, was a participation in the authority of the Messiah· "The sceptre shall not be taken away from Judah, nor the ruler's rod from between his feet, until he comes to whom it belongs " (Gen. xlix 10.)

[66] Between Christ and the people there is a sort of sharing of properties which is explained by the fact of the Messiah's presence in the flesh of Israel. The people were the sons of God (Gen. vi 1–4; Exod iv 22) because they were the messianic race Both Israel and the Messiah were called the Servants of the Lord, sometimes in the same chapter of Isaiah (xlii), sometimes in successive chapters (xl–liii).

If the greatness and glory of the community of old sprang from that deep womb in which it bore Christ, its inferiorities and failings in turn bear witness to the precision of the Johannine definition. This Church which was of Christ by being his mother according to the flesh, remained imprisoned in the sphere of sinful flesh, for of itself Christ's flesh could divinize no-one (John vi. 63.)

The constitution of the Jewish community was that of a natural society, and while in the Christian economy, man stands at the summit of creation and gathers up the universe in himself to bring it to God, the ancient religion remained subject to the world, ruled by the forces of nature, those elements of this world spoken of by St. Paul. Their religious life grew up round feasts which depended on the positions of the stars; the worship ordained by the Law was expressed by material means, "ordinances of the flesh" (Heb. ix. 10), which sufficed only "to the cleansing of the flesh". (ix. 13.) Then too, cleanness and uncleanness were both determined by material actions and contacts, and physiological phenomena. The great sacrament of this Church which was of Christ by its flesh, was itself carnal; it expressed and confirmed membership to the messianic race by a sign "made by hands" (Eph. ii. 11; Col. ii. 11), an excision of the flesh. The Jewish forms of worship were no better, either by their nature or their efficacy, than the rites of the pagan nations: Paul realized this, and with incredible audacity he set them both among "the weak elements of the world". (Gal. iv. 9; Col. ii. 8)

As the promise came to rest upon a single family, the prerogative of sonship was settled upon them, and the Son of David became personally the Son of God (2 Sam. vii 12–14.) The poets surround the Davidic kings with a halo of glory from their illustrious descendant; they give them the title of Elohim, and declare that their throne is for ever (Ps xlv 3, 7). And while the Messiah's titles are bestowed on members of the kingly family, David's name in turn is given to his great descendant (Ezek. xxxiv. 23) Haggai and Zechariah confer the title "Branch" upon Zerubbabel (Zech. iii 8; cf. Hag ii. 23)—a strictly messianic title. (Cf. Isa. iv 2; Jer. xxiii. 5; xxxiii 15.) Liberal exegetes explain this as simply a mistake. These two prophets thought that with the return from exile and rebuilding of the Temple, the messianic era had come, and Zerubbabel was the Messiah. Theodoret of Cyrus was not surprised by the apparent confusion between these two sons of David. (*In Zach.*, P G., lxxxi, 1896.) Zerubbabel, he says, bore Christ who was to come in his flesh, and thus he had good right to claim the messianic title. This is a sound piece of exegesis, for it was because of his descent that the prince was called "Branch". (Cf A van Hoonacker, *Les douze petits prophètes*, Paris, 1908, p. 581)

Because its links with Christ bound it only to his flesh, which was itself under the banner of sin (Rom viii. 3), the ancient Church remained "concluded under sin" (Gal. iii. 22): "For we have proved both Jews, and Greeks, that they are all under sin" (Rom. iii. 9), the Jews remaining as they did "by nature, children of wrath, even as the rest", the pagans. (Eph. ii 3.)

The sonship in which the Jewish people gloried was of a lesser kind. Christ was not Son of God by virtue of his flesh, and no relationship with him achieved by "the will of the flesh" (John i. 13) could raise anyone to the rank of a child of God. Israel was more a slave than a son, vowed to serve the Law",[67] as Christ himself was in his state of flesh. (Phil. ii. 7; Gal. iv. 1–7.) The inheritance of these sons was of the "carnal" order. the earth and its riches, the kingly power of the House of David.

The difference of meaning in the same text, "The just shall live by his faith", when applied to that Church which is of Christ according to the flesh, and to that which is of Christ according to the Spirit, shows the gulf that separates the life bestowed in the Old Testament from that in the New. Amid the Chaldean invasions, only the just would stand, the Israelite who believed in God's protection; that is the prophet's meaning. (Hab. ii. 4.) It is his faith in the Redemption which is in the Christ of glory that assures man the justice of eternal life; that is St. Paul's meaning. (Rom. i 17.) There is the same gulf between the faith of Abraham and Christian faith. The first believes the promise of a carnal birth, the second the gospel of the divine life springing up in Christ. (Rom. iv. 17–25.)

That People of God remained bound within the enclosure of one race, of one national Church, with no perspective upon the world at large. To belong to it one had to join this community of the flesh by imprinting on one's own flesh the mark of membership. The Gentiles could belong neither to the Church nor to Christ: "Be mindful that you, being heretofore Gentiles by birth ... were at that time without Christ, being aliens from the society of Israel." (Eph. ii. 11–12.) There was a wall around this Church which was of Christ according to the flesh, suitably symbolized by the enclosure which forbade access to the Temple (Eph. ii. 14) which no Gentile

---

[67] Then, too, the Hebrews did not have any right *individually* to the title of son. It was the nation that was son because it was the bearer of the promise The only exception to this was found in the descendants of David who were more personally related to Christ

could pass unless he wished to "bear the responsibility for the death which should follow for him".[68]

"The spiritual man", the Christ of glory, who came after "the natural man" (I Cor. xv. 46), was not yet present in the history of that people He manifested himself by signs of a lower order—"the rock was Christ" (I Cor. x. 4)—which were a kind of shadow thrown by his body,[69] a clumsy carnal tracing of the "spiritual" reality, the letter which goes before the Spirit and does not yet give life.

Thus we have a Church which is of Christ according to the flesh, as St. John shows us, bearing within her the Christ of the flesh. "Jesus is the substance of that people, for from it he drew the nature of his flesh", says St. Augustine.[70] Hence both their greatness and their subjection.

ii. THE END OF THE OLD TESTAMENT PEOPLE

That Church continued in existence as long as Christ was in the world. It is true that the grace of the New Testament was already beginning to infiltrate; the foundations of the spiritual economy were present, but hardly appeared on the surface. Far from being ended by the Incarnation, the Church in its ancient form reached its summit then, for having been pregnant since the time of Eve, its pregnancy had come to term with the birth of Christ. The prophecy of the Messiah, addressed to all mankind, and gradually narrowed down to the race of Shem, the people of Abraham, the tribe of Judah, the family of David, had been concentrated into a supreme annunciation made to Mary. The whole of the people of old culminated, were summarized and were fulfilled in this Virgin of Israel. In her the long pregnancy of the race was crowned[71]; Israel

[68] Part of the inscription attached to the wall, found in 1891 by Clermont-Ganneau.

[69] Col ii. 17: "Which are a shadow of things to come, but the body [which casts the shadow] is of Christ" Cf L. Cerfaux, *The Church*, p. 327.

[70] *De Civitate Dei*, xvii, 11, *P.L.*, xli, 544.

[71] Clearly it was a true instinct that led the Christian people to apply to our Lord's mother all the praise Iahweh had bestowed on the community of Israel (Ps. xliv; lxxxvi; Canticle of Canticles), and the promise he had given to Eve, who also summed up in herself the maternal role of that community as Christ's first ancestress: "I will put enmities between thee and the woman" (Gen. iii. 15) But the promise applies to Mary in a richer sense because she is more fully Christ's mother.

truly bore Christ in its womb, the Messiah dwelt amidst his people, their son and their brother.

Though they had achieved this glory, Israel had not stripped off their imperfections; they remained in the closed circle of the flesh, for their centre, the bodily Christ, himself was living in the flesh, a flesh of sin, weakness and slavery. So embedded was he in this house of flesh, that he adapted himself with native ease to the "poor and weak" rites, even going so far as to limit his apostolate specifically to Israel. As long as he was in the flesh, the Law held good—"I was not sent but to the sheep that are lost of the house of Israel" (Matt. xv. 24)—and this command stood: "Go ye not into the way of the Gentiles, and into the city of the Samaritans enter ye not, but go ye rather to the lost sheep of the house of Israel " (Matt. x. 5–6.)

Christ's death in the flesh constituted the last act of the Old Testament. Christ was succumbing to the imperfections of the economy of the flesh. He died by sin, by the weakness of the flesh, by the Law. (Cf. ch. ii.) These evil forces had come to the high point of their power to harm, in attacking the greatest of the children of Israel.

But while he was succumbing to the conditions of carnal life he was also freeing himself of them; he was dying to sin, to weakness, to the Law. Thus his death detached Christ from the economy of the flesh, and that economy immediately ceased to exist. According to the Epistle to the Hebrews, the veil of the Temple symbolized the flesh of Christ (Heb. x. 20.) At the instant when Christ passed through the rent in that flesh to leave the life he held from his people, the veil hanging before the sanctuary tore too, thus declaring the end of the old economy of which the Temple was the figure. (Heb. ix. 8ff.) The mystery of the "Presence" (of God) in Sion was thrown open; the Temple was to all intents and purposes in ruins (John ii. 19); Israel was emptied of its substance; the Israel of God was no longer one with the Israel of the flesh, for Christ was gone from them. "Behold your house is left to you, desolate." (Matt. xxiii. 38) It is emptied of Christ, God has become indifferent to it, it is now merely "your" house.[72] The whole of the old economy died in the flesh of Christ.

---

[72] "In Jer xii. 7—'I have forsaken *my* house'—there still remains a hope that God may return to his house. Here, 'your house' leaves no link with him." (Lagrange, *Évangile selon saint Luc*, Paris, 1921, p 396)

The messianic community is born young and new with Christ,
still united to his body, but united now in the Spirit to a body vivified by the Spirit.

St. John brings the motif of the Exodus into his gospel; he shows
the paschal mystery, which is a passing-over, effected in the death
and glorification of Christ, and he suggests that the change from the
Old Testament to the New is effected in that death and glorification
The changing of the water into wine which Christ is asked to perform, brings to his mind the deeper change which it is his mission
to carry out; and he protests, "My hour is not yet come." (ii. 4.)
The hour will come. The old temple will crumble in the dying
body of Christ, and the new temple will rise in its resurrection
(ii. 19).

St. Paul clearly shows us this passing of the people of the Old
Testament to the new Church. He sees the Mosaic economy, with
all its particularism, abolished in the dying flesh, to be reborn a
new people in the glorious body: "He is our peace, who hath made
both [peoples] one, breaking down the wall of partition between
them, enmity, having annulled in his flesh the law of the Com-
mandments with its prescriptions in order that both [peoples] may
form one new man in him, by establishing peace, so that he may
reconcile both to God in a single body." (Eph ii. 14–16.) The wall
of separation put up by the differences of nationality, and made
perceptible by the intransigent particularism of the Law, has been
overthrown in the dying flesh of Christ. Henceforth the two enemy
peoples are to dwell together and fuse into "a single body", the
glorified body of Christ, which is the Church.[73] The unity of this
"new man" is brought about not in the flesh, but in the Spirit.
(Eph. ii. 18.)

From now on the Jew was no closer to Christ's body than the
Gentile; he was no longer a blood relation of the Messiah, for in
his new existence the Lord was a spiritual being, a universal man,
free of all bonds of the flesh, belonging to no one race. The kingdom

[73] P Benoit, on Eph. ii 16 (*Bible de Jérusalem*): "This single body in which
Christ reconciles the enemy peoples is first of all his individual and physical
body, sacrificed on the Cross. But it is also the Mystical Body, whose centre
or head is that physical body, in which all the members are gathered together,
once Jews and Gentiles, now at last reconciled "

which had developed in an unbroken line, as it were horizontally, up till Christ's coming, had suddenly been caught in a vertical upward movement and lifted up to the level of the Spirit.

In the Epistle to the Galatians, Paul sees the blessing of Abraham being loosed in the dying Christ from the bonds of a single nation, to be placed, in the glorified Christ, at the disposal of the Gentiles: "Christ hath redeemed us from the curse of the Law, being made a curse for us ... that the blessing of Abraham might come on the Gentiles through Christ Jesus: that we might receive the promise of the Spirit by faith." (iii. 13–14.) Christ took upon himself the burden of the curse laid upon those who transgressed the Law, and by submitting to it upon the Cross, he wiped it out. St. Paul does not say in so many words that the Law itself was destroyed along with the curse; but he must mean us to understand this, for as long as the Law stands, the curse remains. (iii. 10.) By this doing away with the old economy, the messianic blessing promised to Abraham became freed from its limiting conditions. This blessing had always been dependent upon Christ, but in the past it was dependent upon a Christ belonging to the Jewish nation, and all Gentiles were excluded from it. Henceforth it was placed in an "open" Christ, "in Christ Jesus" in glory, in whom it is offered to us in the form of the gift of the Spirit. (iii. 14.)

When they had realized that the Kingdom of God had changed places, the true children of Abraham would move with it; they would emigrate with Christ into the world of the Spirit. The Old Testament was to be annexed to the new body of Christ.

This changeover began in the depths of *sheol*. During the three days he was dead, Christ, already "raised above the earth", used his power to draw the beings whose mode of existence he shared, the dead.

The teaching of the Apostles gave an important place to the doctrine of the descent into hell. Even in his Pentecost discourse St. Peter mentions Christ's visit to *sheol* (Acts ii. 27). He makes allusions in his first epistle which presuppose that his readers are familiar with the fact and its meaning. After a passage whose sense is still obscure (1 Pet. iii. 18–20),[74] he goes on: "They [the pagans] think it

[74] "Christ . being put to death indeed by reason of the flesh, but being enlivened by reason of the Spirit, in which also coming he preached [first of all] to those spirits that were in prison, which had been some time rebellious" at the time of the Flood

Exegetes wonder whether the descent into hell here means to the dead or

strange that you run not with them into the same confusion and debauchery, and they speak evil of you. But they shall render account to him, who is ready to judge the living and the dead. For, for this cause was the Gospel preached also to the dead, that although they might be judged, according to men, in the flesh, they may live, according to God, in the Spirit.'' (iv. 4–6.)

The passage seems to mean this: The pagans abuse you now, but they must give an account to him who judges the living and the dead. The last word suggests the descent into hell Christ's activity among the souls of the dead was a proof that one day he would re-establish justice in everything, for by it he was inaugurating his action as judge. He brought them the good news that these dead, once damned by the judgement of men, like these Christians, might receive life by the power of the Spirit.

It was only the just whom he visited, those who had been falsely judged on earth. The Lord appeared to them in his spiritual glory (iii. 18) and took them good news[75] "that they may live by the Spirit", a message of life and of redemption. This "preaching the Gospel" to the dead was not simply words that would set them free; it bore with it a saving life. The souls of the Patriarchs were made Christian by it.

If his preaching bore life—that life of the Spirit which enlivened Christ himself (iii. 18)—it does not seem over-bold to say that it effected in the just a new attitude of soul, the faith that cleaves to the Lord and makes man open to the life of glory. We may think, as did several of the first Christians,[76] that "the announcing of the good news in hell could be for those who believed it the occasion for an act of faith".[77] Whether this be so or not, life came down

to the fallen angels. It is possible, though it remains uncertain, that these spirits are the unbelieving angels whose defection was always connected with the story of the Flood in the minds of the Jews. Christ would thus have come to proclaim his dominion over them and subject them to himself But it is also possible that this descent into hell is a visit to the dead to bring them the message of the good news (this is the usual sense of κηρύσσω in the New Testament).

[75] "The soteriological significance of the descent into hell is bound up with the goods news." E. Stauffer, *Die Theologie des N.T.*, Stuttgart, 1941, p 114.

[76] Their ideas are quoted by U Holzmeister, *Commentarius in Epistulas SS. Petri et Judae*, Paris, 1937, vol. 1, pp 327–30 They believed that the just who had died had to make an act of faith in Christ to be saved Some thought of this act of faith as a real conversion.

[77] J Chaine, "La Descente du Christ aux enfers", *D.B. Suppl.*, col. 423. The author adds, "The souls of the just . . kept the virtue of faith as long as they

into their prison, and we may believe that those souls were linked
to Christ in glory in a living union. Thus they were baptized in
the soul of Christ, the first fruits of the new Church."[8]

The Old Testament had hardly died in the flesh of Christ before
all the multitude of those who had been just in the past made the
first move to transmigrate into the Kingdom of God in its new
form.

The old economy was thus "fulfilled" not only in its institutions,
but in its deeper reality, in the people themselves. The children of
Abraham became more closely united to Christ, and received from
him the Spirit of which the faith of Abraham had given them the
merest glimmer. They had rested upon the one foundation of Christ
who was to come; henceforth they were truly taken up unto him.
In the past they were the "fathers" (Rom. ix. 5), this title, and the
descendant from whom it derived being their sole *raison d'être*.
Now they were receiving life from him; Christ was begetting his
fathers "In all things he holds the primacy", he who is the principle
of all."[9]

did not enjoy the Beatific Vision   We can readily understand that their
adherence to Christ as he revealed himself explicitly to them would be an
act of living faith, an act not in itself meritorious, but one which they had
merited to perform while they were on earth "

[78] St. Ignatius of Antioch: Christ is the door by which "Abraham, Isaac,
Jacob, the Prophets, the Apostles and the Church enter". (*Philad*, iii, 1, cf v,
2.) The *Shepherd* of Hermas, *Sim.* xvi, 2–4, takes the view that the Patriarchs
received Christian baptism at that moment.

[79] Just as the Israelite community is carried on in the Church—so much so
as to form a single Church with it, as the Apocalypse tells us (ch. xii)—so
the messianic function of Christ's mother is carried further, according to
Catholic thought, beyond the maternal role in which the role of Israel was
summed up and culminated Her function is transformed in the same way
as is the Church's Just as the Church was first of all Christ's mother according to the flesh, and became his bride in the Spirit (Eph. v. 25) and the
mother of the faithful, so too, Mary is henceforth considered in the Church
of Christ as mediatrix of life in her union with Christ in the Holy Spirit;
once again she sums up the whole Church, but the Church in its new form
as bride and mother of the faithful Cf. Olier, *La Vie intérieure de la très-
sainte Vierge*, ed Faillon, Paris, 1866, vol. ii, p 126: "Having been granted
by God in his resurrection to have life in himself to give to all men . . . he
[Christ] takes the blessed Virgin as a new Eve, as his assistant, and at that
instant, he communicates to her all he has received from his Father, to make
her the mother of the living."
While Christ is the source of the Church, first as carnal, then as spiritual,
because he became her son according to the flesh and then her bridegroom
in the Spirit, the Virgin Mary *is* that Church in the two successive forms as
the summing up and expression of her.

The New Testament is united with the Old into a single essential unity, in Christ's body, which is the substance of both. There is not merely a permanent cohesion between them, but a unity, the unity of the body of Christ, there is not a break, but the transformation of an existing reality, and the same difference that exists in Christ's own body before his death and after his resurrection.

Thus all the members of the Church are of the race of Abraham; there is no inheritance but Abraham's (Eph. iii. 6); there is no messianic race but Israel. (Eph. ii. 19.)

The older people was the first to enter the spiritual kingdom, in the person of Christ, in whose body their substance was concentrated. And the first to follow him were also Israelites; it was fitting in the order of things that he should first take with him those who were united to his carnal body. It was they whom he addressed, bearing the blessing of Abraham (Acts iii. 26) made spiritual in him. From Jerusalem, the centre of Israel, the Kingdom spread over Judea, then Samaria, then the world at large. (Cf. Luke xxiv. 47;

To be united to Christ in the Resurrection, she had to realize in herself what the whole Church has to accomplish in each of her members: to pass from the flesh to the Spirit She was present upon Calvary as Christ's mother, standing for the Old Testament people and their maternal role. She was God's Israel at the foot of the Cross. In her, at least, the Jewish people accepted the agony of the Cross, and consented to the death of their son according to the flesh, of all earthly messianic hopes and of the whole ancient dispensation. In Mary, the Church of the Old Testament consented to die in Christ.

Every believer takes part in the act of redemption, by associating himself in mystery with the actual act of dying and rising again (cf. below, p. 221), either for his individual salvation, or for the Church of which he is an apostle (cf below, p 344). Having taken part in Christ's death as his mother, as the personification of the community of Israel, Mary, in Christian thought, received in herself the fullness of life of the risen Christ, once again summing up in herself the whole saving function of the Church and all the phases of her sanctification, right up to the final one of bodily glorification.

In a single lifetime, the Mother of Christ lived out the long history of the Church Sacred history began with the first messianic announcement—"I will put enmity .." and it is completed in the bodily glorification of the Church; Christ is its central point, the Christ according to the flesh brought into the world by the Old Testament, the dead and risen Christ to whom the New Testament Church is united. The beginning and end of Mary's life coincide with the beginning and end of the life of the Church; and the history of salvation which takes place between that beginning and end in the life of the Church, was perfectly fulfilled in Mary

The Church saved by Christ—it is also his mother and his assistant—is, as it were, condensed in the individual, Mary. Cf. C. Dillenschneider, "Toute l'Église en Marie", *Bulletin de la Société française d'études mariales*, 1953, pp. 75-132.

Acts 1. 8.) The solicitations of grace were always to respect this priority (Acts xiii 46); and the tentacles of the Spirit were to reach out to the Gentiles by way of the Jewish Christians The glory of the Gentiles was to be "co-citizens with the saints" (Eph. ii. 19) and share in their riches. (Rom. xv. 27; 2 Cor. viii. 14.)

However, there stands between the people of old and the new Church a death and a resurrection, a profound transformation through the renunciation of the life of the flesh. In the new Church, the old is dead and remains so, because Christ's life sanctions forever the death of the flesh. The mass of the Jews rejected the agony of the Cross. They tried to snatch their people from the toils of death in which they felt them to be caught by this Jesus of Nazareth But it was not possible, by suppressing Christ, to keep them back in the flesh, for Israel was wholly bound up in Christ. While for Christ, death was a stripping away of his carnal body and a passing into the life of God, for the Jewish multitude it was an obstinate clinging to their carnal state and a rejection of the Spirit. For Christ and those who believed in him, the Cross was both the end of the life of the flesh, and the root of the new life; for the unbelieving Jews it was an end with no beginning to follow, a casting-out from the Kingdom. That is why "the turning away from the Cross remained essential to Judaism." [80]

Because the two Testaments run into one another, the vision of prophecy can turn a single gaze on them both. The prophecy of the Bible bears upon past and present as well as future; it is an intuition of the messianic importance of institutions, persons and events. From their place at one or other end of the history of God's kingdom, the prophets of the old and new eras unite both peoples in a single concept; it is only the perspective that changes, depending on whether the Kingdom is seen in the forefront of the vision as being in its carnal or its spiritual state. [81]

---

[80] C Journet, *Destinées d'Israël*, Paris, 1945, p 151

[81] Christ standing between the two testaments, sees them both in one glance In the parable of the wicked husbandmen, the son is taken prisoner, and according to Matthew (xxi. 39) and Luke (xx. 15), first taken outside the vineyard and then killed. The parable imprints the image on the reality with this transparent allusion to him who "suffered without the gate". (Heb. xiii. 12) We see the Son captured in Jerusalem, dragged outside the walls and there killed The vineyard represents the Kingdom, historically, as it then was, the earthly Israel, a political as well as a religious society, and Jerusalem in particular, the capital of that earthly kingdom. (Cf. D Buzy, *Les Paraboles*, 3rd ed., Paris, 1932, p. 420.) And if the master kills the husbandmen, the

To make the proper distinctions in our interpretation of the messianic texts[82] and give each of the two peoples their just place, they must be understood first in a "carnal", then a "spiritual", sense. We must grant the old economy the earthly promises they gave it, and then make these texts die to their carnal significance, burying them with Christ to raise them up with him in the Spirit, and thus give them to the Church.[83]

The death and resurrection of Christ were the same for the messianic race and for the whole of the old dispensation as they were for Christ himself; they were a pasch, a passover.

---

vineyard itself is not devastated, but remains the Father's vineyard, ready to be let out to other husbandmen

The seers of the past saw the Israel of the future in the perspective of the Israel of the flesh. The outlines of Iahweh's house drew their gaze to the vision of the messianic temple (Ezek. xlvii), but did not give them any clear understanding of the change between one point of the perspective and the other; so much so that they applied anticipated messianic praises to Zerubbabel who, after the Exile, raised the Temple from ruins (Zech. iii 8; vi. 12) In the City of David, built of stones, and narrowly enclosed, they already contemplated Sion the mother of many nations (Ps lxxxvi); the reign of Solomon carries on in the eternal kingship of the Messiah (2 Sam vii. 12-16; Ps xlv; xlix), and "the land" (the land of Israel) figures as the messianic inheritance of all who believe (Ps. xxxvii. 9.)

Whereas the prophetic perspective of the past starts with the carnal reality, the Epistle to the Hebrews reads the Bible as it were backwards, starting with the Christian reality with which that perspective ends (Cf J Van der Ploeg, "L'Exégèse de l'Ancien Testament dans l'épître aux Hébreux", R B., liv, 1947, 187-228) It applies to Christ, literally and in their strongest sense, praises which in their first literal sense belonged to individuals in the past It grants to Christ alone the honour of divine sonship in a text which allows it, in a weakened sense, to the whole seed of David (Heb i 5; 2 Sam vii. 14.) To him alone it attributes the title "Elohim", which was given to a king of David's line in an epithalamion by a Court poet. (Heb i. 8-9; Ps. xlv 7) The author takes these texts always in the fullest sense which they have come to have now that the reality they express has attained to its full perfection.

Perspective changes—now carnal, now spiritual. The reality is wholly messianic

[82] I mean the greater number of messianic texts which refer not to Christ alone, but to the messianic reality in its earlier form before it came to fruition in Christ.

[83] We must not, however, make them undergo any kind of discarnation, but a spiritualizing bodily resurrection. The messianic prophecies we call "temporal" are an integral part of prophecy as a whole, and were in no way different in the Prophets' minds from those we call "spiritual" Just as Christ did not become discarnate, but was raised up bodily, not in the flesh but in the Spirit, similarly these prophecies have been fulfilled, or have yet to be fulfilled, as an integral whole, not according to the laws of the flesh, but of the Spirit of God.

VI

THE CHURCH'S LIFE IN THE RISEN CHRIST

Here again we shall be enumerating the effects of "the power of his resurrection". (Phil. iii. 10.) It is not enough to have studied them in their central point, the individual Christ; we must also measure them as they spread outwards. The Church has sprung up in the body of Christ, sown in spirit from the first, but needing the husbandry of the Passion to make it bear fruit. She forms one body with that body; she was born in the same act which brought forth her Saviour to a new existence. The full riches of this life of glory can only be gauged from Christ's body, which is also the Church.

1. Indications of a New Life in the Synoptics and the Acts

From the Resurrection onwards, a change could be seen in the Apostles which became more and more marked, as though their souls had become fruitful.

Their attitude to their Master altered. During his natural life, Christ was the object of their human knowledge; he was perceptible to sense, part of ordinary human history, caught up in a net of family and social relationships; he called forth the admiration of those about him, and provoked affection, but these feelings hardly deepened into adoration and charity. In the evening after his great day of parable-telling, our Lord said to his Apostles: "Let us pass over to the other side " "And they take him", the passage goes on, "even as he was in the ship." (Mark iv. 35ff.) We feel the rough friendliness of these men. If he wanted to cross the sea they were the men whose job it was When they saw him asleep during the fearful storm: "Master, doth it not concern thee that we perish?" This was certainly not the infinite respect they showed later speaking of the "Lord Jesus" (cf. Acts i. 21) after the Ascension. Their rabbi was so much a part of mankind on earth that they could speak to him without realizing that they were speaking to God, could call him their brother without knowing him for their Lord, could sin against him without sinning against the Holy Spirit (Matt. xii. 32.)[1] The disciples had not yet got beyond the sphere of flesh and blood, whose vision went no further than the Christ of flesh and blood.[2]

After the Resurrection, Christ still appeared in his ordinary earthly form, but he was no longer the same man as formerly, the object of a purely natural knowledge. St. Peter declares that it "was given to him [Christ] to be made manifest not to all the people, but to witnesses preordained by God". (Acts x. 41.) The sight and companionship of the risen Christ were reserved to the company of those who believed.

The souls of the disciples opened out at contact with him. Christ himself "opened their understanding that they might understand" (Luke xxiv. 45); the meaning of the enigmatic things they had heard before became clear to them (Luke xxiv. 8); their hearts burned within them by simply being in his presence, even before they recognized him (Luke xxiv. 32), and in a mysterious shared meal, our Lord revealed himself so that their eyes were opened (Luke xxiv. 31, 35). St. Peter, whose mind was once so closed to the mystery of the Redemption, showed, in his discourse to the brethren in the upper room, that he had begun to see the capital importance of Christ's resurrection. (Acts i. 22.) Lifted as he was into another sphere, our Lord drew their souls gradually, gently up to it, leaving to the Spirit of Pentecost the task of bringing this still faint light to its full brilliance. (Cf. Acts i. 6–8.)

Their whole psychology altered. The disciples lived in joy and simplicity of heart (Acts ii. 46); joy was their dominant sentiment. (Acts v. 41; viii. 39; xiii. 48.) Even during Christ's earthly life, the Apostles' affection for him had deepened to the point of being unable to be happy away from him; and since now their joy was intense, and reached its peak at the moment when our Lord in his sensible form finally left them (Luke xxiv. 52–3), it must be that his very leaving them made him more closely present to them. This

[1] Even after Christ's resurrection, it was possible to "speak a word against the Son of Man" without speaking against the Holy Spirit, as long as one only knew Christ according to the flesh, according to the historical appearances. This was St Paul's situation before his conversion. (2 Cor. v. 16.)

[2] More than once, however, the Apostles were lifted by some higher principle to a more spiritual knowledge of their Master; cf. Matt. xvi 17.

presence, preserved and indeed intensified as it was by his leaving, must have been of a totally new kind.

Their earlier hopes were emptied of all selfishness[3]; a new sort of brotherhood was established among the disciples[3] (Acts ii. 42–6, iv 32.) A new sort of society had been born.

2. THE NEW LIFE AS SEEN BY THE FOURTH GOSPEL

To St. John, salvation was of the order of knowledge as well as of life, and the first effect of the Easter mystery was an illumination. Christ had long ago declared that his paschal exaltation would be the beginning of a new knowledge· "When you shall have lifted up the Son of Man, then shall you know that I am he " (viii. 28; cf. iii. 14–16.) On the eve of his death, he prayed that the light which should make him known be enkindled in him. His prayer can be paraphrased thus. "Father, glorify me, for thou hast given life to me to give to men. And this life is to know thy unique Godhead and that of him whom thou hast sent—a knowledge that can only dawn upon men by means of my glorification." (xvii. 1–3.)

Only then will Christ's deepest being be revealed, and the features of the Father will appear in the regained glory of the Son, once the Father has absorbed the Son into his divine holiness. (xvii. 10.) "In that [great] day you shall know that I am in my Father." (xiv. 20.)[1] A torch will be lighted in them: "And in that day you shall not ask me anything" (xvi. 23); in its light they will have no more need to ask, "What is this that he saith?" (xvi. 17.) That day is the day of the Resurrection (xvi. 22–3); and it does not seem that the sun will ever set on it (Lagrange.)

It is a knowledge that is not merely notional, but a life filled with light: "Now this is eternal life, that they may know . . ." (xvii. 3); it is also a source of love. (xvii. 26.)

With this living knowledge there was to go a new sort of presence of Christ: "I will not leave you orphans, I will come to you." (xiv. 18.) "A little while and now you shall not see me, and again a little

[3] L Beirnaert, *Pour un christianisme de choc*, Paris, 1942, p. 21 "The death of the loved being marked the collapse of their selfish love With him they were crucified to the letter on Calvary."

[4] According to xii 45 and xiv 7–9, the disciples could already see the Father in the Son. This may be an anticipation. It is true that even during Christ's time on earth, the Apostles knew the Father in the Son, but more or less perfectly according as his oneness with the Father was manifested before the Resurrection.

while and you shall see me." (xvi 16.) Our Lord was to disappear, but only in order to make himself seen Easter morning brought him back to his disciples, and this time his presence would remain, for the Apostles were not to be left orphans[5]; at first it was still perceptible to sense, though so transfigured that it was not accessible to the perception of the senses alone: "Yet a little while, and the world seeth me no more", for the world is only in touch with sensible things[6]; "But you see me, because I live, and you shall live." (xiv. 19.) Do the tenses used here make a difference? Speaking of his own life, Christ uses the present, but of his disciples', the future. The Apostles undoubtedly "did not receive the whole spiritual life at once at the Resurrection, it being, rather, a starting-point".[7] Because of this life they shared, the disciples' gaze, raised to the level of the life of the risen Christ, was filled with a supernatural vision.[8] The Lord would come back to whoever loved him, to dwell in them and reveal himself to them. (xiv. 21, 23.)

The Spirit would have a part to play in this new knowledge, this close presence and this life. He was to give witness of Christ and bring the knowledge. (xv. 26; xvi. 13–14.) It appears that it was also to be he who would make Christ present, for, having announced the Spirit's coming, Christ adds as if in conclusion: "I will not leave you orphans. I will come to you." (xiv. 18.)[9] And the life to be given to believers by the glorified Christ, was none other than the Holy Spirit. (vii. 37–9.)[10] "The day" when this new relationship was formed dawned with Christ's resurrection, but in this Easter daybreak Pentecost was already dawning too.

---

[5] We understand it [this coming in the Resurrection] as the beginning of a closer union between the risen Christ and his disciples, indeed of an intimate and mystical coming." (Lagrange, *L'Évangile selon saint Jean*, 3rd ed., pp 384-5.)

[6] St. Cyril of Alexandria, *In Jo.*, xiv, 19, *P.G*, lxxix, 264: "They will not see Christ in them, for their hearts are without the Spirit "

[7] Lagrange, *L'Évangile selon saint Jean*, p 385.

[8] To the Jews, our Lord had spoken of a lesser knowledge according to the flesh (viii 15), and a few moments later, he told them: You do not understand my words, for "You are from beneath; I am from above". (viii 23)

[9] This is the explanation given by St Cyril of Alexandria, *In Jo*, xiv. 18, *P G.*, lxxiv, 261 and 264, linking John xiv 18 with Rom. viii. 9.

[10] It is true that this is not affirmed so strongly here as in St. Paul; it is suggested by vii. 37–9, by the literary resemblance of xiv. 17–18, by the similarity between the coming of the Spirit and the return of Christ, both of whom were to pass unseen by the eyes of the world and be seen by the disciples because of the life they possessed (xiv. 17, 19.)

The new psychology of the disciples was marked by peace and joy. When he left them, our Lord left his Apostles the gift of peace (xiv. 27); his return in the Resurrection was the beginning of an era of joy that was to be unending. (xvi. 22.)

"That day" a new sort of prayer came into existence, a prayer in the name of Christ: "In that day you shall ask in my name." (xvi. 26.) Up till then the disciples had not asked for anything in Christ's name. (xvi. 24.) To pray thus did not mean simply to put forward his name, declare oneself his disciple, and refer to his merits in the fashion of the Jews, who reminded God of the Patriarchs and his friendship for them. This was a completely new sort of prayer, and the context in which Christ spoke of it raises us far above the formulae of the past, for prayer in the name of Christ could be addressed to Christ personally (xiv. 14), and even when addressed to the Father, it was heard by Christ (xiv. 13) as well as the Father. (xvi. 26-7.)

The name indicates the person. Therefore, and from the context, with the close presence it speaks of, the method here recommended approximates to a prayer "in Christ", which fits in with the teaching of St. Paul. (Tillmann, Huby.) Our Lord paraphrased the formula himself when he gave the disciples the same promise that they would be heard as long as they remained in him and his words remained in them. (xv. 7.) Prayer in the name of Christ sprang from an intimate communion with him, from those depths of the soul in which he lived in them. That is why this prayer could only come into existence "in that day". The living union had first to be established and the Apostles to become conscious of it.

Every prayer spoken in the risen Christ, the house of prayer for the new people (ii. 19), would be heard by God far more surely than any said in the Temple of old[11]; for prayers said in this dwelling-place of the Spirit were valid, "the hour being come when all true adorers would adore the Father in spirit and in truth". (iv. 24.)[12]

This prayer, then, was to be efficacious by its very excellence. But there were other reasons too: since Christ had returned to the

[11] After reading the discourse at the Last Supper, given so shortly before the inauguration of the new temple, the body of Christ, it is moving to read Solomon's prayer at the dedication of the other temple, beseeching that all who were to pray in that place where God's name dwelt, should be heard (1 Kings viii 27-53.)

[12] St. Paul (Eph ii 18) re-echoes Christ's words; by the Son in the Spirit—this is the proper way to pray in the new dispensation.

Father, the prayer would come to him as well; he would intervene and grant whatever the faithful wanted in him, for power to do so would be given to him: "He that believeth in me, the works that I do, he also shall do; and greater than these shall he do; because I go to the Father. And whatsoever you shall ask the Father in my name, that will I do." (xIV. 12–13.) Once they had realized that Christ and his power were thus present in the Father, the disciples would address their requests to their Master himself: "If you shall ask me anything in my name, that will I do." (xiv. 14.) A wholly new prayer, this—said in Christ and addressed to Christ in the Father. Our Lord could not shut his ears to this prayer said within himself, for he would be making a break in his own being did he not hear the longing breathed out from within it.

Events confirmed what had been foretold, as Easter Day inaugurated a new knowledge and a previously undreamt-of relationship with Christ was established.

The first effect of the Resurrection which the disciple recognized in his own mind, was faith: "He saw and believed." (xx. 8.) It was the fact of the Resurrection that he was believing, but this new knowledge was an essential contribution to the faith he had had before· "He believed."

"Do not touch me," said Christ to the Magdalen on Easter morning, "for I am not yet ascended to my Father." (xx. 17.) "A mysterious saying"[13] which exegetes, St. Augustine in particular, have discussed with the most passionate curiosity.[14] When she recognized our Lord, Mary Magdalen must have clung to him with all the violence of her love. Christ had once commended this gesture by the sinner and by Mary of Bethany; now he cut short this evidence of love. He was not yet wholly ascended; he appeared in so purely human a form that Mary at first mistook his identity. Yet there had been an essential change, and the contacts of the past were no longer possible. The intimacy and familiarity of love must wait for the day when our Lord should no longer appear in earthly form, when Mary could no longer put her arms round him, but would grasp him in the embrace of faith. His death and resurrection

[13] St Cyril of Alexandria, *In Jo.*, xx, 17, *P G.*, lxxiv, 692
[14] *Serm.*, ccxlii–ccxlvi, *P.L*, xxxviii, 1143–55; *In Jo Tract.*, cxxi, *P.L*, xxxv, 1957.

had laid in Christ the foundations of a new relationship. Once he had ascended, the Magdalen might hold him in her embrace.[15]

Here, for the first time in John's gospel, our Lord called the disciples his brethren, children of his Father. He made an intimate bond between them, brought them into the family of his Father: "Go to my brethren, and say to them: I ascend to my Father and your Father, to my God and your God." (xx. 17.)[16]

On his return, Christ freely gave the peace he had promised. "Peace be to you" was his greeting, every time he came to his disciples. (xx. 19, 26; Luke xxiv. 36.)

On the octave day of the Resurrection, Thomas, the doubter, uttered a profession of faith so complete and so spontaneous, that it exceeded all those made before Christ's death.[17] No-one had as yet given Christ the actual title of God. But, as with Mary Magdalen, Christ urged his disciple towards a more spiritual sentiment, to a faith going further than the experience of sense: "Because thou hast seen me, thou hast believed. Blessed are they who have not seen and have believed." Once again we see John as supremely spiritual, in spite of his insistence on the bodily reality of Christ. The bonds of our relationship with Christ must be fixed far above our senses.

The "coming" of the Incarnation, then, has not been ended by Christ's return to the Father, but completed: "I go away and I

[15] In John vi. 62–4, Christ also referred his hearers to the Ascension to indicate that the union the faithful were to have with his flesh would be spiritual This is the exegesis of Theodore of Mopsuestia; cf. R Devreesse, *Essai sur Théodore de Mopsueste*, Vatican City, 1948, pp. 415ff.; St. John Chrysostom, *In Jo. Hom*, lxxxvi, 2, *P.G*, lix, 469; St Cyril of Alexandria, *In Jo.*, xx, 17, *P.G.*, lxxiv, 692, 696; St. Leo the Great, *Sermo II de Ascensione*, *P.L.*, liv, 399. J J. Olier puts it very well: "To understand this passage aright, we must remember that our Lord was present to St Magdalen in a human and corporeal form; and he makes clear to her that he was deferring intimate union till the time.. when he should be in his spiritual state." (*Lettres*, pp 481–4, quoted by H. Bremond, *A Literary History of Religious Thought in France*, vol. iii, pp. 433–4) Among modern writers, cf Lagrange, F. Tillmann; F. Prat, *Jésus-Christ*, 5th ed., vol. II, Paris, 1933, p 436; P. Benoit, "L'Ascension", *R.B.*, lvi, 1949, 183.

[16] Matt xxviii. 10 records the same words in the same context. But our Lord had called the disciples his brethren earlier, in Matt. xii. 46–50. It seems, however, as though the word did not then have the fullness of meaning it came to have; cf. F. M Catherinet, "Note sur un verset de l'évangile de saint Jean xx, 17", *Memorial J. Chaîne*, Lyons, 1950, pp 51–9

[17] "St Thomas' confession goes further than even that of St Peter." (F Prat, *op cit*, p. 448.)

come unto you." (xiv. 28.)[18] From now on the Lord was to radiate his light-giving life, and himself penetrate into souls, the Incarnation was spreading out to the disciples. "As the Father hath sent me, I also send you." (xx. 21.)

3. THE NEW LIFE IN ST. PAUL

1. THE NATURE OF THAT LIFE

In St Paul, the life of the Church is characterized by the double sphere in which it develops: "in Christ" and "in the Spirit", and by its association with the destiny of Christ ("with Christ").

(a) In Christ

(a) We realize that the phrase "in Christ" has a great variety of meanings. It may indicate no more than "a relation of some sort between the faithful and the person of Christ", and can often be replaced by the adjective "Christian".[19] "The Churches of Thessalonica which are in God the Father and in the Lord Jesus Christ" (1 Thess. i. 1) means simply the Christian Churches. (Cf. Gal. 1. 22.) Elsewhere, the sense of the phrase becomes deeper and more mystical; it indicates a vital relationship formed between the believer and the person of our Lord. The Church is in Christ; this means that there is an interpenetration of life between the Church and Christ.

A. Deissman[20] favours the idea that the Christ in St. Paul's mind takes a certain spatial form, like a sort of outspread power which the Christian enters locally. Certainly the preposition "in" suggests the notion of a presence, but it is not a local one. There are cases where any visual representation of our presence in Christ is impossible[21]; where the reality is quite outside the spatial order and beyond the reach of imagination. The notion of a "fluid Christ", based on a false exegesis of "the Lord who is a spirit" (2 Cor. iii. 17) is one of the most unpardonable of all the errors made in interpreting St. Paul. We need not dwell on it.

[18] Similarly, in xvi. 16-17, the two themes of the return to the Father and the return to the disciples are linked.
[19] L. Cerfaux, *Theology*, p. 213.
[20] *Die neutestamentliche Formel in Christo Jesu*, Marburg, 1892.
[21] How, for instance, could we imagine a spatial "sitting together in Christ"? (Eph. ii. 6)

The phrase "in Christ" suggests the image of a sphere of life; but while we must strip it of any spatial ideas, we must not simply take it to mean a sphere of influence Christ has. It is a sphere of existence in which man's whole being is taken up by a new principle, created afresh (Eph. ii. 10) to make a "new creature" (2 Cor. v. 17; Gal. vi. 15), a kind of man that has not existed before (Eph. ii. 15; iv. 24). Man enters it not by being as it were poured into a mould, but by a change transforming him into "one man, one body" (Eph. ii. 15–16)—into the bodily Christ. "As many of you as have been baptized in Christ, have put on Christ", wrote St. Paul to indicate this. (Gal. iii. 27.) The metaphor is one borrowed from the speech of the time, meaning that one enters into the dispositions of someone else, and the earlier context does not strictly demand any more literal interpretation. We are the children of God because we have put on Christ. But the conclusion Paul draws from this entry into Christ who is henceforward to clothe us, shows that in his mind our union with Christ becomes an actual identification of being. "There is now neither Jew nor Greek ... neither male nor female. For you are all one in Christ Jesus." (Gal. iii. 28; cf. Rom. xii. 5.) His meaning is clearly this: "You are one among yourselves, and one with him, and that one is himself."[22] Christ has taken us up into himself; our presence in him is an identification in the order of being.[23]

There are several other cases where the phrase lets us suppose, and indeed suggests, a community of being at the root of this relationship. Life in Christ (Rom. vi. 11), the riches to be gained there (1 Cor. 1. 5), our sitting in heaven in Christ (Eph. ii. 6)—all these

---

[22] L. Malevez, "L'Église, corps du Christ", *Rech. Sc Rel.*, 1944, p. 63 Gal. iii 27 is thus related to 2 Cor v. 4, which refers to the body of glory we put on.

[23] Up till now we have scarcely spoken of more than a mystical union. Several authors find this too weak a term and have justifiably used the word "identity": F. Prat, *The Theology of St. Paul*, vol. ii, pp. 19–10; L. Cerfaux, *Theology*, p 343; L. Malevez, "L'Église, corps du Christ", p. 63, and "Quelques enseignements de l'Encyclique Mystici Corporis Christi", *Nouv. Rev. Théol.*, lxvii, 1945, 390; J. Huby, *Mystiques paulinienne et johannique*, Paris, 1946, p. 27, C Spicq speaks of "community of being and of life", *La Sainte Bible, Épîtres aux Corinthiens*, Paris, 1949, p 211; P. Benoit, in "Mélanges Jules Lebreton", *Rech. Sc. Rel.*, xxxix, 1950, 272, says: "Union with the risen Christ takes place in the order of being." These are bold formulae; they would be excessive did we not allow them an enormous flexibility. But they correspond better than any to the language of St. Paul.

seem to be rooted in an existence in Christ out of which the
Christian life and its manifestations grow· "You are in Christ"[24]—
this is the fundamental thing—"who is made unto us wisdom
through God, and justice and sanctification and redemption"—
these are the consequences that flow from it. (1 Cor. i. 30.) "There
is now therefore no condemnation to them that are in Christ Jesus."
(Rom. viii. 1.) And again, "If then any be in Christ, he is a new
creature." (2 Cor. v. 17.)

The first result of this fundamental union is a sharing of life: "So
do you also reckon that you are alive unto God in Christ Jesus."
(Rom. vi. 11) "The grace of God is life everlasting in Christ Jesus
our Lord." (Rom. vi. 23; cf. viii. 2.) The life of the bodily Christ
informs the multitude that are in him. Indeed we generally explain
our identification with Christ by just this transfusion of the one
life. But it seems that it is more radical than this—we are already
in Christ—it goes so far as to identify us with Christ in the order of
being, so that he becomes our life.

(b) Sometimes St. Paul reverses the formula. Instead of our existing in Christ, he sees Christ as present in us: he dwells in our
hearts. (Eph. iii. 17.) "Know you not that Christ Jesus is in you?"
(2 Cor. xiii. 5.) Because of our presence in the Lord, Paul has denied
all differences of race and declared the faithful to be one among
themselves and with Christ. Christ's presence in us effects the same
unity: "There is now neither Greek nor Jew ... But Christ is all,
and in all" (Col. iii. 11); it is rather that Christ exists in us than
that he is merely present, for he is born in us and grows in our
substance "until Christ be formed in [us]". (Gal. iv. 19) "Christ
in us" is simply another way of expressing the community of being
between Christ and those who believe in him.

Here, as in the framework of the formula "in Christ", identification with our Saviour brings with it a communication of life. "I live
now not I, but Christ liveth in me." (Gal. ii. 20.) Our life is not
added to Christ's—it is his to such a point that he is the subject of
it. We can gauge how far St. Paul extends Christ's possession of us
by the fact that he attributes our life to him, not because of our
Lord's supernatural universal causality, but because he is the subject of it: "I live now not I, but Christ liveth in me " "Strange

[24] Various exegetes here follow the Greek Fathers (cf. Allo and the authors
he quotes) in giving the verb "to be" here the sense of "to exist". Allo translates, "You exist in Christ."

though such a teaching may seem, hard though it may appear to reconcile it with the absolute distinctness of Christ and of the Christian, St. Paul does, without doubt, say, "It is Christ who lives in me."[25] Christ superimposes his own personality on ours; our Christian being and our life belong to him before belonging to us, he "identifies our new self with him".[26]

As A. Wikenhauser has pointed out,[27] we find Christ and the believer each having attributed to them actions, feelings, modes of being, which, outside this identification, are strictly incommunicable. The Apostle is animated with a charity which is personal to Christ. "The charity of Christ presseth us" (2 Cor. v. 14)—not the love the Apostle bears for Christ, but Christ's own love. The personal sufferings of our Lord are undergone by the believer, and the apostolic sufferings of Paul are those of our Lord. (2 Cor. i. 5; iv. 10; Phil. iii. 10; Col. i. 24; Gal. vi. 17.) His personal death and resurrection are our death and our resurrection.

In the Apostle's mind, the union between husband and wife not only illustrates the love between Christ and the faithful but also reflects the impress of Christ's personality upon the Church. St. Paul, indeed, stresses the lines of the image rather surprisingly, so taken up is he with the reality it expresses. According to him, the husband subordinates the wife in a subordination of being as well as of will to such an extent that his bride becomes his body and, in loving his wife, the husband is simply loving his own person.

"This is a great sacrament." It is a mystery of two persons in which one takes to himself the other so as to be identified with him in his very being, and to become the subject of attribution in the life that has become common to them both. And yet there is no lowering of the personal barriers between Christ and the members of the Church. Paul remains himself; the life animating him is lived by him—not only the life of his flesh (that "if I live now in the flesh" of Gal. ii. 20) but also the life of his Christian being. Though the idea of Christ living in us appears to dispossess the Apostle— "I live now not I, but Christ liveth in me"—the complementary idea of life in Christ in turn attributes to the faithful the Christ-life they live: "You live unto God in Christ Jesus." (Rom. vi. 11.) Christ is

[25] L. Malevez, "L'Église corps du Christ", p. 64
[26] Malevez, "L'Église", p 62
[27] *Die Christusmystik des hl. Paulus*, Freiburg-i.-B., 1956, pp 16–18, 108ff.

the subject of Christian existence, but the believer never ceases to be himself.[28]

What we must remember is that the faithful are in a community of being and life with Christ in glory, that they are in a mysterious way taken up into him. Yet the identification with Christ does not extend to Christ's whole being. We can discover the precise extent of the phrase "in Christ" by what we know of the Church's relationship to the body of our Lord. It is never said of the Church that she is Christ; she is "his body, the fullness [*pleroma*] of him who fills all things whatsoever". (Eph. i. 23, Osty's rendering.)

The elements in this definition, which are meant to complement each other, are both deeply mysterious. What does it mean to say that the Church is Christ's body, his *pleroma*?

Since the studies of the *pleroma* which have been made recently,[29] we need no longer hesitate to recognize that both in the word and in the idea it expresses the Apostle was borrowing from Stoicism. In the philosophy of the Stoa as popularized, it indicated the universe as a whole, filled and animated by the divine principle. Not long ago there was argument as to whether the *pleroma* should be interpreted as having an active or a passive sense. For those who upheld the former,[30] the Church was to fulfil Christ, to be an active fullness, giving him his final perfection, the consecration of his being and his glory.[31]

[28] Christ's invasion of the believer takes away nothing of his personality but an imperfection. To be closed in upon itself is an imperfection of the human person; the divine persons are opened out one to another. Man becomes open to the person of Christ because the Spirit raises him to the divine mode of living

[29] Particularly J. Dupont, *Gnosis*, Louvain, 1949, pp. 453–76

[30] Cf. the commentaries of Armitage Robinson, T. K. Abbott, P. Ewald, J M Vosté, A Médebielle, F Prat, *Theology*, vol ii, pp. 283-4, P. Benoit, "L'Horizon paulinien de l'épître aux Ephésiens", *R.B.*, xlvi, 1937, 354, "complement", p 514, *n.* 2, "completion"; J. Bonsirven, *L'Évangile de Paul*, Paris, 1948, pp. 228ff.

[31] To attribute so important a role to the Church appears from the first as incompatible with Pauline thought. But if the *pleroma* is to be given an active sense, then the Church must be allowed this tremendous function; it would not be enough to say that the Church is complementary to Christ, for a complement may be an extra, whereas the *pleroma* indicates fullness, complete perfection.

Even limiting ourselves to St. Paul's usage, the fullness of God (Eph iii. 19; Col. ii 9), the fullness of time (Gal. iv 4; Eph. i. 10), the fullness of the nations (Rom xi. 25), the fullness of the Law fulfilled in love (Rom xiii. 10), signify God, time, the nations as a whole, the Law in its full realization; they do not mean the completion of all these things

For the others[32] it did not add anything to our Lord, but simply received from him, and contained the fullness of his power and his redemptive riches

In the context of Stoic literature from which it was drawn, the word *pleroma* always designated a divinely fulfilled reality.[33] And the evidence from the rest of Pauline theology is in any case quite sufficient to cut short the debate in favour of the "passive" interpretation. The Church does not claim to give her head any sort of supreme fulfilment[34]; she is the body and the bride, the body filled with the riches of Christ, the bride wholly existing to contain her Lord who acts in her and through her.[35]

If the Church were Christ's *pleroma* in the active sense of the word, she would give Christ his perfection, which would be a contradiction of the whole of Paul's teaching.

[32] Cf. particularly J. B Lightfoot, *Epistles to the Colossians and to Philemon*, London, 1892, pp 255–77; the commentaries of J Knabenbauer, M. Meinertz, J Huby, C. Masson, L Cerfaux (*The Church*, p. 323; *Christ*, pp. 426–9); P. Benoit, "Corps, tête et plérôme dans les épîtres de la captivité", *R B*, 63 (1956), 7–22, A. Feuillet, "L'Eglise plérôme du Christ d'après Eph. i, 23", *Nouv. Rev Théol*, lxxviii (1956), 449–59

[33] Cf J Dupont, *Gnosis*, p. 468

[34] To support the idea of a Church that completes Christ, such authors as Armitage Robinson, T K Abbott, and even St John Chrysostom, put forward the comparison of Christ as head and the Church as body. The head is incomplete, and the body completes it. The body completing the head is a strange comparison, to say the least. Christ, according to Ephesians and Colossians, is the whole Church as well as being the head Cf. K L Schmidt, *Th. W. N.T.*, vol. iii, p 512; E Percy, *Der Leib Christi in den paulinischen Homologoumena und Antilegomena*, Lund, 1942, p. 50 "If he is the head, it is because he is the *pleroma*" (Col. 1. 18), writes Y. Congar (*Esquisses du mystère de l'Église*, p 22); because he is the total principle and the fullness.

[35] The discussion is one of capital importance and is indeed a cross-roads in Pauline theology. Though it seems to me quite clear that it must be settled in favour of the passive interpretation (which I should prefer to call "receptive"), it may be as well to reiterate it.

Ephesians and Colossians, which make up the context of the definition, look upon Christ's activity as head as a movement whereby the divine life is poured out upon the Church: "In him dwelleth all the fullness of the godhead corporeally, and you are filled in him." (Col. ii 9–10.) The totality of divine life, permanently in the body of Christ, passes into the Church; it is the Church which is filled, not the other way round Christ is all in all. (Col iii 11; Eph. iv 10.) The Church yearns for this total realization of Christ in her, "for the building up of the body of Christ, until we all meet into the unity of faith, and of the knowledge of the Son of God, unto a perfect man, whose maturity is proportioned to the fullness of Christ." (Eph. iv 12–13.) The building up of the body of Christ consists in a steady growth until the measure of Christ is attained; then the Church will contain Christ in his fullness It is she who will reach the stature of the perfect man. The formulae make no suggestion that Christ is in any way fulfilled by the

Since the totality of the riches of God has become concentrated in Christ, in his risen body, for the salvation and consummation of the world (Col. i. 18–20; ii. 9–10), the Church in her turn is divinely filled, for she is the body of the risen Christ and in her this salvation and consummation are worked out.

The definition of the Church as the body of Christ thus takes into account the presence of Christ's riches in her. It also determines the extent to which the Church is identified with Christ, for the Apostle in fact limits to the Lord's body this identification which he elsewhere seems to extend to the whole Christ.

It is easy to see the reason for this limitation. For one thing, in the basically Semitic thought of St. Paul, the body represents the totality of the human complexus; and for another, our identification with Christ does not take place in the sublimity of the Godhead, but in that bodily humanity in which he underwent death and resurrection and in which he received the glories of salvation. In it, he took to himself our sinful condition and was justified in the Spirit (1 Tim. iii. 16); henceforward he takes us to himself, who has become for us justice and redemption (1 Cor. i. 30), and in us he lives the identical life of his bodily humanity. Thus we can understand why the Apostle identifies us with Christ and to what extent: to the same extent as the bodily humanity of our Lord is identified with our Lord himself without being equal to him. The Church is Christ; she does not realize his complete identity, but she is his body,[36] she is identified with his bodily humanity.

(b) In the Spirit

The formulae we have studied so far reveal only one aspect of the Church's life. There are parallel texts which establish between the Church and the Spirit a relationship similar to that which unites the Church to Christ. It is natural that our life in the glorified Christ should be seen in the framework of the action of the Spirit, since Christ in his glory lives by the Spirit. The whole work of justification, and all the manifestations of the divine life, take place at once "in Christ" and "in the Spirit".

addition of the Church, they indicate a spreading out over the Church of Christ's riches of being and of life, and a growing of the Church in her Saviour until there is total assimilation.

[36] Cf L Malevez, "L'Église corps du Christ", *Rech. Sc. Rel* , 1944, p. 64, n. 1

The Fathers were early struck by the apparent synonymity of the two phrases.[37] Some modern writers have taken them to mean the same thing, in fact. But though the two phrases are, in many cases, interchangeable, there are subtle nuances to distinguish them, which tell us about the difference between our relationship with Christ and with his Spirit.

(a) The formula "the Spirit in us" is parallel with "Christ in us"; Christ and the Spirit dwell in our hearts. Paul asks "that Christ may dwell by faith in your hearts" (Eph. iii. 17); and he says that "God hath sent the Spirit of his Son into your hearts". (Gal. iv. 6; Rom. v. 5; viii. 9, 11; 2 Cor. i. 22.)

But each of our guests is established in us in his own fashion: "Know you not that your body is the temple of God and that the Spirit of God dwelleth in you?" (1 Cor. iii. 16.) Our body is a sacred dwelling of God because the Spirit lives in it. The Apostle says this even more clearly: "Know you not that your body is the temple of the Holy Ghost?" (1 Cor. vi. 19.) No ear attuned to the Epistles could admit of anyone's saying that Christ dwells in us as in a temple. As long as we consider him in his bodily humanity, Christ our head is not present in us in the manner of a divine person; the image of indwelling is better suited to the presence of the Spirit. St Paul uses it only once to characterize Christ's presence in us, and that in a context which makes this indwelling a presence of identification, for the faith which, according to Eph. iii. 17, makes Christ dwell in our hearts, is the same faith that grafts us into his body and identifies us with him. (Gal. iii. 26–8.)

Whereas the Spirit "is given to us", and we possess him as a living pledge, as the root that will grow into the fullness of life,[38] we *are* Christ. The latter is with us by identification, by assimilation to his divinized humanity; we are not his temple, but his body—Christ himself. Paul chooses his words with care: we have the Spirit, but we belong to Christ (Rom. viii. 9).

Whereas our bodies are the temple of the Spirit, they are the members of Christ. (1 Cor. vi. 15, 19.) Our Lord is present to the temple as we are—as going with us to make up the fabric of it. He himself is the whole temple (cf. John ii. 19), its foundation stone (1 Cor. iii 11) and corner-stone. (Eph. ii. 20.) The Holy Spirit

---

[37] St. Cyril of Alexandria, *In Jo.*, i, ix, *P G*, lxxiv, 261.

[38] Rom v 5; viii 9, 11, 23; 1 Cor ii 12, vii 40; 2 Cor. i 22; iv 13; v. 5; Gal iii 2; iv 6; Eph 1 17, 1 Thess iv. 8.

dwells simultaneously in Christ and in us (Rom. viii. 11) who are the body of Christ.[39]

(b) There are similar nuances to distinguish the complementary formulae, "in Christ" and "in the Spirit", which prevent their being arbitrarily interchangeable.

In the doctrinal context of this subject, the word *pneuma* may indicate either the person of the Spirit, or a communication of the Spirit—in other words sanctifying grace. This latter signification lends itself to a great many different shadings, since "the spirit" may indicate the principle of supernatural life, of grace; or a sphere and way of life as opposed to carnal life; or, again, the spirit of man divinized by grace. But if we take the phrase "in the Spirit" to mean the person of the Spirit, and "in Christ" to mark our identification with Christ, then the two cannot possibly be interchanged. We are identified with Christ alone, not with the Holy Ghost When God predestines us, chooses us, and loves us (Rom. viii. 39; Eph. i. 3–12), it is "in Christ", as Père Prat points out,[40] not "in the Spirit". God has heaped up for us a wealth of graces because he has seen us in his Son, identified with him. St. Paul does not suggest any identification with the Spirit.[41]

The presence of the Holy Spirit acting within us is not seeking

[39] These statements have nothing in common with the opinion condemned in the encyclical *Mediator Dei* (*A.A.S.*, 1947, p 393), that the bodily Christ is present in the believer by indwelling I speak of the presence of the bodily Christ in the same way as Paul does, a presence by identification; this is a very real and intimate presence, but quite different in kind to the indwelling of the Spirit The Eucharist makes this distinction clear. By Communion, the body of Christ is present in the believer as in a physical place, as well as in an identifying and living union The first presence is fleeting, and is simply a means, the second, the end to which the first is the means, persists.

[40] *Theology*, vol. ii, p 394

[41] Père Malevez, "L'Église corps du Christ", p. 70, does not think the idea of an identification with the Spirit is foreign to St. Paul's mind As proof of this he puts forward 1 Cor. vi. 17. But he rightly adds: " . is the Spirit named here really the Spirit of God? Is it not rather the spirit of the man Jesus, or the spiritualized man, the risen Christ? It seems as though it is not an identification with the Holy Spirit that is meant here, but one with the Christ of glory." He also quotes, with reservations, in favour of identification, the prayer that the Spirit cries out in our hearts (Rom. viii. 15, 26; Gal. iv. 6) The Spirit is the subject of one of our actions and thus we are integrated into his personality. This seems very tenuous evidence beside the texts which explicitly identify us with Christ. In any case, the Spirit's prayer in us can be explained in other ways just as well as by identification with him. And further, what is the testimony that the Spirit gives in our hearts? He does not tell us that we are the Spirit of God, but "that we are the sons of God", that we are assimilated to Christ

to take possession of our humanity; St. Paul never suggests a "body" of the Holy Ghost. The work he dwells in us to perform is an inward work of incarnation, but it is on Christ's behalf, integrating and assimilating us into him.[42]

Indeed, the presence of Christ's being in us is the effect of the Spirit· "You are not in the flesh but the Spirit, if so be that the Spirit of God dwell in you. Now if any man have not the Spirit of Christ, he is none of his [Christ's]. And if Christ be in you . . ." (Rom. viii. 9–10.)[43] To St. Paul, the presence of the Spirit means belonging to Christ and having Christ present.[44] Whoever possesses the Spirit is of Christ and Christ dwells in him. Hence the Holy Spirit can give us the assurance that we are true children of God (Rom. viii 16), united as we are to the Son of God. The water of baptism, a symbol of the messianic giving of the Spirit, consecrates us to the body of our Saviour: "In one Spirit were we all baptized into one body." (1 Cor. xii. 13.) The Spirit is the agent (ἐν), Christ the object of the action (εἰς). He is a Spirit who incorporates us. Clearly, then, "no man, speaking by the Spirit of God, saith Anathema to Jesus" (1 Cor. xii. 3), for by the Spirit of God, Christ is in us.

The life which grows up from the basis of our identity with Christ proclaims a twofold origin: it comes from Christ, and it comes from the Spirit It could not claim to belong to Christ without at the same time originating from the Spirit, for it is the life of Christ raised up in the Spirit. We live in Christ, Christ himself lives in us (Gal. ii. 20), and we live by the Spirit (Gal. v. 25), the principle of new life. (Cf. 2 Cor. iii. 6.) Yet in spite of its duality of origin, our Christian life does not belong in an equal sense to Christ and to the Spirit. It springs from the Holy Spirit, but it is lived personally

[42] The Spirit is love and communication. He plays a disinterested part, working not for his own benefit; he is, as it were, the humility of God. "I should say without hesitation that the outstanding mark of the Spirit is his perfect secrecy, his complete humility." (T. Preiss, "Le Témoignage intérieur du Saint-Esprit", *Cahiers théol. de l'Act. Prot*, no. 13, Neuchâtel, 1946, p. 26)

[43] Eph iii 16–17 is probably an expression of this same presence of Christ in us through the power of the Spirit. F. Prat (*Theology*, vol ii, p. 433) comments: "Paul asks the *Father* to send *his Spirit*, that Christ may dwell in our hearts."

[44] This does not mean that Christ's presence in us is the same thing as the presence of his Spirit. One is present through the other, because there is a mutual causality, but each is truly present, each in his own fashion; the bodily Christ, by identification—the Spirit, by indwelling

by Christ (Gal. ii. 20); the Spirit is its cause (we live πνεύματι in Gal. v. 25, ἐκ δυνάμεως in 2 Cor. xiii. 4); Christ is its subject. The life-giving communication of the Spirit and the personal life of Christ, it becomes our own life when the Spirit incorporates us into the glorified humanity of our Lord.

Christ is not, however, merely a passive power, a foundation stone on which the Spirit builds. He takes an active part in the construction. Clearly St. Paul sees the mission of the person of the Spirit, whose presence in us is the root of life, as being the Father's concern; it is he who sends the Spirit who makes us his sons, just as it is he who raises up Christ and the faithful. Yet the Spirit is sent "through Jesus" (Tit. iii. 6), and is the Spirit of Christ. The sending of the personal Spirit indeed presupposes that we have first been integrated into the Son—at least if the most natural rendering of Gal. iv. 6 is also the right one: "Because you are sons, God hath sent the Spirit of his Son into your hearts "[45]

Furthermore, the grace which sanctifies us and which is a communication of the life of the Spirit is given to us by Christ at the same time as by the Spirit. Christ's instrumentality, expressed by the preposition διά, is frequently affirmed (cf. Rom. v. 17–21); Christ is the quickening spirit (1 Cor. xv. 45) who engenders the life of the spirit. The single work of our sanctification can be attributed to both principles, but each supplies a different element in their co-operation: Christ himself first receives the divine life and the power to transmit it, and he works by the power of the Spirit, in which he has been raised from the dead.

The Spirit and the life of Christ are transfused into us as we come in contact with the bodily Christ. Just as "he who is joined to a harlot is made one body with her . . . he who is joined to the Lord is one spirit with him" (1 Cor. vi. 16–17), becomes one thing with him in a single body and in the participation of his Spirit. It is necessary that we have this existential contact, this identification with Christ's body filled with the Spirit; this is clear from the Eucharist, whose "spiritual" effectiveness is due to the union it establishes between Christ's body and ourselves.

Here St. Paul appears to contradict himself. The Spirit is the

[45] However, a good many authors prefer: "The proof that you are sons is that God hath sent. ." Though this may be a possible translation, it should not be retained simply because Rom. viii 14–15 makes the Spirit the principle of filiation There would be no contradiction in St Paul's making the sending of the Spirit come first in one place and the filiation in another.

principle of filiation (Rom. viii. 14–15); he makes a contact between us and Christ, identifying us with him. Yet elsewhere it is the filiation we already possess which seems to produce the presence of the Spirit in us (Gal. iv. 6), the Spirit is communicated to us in Christ and in our union with him. Theology has no fear of such antinomies, and generally they can be resolved easily, since two principles may change places as cause and effect when viewed from a different aspect.

The relations existing between the Spirit, Christ and the Church are immensely complex, because of the collaboration between Christ and the Spirit of God, and the dynamic way in which Christ is penetrated by the life of the Spirit. St. Paul sees them under different aspects, but does not trouble to show how they fit together. However we can, from a study of these relations, formulate this conclusion: the Spirit, who invaded the bodily humanity of Christ at Easter, is for mankind a force of incorporation into the Son of God; he effects our salvation by grafting our humanity into that of our risen Saviour.

(c) With Christ

The two phrases "in Christ" and "in the Spirit" show us that the Church is the body of the Christ of Easter. There is another phrase common to the Epistles which brings a dynamic element into our idea of the Church; it gives her a share not only in the *being* of the paschal Christ, but in the very action whereby he died and rose again.

At the root of everyone's life in Christ and in the Spirit there is to be found a death and resurrection "with Christ": "Buried with him in baptism, in whom also you are risen again ... God hath quickened you together with him." (Col. ii. 12–13.)

There are two groups of texts which embody the phrase "with Christ", each of which puts a sharing in the act of redemption at the origin of the new life, but each doing so in a different way.[46]

The first group, which does not need any special stress here, refers to baptism. (Rom. vi. 4–8; Eph. ii. 5–6; Col. ii. 12ff., 20.) The

---

[46] Here I am keeping to those texts which use the phrase for our union with Christ in this world. In Chapter IX I will consider those where the phrase is used to indicate our association with Christ in the next

moment the sacramental rite has taken place, we are brought into contact with Christ's death and resurrection.

The other group refers to a permanent participation in the act of redemption. After baptism, the contact with Christ's death is preserved, for instance through the sufferings the believer undergoes (Rom. viii. 17), at the moment of his own death (2 Tim. ii. 11), in the labours of the apostolate (2 Cor. iv. 10–12), and indeed, at every moment of life: "With Christ I am nailed [perfect tense, an act which continues] to the cross " (Gal. ii. 19.) Similarly, the believer has a permanent participation in the Resurrection. Rom. vi. 3–11 assumes that a contact with the Resurrection has been established by baptism (cf. verse 11), though it only affirms this communion explicitly for the future, a future which will culminate in the final resurrection of the body. But the ease with which Paul passes from the final resurrection to a resurrection which spreads out over the whole of the believer's life, presupposes that that entire life is subject to God's action in raising up Christ. St. Paul says it again in other terms: he lives divinely in a permanent crucifixion with Christ (Gal. ii. 19–20), day by day, though he is advancing towards death, he is renewed in the life of Christ (2 Cor. iv. 16); he experiences the power of the Resurrection in himself at the same time as "the fellowship of his sufferings" (Phil. iii. 10); he thus unceasingly benefits from God's vivifying action upon Christ.

The principle of all Christian existence is this constant participation in Christ's death and resurrection. By baptism the believer is brought into the mystery of redemption; there he remains, and will continue to enact his union with Christ in the death and glorification until the day when that union will become complete, when the believer will sleep the sleep of death with Christ (2 Tim. ii. 11) and rise with him on the Last Day (Rom. vi. 8). The Church does not appear as merely a static entity, identified with the being of Christ in glory: she is transformed into Christ in his redemptive act, in the death which brought him into that glory.

The phrase "with Christ" is generally understood to mean a communion in his death and resurrection, which is not merely a relationship of similarity, but a real participation in the acts themselves.[47]

[47] Cf F. Prat, *Theology*, vol. 1, p. 222; vol ii, p. 257; K. Mittring, *Heilswirklichkeit bei Paulus*, Gütersloh, 1929, p. 39; O. Schmitz, *Das Lebensgefühl des Paulus*, Munich, 1932, p. 39; W. T. Hahn, *Das Mitsterben und Mitaufer-*

This interpretation is clearly correct. It is said that God "hath quickened us together with Christ" (Col. ii. 13)—Christ and his faithful are objects of the one vivifying action; that he has made us sit together with Christ in heaven (Eph. ii. 6)—there is only one elevation into heaven, and that is Christ's; that the believer benefits from "the operation . . . which he wrought in Christ, raising him up" (Eph. i. 19–20), from "the power [which effected] his resurrection". (Phil. iii. 10.) When he declares that the believer "is baptized in [εἰς] the death of Christ" (Rom. vi. 3), he is affirming our communion with Christ in the act of his death.

To define the Church as the body of Christ is thus to define her incompletely: she is the body of Christ *redeeming us,* joined to our Saviour in one special moment of history, in the instant of the Redemption. She is the body of Christ in the act of his death and resurrection. The identification is dynamic as well as existential, for it is effected by participation in the same action in a shared being.

Two problems follow from this: how are we to explain how persons separated in time participate simultaneously in the same action? And how can the faithful become the subjects of actions which are so completely personal to Christ?

There are various possible solutions of the first problem.

(a) It is conceivable that there is a repetition of Christ's death and resurrection to make them present to the believer. According to many historians of religion, St. Paul's teaching was strongly influenced by the mystery religions. In those religions, they tell us, the believer sought his salvation by taking part in a symbolic drama which reproduced the death and resurrection of his god, Osiris, say, or Attis. This symbolic action was not simply a representation, it would have been a reproduction of the life story of the god, allowing his death and entry into a new life to be repeated both in himself and in the initiate.[48] Similarly, to St. Paul, baptism is a drama making Christ's death and triumph once again present.

In spite of their efforts, this theory is supported neither by the

stehen mit Christus bei Paulus, Gutersloh, 1937, pp 65–6, 93, 100; E Percy, *Der Leib Christi in den paulinischen Homologoumena und Antilegomena,* Lund, 1942, pp 25–6; R Schnackenburg, *Das Heilsgeschehen bei der Taufe nach dem Apostel Paulus,* Munich, 1950, p. 206.

[48] W Bousset, *Kyrios Christos,* 4th ed , Gottingen, 1935, p 138, says· "The fate of the god who succumbs and then triumphs becomes the pattern of the fate of the believer. What takes place here is not something that happens once for all, but something ever renewed."

Pauline text, nor by the evidence of secular documents. Its historical basis is more than problematic. These historians force the evidence, interpreting pagan rites in the light of Christian ideas.[49]

In any case, Paul's thought cuts clean across any real or supposed significance of the pagan rites. Whereas the story of the god is a vegetation myth, bound up with the cycle of the seasons and un-related to historical fact, our Lord's death and resurrection are definite events, part of human history. Christ died once and for all (Rom vi. 10), at the time of Pontius Pilate (1 Tim. vi. 13), and rose again the third day. (1 Cor. xv. 4.) The events are not repro-duced or made present in the rite of baptism; it is rather the believer who is caught up by the rite and brought into our Lord's death and resurrection. And the phrase "with Christ" does not admit of being turned round to read "Christ with us"[50]; our Lord does not die along with the believer. Furthermore, this theory does not explain how our communion in the redemptive act can be effected quite apart from any ritual of worship, in our own physical death and final resurrection, and throughout our life.

(b) If the rites of initiation do not make the events of our redemp-tion present now, do they then carry us back into the past, spiriting us into Christ's last breath and reawakening to life? This is the explanation current among certain Protestant theologians.[51] They speak of a mysterious contemporaneity with Christ, of synchroniza-tion with a past act of history; the agent and medium of this opera-tion is the Spirit, in whose timeless being all moments are one.

It is certainly the death and resurrection that took place under Pontius Pilate in which the believer shares, for Paul knows no others. But the synchronization of our historic acts with the historic acts of Christ belongs to the realm not merely of the mysterious,

---

[49] J Coppens, "Eucharistie", *D.B. Suppl*, col 1206, writes: "It is not certain that the saviour-gods of Graeco-Roman syncretism were gods who literally died and rose again; or that the mysteries were intended to be efficacious commemorations of their sufferings, or that the initiates attributed any salutary power to those sufferings or their commemorations." Cf. *id.*, "Baptême", *D.B. Suppl*, col. 917ff.; Lagrange, *Orphisme*, Paris, 1937, p. 199.

[50] Cf. W. T. Hahn, *Das Mitsterben*, pp. 97–100 The phrase "in Christ" does allow of such an inversion.

[51] Thus Kierkegaard and his "contemporaneity", quoted by O Cullmann, *Christ and Time*, p 146, n 2. This is W. T. Hahn's thesis According to Dom V Warnach ("Zum Problem der Mysteriengegenwart", *Liturg Leben*, v, 1939, 9–39), the liturgical drama takes us out of the present, and unites us to the work performed by Christ in the reign of Tiberius Cf E Dekkers, "La Liturgie, mystère chrétien", *La Maison-Dieu*, no xiv, p. 56.

but of the unintelligible. And, further, it completely contradicts the early Christians' idea of time, which envisaged no such moving backwards or any other breaking down of the barriers of time.[52] The Christian is firmly embedded in successive time, living and working out his salvation in it. The time elapsing between Christ's resurrection and his *parousia* is a time of salvation; redemption is not offered to man at a single point of time which he must attach himself to in the past; it is always at man's disposal in the glorified Christ present throughout history.[53]

(c) This gives us our solution. It is "in Christ", Paul tells us quite definitely (Col. ii. 11–13; Eph. ii. 5–6), by incorporation into the glorified Christ, that the believer comes to salvation through a sharing in the redemptive act; he is baptized into the death of Christ because he is baptized into Christ himself. (Rom. vi. 3.)[54]

We must hold firmly to both principles: the believer communicates in acts which were accomplished in the past, and he does so by being united to the Christ of the present. The Apostle does not explain how the two things fit together in his thought. He was not formulating his personal doctrinal system, but a divine reality whereby he himself lived, and he may well have had an intuitive understanding of how to synthesize a complexus of facts without working it out rationally. The theologian's job is to find the point in that reality at which the individual concepts which appear to be contradictory intersect.

The key to the solution is to be found in the life of Christ in glory, for it is there that the believer communicates in the redemptive act. In fact, the risen life assumes and maintains in our Lord the state of being dead to the flesh, and whoever is incorporated into Christ shares not only that life, but also that state; the actual fact of being incorporated thus constitutes a death and resurrection for the believer.

However, this is not a sufficient explanation. The texts go further: they demand a participation not merely in the state, but in the very act of death and resurrection. We saw earlier (cf. Chapter IV) that

---

[52] For instance, an anticipation of existence in the time of the *parousia*

[53] This is shown by O. Cullmann, *Christ and Time*, pp. 144–74

[54] Cf L. Malevez, "L'Église, corps du Christ", *Rech. Sc Rel*, 1944, p. 46; E Percy, *Der Leib Christi*, pp 25–9, truly says that communion with the death and resurrection of Christ presuppose incorporation into Christ, and that the two formulae, "in Christ" and "with Christ", are realized simultaneously

the Father's life-giving action upon Christ, as described by St. Paul, must be looked upon as continuing in a permanent actuality, though historically it belongs to the past. Whoever is united to Christ in life is caught up in him into the life-giving action of the Father.

And Christ's death is also permanently established in this everlasting glorification, for the latter is none other than the conclusion of that death, the act of dying achieving its goal; his death coincides with his glorification just as in any transformation the losing of the first status coincides with the gaining of the second. It becomes eternal in the eternal actuality of the glorification which consummates it.[55]

Thus the believer can communicate in the act of the death of Jesus at the same time as in his resurrection. He communicates in the death in as much as it is concluded in glory, in as much as it achieves renunciation of the flesh in glory. But in so far as it is a process of disintegration he does not communicate in it; for it is to this extent in the sphere of the flesh, belonging exclusively to the past, and therefore neither communicable nor worthy of being communicated.

This death and resurrection are not, as it were, prised out of the past in order to be transplanted into the present; neither does the believer leave his place in the present to be linked to the act of redemption in the past. This action, performed once in the past, remains fixed in an everlasting actuality in the Christ of glory, where all the ages with which he coexists flow together, accessible to all who seek redemption. When Christ was in the world it was subject to being measured by successive time; it still is—not in our Saviour, but in his body, the Church, until the Easter mystery be consummated in the *parousia*. The death and resurrection which took place once for all under Pontius Pilate continue to take place in the Church because we are incorporated into Christ who is forever fixed in the act of redeeming us.

The first question of how we can explain the simultaneous participation in a single action of persons separated by time is thus answered, the answer taking away nothing of the mystery. We already have the answer to the other problem of how the believer can be the subject of acts as personal to Christ as those of his death and resurrection. It is "in Christ" that we die and come to life

[55] Cf above, pp 148–50

again with him; there is a quasi-identification with him. This identification involves a communion in the two acts which form the permanent basis of the Saviour's new existence[56], it is the logical preliminary to our sharing in the redemptive act and the cause of it.[57]

If this being "with Christ" takes place "in Christ", it is also true that our identification with Christ is only effected through his death and resurrection.[58] It is in this moment of Christ's existence that the believer is united to his Lord, in baptism and throughout his life. We do not share in any of Christ's modes of being, actions or sentiments other than those proper to our Lord as Redeemer. his death, his life, his weakness, his strength, his love and his humility. And Christ is never the subject of any action or state of ours apart from our sharing in his death and his glorification.[59] The Church is not the body of Christ pure and simple, but the redeeming body of Christ, in the moment of his death and resurrection.

St. Ambrose had a superb realization of this when he wrote that the Church penetrates into the bridal chamber of Christ's body and is united to the King in the sleep of his death and the power of his resurrection.[60]

The Church therefore stays young throughout her existence. Living in Christ, in a perpetual communion with his death and resurrection, she grows no older than the day of Christ's birth in heaven and her own birth in Christ.

The Church, the *pleroma* receiving Christ, his body and his fulfilment, might seem to be simply submitting to the honour of being identified with Christ, simply the passive subject to be filled by

---

[56] This is sufficient proof that our being with Christ is not the result of a synchronization, but of an existential contact with Christ in his death and resurrection.

[57] Since our identification with the risen Christ is itself a result of the Father's action of raising Christ by the Spirit, we can see here, as so often, an interaction of causes: communion in the redemptive act presupposes an identification with Christ, and this in turn presupposes a communion in the Resurrection.

[58] Cf E. Percy, *Der Leib Christi*, p. 32

[59] Actions which have no part in the redemptive act may be performed "in Christ" (one can marry in the Lord, for instance—1 Cor vii. 39) But Christ is not the subject of such actions However, it is quite in line with Pauline theology to say that Christ is the principle of every Christian action in so far as it contributes to the death of the old man and life in God

[60] *In Ps CXVIII*, sermo i, 16, *P.L.*, xv, 1207

Christ with his own fullness.[61] But since her assimilation with Christ takes place through sharing in an action, in a totally free and completely personal engagement in the act of redemption, it is clear that the free collaboration of all who believe is essential to the nature of Christ's ecclesiastical body. The Church is not the body of Christ pure and simple; she is the body of Christ the Redeemer in the total gift of his love. In order that the body of Christ may be built up in us, each of us must reach the high point of free activity where we join our Saviour in his supreme perfection, in love. Thus Christian history is a channelling of human riches towards our Lord, who is yet also their source.

ii. THE CHARACTERISTICS OF THE CHURCH'S LIFE

The Church's life is rooted simultaneously in the Spirit and in Christ, and in a Christ who is both dead and risen. It bears the mark of this complex origin. Its characteristics are spiritual and flow out of Christ as source; they speak of Christ's life and of his death.

(a) Spiritual

The faithful are spiritual beings. Paul would be quite willing to give them the name "spirituals" if that was not a term reserved for charismatics and those who had come to a higher stage of perfection; he is saying the same thing when he says they are no longer in the flesh but in the Spirit. (Rom. viii. 9.)

(b) Christ-like

The "spiritual" characteristics of our life in Christ do not derive exclusively from the Spirit but belong equally to Christ, for the life of the Spirit is also that of Christ. (Rom. viii. 2.) Every spiritual gift is a Christ-gift; it is given in a way that is proper to the body of Christ: "The Spirit does not move indeterminately, but in the way in which he moves in raising up Christ."[62] The grace of the

[61] This would mean that her centuries of giving witness to the world, her charity and her patience, her heroism and her repentances add no further human richness to Christ.

[62] "The Spirit of God who raised up Christ, in other words, is both given us *by* God through the raising up of Christ, and as it were blowing and driving us *to* God—not indeterminately, but as he raised Christ from the dead." Cajetan, *Epistolae Pauli et aliorum Apostolorum, In Rom* vii, 11, Venice, 1531.

Spirit, springing from the body of Christ, is comparable to those springs which preserve the qualities of the earth from which they flow.

(c) A Life in Death

In Christ the spirit is a life in death, a life that rises from the depths of the Son's dignity because of his death to the flesh and which remains rooted in that death. The spirit comes to us as the life of Christ who has died,[63] as a power of life and of death; he gives life by bringing about the death without which he has no way of entry into man.

The believer lives in death to himself. St. Paul says of himself that he lives no longer (Gal. ii. 20), that he is permanently crucified (Gal. ii. 19), and that he is dead (Col. iii. 3), that he has received the circumcision of Christ and the Spirit, which is no mere surface excision, but a "despoiling of our body of the flesh". (Col. ii. 11; Phil. iii. 3.)

In our Lord, life consummates and consecrates death, and similarly in us death is brought about by a life. It is death by absorption into another's life. This death is not a separation of soul and body; it is the end of one life by being lifted into a higher life whose nature is incompatible with the first.

(d) The Death of the Flesh

Hence everything to which Christ has died is dead in us as well. To describe our death is merely repetitive; all has been said in Christ.

Christ has died to the flesh; the believer in turn is no longer in the flesh (Rom. viii. 9), he has become detached from Adam in whom all die (1 Cor. xv. 22), and he lives in the Spirit. The Holy Spirit and his life have done away with the rule of the flesh. (Rom. viii. 9.) The fact that Paul calls some believers carnal (1 Cor. iii. 3), and even says that we all still walk in the flesh (2 Cor. x. 3), is because our death is progressive It is absolute only in principle;

[63] Several authors (cf. L. Cerfaux, *The Church*, p 223) give this rendering of 2 Cor v 14–15: "One man has died for all, therefore all are dead. He died for all so that those who live might live no more by themselves but by him who has died and risen for them"

no one has yet wholly left the sphere of the flesh, and some are far too slow in quitting it. But the flesh is dead in principle, for the principle of the carnal state is sin.

The Apostle uses a truism of human justice to show that the believer is discharged as regards sin: "He that is dead is absolved from sin." And "we are dead with Christ". (Rom. vi. 7–8.) The imprint of sin was removed from Christ at the moment when death transferred him from the state of flesh into the existence of the Spirit. The same is true of the believer, when he joins himself to our Lord's body in the act of dying. But neither here nor in Christ are we concerned with a static death, with death in itself; this is a death which is life in God: "So do you reckon that you are dead to sin, but alive in Christ Jesus." (Rom. vi. 11.)

Man, in his state of flesh, is not only bogged down in sin, but imprisoned in a natural universe marked by sin and closed to grace. The carnal man is wholly one with this world where the Spirit cannot penetrate, and he is subject "to the elements of this world". He is ruled over by the stars as they dictate his seasons, and he is the prisoner of the thousand natural forces on which he is dependent. Thus the man not yet raised to familiarity with his Creator by the spirit of sonship thinks he owes homage to the beings who govern the cycles of nature, to the powers and principalities, and follows a religion of festival days, new moons, sabbaths and food laws. (Col. ii. 15–23.)

But the faithful "are dead with Christ from the elements of this world". (Col. ii. 20.) The world has been crucified in the flesh of Christ (Gal. vi. 14)[64] and all its obligations discharged there By being made part of the new creation in the risen Saviour, the faithful are set apart from this lower world and set free from its enslavements.

Specially mentioned as belonging to this natural worship are the observances of the Mosaic law, which were made known by the ministry of angels (Gal. iii. 19; Heb. ii. 2), the rulers of this world. St. Paul, the former Pharisee, was inspired to link the pagan religions and Judaism together in the one slavery. To him, observance of the Law was a carnal worship, a subjection to the

[64] The "world" here is not mankind at enmity with God, but the whole world of the flesh, the physical universe lacking Christ, and all the laws and maxims that went with it . Cf. Sasse, *Th. W. N T.*, vol iii, p. 894, A Oepke, *Der Brief des Paulus an die Galater*, Leipzig, 1937, p. 122

elements of this world; it stands in opposition to union with Christ, for it grapples man to the world of sin, which is closed to grace.

The believer becomes detached from the Law as well as from the world, by being united to the immolated body of Christ: "I am dead to the law ... I am crucified with Christ." (Gal. ii. 19.) With Christ I am dead to the Law, for I am crucified with him.

But Christ's death set him free only because it brought him into the liberty of the Spirit and an existence beyond the racial distinctions which placed him out of reach of the Jews' law. Had Christ not risen he would still be subject to sin and the Law. The believer has entered into this death which concludes in resurrection: "I am dead to the law that I may live to God. I am crucified with Christ, and I live ..." (Gal. ii. 19–20.) "You are become dead to the law by the body of Christ; that you may belong to another who is risen again from the dead." (Rom. vii. 4.) Death ends in life; the first is redemptive only because of the second: "The law of the spirit of life in Christ Jesus hath delivered you from the law of sin and of death." (Rom. viii. 2.)

(e) A New Race, neither Jew nor Greek

There were in the past "pagans in the flesh" and also those who had received "circumcision in the flesh". (Eph. ii. 11) Now that men are no longer "in the flesh" there is no such distinction, "There is neither Jew nor Greek; there is neither bond nor free; there is neither male nor female" (Gal. iii. 28; Col. iii. 11), for all have put on the one spiritual body of Christ and constitute but one man (Eph. ii. 15), the risen Christ.

A third race of men has come into being, "a new creature" (2 Cor v. 17), outside the categories of the circumcised and uncircumcised (Gal. vi. 15), the *"genus christianum"*, the Christian race. Baptism has not uprooted their own individuality, but has as it were opened them out from above to a single principle, the Spirit, who unites them and identifies them with the one body of Christ, in which every principle of division is abolished.

(f) Sonship of God

The new race is a race of children of God. Christ "was constituted Son of God in power ... because of the resurrection from the dead" (Rom. 1. 4); for him glorification was a full flowering of his sonship by the working of the Holy Spirit. The identification of the believer with the body of Christ extends to him this birth as son; from being a servant he becomes a child of God: "You are all the children of God . . . for as many of you as have been baptized in Christ have put on Christ." (Gal. iii 26–7.) The marks of past servitude are effaced and a likeness to the Father takes shape: "You have stripped off the old man . . . putting on the new . . . according to the image of the Creator." (Col. iii. 9–10.) The Father's action of raising is a generation; by it Christ becomes the firstborn of many brethren. (Rom. viii. 29.)

The Spirit is the principle of that birth: "Whosoever is led by the Spirit of God, he is the son of God", for it is the "spirit of filiation, whereby we cry: Abba, Father!" (Rom. viii. 14–15.)[65] Thus it is the Spirit who brings about the state of sonship in us. However, according to Gal. iv. 6, the filiation seems to precede and bring with it the reception of the Spirit: "Because you are sons, God hath sent the Spirit of his Son into your hearts." We can see why the filiation and the possession of the Spirit can each in turn be said to come first in the believer, for we are given the Spirit by being grafted into the Son, and we are grafted into the Son by the Spirit.[66]

If we are sons in Christ, we are co-heirs with him (Rom viii. 17), in possession of the divine riches bestowed on the risen Christ; but our possession of them remains imperfect as long as our death and our adoption remain incomplete. (Rom. viii. 17 and 23.)

(g) The Dominion of the Church

With Christ the Church is brought to the pinnacle whence all things are dominated; she shares with him his universal sovereignty.

---

[65] Verse 15 might be understood in this way: we have received a spirit proper to filiation (Lagrange, Cornely, O. Kuss) In this case, verse 15 does not affirm the Spirit's causality in the state of filiation However, the rendering "the Spirit of filiation" in fact seems preferable. (St. Thomas, J. Sickenberger, J. Huby)

[66] According to E Tobac, the opposition between the texts can be resolved in this way: Christ's death gives us the right to be adopted as sons, and the Spirit communicated by Christ in glory confers this adoption upon us (*Le Problème de la justification dans saint Paul*, Louvain, 1908, pp 204–5) But the filiation spoken of in Gal iv. 6 is real, not merely juridical The Cross has given all men the right to be adopted, but there are many to whom the Spirit is not given.

Not merely is she not subject to the world and its powers; she is
mistress of them, for Christ's exaltation affects her as well: "He has
raised him up from the dead and set him on his right hand in the
heavens, above all principality and power . . . And he hath subjected
all things under his feet, and he hath given him to be head, over
all things, of the Church which is his body." (Eph. i 20–23.) Having
subjected all things to Christ, God gave this Christ to the Church
which, having become his body, is in turn "made to sit in the
heavens" (Eph. ii. 6) above all things.[67] This sovereignty, of course,
is still imperfect, for the Resurrection is still in progress. There will
come a day when Christ has conquered all his enemies in fact, and
then the Church, identified with her head, the Lord of all, will judge
the world (1 Cor. vi. 2), all intelligent creatures, men and angels.
Paul lays special stress on this latter incredible jurisdiction· "Know
you not that we shall judge the angels?" (1 Cor. vi. 3.)[68] That the
Church is to be elevated even above the angels shows how real is her
identification with our Lord.

(h) Resurrection Space and Time

This exaltation brings about a displacement of the believer which
the Apostle pictures according to the dimensions of space and time.
The Church is in the Lord, and thus detached from carnal space;
she is deep in the eternal Spirit, and thus stands outside this world's
time.

According to the Epistles of the Captivity, Christ's glorification
immediately put him in the heights of heaven. The believer, too,
is granted not only a resurrection, but also an ascension. The
Father's action upon Christ lifts the Christian out of this world too
(Col. ii. 20), out of the lower sphere where he is separated from
God, and transfers him to heaven. That is the homeland of which
he is a citizen. (Phil. iii. 20.) He has not entered it merely by proxy
in the person of Christ, but is himself seated in heaven, for he is
in Christ, and Christ is the heavenly dwelling of all believers [69]

---

[67] "The exaltation of the Church is the goal of the exaltation of Christ—
that all things in heaven and on earth may be subject to the Church " (J. M
Voste, *Commentarius in Ep ad Ephesios*, Rome, 1921, p 125)

[68] Present-day writers take this verse to mean all the angels, as did
Ambrosiaster, St. Thomas, Cornelius a Lapide, cf Allo.

[69] Eph. i 3 seems to demand this kind of literal interpretation. "We have
been blessed . . in the heavens, in Christ." Similarly, Eph ii. 6 indicates that

The believer is also transferred in time, passing from "this world" into "the world to come"

The opposition between the two worlds was familiar to the Jews. Our Lord himself had made use of it. (Luke xvi. 8, xx. 34.) "This world" and "this age" are so closely related as to become interchangeable (1 Cor. 1. 20; iii. 18–19.) The present world is for St. Paul the temporal dimension of the sinful world (Gal. i. 4; Rom. xii. 2); it is the era of Satan, empty of God. (2 Cor. iv. 4.) "We have been delivered from this present wicked world" (Gal. i. 4) and we are living in the world to come (Eph ii. 7; Heb. vi. 5), which is the temporal dimension of the Kingdom of God. The age to come is the age of the Resurrection (Luke xx. 35). The turning-point of the two ages is Easter. In Christ the Spirit has established a new time as well as a new space. All who are united to Christ enter this twofold newness. "You were heretofore in darkness, but now light in the Lord." (Eph. v. 8.) This "now" begins a new era in a new space. Though Christian time begins with the Resurrection, it must not be identified with the centuries following upon that event; it cannot be separated from the reality it measures: it is the time of the risen Christ and those who share in his resurrection. That is why "this age" of wickedness still runs on, and the Christian "now" starts for every believer at the moment of his own justification. (Eph. v 8.) Yet the new time also dates back in all believers to the moment of the Resurrection, for their justification belongs to that moment (remembering the formula "with Christ").

The Resurrection is not merely the historical beginning of the new time, but the ontological centre in which it is fixed[70]; the opening of Christian time occurs both at a date in history and in a reality that remains ever present, namely the resurrection that is in Christ

This new time carries on from the old. According to the Greek idea of time running in cycles, the eternal returning of things means

to be in Christ is to be in heaven. This suggests that the reality of heaven as a whole was inaugurated by the glorification of Christ, and that Christ in glory *is* the sphere of heavenly life for the believer. We get this idea also from the fact that Christ's entry into heaven and the glorification of his body are simultaneous

[70] I am in disagreement on this point with O. Cullmann (*Christ and Time*, pp 81–93) who considers that the redemptive act is at the centre of time in a purely chronological sense, as the dividing point between the old time and the new

that time never achieves any goal other than itself, and to find salvation one must escape upwards from it. Christian thought has inherited the Jewish idea of linear time, in which history is a preparation for salvation, which lies at its term But the Christian notion
is more complex than this. The new age is certainly in continuity
with the old, for it is the age of the resurrection of Christ which is
the result of his death. Christ's death is the goal of earthly time
and its conclusion. (Cf. ch. vii.) Thus the new age comes at the end
of "that time" as a prolongation of it, in line with Jewish thought.
Yet in another sense it stands above "this world" as in Greek
thought. Between the two eras there is both a continuity and a
break, for their point of contact is death. They are continuous in
the same way as the realities they measure: existence in the flesh
and in the Spirit. Since Easter the two have coexisted in the world,
the one set over and against the other. They come together in the
believer, for he lives both in the flesh and in the spirit, and goes
from one to the other. Salvation takes place in "this time", but it
does so by constantly getting beyond it.

Christian time is still developing towards a reality yet to come,
although it has already achieved its fullness in Christ; for though
the goal is already attained in us, it is only attained imperfectly; the
history of salvation does not conclude with the Resurrection, but
moves on to the *parousia*. But whereas, before Christ, it was advancing towards a reality that stood wholly ahead of it, it is now moving
towards a reality which, though still to come, is yet also already
present· the risen Christ who is the Christ of the future world. It
is a movement both forwards and inwards, an advance to a reality
that is present. In as much as it measures our life in Christ, Christian
time belongs to the end of the world; but in as much as it measures
this existence in its imperfect state, it is still developing towards
final salvation. On one hand it is advancing towards the *Parousia*,
on the other it already touches the end of time. The head of the
Church, the risen Christ, has already broken through to the Last
Day. The whole body must follow.

(1) *Power*

That the faithful are exalted in the lordship of Christ is the effect
of an outpouring of *dynamis*, of power. The new life of the risen
Lord is a tremendous force, for its principle is the Spirit, who is the

driving power of God. "The power of the Resurrection" (Phil.
iii. 10) acts in Christ's mystical body just as in his individual body.
The Church is charged with an irresistible power which showed
itself in the Apostles' might, capable of "pulling down fortifications" (2 Cor. x. 4), in their dazzling manifestations of charismata,
and in the moral energy whereby believers gradually repress "the
old man". Just as Christ's risen body is the principle of the diffusion
of the Spirit, so the Church identified with that body is a leaven of
life by the force of her apostolic charismata, and the power of her
rites of sanctification Christ's body is a source of the Spirit for this
world through her who makes him present in the world.[71]

But the exercise of this power starts from the Church's death to
the flesh, and makes that death ever more complete. The Church
will not triumph over the world on the world's own ground· she
will have no era of earthly grandeur, which to her could only be
an artificial grandeur. She is a gathering of those who have been
raised up in the Spirit, and therefore a gathering in the death of
Christ. Her true triumphs are celebrated in her martyrs.

(1) Victim

This state of divine life in death to the flesh imprints on the
Church the character of a victim. In the strictly Pauline epistles,
Christ's passing from a carnal state into the divine life is never
really expressed in sacrificial terms. But this same transformation,
when seen in the faithful, appears as a sacrifice. Believers "present
[their] bodies as a living sacrifice, holy, pleasing unto God". (Rom.
xii. 1.) The action of the sacrifice consists in stripping off the form
of this world and being renewed in the Spirit. (xii 2.) Paul is the
minister of this rite; the Gentiles he offers to God are sanctified in
the Holy Spirit and accepted by God (Rom. xv. 16, cf. Phil. ii. 17)

---

[71] This privilege whereby Christ's mystical body is a source of the Spirit
like his individual body, which is implicit in the Pauline epistles, is stated
explicitly by St. Irenaeus (*Adv Haer* III, xxiv, 1, P.G. VII, 966) with reference to John vii. 38: "For where the Church is, there also is the Spirit of
God, and where the Spirit of God is, there is the Church and all grace
Wherefore they who have no part in him, are neither nourished with life
from the breast of their mother, nor receive of that crystal stream coming
from the body of Christ " The Holy Spirit flows from Christ's body taken in
both senses Cf St. Cyprian, *Epist. LXXIII*, 10ff., *De Haer. Bapt., P.L* , iii,
1116-7; cf G Bareille, art. "Irénée", *Dict théol. cath* , col 2425ff ; H Rahner,
"Flumina de Ventre Christi", *Bibl* , xxii, 1941, 368-74, 384-5

The light cast by these texts is dim and blurred; they do not seem to mean to express the whole tremendous idea of a Church immolated in herself, offered to God and hidden with Christ in the divine life (Col. iii. 3; Gal. ii, 19); yet the idea of sacrifice applied to Paul's thought brings out these riches.[72]

(k) Holiness

Because the Church is consecrated to God in Christ, she is essentially holy. The faithful are the saints. (Rom. i. 7 and *passim*.) What does St. Paul take this holiness to mean? Clearly he takes it in the biblical sense, whereby holiness is primarily a property of God, who is holy because of his transcendence and inaccessibility; the creature shares in this divine attribute when it is set apart from the profane world and enters the sphere of the sacred The holiness of the creature is in the order of worship; it is brought about by a consecration. "In calling those who are in Christ 'saints', Paul sees them as cut off from the world, from its space and its time, as beings consecrated to the Divinity . . ."[73] This fact of being cut off obliges the believer to be morally pure; thus holiness is sometimes taken in an ethical sense (Eph. 1. 4; v. 26; Col. i 22), but even then it remains something called for by a deeper holiness, a consecration of the being.

The faithful have a share in divine holiness because they belong to the risen Christ—they are holy "in Christ" (1 Cor. ii. 2; Phil. 1. 1) —and because the Holy Ghost, who is the expression of God's transcendence, is present in them. (1 Cor. iii. 16–17; Eph. ii. 22.) The Christ of the fourth gospel declared that he sanctified himself that his Apostles might also be sanctified (John xvii. 19); that he consecrated himself to God in the immolation of his human life

[72] A reference to the ideas of sacrifice would make it possible to conceive the Church in the image of the Lamb standing immolated (Apoc. v 6) Like Christ, with whom she is identified, she is the paschal victim immolated in herself and living in God The Church makes the whole world a Calvary where Christ dies and rises again. In her Christ unceasingly passes from this world to the Father, "sanctifies himself", immolates himself that he may only live in God Although in Christ as an individual this same unique sacrifice has achieved its goal, it is preserved in the Church in an ever actual state of becoming, under the *parousia*

[73] L Malevez, "L'Église, corps du Christ", *Rech Sc Rel* , 1944, pp 56–7; cf R Asting, *Die Heiligkeit im Urchristentum*, Gottingen, 1930, p 144; Proksch, *T. W. N.T.*, vol 1, pp. 107–14

THE CHURCH'S LIFE IN THE RISEN CHRIST

that they, in their turn, might be consecrated. In Pauline theology too, the holiness of the faithful is a consecration "in Christ" (1 Cor. 1. 2), a participation in God's holiness in Christ, who is sanctified by the Holy Spirit of the Resurrection; they are "sanctified" in the "sacrifice" of Christ, made sacred along with him, in their baptismal sharing in his death and resurrection.

There is one aspect of this holiness to which St. Paul refers several times. it is the holiness of a temple, with its two elements of consecration and divine presence. "You are built upon the foundation of the Apostles and Prophets, Jesus Christ himself being the chief corner-stone; in whom all the building, being framed together, groweth up into a holy temple in the Lord. In whom you also are built together into a habitation of God in the Spirit." (Eph. ii. 20–22.)

Notwithstanding this, the Church is not seen as a building of whom Christ is merely the corner-stone. The physical image suggested this mode of expression to St. Paul. But according to 1 Cor. iii. 11, the Lord is also the foundation, and the Apostles who are its foundation and the faithful who are its walls, only grow into a temple "in the Lord", that is to say, in their union of identification with Christ. Indeed in the Epistle to the Ephesians, St. Paul "makes an implicit comparison between the city-temple of heaven and the body of Christ in which the keystone of the building corresponds with the head of the body.[74] In the temple as in the body, the Lord is the principle and the totality.

This building is God's dwelling "in the Spirit". It is inhabited by God because the Spirit who is the communication of the Godhead, is present in it. The Church is "in Christ", she is his body; as such, she is the receptacle of the Spirit; as such she possesses the divine presence. (Cf. 1 Cor. vi. 15–20.)

(l) Unity

The fact that all are consecrated to the holiness of the one God imprints on this people their mark of unity. One God, by whom, and for whom all the faithful live—one people. (1 Cor. viii. 4–6; xii. 4–6, 11; Eph. iv. 4–6.)

Consecration to the one God of heaven had cemented the unity of God's people in the past. But the new Israel is consummated in

[74] L Cerfaux, *The Church*, p 378

a more perfect unity by a fundamental sanctification, by being physically related to the transcendence of God; they are of God by the physical life that they live, for the Holy Spirit, God's transcendence and holiness, is their vital principle.

The life of the Spirit, one in itself, is primarily the life of one man, and it remains the life of that one man, the risen Christ, even when laid open to mankind at large: "In one Spirit were we all baptized into one body, whether Jews or Gentiles, whether bond or free" (1 Cor. xii. 13); ". . . one body and one Spirit". (Eph. iv. 4.)

This, then, is the Church of our glorified Saviour· identified with the one Christ, living in him by the one Spirit, consecrated to the indivisible God.

The unity of the Church is the natural consequence of the Resurrection, for Christ's glory is a mystery of communion. Though Paul does not use this sacrificial terminology in speaking of Christ himself, he recognizes that the Church of the risen Christ is gathered together in a sacrificial banquet: "Christ our Pasch is sacrificed. Therefore let us feast." (1 Cor. v. 7–8.) The whole of the Church's life is a communion, the feast of the Lamb. Those who feast at the same sacred table are brothers, nourishing their life with the same food, and, what is more, with a divine food; God is the bond of relationship between them and the seal of their brotherhood. This paschal meal, which *is* the Church, is wholly realized in the rite of the Eucharist. That is why St. Paul cannot speak of it without also mentioning the unity of the Church. (1 Cor. x. 16–22)

(m) Grace in the Old Testament

Here a question presents itself: What, to Paul's mind, was the nature of the grace of the Old Testament as compared with God's grace in Christ? The comparison from the first is unfavourable to the Old Testament. If the just man in the new law has to die in Christ in order to be vivified in him by the Spirit, it appears that the just man of the old law, who never entered into any such communion, cannot have participated in the Spirit in the same sense.

Western theologians, with their inheritance of a moral and juridical notion of the Redemption, seem to have ignored the problem, for they thought it necessary to establish an essential continuity between the two graces. The Eastern Fathers, who saw the Redemption as a raising of man to the dignity of sonship by the gift of the Spirit, were either hesitant in allowing that the just of old had the personal gift of the Spirit and the grace of sonship, or denied it to them altogether.[75] They conceived of the Spirit as having dwelt in mankind only since the Incarnation and being communicated only by Christ in glory.

Modern theologians, aware of the connexion of sonship and the gift of the Spirit with the glorification of the immolated Christ, have tried to define the degree of inferiority of the Old Testament grace.[76] Whatever the definition they may have arrived at, a merely quantitative difference does not appear to give a sufficient expression of Pauline teaching. To Paul, the life of the believer is essentially the life of Christ, the same that sprang up in Christ's own body after his death; the Spirit is present only in Christ and those who are united to his glorified body; the faithful are sons by being identified with the Son, and outside Christ there can be neither communication of the Spirit nor sonship. Thus the ancients lived the life of servants; the Spirit was not in their hearts to cry, "Abba, Father!" (Gal. iv. 1-7); they were not to enter into rest at the end of their labours (Heb. xi. 40), for the inheritance was not for them. They lived at the level of the flesh, subject to the elements of this world, and affected by the racial differences in their flesh.[77]

[75] Thus Irenaeus and, following him, Tertullian, Athanasius, Chrysostom and, above all, Cyril of Alexandria Cf. G Philips, "La Grâce des justes de l'A. T ", *Eph. Theol Lov.*, xxiii, 1947, 521–56; xxiv, 1948, 23–58.

[76] According to Petau, *De Trinitate*, i, viii, ch vii, ed. Vivès, 1865, vol iii, p. 493, the ancients only had the energy of the Spirit. E Tobac, in "Grâce", *Dict apol for cath.*, col 329ff, tends to think that the justice of the ancients consisted in being numbered among the future members of the Kingdom. There must have been a real inner holiness to explain the intimacy existing between some of the just and their God (Cf. Ps. lxxiii 25–8) The Bible speaks of a gift of the Spirit (Ps li. 12–14) and wisdom (Wisd. vii. 27) which transform men inwardly. But when we examine the nature of this sanctification we must note that God did not reveal the Trinity in the Old Testament, and the Spirit does not appear there as love, as the gift of God communicating himself, but only as the power of God. Cf P Van Imschoot, "L'Esprit de Yahvé, principe de vie morale dans l'A T.", *Eph Theol. Lov.*, xvi (1939), 467 Surely the revelation and the gift go hand in hand.

[77] As an introduction to Christ, the old dispensation had brought forth a prophet greater than the rest: "There hath not risen among them that are born of women a greater than John the Baptist", but, added Christ, "he that is the least in the Kingdom of Heaven is greater than he." (Matt xi 11) The slightest subject of the Kingdom is raised above the highest dignitary of the past, for he is drawn up to the height of Christ According to St Cyril of Alexandria, *Comm in Jo*, i, v, 2, *P G*, lxxiii, 757, he was neither baptised by Christ, nor born of God, nor possessed of the person of the Spirit

Can we allow these differences and still claim that there is a unity between the grace of the Old and New Testaments? The Christian knows from experience that one and the same grace may be subject to limitations, for during his life on earth the carnal state coexists with the life-giving Spirit, and the life of faith must wait for vision. This is true. It remains that, for St. Paul, the life of the New Testament is the physical life of the risen Christ, and its presence in those who believe is only explained by their real union with Christ. It would seem that as far as the grace of the Old Testament is concerned we can only admit ignorance.

iii. THE NEW LIFE IN THE CONSCIOUSNESS AND CONDUCT
OF THE FAITHFUL

(a) A New Knowledge

The newness of life that the believer bears within himself is realized immediately as a new knowledge. This is how the Apostle himself experienced it: as a revelation, an illumination comparable to the physical miracle which marked his entry into the community of believers: "There fell from his eyes as it were scales." (Acts ix 18.)

The whole of the inward renewal tends towards this knowledge: "You have stripped off the old man with his deeds, putting on the new, who is renewed unto knowledge, according to the image of him that created him." (Col. iii. 9-10.) Indeed, it may be said that God's gradual assimilation of the believer, by the stripping off of the old man and putting on of the new, is accompanied in the conscious mind with an ever deeper vision of the Christian mystery.

Paul confirms this idea in Ephesians: "May Christ dwell by faith in your hearts; that being rooted and founded in charity, you may be able to comprehend . . . what is the length and breadth, and height and depth; to know also the charity of Christ, which surpasseth all knowledge, that you may be filled unto all the fullness of God." (iii. 17-19.) Christ's presence brings about the ripening of knowledge in the believer, while, at the same time, the knowledge of the dimensions of the mystery fills him with the fullness of God —in other words, with the life of Christ.[78]

---

[78] Similarly, according to Phil. iii 9-10, "the justice of faith" becomes a knowledge of Christ and his mystery of death and resurrection.

This knowledge is more than something intellectual: it is a living grasp of its object by all our faculties, a seeing with "the eyes of the heart" (Eph. i. 18), with an understanding imbued with love; and it is also the object seizing all our faculties and giving life to us. It is the experience of a life taking possession of us.

The object of this knowledge is "him" (Phil. iii. 10)—Christ. There are two ways of knowing: the first comes from flesh and blood—to this Paul "condescended not" (Gal. i. 16), the second originates in the Spirit. Paul had experienced both: "If we have known Christ according to the flesh; now we know him so no longer." (2 Cor. v 16.) He had known Christ in a human manner (though the text says nothing of direct knowledge of our Lord during his life on earth); he had judged him by the events and human appearances of his life, without penetrating the secret of his glory. This secret could only be open to a vision according to the Spirit, for that alone could see beyond the Christ of flesh to take hold of the Saviour as revealed by the Resurrection [79] The object of Christian knowledge is "the Lord of Glory" (1 Cor. ii. 8), the Christ who lives in us (2 Cor. xiii. 5), the mystery of his death and resurrection (Phil. iii. 10), the Christ-Spirit whom the believer contemplates with his face uncovered (2 Cor. iii. 17–18), the omnipotent power of God displayed in the Resurrection and the riches of glory destined for the saints. (Eph. i. 18–20.)

Since "the mystery", God's plan of wisdom for the world, is realized in the dead and risen Christ who thus becomes the personification of God's wisdom (1 Cor i. 30), the believer embraces the whole world in the knowledge of Christ, and turns a wholly new gaze upon it. Since the Saviour died and rose again for all men, Paul knows no-one according to the flesh now, any more than Christ, for all has been made new (2 Cor. v 14–17); he sees the world in the light of death and resurrection

But the ideas of Saul the Pharisee had to undergo a death to arrive at this knowledge. "The things that were gain to me [as a Pharisee], Christ hath taught me to count but loss for the excellent knowledge of Jesus Christ my Lord." (Phil. iii. 7–8.) The believer's knowledge, like his life, is a sharing in Christ's resurrection from the dead.

[79] F. Prat, *Theology*, vol ii, p 25, *n*. 1, says *à propos* this: "To know him according to the spirit, is to know him as his resurrection and glorification have taught us to know him, in the light of the Holy Spirit "

Since it is of the spiritual order, this knowledge is linked with charity, the prime result of the presence of the Spirit. Outside Christ, knowledge is purley notional· it "puffeth up" without filling or edifying, for it lacks charity. (1 Cor. viii. 1.) The believer's knowledge is a seeing with his heart (Eph. 1. 18); it is a lamp lit by the Spirit of love. "rooted and founded in charity, that you may comprehend . . " (Eph. iii. 17–18.)

Indeed, there is no very clear distinction between knowledge and charity. Our life in Christ is expressed wholly in both; they advance, as it were, hand in hand: "May your charity more and more abound in knowledge and in all understanding." (Phil. i. 9.) But charity is more fundamental; it is present first and is what is enlightened to become knowledge. Eyes are opened in the heart. But even before charity the Holy Spirit and his life are in us by existence in Christ. Historically speaking, the source of the believer's faith is the preaching of the Apostles (Rom. x. 17), but the truth of faith originates in the life of God and when the believer, by being joined to Christ through faith and living in him, begins to share the life of God, it is in this life that his faith has its origin.[80] He still believes in the Apostles' words, but those words are henceforth the expression of his own life.[81]

That the Spirit is at the basis of our knowledge, is not because he is the light and wisdom of God, but because he is power and the bond of our union with Christ. He unites us to Christ, the light and wisdom of God, and gives us the power of understanding, for he fills us with charity, the intelligible bond of our union with Christ. Because of charity our minds are illuminated by the light that is in us [82]

(b) A New Morality

With Christ's resurrection a new race of men was born, a third race different from the other two, and with it a totally new morality

---

[80] This is perhaps how we are to understand St. Polycarp, *Phil iii, 3* "[Faith] is the mother of us all, it is followed by hope, and preceded by the love of God."

[81] That being and life come before knowledge is made clear by St John· "Every one that is of the truth, heareth my voice" (xviii. 37); the unction which is in the believer is a source and criterion of truth (1 John ii 27.)

[82] The working together of Christ and the Spirit which I have so often mentioned appears here in the psychological sphere also.

The Greeks and Jews had each had their own moral law, the former dictated by reason, the latter imposed by God from Mount Sinai.

Greek morality was a humanism, a seeking for perfection in the order of reason. The Greek man recognized only the eternal laws of nature, which were those of reason. To be subject to these was to remain free, for it was but to be subject to oneself. He had no idea of a holiness consisting in a consecration to God and submission to his will; and because he did not renounce self and open himself to the redeeming power of God, he succumbed to the laws of this world in which he was imprisoned.[83]

The Christian law was not this law of nature. Christ refers to it only to indicate its inadequacy. (Matt. v. 47.) To St Paul it is a law only by analogy: it is equally true to say that the Gentiles are a law unto themselves (Rom. ii. 14); they are in fact simply "without the Law". (Rom. ii. 12; 1 Cor. ix. 21.) Paul condemns their ideal and relegates it to the order of the weak and accursed flesh.[84]

The morality of the Old Testament is not of the order of reason; it is to obey God. The Jews recognized the precepts of the natural law, but they were imposed on them by God. The whole of Jewish law, whether moral or ritual, came from Sinai. Obedience to the Lord was the principle of all wisdom.

As compared with natural morality, governed by its own inherent principles, Jewish morality was from one point of view inferior: St. Paul speaks of it as servile. In the Old Testament, man was obeying an exterior principle, a commandment from God on Mount Sinai he was God's slave.

Christian morality is also a morality of submission to God, for Christ had not come to destroy the Law, but to urge its observance and bring it to perfection. (Matt. v. 17.) The whole of Christian life is an "obedience to the faith" (Rom. i. 5), a servitude to God and his justice. (Rom. vi. 16–18.)[85] But whereas in the past God spoke from

[83] A J Festugière, *La Sainteté*, Paris, 1949. The Greek ideal was personified by the sage and the hero The first sought the "divine *gnosis*", trying to act always in accordance with that wisdom; his ideal was of the order of reason With the hero, the quest for greatness was an end in itself, it was the noblest form of egocentrism.

[84] According to Aristotle (*Ethic Nic.* x, 9), the sage is loved best by God, whereas to Paul the wisdom of this world is folly to God (1 Cor iii 18–20) whose call goes rather to the little ones whom he justifies in Christ.

[85] In 1 Peter i. 14, Christians are called "the children of obedience" Those who refuse to belong to Christ are the "children of disobedience" (Eph v 6)

the top of Sinai, he now reveals his law in Christ the Redeemer, and man submits to him by his life in Christ.

The Synoptics recall the memory of the "Holy Mount" in relation to our Lord[86]; the shadow of Moses indeed is never absent from him.[87] The law he gives is one that presupposes man's being re-created in holiness.[88] Bit by bit he shows that he himself is the principle of morality, and that men are to be judged according to their attitude to him (cf. Matt. xxv. 35–45).

St. Paul speaks of "the law of Christ" (Gal. vi 2; 1 Cor. ix. 21), of the "ways in Christ" that are taught in every church (1 Cor. iv. 17), of a "rule of doctrine" which must be obeyed. (Rom. vi. 17.)

He gives us no clear pronouncement about this Christian law. It includes a collection of rules of behaviour taught catechetically, lists of virtues to be practised and vices to be condemned (Gal. v. 19–23; 1 Cor. vi 9–10)—no doubt gleaned from the sayings of Christ, for he is the unquestioned ruler of souls, and any case of conscience is instantly resolved if there is "a commandment of the Lord" on the subject. (1 Thess. iv. 15; 1 Cor. vii. 10, 25)

But these Christian codes of life merely put into words an inherent life. There is a living force in the faithful which is the principle of holy actions, the same force that dwells in the body of the risen Christ whereby the faithful live. The risen Christ is the principle of Christian morality. For it is our belonging to the body of the risen Christ which takes us away from the Law into newness of

---

[86] There is a very real analogy between Christ's transfiguration and the theophany of Sinai. Like Moses, Christ went up a high mountain, accompanied by disciples and leaving the multitude behind The glory of God came down over both mountains, the faces of both Christ and Moses were illuminated; and a voice was heard Elias and Moses, the two men of Sinai, were talking with Christ God declared "This is my Son   . hear ye him", fulfilling the promise made to Moses when he came down from Sinai: "The Lord will raise up a prophet like unto me [Moses]: hear him " (Deut xviii. 15)

But the Transfiguration was only an announcement; the glorification was a fleeting one, and the death Christ was speaking of with his companions was yet to come The Synoptics give us several anticipations of Easter during Christ's life on earth (his baptism, his entry into Jerusalem, the Last Supper). Christ dead and risen was to be the Sinai of the New Testament Cf "La Transfiguration de Jésus", *Vie Spir.*, lxxxv, 1951, 115–26.

[87] J. Daniélou, *Sacramentum Futuri*, Paris, 1950, pp 135–43; J. Jeremias, *T W.N T* , vol iv, pp. 871–8

[88] Whereas the Mosaic Law was adapted to man's fallen state (Matt. v. 31, 38, 43; xix 8), Christ's demands assume a humanity restored to paradisal innocence (Matt xix. 8)

life, and makes us "bring forth fruit to God". (Rom. vii. 1–6.) It is
our participation in Christ, in his death and resurrection, that makes
us subject to the demands of the new life. (Rom. vi. 1–11.) The
opposite of sin is not integrity in human virtues, but the faith that
unites us to our Saviour, and justice consists in our being present
in Christ. (Rom. viii. 1.) Fornication is to be condemned because
it impairs the dignity of man. (1 Cor. vi. 18.) True. But this is above
all because it takes a member away from the body of Christ to unite
him to the flesh of a harlot. The cult of the Sabbath, once glorified
by God, and trust in the works of the Law, are just as much to be
condemned as fornication, and for the same reason. (Phil. iii. 7–9,
19; Col. iii. 20–22.)

The life that animates the body of the risen Christ is none other
than the Holy Spirit, who, in his power and holiness, gives life
and holiness to all who are in Christ: the Spirit of the risen Christ
is the law of the New Testament. The Mosaic law has been replaced
by "the law of the Spirit of life" (Rom. viii. 2); the injunctions of
the dead letter have been replaced by a life in the newness of the
Spirit (Rom. vii. 6); those who are led by the Spirit are no longer
under the Law. (Gal. v. 18.) The Spirit, the antithesis of the Law
of the time of prefiguration, is the principle of the morality of the
new age.[89]

The new law, in the body of Christ, is thus not merely a code,
but a life, a force: it is the Spirit who raises Christ from the dead.[90]
The believer as a new creature is subject to the law immanent in
his new nature.

But whereas the natural law makes its demands without pro-
voking any reaction from the recalcitrant flesh (Rom. vii. 23), the
law of the Spirit asserts itself with a living power It is a power of
resurrection; it has thrusts and instincts for life (Rom. viii. 6) whose
direction is indicated and whose meaning is put into words by the

[89] St. Thomas, *Com. in Rom*, viii, lect. 1: "The Law of the Spirit is called
the new Law, and is the Holy Spirit himself since it is placed in our hearts
by the Spirit" *Summa Theol.*, 1a iiae, q. 106, a.1 · "The most important thing
in the law of the New Testament, the thing from which all its force comes,
is the grace of the Holy Spirit, which is given by faith in Christ Therefore
the new law is first of all that same grace of the Holy Spirit given to all
who believe in Christ . It must therefore be said that the new law is above
all an interior gift."
[90] A M Ramsey, *The Resurrection of Christ*, 3rd ed, London, 1950, p. 8:
"Christian ethics are Resurrection ethics, defined and made possible by men
being 'raised together with Christ'."

precepts of the Apostles' teaching The Spirit moves the believer
(Rom. viii 14; Gal. v 18), he is the principle of Christian acts (cf.
1 Cor. xii. 3); he brings forth the virtues as a plant its fruits. (Gal.
v. 22)[91]

The Spirit moves the faithful as he raises Christ, by permanently
consecrating the death of the flesh The new morality is governed
by the paschal mystery; it is a law of death and resurrection. What
happened at Easter now orders all moral activity by transplanting
the faithful from the carnal level to the sphere of the Spirit. (Cf.
Rom vi. 2–5; Col. iii. 1ff.) Christian life is declared a death and a
new reality; it is a renunciation of the characteristic vices of carnal
man, self-indulgence, idolatry, and hatred, for the pursuit of justice,
goodness and chastity (Gal. v. 19–23): "They that are Christ's have
crucified their flesh with its vices and its concupiscences. If we live
in the Spirit, let us also follow the Spirit." (Gal. v 24–5.) The flesh
must no longer bring forth in its works now that the Spirit is in us
desirous of bearing fruit in the love of God. We must now live our
baptismal consecration, we must become what we are: "Purge out
the old leaven . . for you are unleavened bread." (1 Cor v 7.)

The paschal life of the Church is most characteristically expressed
in the virtue of charity.

The Church's very being demands charity, even before her teaching does, for her being is in the Christ of Easter who is eternally a
renunciation and a giving.

Caught up in Christ and his gift of himself, the believer can no
longer "seek to please himself" (Rom. xv. 3), but considers the good
of his neighbour, having the sense of renunciation for the sake of
his brethren that rises out of his union with Christ the Redeemer.
(Phil. ii. 4–5.)

Charity assumes and, indeed, effects the death of the old man[92]—
it is the very opposite of the flesh closed in upon itself in the selfishness of its pride and its weakness; it is a new and overflowing life.

---

[91] To break the laws of our new life threatens the growth or even the
very existence of that life Just as "flesh and blood" cannot enter the Kingdom
of God, neither can sin (1 Cor. vi 9–10; Gal. v 21; Eph v 5), for sin is a
return to the order of flesh and blood and brings the life of the Spirit in the
believer to an end. The immoral life, which, as St John Chrysostom tells
us (Hom , xlvii, 4, P.G., lx, 331), strikes even at the dogma of the Resurrection, deals a mortal wound to the risen life, for it is a violation of its law

[92] The qualities of charity listed in 1 Cor xiii are largely negative

It is an invincible force (1 Cor. xiii. 4–8); it can do all things and never passes away; it is the life of the risen Lord.

It is like a sap poured into the believer, for the Christ of Easter who is the root of his life, is a "living Spirit", and the Spirit he communicates is "the charity of God poured forth in our hearts". (Rom. v. 5.)[93]

Charity coincides so closely with the new life of the Spirit that we hardly notice if the phrase "in the Spirit" is replaced by "in charity". We walk in the Spirit, and also in charity (Rom. viii. 4; Eph. v. 2); we are sanctified in both (Rom. xv. 16; Eph. i. 4); both are the principle by which the body of Christ is built up. (Eph. ii. 22; iv. 16). Charity fulfils the same function in the body of Christ as does the Spirit. (Eph. iv. 16; Col ii. 2.)

Because the Spirit is both power and charity, the divine force which bursts forth in Christ and in the Church does not create supermen. The force of Christianity lies in charity; "benignity" (Gal. v. 22; Col. iii. 12) and "humility" (Eph. iv. 2) are the fruits of the Spirit and "the mark of Christianity".[94]

Because the Spirit is charity as well as the fullness of reality and the holiness of God, charity is "the fulfilment of the law" (Rom. xiii. 10; Gal. v. 14),[95] "the bond of perfection". (Col. iii. 14.) All justice is "fulfilled" in it.

The new life which is our law gives birth to a specifically Christian moral knowledge which orders the will to act in accordance with the instincts of that life, which makes judgements in the body of Christ according to that life of the Spirit: "Be of one mind, having the same charity . . . Have this mind among yourselves which [you have] in Christ Jesus" (Phil. ii. 2, 5); in your relations with each other, be guided by the life you live in Christ Since this life is the

[93] This text identifies the charity of God with the Spirit, or rather, it makes charity the formal effect of the presence of the Spirit in us. In biblical writings it is the Spirit who is "poured forth", and the Apostle speaks of an outpouring of charity because that charity is given in the same gift as the Spirit Charity is always linked with the Spirit Sometimes Paul relates it to the Spirit as to its cause (Rom. xv. 30), as the fruit to its root (Gal. v 22; cf v 13–16), as the principle that animates it (Col i. 8); sometimes he simply puts them side by side (2 Cor vi 6); sometimes he declares charity to be the supreme charism of the Spirit. (1 Cor xii. 31, xiii, *passim.*)

[94] St Macarius of Egypt, *Hom*, xv and xxvi, *P.G.*, xxxiv, 593, 681; Hesychius, *De Temperantia et Virtute*, cent. 1, *P.G.*, xciii, 1505.

[95] St. Thomas, *Com. in II Cor iii*, 6: "The Holy Spirit, when he produces charity, which is the fullness of the Law, in us, *is* the new Testament, not in the letter . but in the spirit, that is by the spirit which gives life"

"charity of the Spirit", as charity advances so will the Christian conscience become more sensitive. "... that your charity may more and more abound in knowledge and in all understanding, that you may approve the better things, that you may be blameless". (Phil. i. 9–10; Rom. xii. 2.)

The moral ideal towards which the believer must tend is not that of Greek wisdom and mysticism, for which ultimate perfection lay in divine *gnosis*, nor does it consist in the heroic practice of human virtues: one might possess all knowledge and all heroic virtue and yet be nothing. (1 Cor. xiii. 1–3.) Nor is the ideal one of justice as conferred by the Law. It consists in the dead and risen Christ, the ideal of the only true justice, and in participation in the Spirit of love that animates him Christian justice is "a justification of life" (Rom. v. 18), and is conferred in the reality described as "the grace of God through the redemption that is in Christ Jesus". (Rom. iii. 24.)[96]

Christian morality is therefore something wholly new. It is not imposed by God from without, nor yet is it something demanded by human nature from within. It is a "new commandment", the law of the new and final creation in Christ. It does not, however, replace the law of Sinai nor the law of reason; it includes them both[97] and yet goes beyond them: it is the law of God just as was that of Sinai, yet it comes from within just as did that of the Greeks.

Man is thus free in Christ "Where the Spirit of the Lord is, there is liberty." (2 Cor. iii. 17.) He can submit to God without compromising his own liberty, for he is obeying the laws of his own proper being, the instincts of his Christian life. Even more free than the Greek who obeyed reason, the Christian obeys love. He does what he likes. Nothing is forbidden him save falling under a law outside himself. (1 Cor. vi. 12.) The law of life does, certainly, impose a constraint, but only upon the flesh.

Though it comes from within man, the new law is still a law from another being, like the law of the Old Testament, it is a complete obedience to God. For the Spirit, the gift of love is also a law —the will of God expressed in the depths of our hearts. In the risen

---

[96] To St. Paul, whose moral preoccupation was directly religious, there is no moral perfection other than that which justifies us before the tribunal of God It is not that he condemns pagan or Jewish virtue—except perhaps for inadequacy—but simply that, for him, only he who believes in Christ is just

[97] Just as spiritual knowledge includes natural knowledge (1 Cor ii. 15)

Christ and those who believe in him the dominion of God is complete. For Christ and all who are of Christ are dead to themselves, and their life is the life of the Spirit, God's power and his sovereign will.

Christian morality is a morality of total freedom and total obedience.

We might say that Easter is the Christian Sinai, and that the dead and risen Christ is the table of the new law, except that Easter is more than the voice of God upon the mountain and Christ greater than any table of law. But Easter is the bursting forth of the holiness of the Spirit of God in a man, Christ, and the transformation of that man into the holiness of the Spirit of God, and our progressive transformation into that man. Such is Christian morality· the mystery of Christ dead to the flesh in the divine life of the Holy Spirit, growing ever stronger in us.

THE PROGRESS AND CONSUMMATION OF THE
PASCHAL MYSTERY IN THE CHURCH

The description of the Church's life (Chapter VI) seems all opti-
mism: the Resurrection has happened, redemption is won. Reading
these texts we feel a certain surprise Our own personal experience
tends to contradict them. And St. Paul himself recognized this difficulty as much as we do His mind was also divided, he will give an
unqualified declaration and then seem to unsay what he has said.
When we raise the question of whether our resurrection in Christ
is already accomplished, or still awaits completion in the future, we
find ourselves faced with two quite different sets of texts.

The energies of resurrection are still locked within the hearts of
the faithful. We must wait for the day when they burst forth, when
the Lord will bring the whole of "his power of resurrection" to bear
upon the world.

The Church moves ever deeper into the splendour of Easter, looking forward to the perfection of that splendour in the *parousia*; it is
as though Easter is for her only the morning, and the day is yet to
come. This leads us to consider what the relationship is between
Easter and the *parousia*.

1. Christ's Resurrection as the Consummation of the World

i. THE SYNOPTICS

It is always our Lord's claim that he is leading the world to its
goal and opening a new era.

The story of the Annunciation shows him as a heavenly being
bearing within him the promise of a new humanity. God has raised
him up in Israel through the Spirit's creative power, and inaugurates
the new things foretold for the end of time

The eternal Kingdom (Luke 1. 33) promised to this Child is the

new age, foretold by prophecy as bringing the history of the world
to its close.

Long before, the Spirit had hovered like a bird over the primal
waters, and he now comes down again, in the form of a dove, as
Christ emerges from the waters of the Jordan. St. Luke senses this
to be an analogy with the story of the first creation, and it is here
that he brings in Christ's genealogy, taking it right back to the
creation of Adam, thus setting Christ alongside the earthly father
of mankind. (Luke iii. 23ff.)

Very early in his public life, our Lord applied to himself that
great and mysterious title whose meaning he was not to reveal till
the day of his death—"Son of Man".

Time was when a great many exegetes saw this name as expressing the human simplicity of Christ, as the title belonging to his
humiliation. A deeper study of Jewish messianic literature shows it
to be a statement of the highest claim a man can make. Long before,
Daniel (vii) had been present, in an apocalyptic vision, at God's
judgement of the empires of this world and their rulers. Once these
empires had in turn been eliminated, and the Syrian, the cruellest
of them all, duly condemned, there appeared on the clouds "one
like the Son of Man", head of the nation of the saints of the Most
High, whose kingdom was given to them for ever and ever.

Daniel goes on to reiterate the theme of the successive empires,
but this time the Syrian reign is succeeded not by the kingdom of
the saints, but by the resurrection of the dead (xii. 1–2); for the
nation of the saints is a risen nation, and the Son of Man an eschatological being.

Later Jewish apocalyptic writings preserved the vision of a Son
of Man coming at the end, head of the community of saints who
was, on that day, to be "sown" and to live forever. (Enoch lxii.
7–8.) This expectation has a certain analogy with the older
prophecies which crystallized round the birth of a child, an eschatological saviour, prepared from all eternity (Micah v. 1) and destined
to renew the world in primitive innocence. (Isa. vii, ix, xi.)

Christ was claiming this title and this function for himself. He
inaugurated his ministry by proclaiming that it was he who was to
perfect the world. The Spirit was upon him to bring about the
liberation of the world to come. (Luke iv. 18–19.) When asked "Art
thou he that is to come?" (Luke vii. 19), he replied by quoting

prophecies of the end of the world (Isa. xxxv. 5; lxi. 1.) The marriage feast he was celebrating meant, to his hearers, the coming of the end.

In the power of the Holy Spirit, he entered into combat with the forces of sin and death that lay heavy on mankind. He confronted the prince of this lost world in the desert; three times he wrestled with death (Luke vii. 11–15; viii. 49–55, John xi. 1–44), undermining its tyranny and giving mankind a promise of liberation. He cleansed the Temple in order to begin a new worship. Furthermore, the Temple of Jerusalem, the centre of his hearers' world, was soon to be destroyed, with the whole world falling into ruin around it. (Matt. xxiv. 2.)

But the things he did on earth were still no more than presages, signs of the things to come. The young man of Naim, Jairus' daughter, and Lazarus, received only a renewal of mortal life, yet these were a prefiguring of the immortal resurrection. The Son of Man was not yet "come" in the fullness of his power, and the setting up of the kingdom of the saints upon the clouds had not yet come about. Time and again Christ repeated, "The Son of Man will come", the Kingdom will arrive soon.[1]

As his death approached, he announced his coming more forcefully: "Amen, I say to you, there are some of them that stand here, that shall not taste death till they see the Son of Man coming in his kingdom." (Matt. xvi. 28.) This statement follows immediately upon the proclamation of the Last Judgement: "The Son of Man shall come in the glory of the Father with his angels: and then will he render to every man according to his works." The forthcoming *parousia*, which some of his hearers were to witness, bears an undeniably eschatological character.[2]

[1] The Christ of the Synoptics and the early preaching "comes" in the *parousia*. To translate ἔρχεσθαι as "return" and ἀποστέλλειν as "send back" (Acts iii. 20), is to miss the nuances. The material imagery of the parables might lead us to conceive the coming of the master of the house as a return; but when Christ moves away from metaphor to direct statement, it is clear the Son of Man "is coming". The coming certainly follows a departure, but Christ is going in order to come, not to return. The Messiah is "he who is to come" (Matt. xi. 3) and "the coming" is the coming of the Messiah. Though it may have begun on earth (Matt. ix. 13), there is only one true coming, on that unknown day in the future when the *parousia* takes place.
[2] It is true that in Mark ix 1, the two sayings are divided by the phrase, "he said to them", which suggests the possibility of their having been brought together by the writer. However, Mark certainly means to put this coming in an eschatological perspective. His exact words are, ". . till they see the

Our Lord stated three times that the Son of Man must die and rise again. Daniel's vision of glory was incomplete, for it left out the humiliation which must precede the Son of Man's coming. Our Lord completed it, combining in one picture the features of the Son of Man and of the Servant of Iahweh, Isaiah's suffering Servant who was also to inaugurate a new humanity. (Isa. liii. 10.) The coming in glory was to take the way of suffering and be completed in a resurrection from the dead.

In the middle of a discourse about the day which was to appear like lightning, Christ brought in the reflection that "first [the Son of Man] must suffer many things and be rejected by this generation". (Luke xvii. 25.) He related the suddenness of his glory to his humiliations just as later he was to relate the Resurrection to them: "Ought not Christ to have suffered these things and so entered into his glory?" (Luke xxiv. 26.) The *parousia* and the Resurrection follow equally closely upon the death.[3]

It is in the eschatological discourse that we find that mysterious passage: "When they shall persecute you in this city, flee into another. Amen I say to you, you shall not finish all the cities of Israel, till the Son of Man come." (Matt. x. 23.) This certainly makes the interval a short one.

And indeed, the persecuted believers had not gone through all the towns of Israel before Christ did come, delivering a resounding sentence upon Israel. The flames that destroyed the Temple lit up a Christophany. The *parousia* was now in the world.

All the faithful must await the Master's coming, for it will affect them all and all will be taken by surprise. Happy will be those servants whom it finds watching, their loins girded and their lamps burning.

Theologians today, aware of the delay in the final coming and the complexity of the mystery of the *parousia*, see a succession of *parousias*: that of the judgement on Jerusalem, that which takes the Church by surprise in each of her members, the coming of grace into the hearts of the faithful and finally, the last coming. But it would be arbitrary to make such distinctions in the texts. The Prophets, John the Baptist and the Gospels all saw but one Kingdom of God coming in power". Glory and power are marks of the Last Day, and indicate that this kingdom is eschatological.

[3] C. H Dodd, *The Parables of the Kingdom*, London, 1950, p. 97, thinks that for Christ the death and resurrection of the Son of Man were eschatological events.

coming[4]; we know it as multiple in its manifestations, but in itself it is one, and Christ announced it as coming soon.

Having often foretold the coming of the Son of Man, our Lord, the night before the day he died, declared to his judges "Nevertheless[5] I say to you, hereafter you shall see the Son of Man sitting on the right hand of the power of God and coming in the clouds of heaven." (Matt. xxvi. 64) The time of this world had come to an end, and the Son of Man was now coming and bringing the new age into history. The *parousia* was to shine forth into the world from that day forward, and the power of this immediate coming contained the whole dynamic force of the final coming.

The death and resurrection of Christ are cosmic in dimension: they stand for the end of this world and the beginning of the resurrection of the dead.

It was not for nothing that the sun was darkened when Christ died, that the earth quaked and the rocks were rent: the world as it then was was mortally wounded in the dying Christ; the end of the world had come, and with it the upheavals that had been foretold. (Isa. xxiv.; Amos viii. 8–10.)[6] Not for nothing was the veil of the Temple rent across, a sign that the sanctuary was destroyed, a symbol of the abrogation of a worship adapted to the earthly state of sinful man. (Heb. ix. 9.)[7]

The old world was crumbling, *sheol* was defeated, and the power of the world to come had burst forth. our Lord rose from the dead, and all round him, "the bodies of the saints that had slept arose" (Matt. xxvii. 53).[8]

Thus, from the moment of his glorification, Christ's *parousia*

[4] E Walter, *Das Kommen des Herrn*, vol ii, Freiburg-i -B , 1947, p. 65: "There is never any question of a double coming" See also C K Barrett, *The Holy Spirit and the Synoptic Tradition*, London, 1947, pp 157, 160

[5] The adversative preposition πλήν contrasts the manifestation of the *parousia* with Christ's present situation. Cf also Luke xxii 69. The *parousia* is thus linked to the Passion, as in Luke xvii 25

[6] Matt xxvii 52–3 is quite clearly meant to show our Lord's death as an eschatological event

[7] Of course the world of earthly realities did not collapse all at once; nor did the Temple of the liturgy of shadows, whose destiny was bound up with that of Our Lord, disappear at the moment of his death. The plant was still green, the world still stood as before and sin seemed triumphant· but the root had been cut, for already, "the form of this world passeth away" (1 Cor. vii 31)

[8] For the eschatological significance of Matt. xxvii 52–3, cf. H Zeller, "Corpora Sanctorum (Matt xxvii 52–3)", *Z.f Kath. Theol*, lxxi (1949), 385–465

has been in the world. It overtakes different men at different times, some soon, some in the distant future; in the course of history it becomes multiplied, but in itself and in the mind of Christ, it is a single reality and already present. Now while it is true that this statement requires further proof, even at this point we are entitled to say that Christ's resurrection and the manifestations of his glory, together with his final coming, form a single mystery of the *parousia*, revealed gradually in the course of history. Time, which for us flows continuously between Christ's resurrection and the *parousia*, is at it were contracted in Christ's exaltation; for us on earth it shows one by one the effects of the *parousia* of Christ which will eventually be revealed as a whole.[9]

ii. THE ACTS

The outpouring of the Spirit at Pentecost, is, as far as the Acts is concerned, the characteristic event of the last age of the world

Israel had already known the Spirit. But the Prophets had foretold that in the last age the outpouring of the Spirit would exceed anything known before; that the Spirit would do greater things than ever, establishing a more sublime creation than the one he had produced when the world began. "In that day", he was to sanctify the messianic community and cleanse it of all defilement. (Isa. iv. 4.) He would be poured out upon Israel as a stream on the parched earth, and Israel would blossom so that what had been desert in the time of wrath would become orchard. (Isa. xxxii. 15–18.) Raised up in the Spirit (Ezek. xxxvii. 14) and created in a new pattern (Ezek. xxxvi. 25–8; xi. 18–20), the people would belong to God forever. (Isa. xliv. 3–4; lix. 21.) We are told by Joel that on that last day there was to be a blossoming of charismatic gifts, and on Mount Sion, a community of the saved (iii. 1–5; Douai numbering, ii, 28–32). What was to make the last age new was the outpouring of the Spirit.

Thus, when at Pentecost some of the Jews jeered, "These men are full of wine", St. Peter quoted Joel to them; it was the Spirit who caused their behaviour: the last age had burst into history: "In the last days, I will pour out my spirit . . ." (Acts ii. 17–21.)

In St. Peter's mind the interval separating the Resurrection and

[9] C H Dodd, *The Parables of the Kingdom*, p 28· The Resurrection, Ascension and *parousia* are "all three . . aspects of one idea".

the *parousia* was eradicated. He knew quite well that not until the return of this Jesus who has gone up into heaven shall we see "the re-establishment of all things". But the messianic era foretold by the Prophets was the same era opened by the Resurrection: "For Moses said: A prophet shall the Lord your God raise up unto you, like unto me . . . And all the Prophets, from Samuel and afterwards, who have spoken, have told of these days" (iii. 22-4)—the days of the Resurrection.

III. ST. PAUL

All St. Paul's preaching is dominated by the conviction that, with the Father's action in raising Christ, this last age has burst into the world.

The whole universe, as fashioned by sin, has died in the body of Christ: "The world is crucified for me." (Gal. vi. 14.) That sinful world was still, of course, in appearance, as healthy as ever, but the eye of prophecy saw death at its roots: "The form of this world already passeth away." (1 Cor. vii. 31.)[10]

Christ's resurrection has brought "this present age" to an end, delivering us from Thanatos, Death, from the earthly power of corruption. It has turned the natural universe upside down, for in this man the chain of universal necessity has been snapped and the way of life proper to the last age has been introduced

Only Christ has risen, and yet in him the resurrection of all the dead is fully realized· "He was established Son of God in power by the resurrection of the dead." (Rom. i. 4.)[11] All the power of universal resurrection is concentrated in his glorification. Men will enter the fullness of time when they know the power at work in the one Resurrection—Christ's. (Phil. iii. 10.) On the day of the *parousia* they will be resurrected with him, caught up by the single action of raising which brings Christ into glory; so much so indeed, that the mystery of the *parousia* appears to be not merely bound up with the Easter mystery, but actually identified with it.

All the realities brought into the world by the risen Christ through his rising—the Kingdom (1 Thess. ii. 12), the Spirit, the glory and the power, justice and salvation—are eschatological.

[10] "The world" here is always the sinful world as it is at present.
[11] In the mystery religions, the resurrection of the god never figured as an eschatological fact, because it was simply a reanimation These gods remained involved in the cycle of recurring ends and new beginnings.

The Spirit, imparted to the Church in the Christ of Easter, is the final, heavenly reality. The faithful on earth receive, as it were, an advance upon the sum promised them for the Day. But Christ in glory contains in himself the fullness of the heavenly reality: "The Lord is the spirit." (2 Cor. iii. 17.)

That is why Christ holds in himself all the reality underlying history and the dispensations of this world which were but a dead letter (2 Cor. iii), an inanimate expression of the life-giving reality, a shadow cast back to the beginning of the world, by that glorified body. (Col. ii. 17.)[12]

Christ stands at the conclusion of all things for, because of his glorification, they all centre wholly upon him: all fullness dwells in him. (Col. i. 19.)

Because he contains the fullness of the world and of time, Christ is at the centre of all the change in the universe. Everything stands in him, depends upon him, and takes its origin from him, for he is the fullness of the world to come. The Apocalypse calls him the alpha and omega; he is the principle because he is the goal.

Glory always goes with theophanies, and prophecy has always promised glory for the Day of the Lord. It is Christ's glory that enthrones him in God's universal sovereignty and in the saving power which will be asserted on the Last Day. And that saving will consist in granting us a participation in Christ's own glory (2 Cor. iii. 18; Rom. viii. 18; Phil. iii. 21; 2 Tim. ii. 10); for is not the Gospel announced "unto the acquiring of the glory of our Lord Jesus Christ" at the last day? (2 Thess. ii. 14.) Easter and the *parousia* are for Christ a single "epiphany".

The power with which Christ's splendour is presented to the world is also a reality of the Last Day. Our Lord foretold that the Son of Man would come on his Day with great power and glory. (Mark xiii. 26.) Both attributes were with him in the Resurrection. "The title 'Κυριος', Lord—given at Easter—designates the Christ of the *parousia* in his majesty and glory."[13] The text of 2 Thess. ii. 14

---

[12] The idea that the glorified Christ is the full and final reality of which the realities of the world are only a shadow, can be found in the comparison between earthly marriage and the marriage of Christ and his Church (Eph. v 31ff.); and it underlies the whole of the Epistle to the Hebrews.

[13] L Cerfaux, "Kyrios dans les citations pauliniennes de l'A. T.", *Eph. Theol Lov.*, xx, 1943, 10; *Christ*, pp. 468–9ff Hence the repeated use of the term Lord in the eschatological parables (Matt. xxiv 42–xxv 46)

has preserved the primitive connexion between glory and Lord as between two eschatological concepts. The giving of the title "Kyrios" with the Resurrection is identified with Christ's glorification on his Day, and St. Paul uses the same text from Isaiah (lxv 23) to describe both the exaltation of Easter and the *parousia*, both of which make the whole world bow the knee before the Lord. (Phil. ii. 10; Rom. xiv 11)

On the Last Day, Christ will force his victory upon the powers of this world, bringing powers and principalities to naught, "putting all his enemies under his feet". (1 Cor. xv. 24-5.) But Christ has in fact been their Master since the Resurrection, Lord over all the spirits made subject beneath his feet. (Eph. i. 22)

All is consummated in the man Jesus, the Son of God, raised up according to his divine fullness; in him the resurrection of the dead is complete, power is asserted, holiness is revealed: "He was established Son of God in power, according to the spirit of holiness, by the resurrection from the dead." Our Lord himself said: "Hereafter you shall see the Son of Man coming in the clouds of heaven, sitting at the right hand of the Power." (Matt. xxvi. 64)

iv. CHRIST, DISPENSER OF GOD'S JUSTICE

The function that characterizes the Son of Man on his Day will be that of dispenser of God's justice.

The Son of Man once came only to save that which was lost (Luke xix. 10); but in his glory he will come to judge mankind and decree their fate according as they have received salvation.

After declaring that the stone which the builders had rejected would become the head of the corner, our Lord gave the image a different twist to indicate the harsher side of his glorification: "Whosoever shall fall upon that stone shall be bruised; and upon whomsoever it shall fall, it will grind him to powder." (Luke xx. 18.)

When the parable was about to be fulfilled, as he stood before the judges who were to reject him, our Lord recalled the scene of the judgement as described in Daniel. "Hereafter you shall see the Son of Man seated at the right hand of the Power . . ." The Prophet had seen a heavenly being advancing upon the clouds of heaven towards God who was sitting solemnly in judgement. Thrones figure in the vision; but Daniel does not describe the Son of Man as seated

beside God Christ added this further detail, using another judge-
ment-prophecy to complete Daniel's: "The Lord said to my Lord:
Sit thou at my right hand until I make thy enemies thy footstool."
(Ps. cx. 1.)

God has set the man he has raised from the dead as judge over
mankind—this is also what St. Paul told the Athenians. "He hath
appointed a day wherein he will judge the world in justice by the
man whom he hath appointed [to this task], whom he hath
accredited to all by raising him up from the dead." (Acts xvii. 31.)
The Resurrection is the judge's entry into office and the setting up
of judgement. The same text that is used in Phil. ii. 10–11 to describe
the glory of Christ in the Resurrection, is applied in Rom. xiv. 11
to his function as judge.

The essential function of the risen Christ is the exercise of
sovereign justice: "Him God raised up the third day . . . And he
commanded us to preach to the people, and to testify that it is he
who was appointed by God, to be judge of the living and of the
dead." (Acts x. 40–44.) St. Paul is a witness of the Resurrection, and
in bearing witness to it, he proclaims God's will for justice. Up till
then it had appeared as though God were taking no action against
the sin of the world, but letting evil reign unmolested, not sup-
planted by justice. The age of toleration has come to an end, and
God has determined that now his justice will triumph· "And God
indeed, having winked at the times of this ignorance, now declareth
unto men, that all should everywhere repent." (Acts xvii. 30.) He
wills to "show his justice now, since formerly he allowed the sins
of men to pass without demanding reparation in the time of his
patience; God will show his justice now, I say, that he may be
known to be just and the justifier of him that believes in Jesus."
(Rom. iii. 25–6.)

The justice of God shining out in the risen Christ has two aspects;
it triumphs over evil by justifying and by condemning, as the pillar
of cloud set between two camps which is dark on one side and light
for God's people. The Apostles bear Christ into the world, and are,
as it were, an emanation from him, a "good odour" that is poured
out; with them the judicial sentence contained in the risen Christ
is brought into the world, bearing life for some and death for others.
(2 Cor. 2, 15–16.)

God judges the world through the mystery of Redemption that
takes places in Christ. In the flesh of Christ "this world" and the sin

that was tolerated in the past (Rom. III. 25–6) have been condemned
(Rom VIII. 3; Gal. VI. 14), and henceforward the wrath of God lies
heavy upon them. (Rom 1. 18.)[14]

At the same time God has established, in Christ, the new world
of his justice, and all who belong to it are no longer under condemnation (Rom. VIII 1), but stand in the justice of God· "He rose
again for our justification." (Rom. IV. 25)

God judges the faithful with a justifying judgement, creating
them anew in Christ, communicating to them the justice that is in
Christ, which is his risen life of holiness

To the believer, God's justice is simply a life that is communicated to him. It becomes concrete in Christ's divine glory extending
over us (cf. Rom. III. 22–4), in the Holy Ghost[15] in whom Christ was
"justified" (1 Tim. III. 16), and who is God's love poured out in
our hearts. (Rom v. 5.)[16]

Henceforth this world is split in two, with on the one hand the
flesh and sin, doomed to perdition, and on the other the new
creation. The two are still intertwined in mankind, even in the
heart of the believer who possesses only the pledge of the Spirit
and remains partially subject to the flesh. But from now on the Last
Judgement is in the world and will remain until it is fully revealed.

V. THE FOURTH GOSPEL

Whereas in the Synoptics, Christ foretells his sudden coming, in
the fourth gospel, he is looking forward only to his Hour. In that
hour will the destiny of the world be fulfilled. "The hour now is
when the dead shall hear the voice of the Son of Man." (John v.
25.)[17]

It has been said that to St. John the Incarnation itself is eschatological. From thenceforward judgement is in the world, dividing
it into two, for salvation and perdition "For judgement I am come
into this world." (ix. 39.) But it is only from knowing the fullness
of his glory that Christ claims eschatological privileges, in anticipa-

[14] God's wrath is an eschatological reality. Cf Rom II 5, 8, IX 22; Eph
v. 6; 1 Thess. 1. 10, v. 9, Apoc VI 17.

[15] Rom. viii contrasts the condemnation weighing upon the flesh with the
life of justice in the Holy Ghost.

[16] Thus even God's justice is love, so true is it that God *is* love

[17] "The Hour is also that of the Passion and final consummation " (D
Mollat, "Jugement", *D B. Suppl.*, col 1383.)

tion of the exaltation of Easter, seeing himself as already established in the glory of his Hour.[18]

When the Hour strikes, the final realities are accomplished: "They will look upon him whom they have pierced." (Zach. xii. 10; Apoc. 1. 7; John xix. 37.) But who, one wonders, will thus contemplate him in his immolation? Not the Jews on Calvary, for they have fled. From now on Christ is the man of the vision of the Apocalypse, the man pierced, over whom all the tribes of the earth will lament. (Zach. xii. 10; Apoc. i. 7.)

Our Lord rose in the morning of the first day of the week. Having carefully reckoned[19] the days of Christ's week on earth, John underlines the day of the Resurrection. The new week of creation begins on that day. Having entered into his glory, Christ gives life to all flesh (xvii. 18); that same evening he breathed out the Spirit upon his disciples (xx. 22) just as God breathed upon the waters at the beginning of the world. (Gen. i. 2.)

God's judgement upon the world was given at the moment when Christ's Hour struck: "Now is the judgement of the world; now shall the prince of this world be cast out" (John xii. 31.) But there is in fact only one judgement—the judgement of the Last Day.

As soon as Christ had gone, the Spirit came to reveal that the sentence had been passed and justice done, for Christ had gone to the Father; the unbelieving world was exposed in its essential sinfulness, and the prince of this world was conquered. (xvi. 8–11.)

St. John bases Christ's judicial power on his redemptive work even more firmly than St. Paul: "God sent not his Son into the world to judge the world, but that the world may be saved by him." (iii. 17.) It was not only during his life on earth that judgement was not his task: "I am come not to judge the world but to save the world" (xii. 47), and that "coming" covers the whole economy of the Incarnation. Even on the last day, it will not be Christ himself who pronounces the sentence. (xii. 48.) His mission is only to give life.

The justice Christ has not come to exercise is that of condemnation, for that is the reverse of his life-giving work. Generally, the meaning of "judgement" is limited to this sense—to judge is the

---

[18] In v 21–9, our Lord is talking of his fullness of life and his power of giving life to all flesh, yet he still begs in ch. xvii that he may be glorified in order to be able to give life to all flesh

[19] Cf. above, p 20.

reverse of to save (iii. 17; xii 47); "the resurrection of judgement" is contrasted with that of life (v. 29), for it is the "resurrection of condemnation".

And yet Christ does judge "For judgement I am come into this world" (ix. 39.) By his very presence spirits are separated, for it draws some to the light, while others are cast back into darkness— a darkness made denser by the coming of the Word—and to the condemnation of the Last Day. (xii. 46–7.) There is no need to argue the case, nor prove the guilt; it remains only to execute the sentence.

And, by an extraordinary paradox, this task devolves upon Christ: "As the Father raiseth up the dead, and giveth life. so the Son also giveth life to whom he will. For neither doth the Father judge any man, but hath given all judgement to the Son ... Amen, amen, I say unto you, that the hour cometh and now is, when the dead shall hear the voice of the Son of God, and they that hear shall live. For as the Father hath life in himself, so he hath given to the Son also to have life in himself: and he hath given him power to do judgement because he is the Son of Man. Wonder not at this, for the hour cometh wherein all that are in the graves shall hear his voice. And they that have done good things shall come forth unto the resurrection of life; but they that have done evil, unto the resurrection of condemnation." (v. 21–2, 25–9.) The unbeliever has already prosecuted and condemned himself; Christ steps in to carry out the sentence, and bring him forth to the resurrection of damnation.

How can we reconcile this judicial role with the denials quoted previously? The power to judge is intimately linked with the power to give life; the passage I have just given works out the parallel between the life given by Christ and the sentence he executes. Our Saviour exercises his life-giving power simultaneously with his judicial power.

He who believes is not judged (iii. 18); he passes from death to life (iii. 36)· Christ judges him by giving him life. As for the unbeliever, Christ can claim to be a partial cause of his condemnation, but he can also deny it, for it is only an indirect causality. The sinner himself is the sole cause of a directly willed reprobation; it is he who barricades himself in against the salvation that knocks at his door. And if the Incarnation does not allow of judging (xii. 47), it is possible that in St John's mind, even Christ's positive intervention on the Last Day will only exercise an indirect causality in condemnation. "The resurrection of condemnation" (v. 29) will be the effect of a power to redeem, of the power of life bestowed upon the "Son of Man" (v. 27) come to save us, bestowed therefore for our salvation But this saving power of life will do no more than reanimate those cut off from Christ, without continuing to open out into the divine life; it will remain corrupt and without hope, the living root of the flower from which they have cut themselves off. The power of giving life to all things, granted to Christ because he died for all, has this surprising effect that, in those who shut themselves off from eternal life, it can only produce a life forever unsatisfied and tormented. This is the hell of redeemed man.

Christ's hour, the hour of salvation, is therefore an hour of judgement indeed. At the moment of our Lord's coming to exercise his full right of giving life (xvii. 1–2), condemnation, the stern *other face* of salvation, is revealed as well.

Thus Johannine teaching comes close to the statements of St. Peter and St. Paul. God's justice comes into force with the Redemption; the task of executing it belongs to the risen Christ, and its harshness is the reverse side of his saving action.

Despite often considerable differences in their points of view, the sacred writers agree in seeing Easter as the eschatological event that brings history to a close. They know, however, that time still flows on; they realize that they are caught up in history and they look forward to its end. A theologian who wants to reconcile these contrary ideas would say that God's action in the *parousia* is the same as that action of raising which has been wholly accomplished in the man Christ Jesus, and which will one day be brought to bear upon the entire world.

Since Easter, human time has been advancing towards an event of the past, the resurrection of Christ, and it will only reach it at the end of history.

Our Lord has passed out of our time and become its centre because he is its fullness, its master because he is its end.

VI. THE *parousia* IN HISTORY

The interventions of Christ which mark the history of the Church herald and anticipate the *parousia*.

Shortly after his resurrection, our Lord came to carry out the sentence passed on the Temple of Jerusalem by his death. The

Apostles had thought that the destruction of the sanctuary would coincide with the Messiah's *parousia*: "Tell us when shall these things be? And what shall be the sign of thy coming and of the consummation of the world?" (Matt. xxiv. 3.) Our Lord did not contradict them, but described the destruction of Jerusalem in the framework of his own final coming upon the clouds of heaven.[20]

Before his martyrdom, St. Stephen, filled with the Holy Ghost, contemplated the heavenly realities governing human events, and saw "the Son of Man standing on the right hand of God" (Acts vii. 56), as he will appear on the Last Day. Christ judges history in its very happening.

St. Paul's prophetic intuition also confers an eschatological character upon the events of history. To dispel the Thessalonians' preoccupation with the end of the world, and make them live as men who would be living on earth for an indefinite time, he reminds them that one condition which must precede the *parousia* is not yet present: the appearance of the man of sin, and the great apostasy. (2 Thess. ii. 3–12.) It is clear that the coming of the Antichrist is expected in the near future in this text, for the mystery of iniquity is already at work (verse 7), and in order to delay it, "he who holdeth" must stand in its way. "We get the impression . . . that the adversary is already there, trying to force the door of the house. But there is someone or something holding him back."[21]

If it is natural that two men living the same life of Christ, and brought up on the same Jewish apocalyptic traditions, should judge

---

[20] Despite an intention several times shown of taking away all eschatological significance from those prophecies which admitted of an early realization (compare Mark ix. 1 and xiii. 14 with Luke ix. 27 and xxi 20, 24; note the suppression of Mark xiii 27, 32), Luke has retained in the parable of the talents (xix. 11–29) the simultaneity of the final *parousia* with the prosecution of the rebellious people

[21] D. Buzy, "Antéchrist", *D B Suppl.*, col. 301 The revealing of the Antichrist must be accompanied by an apostasy The Apostle certainly did not envisage the mass apostasy of the faithful as being in the near future; but this does not mean that that revelation must be delayed, for he was not foretelling an apostasy within the Church, but a general religious revolt by those "children of disobedience" in whom "the prince of the power of this air" is at work (Cf Eph. ii 2)
This is in the year 50 or 51, and the Apostle can hardly have spoken so calmly if he envisaged the apostasy of his converts. He saw the Christians of the time of the *parousia* as saved (1 Thess iv 15–17, 1 Cor. iii. 15.) Those who will be dragged down in the fall of the man of sin are not apostate Christians, but those who have refused to accept the truth (2 Thess ii 11–12) Cf B Rigaux, *L'Antéchrist*, Paris, 1932, p. 289.

a situation in similar ways, it is legitimate for us to look for an explanation of this mysterious text from St Paul from what we are told in the Apocalypse of St John.

There too, a mystery of iniquity is at work in the world, a flood of pride passing over the earth, claiming the honours that are God's alone for the "lords" of this world, and bearing them to God's very dwelling. (2 Thess. ii. 4.) St. Paul has been a witness of this. (Acts xii. 22; 1. Cor. viii. 5, of Caligula's attempt to have his own image honoured in the temple of Jerusalem) When John is writing, the iniquity has already borne fruit, the persecuting emperor has appeared, seducing the world with his "lying wonders". (2 Thess. ii. 9–10; Apoc. xiii) The activity of the Beast Antichrist is first of all opposed by the two witnesses (Apoc. xi. 1–13), just as the man of sin is held back by "him who holdeth". These witnesses are they who preach the Gospel, and according to Cullmann,[22] "he who holdeth" is none other than Paul and the Apostles, whose missionary work is holding back the thrust of the adversary. But in the end the Beast wins, the great apostles fall, and it triumphs for a time. (Cf. 2 Thess. ii. 7.) Then Christ appears in his turn, and destroys the Adversary with the sword of his word. (Apoc. xix. 11–21; 2 Thess. ii. 8.) John had seen the adversary of Christ perishing and continually reinstated upon the imperial throne—both a personal and a collective Antichrist, the expression of the pride of the god-state. (Cf. Apoc. xvii. 9–11.) As in St. Paul, the Apocalypse's Antichrist is personal, and as with the Apocalypse, Paul's Antichrist can also be interpreted as collective.[23]

The revelation of Paul's Antichrist—whom the writer of the Apocalypse sees as already at work—is not so far off; for St. Paul Christ's coming seems fairly near, and John hears his step echoing resoundingly in Roman history. Paul does not say that the end of the world will follow upon the revelation of the Adversary. Yet his charismatic insight perceives the end of time, bringing together the whole rebellion of the world and the whole coming of Christ in a

---

[22] O. Cullmann, "Le Caractère eschatologique du devoir missionaire et de conscience apostolique de saint Paul", *Rev. Hist. Phil Rel*, 1936, 210–45

[23] Exegetes recognize an individual Antichrist in 2 Thess ii 3–12. The Apostle's picture is a true one; the events taking place were actually the events of the end, and the present adversary was the final adversary. But it is an incomplete picture, and the theologian might well conclude from the nearness of the revelation of the Antichrist in St Paul that the Antichrist prophesied by Scripture was to consist in a series of adversaries.

single unforeshortened vision which sees the struggles of the end in
the foreground as current facts of history.[24]

Paul may not have adverted to the process of condensation that
his intuition admits of But, as a result, history is asserted to be
eschatological, since Christ is Lord. The end of time is in history,
for the power of Christ is present to it and makes his final victory
part of it even as it unfolds.

When, in the discourse at the Last Supper, our Lord spoke of his
coming, it took an unspectacular form: "When I shall go, and prepare a place for you, I will come again and will take you to myself."
(xiv. 3.) John, the sole survivor of the Twelve, was certainly not
expecting a sensational *parousia* for the Apostles; he appears to have
understood it as that intermediate *parousia* recognized by St. Paul
(2 Cor. v. 8) which takes place in every believer at his death. Even
during men's life on earth, the coming of Christ takes place in the
secrecy of their hearts· "I go away and I come unto you." (xiv. 28.)
This coming is not in the far future, but will start to happen on
Easter Day itself: "A little while and now you shall not see me;
and again a little while, and you shall see me." (xvi. 16.)

Despite its diverse manifestations, Christ's coming remains in
itself a single reality. That one day (xvi. 23) of his return is the day
of his visitation, of his presence in souls, of his giving of the Spirit,
of his final coming.[25]

It seems as though the last appearance of the risen Christ recorded
in the Gospel is meant to suggest his appearance at the end of the
world. Ancient and modern commentators are all struck by the
symbolic nature of the story of that miraculous draught of fishes.
St. Jerome saw this as an eschatological allusion,[26] and St. Augustine[27] Christ appearing at daybreak on the banks of eternity, and
feeding the disciples with mysterious food after they have brought
their net, the Church, safe onto the shore from the restless waters.
The Gospel concludes with this vision, and with one last word from
Christ about his return. (xxi. 22.)

[24] Some modern authors have come to see this Antichrist as a false Jewish
Messiah. Cf. E Cothenet, "La II épître aux Thessaloniens et l'Apocalypse
synoptique", *Rech Sc Rel.*, xlii (1954), 5–39.
[25] Cf Lagrange, *Évangile selon saint Jean*, 3rd ed., Paris, 1927, p. 428.
O. Cullmann, *Christian Worship*, p 116. L Cerfaux, "La Charité fraternelle
et le retour du Christ", *Eph. Theol Lov.*, xxiv, 1948, 324: "All these per-
spectives—resurrection, Pentecost, the actual presence of Christ experienced
in the community, the *parousia*—are mingled together "
[26] *In Dn*, *P L*, xxv, 474   [27] *In Jo*, tract 123–4, *P.L*, xxxv, 1962, 1966

vii. THE THEOLOGY OF HISTORY IN THE APOCALYPSE

The Christ of the Apocalypse has won, in essence, by his death and resurrection, the victory which he now imposes upon the world. Satan is conquered; his battles are now no more than violent rearguard actions. Père Allo has shown this.

Considerations of a more formal nature give a new emphasis to this interpretation Christ appeared to John on Patmos "on the Lord's Day". (i. 10.) It was the first day of the week,[28] the day of the Resurrection, the day when the paschal mystery was celebrated in the assembly. (Acts xx. 7.) This paschal day was also a day of *parousia*, of presence and manifestation. Christ had appeared suddenly amid his disciples who were behind closed doors on this, the first day of the week (John xx. 19), and again a week later (xx. 26). The weekly celebration of the liturgy regularly brought back that presence. And it was also on this paschal day that the Christ of the *parousia* revealed himself on Patmos.

It seems clear to me that the very division of the book is intended to make the eschatological character of the risen Christ and of the events of Christian history stand out.

If, instead of looking for the sort of division that Western logic would make in the Apocalypse, we try to see a plan consistent with the Eastern mind, which advances, as it were, in spirals, from synthesis to synthesis, and consistent also with the sevenfold rhythm which governs the natural development of the book, we must divide it into seven. And each part in its turn is sevenfold, either implicitly, or explicitly (as in the first, second, third and fifth parts). The first sevenfold part, the letters to the Churches, records "the things that are" (i. 19), the rest foretell the future, and make up a complex whole in which the seventh element of each part contains the whole of the next, so that they fit into one another, the first containing all the rest, and the last being contained in all the others.[29]

From this division we can work out a whole theology of Christian

---

[28] Cf. *Didache*, xiv, 1; St Ignatius of Antioch, Magn , ix, 1; *Barn* , xv, 9.
[29] This plan set out by R Loenertz in an article which I have only recently seen ("Plan et division de l'Apocalypse", *Angelicum*, xviii, 1941, 336–56) is one I have always believed in, at least as to the sevenfold division of the book, and the fitting together of the sections of the prophetic part of it I am pleased to find this agreement, since the very fact of it seems to indicate that the interpretation is well founded. Loenertz had been preceded in this, unknown to himself, by J. Levie, "L'Apocalypse de saint Jean devant la critique moderne", *Nouv. Rev. Théol.*, li, 1924, 616–18.

history. The first sevenfold section of the prophetic part presents us with the immolated Lamb, who has become in his glorification the executor of all God's designs which are contained in a scroll with seven seals. The other sections foretell events up till the final consummation, and are contained in the first by the dovetailing I have spoken of. Thus the glorified Lamb presides over the unfolding of history. In the same way, the seventh cycle is contained in those before it. This last describes the final consummation; this consummation is thus present in the midst of the events of history.

On the one hand, the risen Christ presides over events at every stage till they finally reach their goal; on the other, this goal is present in all that has happened since the glorification of the Lamb History is paschal and is also eschatological.

Thus the resurrection of Christ is wholly turned towards the *parousia*, although it is in fact in itself the final coming, the only coming, upon the clouds, at the right hand of the Power. Seen in Christ, the reality of the *parousia* is contained in the Resurrection by being actually present and wholly realized; the glorification, the destruction of death (2 Tim. i. 10), the final resurrection, the judgement, the subjection of the powers—all these are realized in Christ from that time onwards. Seen from the point of view of mankind, the *parousia* is gradually being brought about until it blazes forth on the Last Day; but this is simply the realization in humanity of God's judgement which is already in the world, and of the one resurrection of Christ.

Thus the redemptive act is not the battle that has decided the victory, but to which others must be added before that victory becomes final.[30] It is *the* victory, the only victory, not one to which other subsequent victories can be added; it contains them all, even the final one. The Church is the *pleroma* of Christ in the receptive sense of the word, for she contains his fullness; similarly, history is the *pleroma* of Christ's victory, a victory whole and complete in Christ himself, but which must be accomplished step by step in the world.[31]

[30] This is how O Cullmann understands it (*Christ and Time*, p 141)
[31] According to St. Zeno of Verona, *Tract*, xlvi and xlviii, *De Pascha*, ii and iv, *P.L.*, xi, 489–96, the successive phases of the Church's history are like the different seasons of the year, with spring representing the Church's baptism, summer the prime of her life, and autumn her martyrdom. But all is but one day, the great Easter day of Christ, lived daily by the Church.

2. Towards the Total Possession of the Risen Christ in the *parousia*

The Church does not yet possess the mystery of Easter and of the *parousia* in its fullness. She will move towards possession of it by an innate tendency until she attains it in the supreme revelation of the risen Christ.

1. THE CHURCH LAGGING BEHIND THE RESURRECTION OF HER HEAD[32]

When we see what Scripture has to tell us about the transformation of the Church into the risen Christ, the texts seem to contradict each other. Some see the life of the faithful unfolding as it were within the area of the Resurrection, whereas others show it as caught up in the sphere of the flesh.[33]

On the one hand, the Church has already arrived. As the body of the glorified Christ, she has accomplished the passage from flesh to spirit. Living in the Spirit, she stands outside carnal space and time. All her members have been made anew; their sanctification is complete, they have come into glory. (Rom. viii 30.) The Epistle to the Hebrews, above all, tells us this about the place and time of the new economy: "By one oblation he hath perfected forever them that are sanctified." (x. 14.) "The believer ... is sure that he lives at the fullness of time, at the end of ages (ix. 26), that he is already in the world to come (ii. 5; vi. 5), and that what he enjoys are 'the good things to come' (ix. 11; x. 1)."[34] The Church has outstripped the present world; her existence coincides with the end of the world.[35]

Yet St. Paul confesses that our redemption is not yet consummated: "We groan within ourselves, waiting for the adoption of the sons of God, the redemption of our body; for we are saved by hope." (Rom. viii. 23–4.) He has no doubts about the Redemption;

---

[32] In this section I am considering only Pauline writings.

[33] This has often been pointed out. For a juxtaposition of the texts, see A Wikenhauser, *Die Christusmystik des hl Paulus*, pp. 141–2.

[34] J Bonsirven, *Épître aux Hébreux*, pp 33–4 Cf S. Spicq, *L'Épître aux Hébreux*, vol. i, p. 268, n 6.

[35] The world dies in every believer who enters into Christ, and that death is always present as he grows more one with Christ The end of the world is realized in the believer to the extent that he shares in the Resurrection, just as, in Christ, who is the fullness of resurrection, eschatology is already fully realized

but he declares that the Resurrection, which is perfect in Christ, has reached the faithful only incompletely: they possess it only in germ, and still hope for its fullness.

The Church is still detained in the kingdom of the flesh; through each of her members she enters a body which has gained nothing from the Redemption—our spirit lives because of justification, but our body is dead, because of sin. (Rom. viii. 10.) She exists fully in two different periods of time; she walks in the flesh (2 Cor. x. 3), while she also lives by the Spirit; she dwells in heaven but also journeys upon earth. (2 Cor. v. 7.) She does not exist somewhere between the two times, but actually in both simultaneously. The Spirit and the flesh are not in two separate compartments; there is not one area in light and one in darkness, one wholly redeemed, and one left to the flesh: man as a whole is dominated by the spirit and still in debt to the flesh, is seated with Christ in heaven and exiled far from him.[36]

Thus the Church bears the marks of two opposite states. She leads a mysterious, heavenly existence, and she is also a visible, empirical reality. Her visible life on earth is related to her delay in achieving the full resurrection of her head. Whereas in his individual body, Christ is beyond the reach of sense, in his mystical body he remains in space and time. The fact of being engaged in history is an imperfection for God's people; it indicates an incomplete evolution of their resurrection in Christ.[37]

In her mysterious reality, the Church is indeed the Kingdom of God, the divine dispensation for the end of time in the body of Christ; but as perceived by the senses, she is only its sign and instrument; her appearance is a prophecy of her reality, just as the Chosen People of old were a figure of it. Standing between the time when she was only promised and the time when she will be fully consummated, she "still has something of the Synagogue in her; she still bears part of the promise, is still subject to the pedagogy of a

---

[36] The statements in Rom. viii. 10 and 23 might tend to mislead us, they are to be explained by the fact that the life of God is formed in us as it were from the top down, whereas the life of the flesh grows from its foundation in our material nature, and the influence of both is stronger at its point of origin

[37] The Church's visibility, therefore, is not due to the fact that God is present in her by an incarnation, as is sometimes said, but to the fact that that incarnation is, for the time being, imperfect. Christ himself was also only subject to the senses until the glorious consummation of his incarnation.

certain Law".[38] Though Paul knows she is free in God, the Jerusalem which is above (Gal. iv. 26), he still imposes precepts upon her and regulates the manifestations of her life. (Cf. 1 Cor. xi.; xiv. 26–40.)

The institutions of the Church on earth are suited to her twofold character, spiritual institutions bound up with matter, like the sacraments and the apostolic activity whereby existence on earth comes into contact with the world to come. They are both signs of a time of imperfection and instruments intended to abolish the time of imperfection. They will continue "until we all come ... unto the state of a perfect man" (Eph. iv. 13), and they are preparing for this final achievement. The Eucharist will be celebrated "until he come" (1 Cor. xi. 26), and is a call for his coming: "Maranatha!"[39]

His time on earth means for the believer, as it did for Christ, a limitation of the spirit. Whereas the Spirit of God opens wide the human being, makes it possible for Christ in glory to embrace other existences in his own, the flesh still not wholly eliminated in the faithful preserves whatever barriers it can. St. Paul bewails the fact that it limits our opening out into Christ: "We know that while we are in the body, we are absent from the Lord. For we walk by faith and not by sight " (2 Cor. v. 4–8.)[40]

Even faith, irreplaceable and highly praised as it is, seems here to be a somewhat precarious principle, for it is adapted to our life

---

[38] Y Congar, "La Théologie du dimanche", in *Le Jour du Seigneur*, Paris, 1948, p 168

[39] As an institution, the Church is a sign that our redemption is not yet complete. Unlike the law of the Old Testament, stated from outside, from the top of Sinai, the law of the New is completely interior· it is the Spirit poured into our hearts. The man of the New Testament is free, and in following the law of God is simply following his own law. But in so far as we are still in the flesh, we are still under an Old Testament régime, with the law dictated from outside us through institutions which remain valid as long as we remain in the flesh A sign of the time of imperfection, like the suffering and death of Christians, these institutions are destined to abolish the time of imperfection The Church as an institution leads us to meet Christ through dying to ourselves; she makes us ready for the *parousia* To refuse to submit to her is to refuse to go forward, to remain fixed in this world

[40] I am convinced that the flesh also sets up barriers to prevent perfect fusion among the members of the Church It is in the nature of the flesh to hold us apart from each other. There are many brethren who do not know each other at all, and even among those who do, their union in Christ remains very superficial. When the Church is lifted above her earthly condition, she will discover the presence of children she has never known, and men who never recognized the one true Church will call her "Mother".

on earth by being conditioned by the flesh, and can never consummate our union with Christ.

The carnal state means that the Church remains linked to sin,
for baptism does not destroy all connexion with it. The mortality
of the carnal body is a debt we must pay to sin: "The body indeed
is dead because of sin." (Rom. viii. 10.) The Resurrection will only
do away with sin altogether when it has destroyed death, "the last
enemy". (1 Cor xv. 26.)

Earlier, we saw how Paul denounced the way sin and flesh work
together. Sin has weakened the flesh, and in its weakness, the flesh
opens in man the door to sin. Being in the flesh, the believer would
find it natural to "walk according to the flesh", "according to the
lusts of the flesh", did not the instincts of the Spirit fight against
those desires. (Gal. v. 16ff.) The Christian is not just the zone where
carnal and spiritual meet; they do battle within him, the spirit seeking to destroy the resistance of the world of the flesh This is the
great drama of Christian life; it is engaged both in the flesh and in
the Spirit. The believer has the Spirit ruling above him, and the
empire of the flesh below: the material world which the Spirit cannot
yet penetrate with the dark powers that govern it; and in him the
two worlds come face to face. He is the central point of the world.

As long as the Spirit has not won the final victory in the believer,
the effect of Christ's resurrection will not reach every part of the
universe.

The material world, what Paul calls "the creature", "is full of
expectancy" (Rom. viii. 19), waiting anxiously for the radiance of
divine adoption to be revealed in bodily mankind, for only then will
the light of the Redemption be cast over it.

This sense that the universe is bound up with the fate of mankind
presupposes that St. Paul's conception of the unity of the world is
to be taken quite literally He sees man as firmly fixed into the
whole pattern of creation And indeed, man's life is wholly lived in
the framework of the earth's fertility; it nourishes his existence, and
makes him subject to a thousand-and-one unseen influences whose
effects his mind has always felt, and which in fact shape his destiny.
Then, too, the earth itself is forever coming to life in the humanity
she engenders; it was the slime of the earth that had a living soul
breathed into it; through man it is crowned by receiving the Spirit.
"The universe is not merely a pedestal for man to stand on; it
should rather be likened to an immense stalk whose flower is

humanity "[41] Their destinies are bound together; the fall of man uncrowns all creation.

As long as the glory of sonship is not yet revealed in man, creation groans, having been "made subject to vanity, not willingly, but by reason of him that made it subject—preserving hope; because the creature also itself shall be delivered from the servitude of corruption, to share in the liberty of the glory of the children of God" (Rom viii. 20–21.)

This is a deep anguish at the heart of the created world. It is not merely the result of man's having abused creation in associating it with his sins.[42] "This view of nature from top to bottom"[43] sees all nature wounded to the quick with "every creature groaning" (viii. 22), not merely the few creatures that have been made to serve man's needs.

Sin has thrown the whole world into turmoil; it has deflected nature, cutting short the straight line it should have taken towards God through man; indeed, nature has been completely ousted from its proper place in the divine scheme, for it is no longer related to God in man, nor brought into contact with God's glory through him.

This deflection is not merely in the moral sphere a matter of man's spirit no longer relating it to God; "the creature" suffers in its inmost being, groaning with an actual wound in being brought down to the slavery of corruption. For this "corruption" is of the physical order—that is clear from the Pauline use of the word. Even were all mankind the children of God, virtuously concerned to "help the earth to do God's will",[44] directing the earth's praises to God by turning the material world towards him in themselves. St. Paul would still feel the pain of a creation put into a false position and groaning beneath the yoke of corruption; for it is the same corruption suffered by the children of God themselves. The universe needs to be caught up and set free by "the power of the Resurrection", and to be, in man, brought into contact with the glory of God.[45]

[41] J. Huby, *Épître aux Romains*, 3rd ed , p 297.
[42] Cornely, F. Prat, *Theology*, vol. 1, pp. 238–9.
[43] P Claudel, *Conversations dans le Loir-et-Cher*, Paris, 1935, p 255
[44] P Claudel, *Conversations*, p 268.
[45] This text from Romans is not an isolated instance, for the Apostle's mind was filled with this apocalyptic vision. In this case, he is looking upon creation with sympathy, but in others, he sees the world of corruption not as suffering undeservedly, but as a belonging to sin, as the work of evil

If all creation groans and looks forward, the believer does so most of all (Rom. viii 23–4) and he hopes to have in the future what he has not yet got, his liberty. The liberty he has now (Gal. v. 1, 13; Rom. vi. 20), is different from "the liberty of the glory of children of God". Through man's corruptible body all nature remains in slavery, and man, therefore, most of all.

Though it is crucified (Gal. vi. 14) and its old form destroyed, the world is not wholly so. Though the believer need no longer behave according to the demands of the "elements of this world", he is not yet entirely free of their tyranny. St. Paul proclaims with certainty that Christ and his Church are raised above all the powers (Eph. 1. 20–23), but he also says that the powers at work in the world are still dangerous. Christ's lordship has still to be imposed, there remain victories to be won "until he hath put all his enemies under his feet". (1 Cor. xv. 25.) As long as the Church is in the flesh and has not yet attained to the perfect stature of Christ in the Spirit, she is not ready to subdue the powers that stand against her. Hence her never-ending struggle "against principalities and powers, against the rulers of this world of darkness". (Eph. vi. 12.) The Church will not be wholly protected against the powers and laws of this world until she is wholly freed from this world by the Resurrection. The principalities and death will be conquered together. (1 Cor. xv. 25.)

We thus come to see exactly where the world is nailed to the Cross, and where its transformation must take place: essentially in man. In the dead and risen Christ, the world is already crucified (Gal. vi. 14), the universe is made one (Col i. 20) and the powers are subdued. Similarly all this is accomplished in us, but only to the extent that we too have died and risen again. All this will attain its full realization on the day of the supreme resurrection. In man not yet risen, the powers of this world still have dominion. (Eph. ii. 2.)

The Church's life on earth is like Christ's life on earth in that it contains a principle of resurrection, the spirit of holiness (Rom. i. 4), and that it still has to win its glory. (Phil. ii. 8–9.) In the believer as in Christ, the spirit which demands the Resurrection is a gift of filial life as yet as it were not fully in flower; but in us this grace bears from the beginning the mark of death and resurrection, for only with that mark is the life of sonship communicable to us.[46] There is

powers, and he declares it condemned in Christ (Gal. vi 14, cf. 1 John v 18–19) Cf E Stauffer, *Die Theologie des N T* , pp 56ff

[46] For two reasons: (1) The proximate principle of sanctification is the bodily

a definite limit to the resurrection of the believer; the extent to which he can, by his own effort joined to grace, make again in Christ the journey from sinful flesh to the life of the Spirit. Even after his death in baptism he will still die and gain the risen life which he has received in baptism. Similarly, Christ on earth possessed sonship and the spirit of holiness that went with it (Phil. ii. 6; Rom. i. 3–4), and yet had to win for himself the enjoyment of his sonship and the full outpouring of the Spirit.

11. THE CHURCH BENT UPON THE COMPLETION OF THE PASCHAL MYSTERY IN HERSELF

It is no mere coincidence that the life of the believer is pictured by St. Paul as a movement, while Christ conceived the process of his transformation into glory in terms of a passage, for the two are essentially alike. The believer is on a journey; for him, to live is to walk (Rom. vi. 4; Gal. v. 25), to run towards a goal. (1 Cor. ix. 24–6; Gal. v. 7; Phil. ii. 16; iii. 13–14; 2 Tim. iv. 7.) A favourite image of all the epistles is that of a race; St. Paul was seeing the Greek athlete with his disciplined pace, his mind and body both wholly occupied with his object. All the power that baptism has, as it were, invested in us, tends towards the goal of total resurrection. Everything in us that has not yet reached this goal is pressing towards it; we are wholly eschatological, for everything in us that is not in the world to come in fact is there by inclination.

All things develop; the faith first received grows up (Rom. i. 17) The death and new life given by the sacrament are shown forth in action (Rom. vi. 1–6); the needs of the flesh grow less under pressure from the Spirit (Rom. viii. 13).

In one magnificent text, St. Paul describes his effort, through his life, to achieve the full possession of himself by Christ. "Not as though I had already attained [the goal], or were already perfect; but I follow after, trying to apprehend, because I am also apprehended by Christ Jesus. Brethren, I do not count myself to have apprehended. I do but one thing: forgetting the things that are behind, and stretching forth myself to those that are before, I press

humanity of Christ; now, this only became the connatural principle of sanctification after Christ's death and resurrection; (2) the sinner can only receive the life of sonship if it makes him die to himself in Christ

towards the mark, to the prize to which God calls me on high, in
Christ Jesus." (Phil. iii 12–14.)

The aim of this effort is to achieve the complete conformity with
the risen Christ, realized in the glorification of the body. "What is
meant by 'trying to apprehend'? What he says in the preceding
verse, to attain to the Resurrection from the dead."[47] The force of
the Spirit is directed towards this goal from the first; for the Spirit's
instinct is to take the road of life. (Rom. viii. 6.) Baptism raises
up the believer to a new bodily life, both because the life given in
baptism is bodily in Christ, and because the man who receives it is
an indivisible being. When St. Paul describes the effects of baptism
in Rom. vi. 3–11, he does not separate the resurrection of the body
from the believer's new life.

The life of glory is related to the Spirit of baptism in various ways.
That Spirit is a principle of resurrection, since he brings about the
raising action of the Father, exercising an instrumental causality in
it: "If the Spirit of him that raised up Jesus from the dead dwell in
you, he that raised up Jesus Christ from the dead shall quicken also
your mortal bodies, because of his Spirit that dwelleth in you."
(Rom. viii. 11.) His presence is a kind of first instalment of the
Resurrection in us (2 Cor. 1. 22, v. 5); this is more than merely a
pledge: it is a sum paid on account towards the whole outpouring
of glorification; in the same sense it is the first-fruits of it. (Rom.
viii. 23.) The Resurrection is present in the faithful with the
demands of its efficient cause (Rom. viii. 11) and in its initial reality.

These seeds are already germinating. The final resurrection,
already present in its source, becomes the essential object which the
faithful merit. This is what will crown the efforts of the runner
whose goal is to "attain to the resurrection from the dead". (Phil
iii. 11, 14.)

The believer, by his efforts, acquires more than a right to rise
again; by meriting he is already on the road towards it, already
really disposed to the Resurrection. By his merits he is borne along
from his earthly transfiguration in Christ to final glory. "If you live
according to the flesh you shall die, but if by the Spirit you mortify
the deeds of the flesh, you shall live." (Rom. viii. 13.) What is the
life they are to live? It is everlasting life, and that is bodily. (viii.
11.)

[47] St. John Chrysostom, *In Phil. iii, 12, Hom.*, xi, 3, *P G.*, lxii, 267

Through the believer's efforts to live the death and resurrection of baptism, the Spirit, even on earth, emerges from the sphere of the working of mystery, and makes his presence perceptible in the newness of life. The flesh is dying, even in its outward members: "Therefore put to death your members which are upon the earth" (Col. iii. 5); the Spirit is already beginning to spiritualize them.

The action of the Spirit bears more immediately upon the interior faculties; they also were, in the past, wholly given over to the order of the flesh, but they are the first to be renewed, for the new creature is an "inward man" (Eph. iii. 16; 2 Cor. iv. 16) whose growth starts from the inmost part of the soul. But the whole human make-up is in fact marked by the advance of this resurrection. It is man as a unity who has died in principle in the sacrament, and though the body is the last objective of the invasion of grace, its death and glory are the first to be envisaged, since the body of flesh is at the root of the earthly state. Baptism is meant to be a "despoiling of the body of the flesh" (Col. ii. 11); "our old man is crucified with him, that the body of sin may be destroyed". (Rom. vi. 6.)

Paul's most frequent exhortations are directed towards the sanctification of that body. Now that the body of sin is crucified, ". . . let not sin therefore reign in your mortal bodies so as to obey the lusts thereof. Neither yield ye your members as instruments of iniquity unto sin; but present yourselves to God as those that are alive from the dead, and your members as instruments of justice for the service of God." (Rom. vi. 12–13.) Man is being drawn into the life of the Spirit; his body already has a share in the Resurrection.

There is one state of life that bears witness to this sanctification of the Church even in the body, to the fact that the resurrection from the dead will come, and that is virginity. Our Lord said, "They that shall be accounted worthy of that world, and of the resurrection from the dead, shall neither be married nor take wives . . for they are equal to the angels, and are the children of God, being the children of the resurrection." (Luke xx. 35–6.)

There are some who carry their paschal consecration to its final conclusion. Since baptism has united them to Christ's body, they wish to have no union other than with that body. Their flesh has been crucified and they have risen from the dead; they want to live above this world, by the life of the Spirit, as though the laws of this world had no further claim on them. While the faithful who are married bear witness to our being rooted in the flesh (cf. 1 Cor. vii.

2, 5, 9), those who remain virgins publish the presence of the Easter mystery in the Church St. Paul gives three reasons why celibacy is to be preferred. it makes it possible to belong wholly to Christ (1 Cor. vii. 32–5), it corresponds with the fleeting nature of this world (vii. 29, 31), it avoids the tribulations of the flesh (vii. 28) which trouble those who are involved in the concerns of the flesh and the business of the world. (vii. 26) The virgin is set apart from this world, owes no tribute to the flesh, and belongs only to the risen Lord.

Thus the life of the believer is not entirely "hidden in Christ" (Col. iii. 3), but is outwardly manifested; "the inward man" appears on the surface of "the outward man". Actions which seem quite indifferent to the influence of the Spirit do in fact have their place in Christ: "Whether you eat or drink, or whatsoever else you do, do all to the glory of God." (1 Cor. x. 21.) Even the union of marriage enters the order of grace. (Eph. v. 22–32.)[48]

In this way the temporal itself is beginning to be redeemed in the Church. In the history of Christ's body on earth, we are given the story of the risen Christ as perceptible to the senses. True, that body is not entirely dead and risen, and to that extent, the story is still that of Adam's sin.

The existence of the believer, incomplete and straining to advance, remains unsatisfied, "unquiet", acted upon by a force of redemption which has not yet come to rest in a complete resurrection.

Whereas life as something we possess expresses itself in charity, life as being borne forward expresses itself by hope. This hope starts from the fact of our actually possessing the Spirit. This first gift gives the believer a taste for the things of heaven (Rom. viii. 5) and makes him sure of a fuller outpouring: for the Spirit's presence is a pledge (viii. 23), making us sons and assuring our inheritance (viii. 16–17); it makes our hope certain of fulfilment, since the Spirit we possess is the love of God in our hearts. (v 5.) The Spirit within the believer is himself longing and beseeching (viii. 26–7), for the life of the Spirit instinctively tries to remedy its own state of in-

---

[48] Outside marriage, Christians cannot unite their bodies with other human beings without tearing themselves away from the body of Christ. (1 Cor vi 15–16) In marriage, the union of two human beings is holy, it belongs to the mystery of Christ and the Church of which it is an earthly reflection. But in Christian virginity we find the reality of the mystery, in union with Christ.

completeness. For St. Paul, hope is based upon love, upon our actual, though incomplete, possession of the Spirit.[49]

The goal of that hope is the same as the goal to which the energy of the Christ-life in us is working. complete resurrection: "We groan within ourselves, waiting for the adoption of the sons of God, the redemption of our body." (Rom. viii. 23.) The magnet that draws our desire is not the reconstitution of the human personality after death, and the vision of an unending life in bodies no longer mortal. The union of soul and body is not so precious an advantage that it yields to no other; and St. Paul would gladly "be absent from the body" to be "present with the Lord". (2 Cor. v. 8.) His heart longs for "the hope of the glory of God" (Rom. v. 2; Col. 1. 27), "the hope of his calling" (Eph. i. 18), the fullness of divine life in union with Christ, through a permanent participation in the holy Spirit of the Resurrection.

Hope for St Paul is a paschal virtue both in its origin and its object, a thread drawing the believer from his Saviour's resurrection to his own glorification in Christ.

This, then, is the road taken by the Church as a whole and in her members; she starts from the resurrection of Christ and moves towards the resurrection of Christ, progressing in her participation in divine life until she is wholly filled by it. In the final glorification the association with the Resurrection which began at baptism will be consummated: the Church will be "glorified with him", glorified in the same act that glorifies her Saviour. Thus the Church is moving towards an event which historically happened before she existed, the event of Easter.

iii. THE CHURCH BENT ON ATTAINING THE *parousia*, WHEN THE PASCHAL MYSTERY WILL BE COMPLETED IN HER

Since her first resurrection, the Church has been developing towards the final resurrection by means of the organs through which she gets the life of Christ—the Apostles and the sacraments—and through her own efforts. But these organs are adapted to the Church in her earthly condition; and the faithful cannot extend their efforts

[49] In listing the three virtues, Paul usually puts them in this order: faith, charity, hope (1 Thess. i 3, v 8; Col 1 4–5.)

beyond the sphere of influence of the human will, for the power of the Spirit flows in the human will and does not normally act outside it. A manifestation of divine power greater than any yet known is needed before the Church can pass beyond her earthly condition and the resurrection of Christ be completed in her.

Thus the Church's striving towards her total fulfilment in the resurrection of Christ is accompanied by an equally strong tendency towards the supreme manifestation of God's power on the Last Day.

In the parables given by the Synoptics, the whole of the Church's life takes place between the departure and return of the Master; it is all spent in expectation. The Kingdom of God is like ten virgins, who go out, carrying the lamp of vigilance, to meet the one true bridegroom. (Matt. xxv. 1–13.) Not only is the Kingdom as a whole set between these two poles of departure and return, but the existence of every individual in it; on the day of departure, everyone receives his talent to trade with, and to account for at the return. (Matt. xxv. 14–30.)

Everything the disciple does should be directed towards the Master's coming. This orientation is the criterion of morality during the time that lies between; man will be judged by his desire for that coming, by the extent of his watchfulness and readiness for it. (Matt. xxv. 1–30; Luke xii. 35–46.)

The choice of the hour is God's alone. But the disciple can pray for it to come. He should beg: "Thy kingdom come", and certainly, if the prayer were a vain one, he would not have been told to say it. (Luke xviii. 1–8.) St. Peter, in the Acts, believes that the community has power to hasten the coming of final redemption· "Do penance, that the times of refreshment shall come ... and he [God] shall send him who hath been destined unto you, Jesus Christ." (iii. 20.)[50]

We have seen that, according to St. Paul, Christian life is related to an initial resurrection which is its foundation, and a final resurrection towards which it is developing; similarly, it is set between two *parousias* (presences), the first giving it what one may call the root of salvation, the second, towards which it aspires, bringing it total salvation. The title we reserve for the glorious manifestation of it,

[50] This was a notion familiar to Jewish messianism, and we find it also in 2 Pet iii 11–12 Cf Strack and Billerbeck, *Kommentar*, vol. i, pp 162–5, vol iii, pp 769–75; Lagrange, *Le Messianisme chez les Juifs*, Paris, 1909, pp 189–94.

but the presence is in fact already here: "Christ is in you." (Rom. viii. 10.)

This inward *parousia* coincides for the believer with the end of the world, the new age, final salvation; what distinguishes it from the *parousia* proper is its secrecy and its imperfection. It is imprinted upon the consciousness of the faithful, giving them an assurance that the *parousia* of glory is within their reach, and developing in them what we may call an eschatological psychology "Knowing the season; that it is now the hour for us to rise from sleep; for now our salvation is nearer than when we first believed. The night is passed and the day is at hand. Let us therefore cast off the works of darkness and put on the armour of light. Let us walk honestly as in the day." (Rom. xiii. 11–13.)

So close is the day that the Church is already bathed in the glow of its sunrise. To try to distinguish several days, one when the believer dies, another for the end of the world (as Cornely does), is to distort the Apostle's thought; there is only one Day of the Lord. It would be equally arbitrary to use this text to compute the number of years he thought lay between him and the end of time.[51] The nearness of the *parousia* is of a quite different order from that of time; any purely chronological interpretation will introduce contradictions into the text, for in one breath the Apostle proclaims both dawn and broad day, an antinomy we also find in 1 Thess. v. 7–9 The Apostle's statement refers to the nearness of a presence, that is to a presence incompletely grasped, as well as to the historical coming of an event. We approach this day by the degree to which we participate in its light, as well as by the advance of time. We have already begun to experience it; the *parousia* is as yet hidden and limited—that is why it is not yet given its title—but we feel it to be on the point of bursting forth.[52]

[51] C Toussaint, *L'Épître aux Romains*, Paris, 1913, ad 1 (quoted by Lagrange) "So near does the time of the great apocalypse seem to the apostle that, according to his calculations, there will be "a shorter time before it appears than the period between his conversion and that of his readers, in other words, less than twenty years"

[52] St. Paul is using time as a medium in which to express a thought which appears to be more complex in itself This is not an isolated case Complexities of this sort lie beneath all Pauline theology. He places Christ's death and resurrection, and the *parousia*, in history Yet for him these events are neither purely past nor purely future. At any moment we can come into contact with our Lord's death and resurrection, at any moment the Christ of the *parousia* may reveal himself I have already tried to show how Christ's death and resur-

As the Day approaches, there is in the believer a corresponding assimilation to the Resurrection, for any relationship with the *parousia* is a relationship with the Resurrection. The believer who, since baptism, has been a new man (Rom. vi. 4; vii. 6), becomes ever more renewed as time goes on. (2 Cor. iv. 16; Col. iii. 10.) He grows younger, evolving into an existence younger than the ageing realities of this world, towards the newness of the Spirit (Rom. vii. 6) which is a participation in God's being. He is advancing towards Christ's resurrection as well as towards his *parousia*.

The nearness and actuality of the presence govern the way life is manifested: "Rejoice in the Lord always; again, I say, rejoice. Let your goodwill be known to all men. The Lord is nigh. Be nothing solicitous." (Phil. iv. 4-6.) Christian life is marked by the Lord's presence ("in the Lord") and his nearness, which combine to give the soul joyful certainty.

Both because the *parousia* is already here, and because it is as yet imperfect, the Church goes towards the Day with a great longing of her whole being. Just as she is bent on her fulfilment in the resurrection of Christ, so also she is drawn towards the Day of the Lord; and that she thus tends simultaneously towards two goals situated as it were at opposite poles of time, proves once again that Christ's resurrection and his *parousia* form a single mystery, revealed in different aspects at different times.

It is the gift of the Spirit which bestows this essential relationship upon the being of the Church: "Grieve not the holy Spirit of God by whom you are marked as by a seal unto the day of redemption." (Eph. iv. 30; i. 14.) The mark imprinted upon the believer by the presence of the Spirit shows Christ's right of ownership over him, and puts him in the power of Christ's saving lordship on the day of the *parousia*.

This mark is no mere outward seal. The Spirit communicated to man by the presence of the Holy Ghost is borne on by its very nature towards the Day. We have seen how intimately the spirit and the glory of God (*doxa*) are related. (Cf. ch. iii.) On the day of Christ's epiphany (2 Thess. ii. 8; 1 Tom. vi. 14), the glory of God will fall on the faithful with its "eternal weight" (2 Cor. iv. 17), the

---

rection which are, historically, in the past, remain present in his lasting glorification I think the reason for the latent actuality of the *parousia* is to be found in the fact that the *parousia* is an aspect of the ever-actual mystery of the Resurrection Cf. St. Ambrose, *De Sacramentis*, v, 26, *P.L.*, xvi, 453

same glory whose power absorbed Christ's weakness. (Rom. viii 17–18.) But the believer, who even now contemplates the face of the "Christ-spirit", is already illumined by it; it grows in him from glory to glory until it is transformed into an exact likeness of the Lord (2 Cor. iii. 18), on the day of the *parousia*.

Like the glory and the Spirit granted to the believer, justification is also directed towards the Last Day. The action of God's saving justice upon man is one with the transforming action which the glory of God performs in him. (Rom. iii. 23ff.) Having put an end to the "time of his patience", when he appeared to tolerate evil, God is now showing his justice, and quelling sin by justifying those who believe and rendering justice to the rest (Rom. iii. 21–6; i. 17ff.).

This judicial action takes place in two ages. It opens "in this time" (Rom. iii. 26), and will close with the court of judgement on the great day. The impious, even now, feel the weight of God's anger, delivering them over to the shame of their lusts (Rom. i. 18ff.), whereas in those who believe, he destroys sin by communicating his own justice to them. This first justification is not merely a declaration, but a transformation, producing a life in which there is salvation (cf. Rom. viii.). Man seeks God's life-giving justice in order that he may be just and be seen by God to be so. (Cf. Rom. iii. 20.)[53]

On the Last Day God will call all men to his judgement seat and give his pronouncement on their justice. The texts that speak of this tribunal stress the judicial aspect of divine justice (Rom. ii. 13), but the Last Judgement is more than simply a pronouncement, for it produces in the faithful the effects of actual justification, similar to those of baptism—indeed, they are called redemption (Eph. iv. 30) and salvation. (Heb. ix. 28.)

The two ultimate justifications, of baptism and the Last Day, are set in a single perspective. Though the first is real in itself, it is also eschatological in being wholly directed towards the last, and destined to save us from the wrath to come: "Much more, therefore, being now justified by his blood, shall we be saved from wrath through him." (Rom. v. 9.) The condemnation from which baptismal justification spares us is that of "the day of wrath and revelation of the

---

[53] Père Lagrange defines St Paul's concept of God's justice as "an activity of God's for the purpose of making men just and recognized as such before his tribunal" (*Épître aux Romains*, 3rd ed., Paris, 1922, p 121) Justification is a real judgement

just judgement of God". (Rom. ii. 5.) This thought is taken up again and developed positively. "For if, when enemies [in the objective sense, that is to say out of the favour] of God, we were reconciled to God by the death of his Son; much more, being reconciled, shall we be saved by his life." (Rom. v. 10.) The life of the risen Christ, lived in the believer, opens out onto the salvation of the Last Day: by giving it in baptism, God has even then pronounced a sentence of final justification. Baptism puts into man a seed of resurrection and a verdict of divine justice.

Between these two manifestations—baptism and the *parousia*—God's justice develops gradually; first appearing in the believer as the faith of baptism, it asserts itself more and more, "from faith unto faith" (Rom 1 17) Since it is still possible to lose the salvation of the first justification, God is careful to preserve and strengthen it up till the day of final consecration: "Who also will strengthen you until the end, that you may be without crime in the day of the coming of our Lord Jesus Christ." (1 Cor. 1. 8.) "He, who hath begun a good work in you, will perfect it unto the day of Christ Jesus." (Phil. 1. 6.) The believer, in his turn, is sure of this justification, though he possesses as it were only the preliminaries to it; he works to make himself pure and "without offence" for the last day. (2 Cor. v 9, Phil. 1. 10.) Though he may not approach it entirely without apprehension, he longs for it more than he fears it; for he is destined for justification rather than judgement, set apart as he is, not for the wrath of the Last Day, but for the "purchasing of salvation" (1 Thess v. 9), for ultimate resurrection.

Parallel with this progress of saving justice in the believer, the infidel is "treasuring up wrath" for himself as a preliminary to his final condemnation. (Rom. ii 1–10.)

This life which is carried forward by its own law kindles in the soul the fire of desire. The Church's heart is turned towards the Last Day. The epistles to the Thessalonians, which give us the earliest literary echo of Christian thought, are alive with expectation of the *parousia*.

The coming of Christ is the object of one of the three theological virtues: "Being mindful of the work of your faith, the labour of your charity, and of the enduring of the hope of our Lord Jesus Christ." (1 Thess 1. 3.) The hope of the faithful consists in their longing for and expectation of Christ. From the first moment of

faith, they have been directed towards this goal: "You turned . . .
to serve the living and true God, and to wait for his Son from heaven
(whom he raised up from the dead), Jesus, who hath delivered us
from the wrath to come." (1 Thess. 9–10.) All Christian thought
moves from the Resurrection to the return of the Lord starting
from the one and stretching forward towards the other. The attitude
of expectation is a habitual one with the believer: "We wait", is
the cry of the faithful (Rom. viii. 23; 1 Cor. i. 7; Gal. v. 5; Phil. iii.
20); indeed, their love for Christ's epiphany is the criterion of the
reward they are to receive. (2 Tim. iv. 8.) St. Paul's whole life was
a powerful straining towards the *parousia*, even in the latter part
of it when he was less preoccupied with eschatology. Once again in
his last epistle, the one that has been called his testament, his love
of the Lord's coming is expressed. (2 Tim. iv. 6–8.)

There is still more to add about the Church's moving towards the
goal of the *parousia*. Her activity is far from being merely a preparation for the Day, making it possible for her to wait with assurance. Christ's presence, which has, since the Resurrection, been ever
more firmly asserted in the world, is realized in the Church and
through her. In her Christ becomes present to the world, through
the Apostles he takes shape in the faithful. (Gal. iv. 19.) Though
only God can make Christ dwell in men's hearts (Eph. iii. 16–17),
the Church assists the progress of that presence (Eph. iv. 11–13);
grace is given her to bring the *parousia* to birth. Though it is not
she who will bring about the final revelation of her Saviour, for
this, like the Resurrection, is a work reserved to the Father (1 Tim
vi. 14–15; cf. Acts iii. 20), yet it is in her that Christ's presence is
now actual in the world—circumscribed still, but becoming ever
intensified.

We may wonder whether Paul thought that the hour of the
parousia was to depend on the Church, upon her perfection and her
efforts to intensify Christ's presence in the world. It would certainly
appear as though this hour belongs so exclusively to God's sovereign
power that it must be independent of the Church's efforts, yet the
hypothesis merits consideration. St. Paul realizes that the epiphany
of the Lord is bound up with the kingdom of Christ (2 Tim. iv. 1)
for which he labours. The crown laid up for his own good fight
will be for "them also that love his coming" (2 Tim. iv. 8)—a love
which, in this context, is active and expends itself in working for
the *parousia*. It is not impossible that Paul shared the hope (Acts iii.

20; 2 Pet. iii. 11–12) that that coming might be hastened on by the faithful.[54]

We see then that the Church is borne towards the *parousia* by a movement that is of her essence. And, as we have also seen, she is borne by the same movement towards a complete participation in Christ's resurrection. Though God's action in raising Christ, and the *parousia*, are set at opposite ends, as it were, of time, the Church advances towards both, without the strain of aiming for two separate goals. It is clear that the *parousia* is simply the mystery of Easter as expressed in the fullness of its effects upon the faithful.

At a time when both events still lay in the future, our Lord drew them together in a single vision. (Matt. xxvi. 64.) With the Resurrection and the *parousia* standing, one behind the Church and the other ahead of her, the Apostles' view of them was broken when they were thinking of them only in the relationship they had in time. But for them as well, Easter was a mystery of the *parousia*, and the Christ of the *parousia* is the Christ of the Easter mystery. If we are to recover Christ's singleness of vision and recognize the basic identity the Apostles saw in the two events, we must get beyond their relationship in time and judge them according to their nature. This will bring the Resurrection and the *parousia* together in a single mystery.[55]

However, although for Christ personally the *parousia* and Resurrection are one thing, there is a difference for the Church; for her Easter is a vast potentiality and the *parousia* a full realization. Time can add nothing to Christ, but it enriches the Church with all the treasures of her Saviour.

When Christ is considered in his identification with the Church, then even for him the *parousia* is a different thing from the Resurrection. In Christ's individual humanity the mystery of the *parousia* is complete: the resurrection from the dead is accomplished, the world is crucified, the universe is reconciled, the powers are made subject and all things are re-established—the raising action of God

---

[54] In this case the Church is the arbiter of the continuance of "this world", preparing for its end in herself. Hence the hatred "this world" has for her.

[55] In the second century the *parousia* can even be entitled "the Lord's Pasch" The *Letter to Diognetus* closes with this wish and certainty. "Salvation is appearing, the apostles understand, the Lord's Pasch is coming, the time is fulfilled and order is established in the universe " (Or, following a likely conjecture· " .. the candles are brought and arranged" as for the Easter vigil.)

has attained completion. But to Christ, as identified with the Church, all things are not yet subject (1 Cor. xv. 24; Heb. 11. 8), the material world is not reconciled (Rom. viii. 19–20), the resurrection of the dead is only beginning. Thus Christ's resurrection has not yet achieved its full significance throughout the world, for it is in bodily man that the powers are or are not vanquished, and the material world is or is not crucified and saved.

Because Christ and the Church are identified, their destinies in the world are identical as well. The life of both is hidden; when it is manifested in Christ it will appear in the Church (Col. iii. 3–4), for it is in her that Christ reveals himself to the world. "He shall come to be glorified in his saints, and to be made wonderful in all them who have believed." (2 Thess. 1. 10.)

In short, the *parousia*, both actual and final, adds nothing to God's action in raising Christ; but it bestows on the Church the blessings of that raising action, and in the Church, it manifests the risen Christ to the world—for it is through the Church that the risen Christ is in the world. History enriches Christ, not in himself, but by bringing about the realization of him in the Church.

3 THE CONSUMMATION OF THE EASTER MYSTERY IN THE CHURCH

The coming of the *parousia* will result in the resurrection of men's bodies, the reintegration of the material universe and the Last Judgement

i. THE RESURRECTION OF MEN'S BODIES

Bodily resurrection to eternal life will be the ultimate and necessary consequence of God's action in raising Christ and the grafting of the Church into our Lord's bodily humanity; this is both because Christ and the believers caught up in him are men and not simply souls, and because God's action in sanctifying them is of the order of physical realities. To deny the necessary effect of a thing is also to deny the thing itself, the cause: "If there be no resurrection of the dead, then Christ is not risen again." (1 Cor. xv. 13.)

The glorification of the believer will be the complete realization of Christ's resurrection in him. It is the effect of "the power [which brought about] his resurrection" (Phil. iii. 10); it calls for no new display of God's raising power, nor is it a repetition of the Easter mystery in the bodies of the faithful; they will rise "with him" (Rom. viii. 17; 2 Tim ii. 11), as St. Paul's constant phrase expresses it, as they rose "with him" at baptism, but now their whole being will be subject to that same single divine action that raised Christ: they will be absorbed into the mystery of the *parousia* of Christ's resurrection.

Like that of Christ, the resurrection of the Church is the work of the Father. But the Spirit, the quasi-formal cause of all sanctification, is the immediate principle of it. (Rom. viii. 11.)

Christ the Lord is master of all spiritual power. The resurrection in glory pertains to his lordly power: "He will transform the body of our lowness, made like to the body of his glory, according to the operation whereby also he is able to subdue all things to himself." (Phil. iii. 21.) Christ's power as Lord enables him to triumph over every obstacle, death included, and to make man wholly subject to him. (Cf. Rom. xiv. 9.)

This final working of the Spirit and the Lord will bring life "in Christ" to perfection. In the past the believer was born son of God, by the Spirit, the power of the risen Christ. At the *parousia*, the Father will consecrate our adoption as sons and make it evident: "We groan within ourselves, waiting for the adoption of the sons of God, the redemption of our body." (Rom viii. 23.) It will be the conclusion of a lengthy birth, as the Father's image becomes recognizable in the believer's entire being. The Spirit is the author of this "revelation of the sons of God" (Rom viii. 19); it is he who makes them into the sons our Lord spoke of (Luke xx. 36) who will be spiritual like the angels. By doing so, he brings the children into their inheritance, destroying in them all that lingered in the flesh which "cannot possess the Kingdom". (1 Cor. xv. 50; cf. John iii. 5–6.) At the Resurrection, these children will receive the complete liberty of sons, the "liberty of the glory of the children of God" (Rom. viii. 21), for "where the Spirit of the Lord is, there is liberty". (2 Cor. iii. 17.)

When the faithful are thus supremely identified with the bodily Christ, the definition of the Church will be fully realized as "his body, and the fullness of him who is filled all in all". (Eph. i. 23.) She will become the body of Christ in the fullest reality, for then the life of our Lord will animate even her material being; she will be the *pleroma* of Christ, now she is filled by Christ to the uttermost limits of her being; she will have attained to the stature of the perfect man, that "measure of the fullness of Christ" which fits her to receive the gift of Christ in its fullness. (Eph. iv 13.) When St. Paul gave the Church that famous definition—the body and fullness of Christ—he saw her as wholly caught up, body and soul, in the bodily resurrection of her Saviour. (Eph. i. 18-23.)[56]

"But some man will say: How do the dead rise again? Or with what manner of body shall they come?" (1 Cor. xv. 35.) St. Paul goes on to list four qualities of the risen body· incorruptibility, glory, power, and spirituality (42-4) The last, spirituality, is at the basis of them all. (Cf. verse 45.) The Spirit of God gives man the glory and power of his immortal life.

The Christian will be a wholly spiritual being. The flesh will be abolished by the power of the Spirit—not by the body's being absorbed into the Spirit, for it will be the body that rises, nor by the soul's being replaced by some new principle, for human beings will lose none of their humanity in entering the kingdom of God.[57] But the soul will no longer act simply as a principle of natural life, and the body will no longer be a carnal one The soul as a psyche is principle only of a life adapted to the nature of the body, to the laws of the earth of which it was formed, and the body remains a body of earth. (Verse 47) The Spirit ennobles the power of animation in our vital principle, so that the body is enabled to get beyond the laws of its original elements, and take on spiritual qualities. Whereas the life of man's first body is rooted in the flesh, the life of the second is rooted on high; the Resurrection is the goal of birth on high, birth by the Spirit. (Cf. John iii. 3, 5.) But its roots are established in a body as well as in the Spirit—the body of Christ.

[56] Cf J Huby, *Les Épîtres de la captivité*, p 166 If the translation some scholars would give is correct, 1 John iii. 2 shows the supreme transformation of the believer as a formal result of the *parousia*: "Dearly beloved, we are now the sons of God; and it hath not yet appeared what we shall be We know that when he [the Son] shall appear, we shall be like to him, because we shall see him as he is." (Bonsirven renders it thus.) It is in the Son that the life of God will appear, and it will be communicated in the form of knowledge of the Son (Cf 1. 1-3.) He has been manifested once, and that first appearance has destroyed sin and brought the filial life into being (iii 8-9.) Meanwhile, the Son has only imperfectly revealed himself, we have only an imperfect knowledge of him, and therefore our filial life is barely begun. But when he is revealed in his splendour, we shall see him as he is and because we do, we shall become like him With the revelation of the Son, knowledge develops and the filial being becomes perfect

[57] St Ignatius of Antioch, *Rom.*, vi, 2, says that only then will man be wholly man The human body itself will achieve its specific perfection, since it is a human body whose destiny is to be governed by the spirit

Then the Church will have reached her final salvation (Heb. ix. 28), her complete redemption (Rom. viii. 23), then when God has totally transferred her "from the power of darkness into the kingdom of the Son of his love". (Col. i. 13.)

Then will creation be complete. "The shadow", "the letter", "earthly man" will be replaced by "the heavenly man" who is "spirit". (Cf 1 Cor xv. 45-7.) History passes from the earthly man to the heavenly man, from the shadow to the spiritual reality. The Spirit is the power behind this progressive creation, the Master of history.

ii. THE REINTEGRATION OF THE MATERIAL UNIVERSE

All nature, which has been waiting, will be touched by the redemption on that Day.

The Prophets had foretold the end of the world and a renovation of the universe, and the New Testament sanctions this belief. Our Lord made the day of the *parousia* the date for the transformation of the world, calling it simply a regeneration (Matt. xix. 28), a new birth of all things. The eschatological discourse speaks of a cosmic cataclysm: "In those days the sun shall be darkened, and the moon shall not give her light, and the stars of heaven shall be falling down, and the powers that are in heaven shall be shaken." (Mark xiii. 24-5.) But these are all images familiar in prophecy and apocalyptic writings—Isaiah uses them for God's judgements on Babylon and Edom (xiii 10; xxxiv. 4)—as the necessary accompaniments of any manifestation of God as judge; they are not an assurance that the structure of the universe will be changed.

St. Peter describes this transformation as a restoring of all things; he also makes it coincide with our Saviour's return. (Acts iii. 21.)

What is meant by the terms "rebirth" and the "restoration of all things"? Their choice was no doubt inspired by two things which stood in the forefront of the transformation as envisaged in the minds of Christ and St. Peter· the idea of birth was suggested by the resurrection of mankind, and that of restoration by the triumphant return of Israel (cf. Matt. xvii. 11; Acts i. 6), but both the resurrection and the triumph are seen in the framework of a restoration of the whole universe.[58]

---

[58] Cf Strack and Billerbeck, *Kommentar*, p 19; vol. iii, pp 840-7.

Jewish messianism was turning more and more towards an apocalyptic eschatology along the lines of Isaiah, lxv, 17: "For behold I create new heavens, and a new earth: and the former things shall not be in remembrance, and they shall not come upon the heart." Although this text may be taken in a spiritual sense, Jewish thought, and the later documents of Christian revelation (such as 2 Pet. iii. 13, and perhaps the Apocalypse) continued to interpret it literally. In order to be born to this youth and beauty, heaven and earth must be purified by tribulation. Whatever the nature of the fire whereby "the elements shall be melted with heat" (2 Pet. iii. 10), creation must undergo death before entering the new age of the Resurrection.

St. Paul, who is less vivid in the details he gives us about the fate of the cosmos, fixes it more firmly within the economy of the Redemption. The Epistles of the Captivity, with characteristic insistence, follow the effects of the Redemption to the furthest bounds of the universe All creation is drawn behind the Church in the wake of Christ's exaltation. The texts which talk of a compenetration of the Church by Christ also tell of the influence of Christ's glorification on creation as a whole. "[He will make known to us] the mystery of his will .. to re-establish all things in Christ, that are in heaven and on earth, in him." (Eph. i. 9–10; cf. Col. i. 20.)

The Church is set at the very centre of Christ's radiance, identified with the body of the risen Christ, the perfect recipient of the divine glory. But the radiance extends beyond the faithful. Christ "is ascended above all the heavens, that he might fill all things" (Eph. iv. 10), that he may penetrate "to the ultimate element of all things by his presence and his action".[59] The title of Head is reserved to Christ as principle of life for those who believe in him, and the title of fullness (*pleroma*) for the Church filled with that life; yet, in a different but perfectly real sense, Christ "recapitulates" all creation, and "fills" it with his glory.

The universe owes this to its relationship with the Church, who is the "pleroma" *par excellence*, who contains Christ himself, is his body, the light whose rays are cast on the world; all the power of the risen Christ which overflows to the world is first of all in the Church, "which is his body, and the fullness of him who is wholly fulfilled in all". (Eph. 1. 23.) The glory that extends beyond her is the fringe of her own splendour.

The Apostle says this explicitly: all creation will share in "the liberty of the glory of the children of God" (Rom. viii. 21), when the bodies which bind her to the faithful and to Christ are glorified. The corruption she now suffers, from which she will be set free, is of a physical kind; yet the text seems to say that the liberation which will occur in men's bodies will be enough to assuage the groaning of the rest of creation. The fact that creation is reconciled in the glorified Christ, but is not yet so because of the mortal bodies of the other sons of God, makes it clear that the material world will find its liberation in the body of Christ and of man.

Considering the Jewish and Christian apocalyptic thought to which Paul seems to refer (verse 22), we can hardly interpret this so narrowly as to reject the notion of nature itself sharing in the liberty of the children; the Pauline concept of liberty is flexible enough to fit the material creation as well.[60] Creation is drawn into (εἰς) the glory of the children

To what extent? To the extent of its union with the body of Christ and with the Church. But we do not know what this extent will be. For in the Resurrection man will no longer be earthly, no longer nourished by the earth. Rooted in Christ, he will be nourished by the Spirit. Nature will then be dependent on Christian man; the world will be reversed. man, its summit, will be at the same time its base in Christ, for Christ in glory is both the summit and origin of all things.

Thus the second creation—begun in the Resurrection and completed then, too, in Christ—will be completed in the universe. History, which began with the first genesis of the world, will attain in the world to the fullness of time it has already attained in Christ. This second creation is a continuation of the first, and the two are joined in the body of Christ. Starting with the shaping of the material world, passing through man, gradually narrowing until it reaches the summit of mankind, which is Christ, the history of salvation starts to widen again from this point, until, through men, the whole universe is re-created Its central point is the body of Christ, whose death is both the pinnacle and the end of the mortal world, and whose glory is the source of newness for the new world.

---

[60] Pauline liberty is not the same thing as free will The children of God are free because they are set free from sinful flesh and its slaveries.

This body still bears in its side the wound that pierced it, in which the first creation was immolated and the second consecrated.[61]

iii. THE LAST JUDGEMENT

In the *parousia*, God's justice in the Lord Jesus will be, as it were, formulated once and for all.

At the same time as he inaugurated a new creation in the resurrection of Christ, God also began the process of judging of the world. For the principle of the new life brought in by the Resurrection is none other than the Spirit, who is God's justice as well as man's salvation. Henceforth men are marked out either for justice or for condemnation Those who believe have been re-created in the Spirit, judged with a sentence of life-giving justice. The rest remain in the flesh, which is condemned to die.

[61] To this chapter there attaches a question which present-day thinkers are much concerned with. are human work and progress an advance towards the world to come? New Testament theology seems to make the following distinctions:

(a) "Between man's contribution and the Kingdom there is an absolute ontological break, if in man (in his work and in the progress of civilization) we only consider himself." (L. Malevez, "La vision chrétienne de l'histoire", *Nouv Rev. Théol,,* lxxi, 1949, 257.) From this point of view, as Karl Barth says, the coming of the kingdom is "a transcendent event wholly vertical in direction". (Cf. L. Malevez, *op. cit*, pp 258-9) Flesh and spirit are two different planes. To be convinced of this, we have only to read 1 Cor. i 19-31

(b) Yet civilization can be linked to the world to come. Man's earthly existence will in fact be prolonged in the kingdom, if, through the charity of the Spirit, it already contains within it the world to come. If so, it is moving towards the Resurrection in all its manifestations, although it will not arrive there in its earthly form

In the believer, therefore, but only in him, the present world is linked to the future world. Earthly labour can contribute to the building of the future city, not because of what it achieves, but because of the charity underlying it Labour and progress are part of the Christian map of the world because they are demanded by charity. But apart from charity, the evolution inscribed in man's nature, because of the sin inherent in it, moves downward, towards a death with which it is ever in contact; for only in Christ is man saved from his sin and its goal of meaninglessness in Christ, in whom he finds his humanity completed.

Thus, when in the past a Christian kissed a leper or sucked the poison from an ulcer, it was closer to the act of redemption and richer in the power of the Kingdom than the cures of modern science with less of charity underlying them

In short, the efforts of civilization can be a preparation for the Kingdom, but only in as much as they make man himself ready for it The world will enter the new era of the Resurrection in man, and through charity.

Will the end of this trial, one wonders, coincide with the completion of God's creative action in the fullness of resurrection, with the final sentence indicating the unity of the two powers—of justice and of resurrection? Will the Last Judgement be the completion of this action of raising with its twofold effect of justifying and condemning, or is it to be thought of in the same way as a decree of human justice which, after enquiry, pronounces upon the merits and demerits of the case and determines the punishment?

When Christ, closing his eschatological prophecy and the whole of his public preaching, paints that vivid picture of the Judgement (Matt. xxv. 31–46), he is simply enlarging all the elements of a human tribunal to fit the world. The convoking of the human race, the presence of assessors, the judicial enquiry, the separating of the good and wicked, the delivering of the sentence and the reasons for it—nothing is lacking, even the judge's throne.

But the Synoptics generally put the Judgement quite beyond any comparison with human jurisdiction. In the parables of the Coming, judgement is given by the admission of some into the kingdom and the exclusion of others. (Matt. xxii. 11–14; xxiv. 45–51; xxv 1–13.) In the eschatological discourse there is no judicial apparatus. "Then two shall be in the field one shall be taken and one shall be left Two women will be grinding at the mill: one shall be taken and one shall be left." (Matt. xxiv. 40–1.) Some shall be taken into the kingdom (cf. xxiv 31), the rest shall be left out. The judgement is given in the same act by which justice is done.

A better analogy than in human courts of law for the harsh reality of this judgement is found in the various foreshadowings of the *parousia* in history—in the setting-up of the Kingdom, for instance, and the destruction of Jerusalem—in whose framework our Lord himself saw it.

John the Baptist too saw the judgement of the Messiah as the execution of justice. He summed up the whole work of the Messiah, from Christ's approaching coming to the Last Judgement, in the allegory of the winnower sweeping his threshing-floor, collecting the grain for the barn and the chaff for the fire (Matt. iii 12). And he saw Christ baptising with the Spirit and with fire, immersing men in that divine principle which would sanctify some and destroy others: both an act of judging and an execution of justice.

Thus, although Matt. xxv 31–46 makes it appear to resemble an immense court of law, the Synoptics do not envisage the judgement

of the world by the Messiah as a judicial trial followed by a sentence, but as an effective display of power whereby the Messiah
brings some into the Kingdom and casts others out of it according
to their deserts.

In the fourth gospel, the Last Judgement is in close continuity
with a sentence already passed on earth in every man's heart according to his response to the word of God. In this life final justice is
present, precariously but totally, and it will be unfolded in the next.
Man's faithful adherence to the Son's words carries within it the
sentence in his favour; unbelief bears condemnation and suffering.
(iii. 18; v. 24.) For the believer, the judgement coincides with the
resurrection to the new life—resurrection is not followed by judgement, but contains it. "He who heareth my word and believeth him
that sent me, hath life everlasting; and cometh not to judgement
but is passed from death to life." (v. 24.) The power to give life
and the power to judge are so linked that one seems to involve the
other: "As the Father raiseth up the dead and giveth life, so ... he
hath given all judgement to the Son." (v. 21-2.)[62]

These general statements, valid even on earth, are reiterated in
the succeeding verses, but only as applying to the Last Day: "As
the Father hath life in himself, so he hath given to the Son to have
life in himself: and he hath given him power to do judgement,
because he is the Son of Man. Wonder not at this, for the hour
cometh, wherein all that are in the graves shall hear his voice And
they that have done good things, shall come forth unto the resurrection of life; but they that have done evil unto the resurrection of
judgement", in other words, condemnation (v, 26-9.)[63]

Christ delivers the sentence of the Last Day because he is the Son
of Man, the eschatological Saviour who is re-creating the world for
God. The Last Judgement is simply the goal and high point of the
permanent exercise of his power of life and of justice, the conclusion
of a process of separation which, in the same single action, effects
even on earth, the giving of life or hardening into death.

[62] The γάρ repeated in each verse, from verse 19 on, proves in each case the
statement that goes before it The Son raises the dead, because he has the
power of judging.
[63] We translate this "unto the resurrection of judgement", not "the resurrection that leads to judgement". In the phrase "resurrection of life" the
genitive indicates the nature of the resurrection The believer is raised to life
in the Johannine sense of the word; the unbeliever rises to the existence of
condemnation

Christ will judge the dead by awakening them to life in a twofold resurrection. The faithful will no more undergo judgement than they did on earth (v. 24), but will pass from death to life: "They shall come forth unto the resurrection of life." The condemnation of the unbeliever will be wholly contained in his resurrection: "They will come forth unto the resurrection of condemnation." Daniel had prophesied that some should awake to eternal life, and others to shame and reproach. (Dan. xii. 2.)

Our Lord said that his mission was not to judge (condemn) (xii. 47), but to bring a salvation from which men might, to their disaster, withdraw Thus every resurrection is brought about by a force of life and salvation whose saving effect can be impeded by men's resisting it. Man does not rise again to the same life as he had before; history has passed beyond the first creation, and will not retrace its steps. Since Christ's resurrection, it has been advancing towards a new world. The Son of Man, who is the prince of the era of salvation that comes at the end of the world, imprints a new existence on everyone. (xvii. 2.) The Resurrection is the effect of a vivifying power, but there are some in whom it remains incomplete, unsatisfied, in total contradiction of itself: a life essentially of despair, a second death. (Apoc. xx. 6.)

There are two elements in St. Paul's description. He does indeed draw on the repertory of apocalyptic images for the trumpet that calls the court to assemble (1 Thess. iv. 16) and the judgement seat round which mankind throng. (Rom. xiv. 10; 2 Cor. v. 10.) But the drama enacted is a sober one. The majesty of the divine action whose effects he describes, surpasses all human analogy. It does not take place along the lines of a court of law, with an investigation, an arguing of the case and a verdict. God's justice is an effective force (Rom. i. 16–17); the power to judge is an attribute of the risen Christ's lordship, acting on all things, with power.

In the last rendering of justice, as in man's first justification, we find total reality. The sentence is not only a statement of verdict; it is a reality, a fire—though not a material one. The man who has made God's temple well will be glorified by this fire as he passes through it; the mediocre workman who has used poor materials will be burnt by it. Thus the judgement is a fire which of itself administers justice, an effective act of divine justice. (1 Cor. iii. 13–15.) The sentence delivers some up to vengeance (2 Thess. i. 8) and gives salvation to the others. (1 Cor. v. 5.) This salvation of the last day (Rom.

xiii. 11; 1 Thess. v. 8–9), which is fully realized when the Resurrection is total, is an effect of justice, for it is contrasted with the wrath of judgement. (1 Thess. v. 9; Rom. v. 9.) "On the day of wrath, and revelation of the just judgement" God will distribute eternal life and wrath according to men's merits (Rom. ii. 5–8); everyone "will receive [before the judgement seat of Christ] according to what he has done in the body". (2 Cor. v. 10.) Then the just judge will bestow the crown of justice (2 Tim. iv. 8), that "prize of the vocation" which is one with the glory of the Resurrection. (Phil. iii. 11–14.)

Unless this reality of the effect of the Judgement is an illusion, the destiny of the faithful is not accomplished before the sentence has been pronounced, for their resurrection does not precede it but coincides with it, otherwise there must be an intermediate resurrection of unglorified bodies in which they would appear before the Judge for the final reward—and St. Paul says nothing of any such resurrection. Thus Christ "will judge the living and the dead" (2 Tim. iv. 1; Acts x, 42; 1 Pet. iv. 5), those still alive at the *parousia* and those who are not. All the faithful, whether dead or still alive in the flesh, will be transformed in the power of that judgement: the living by being lifted up to that life (1 Cor. xv. 51–2), the dead by being resurrected to it.[64]

That judgement and resurrection coincide is never stated in so many words; but upon reflection we see it as the conclusion of what St. Paul does tell us. The idea must have underlain his thought. In no description of the Day (1 Thess. iv 15–17; 1 Cor. xv. 23–8) are the Resurrection and Judgement presented as successive events. After the Resurrection, the end has come, Christ's action as lord has attained its objectives.

The practical identification of the Judgement and Resurrection fits in with the Pauline teaching about justification as a whole. Man's justification, in its origin, is identified with the first resurrection, though it has a judicial aspect, it is effected in a physical transformation. This single reality with two facets advances in a single movement towards a double goal that corresponds with its complex character as both justification and resurrection.

[64] If we are to separate the Judgement from the act whereby we are justified, then we must admit one of these hypotheses: God judges the dead either before their resurrection, or after their resurrection to natural life (both unacceptable hypotheses), or after their resurrection to eternal life—in other words, after the carrying out of the sentence.

At baptism, man is justified with a view to his final salvation on the Day of Judgement, and is raised with a view to his total redemption on the day of his bodily resurrection, that justification develops gradually throughout his life, just as the power of the Resurrection gradually unfolds. Clearly, the divine act of justification and resurrection, one in its principle and one in its development, remains in St. Paul's mind one in its goal. Nowhere does he say this in so many words, but one text suggests it: "Much more, therefore, being now justified by his blood, shall we be saved from wrath through him. For if, when we were not in favour with God, we were reconciled to him by the death of his Son, much more, being reconciled, shall we be saved by his life." (Rom. v. 9–10.) The final salvation which concludes the process of our first justification (v. 9) is brought about in the glorious life of Christ (v. 10), in man's participation in the Resurrection.

The resurrection of sinners, though St. Paul mentions it in the Acts (xxiv 15), does not enter the field of vision of the Epistles; we do not know what relation it bears to the resurrection of Christ, nor whether it is held to be an effect of the justice of the Last Day. But Pauline teaching enables us to see in it a total exclusion from the Kingdom of God and a manifestation of that condemnation. The sinner remains fixed in the flesh, to which entry to the Kingdom is denied: "Flesh and blood cannot possess the kingdom of God: neither shall corruption possess incorruption." (1 Cor. xv. 50.) Indeed, corruption and incorruption are synonymous with everlasting life and death (Gal. vi. 8), and those who on the Lord's Day exist only in corruption, in the flesh which is not animated by the spirit, will thus show themselves as condemned forever. The two justices, of salvation and damnation, develop side by side until the final resurrection: "He that soweth in his flesh, of the flesh also shall reap corruption ["final loss, as opposed to eternal life", says Lagrange]; but he that soweth in the Spirit, of the Spirit shall reap life everlasting." (Gal. vi 8.) To rise again in the flesh sets a man forever under the seal of sin, fixes him beyond the reach of the spirit of Christ; it involves the sentence of damnation.

When we have made allowances for the traditional apocalyptic trappings in the drama of the Last Judgement, there remain the unchanging elements of the appearance of the Lord, the separation of the good and wicked, the laying open of consciences, and the

execution of the sentences. All these elements are realized in the
Resurrection—the resurrection of glory and the resurrection of corruption. Whereas, on the other hand, any judgement unfolded when
the destinies of all were already fixed would be no more than a
parade, a kind of decoration added to a real judgement already
put into practice—a far cry from that final judgement foretold by
the prophets, by Christ and the Apostles, that day of threat and of
hope, the flame of wrath and glory of salvation! The *parousia* and
the rendering of God's justice through Christ are united to the point
of being merged together in the notion of the Day[65]; the same is
true of the *parousia* and God's action in raising Christ; and all three
—*parousia*, resurrection and judgement constitute not the three
scenes of the last act of the Redemption, but the one tremendous
scene. The mystery of Easter was at once the action of raising, the
presence and the judgement; and the final *parousia* is simply the
mystery of Easter in the fullness of its effects.

It is not only men who will be judged. The world and the angelic
powers who govern it underwent a judgement at Christ's resurrection, by the very fact of that resurrection's taking place. God's justice
had entered the world and transformed Christ, and in that transformation it condemned everything that was withdrawn from God's
justifying action in our Lord. On the Last Day God's judicial power
will blaze forth in all its mighty force, but it will be in Christ's body,
the Church, that it is revealed. The Church, judged herself in the
raising action which is for her essentially a justification,[66] will, in the
transformation she undergoes, judge the world and the angels. In
her the universe, reconciled, will be set up again in justice; but whatever remains outside her and her light will be cast out into wrath.
The justice of the Church will judge the world. (Cf. 1 Cor. vi. 2–3.)

There is only one resurrection, the resurrection of Easter, and the
Church shares in it at the *parousia*. Similarly, there is only one
judgement whereby man is justified and this world and the prince
of this world are condemned: a judgement pronounced in the
mystery of Easter, but becoming fully effective only when the
Church is wholly caught up in that mystery.

With the resurrection of the faithful, "the operation of the might

---

[65] "The coming" of Christ appeared from the first as a judgement (Matt. iii
11–12; John ix. 39).

[66] This justifying action may be accompanied by suffering for anyone marred
by imperfection at the time of the *parousia* (Cf. 1 Cor. iii. 15.)

of his power which [God] wrought in Christ, raising him up from the dead" (Eph. 1. 19–20) will have attained its final objective. The mystery of Easter will be imprinted on the universe.

And this is what the faithful must desire so ardently. Come, Lord Jesus!

THE MEANS WHEREBY THE EASTER MYSTERY
SPREADS OUTWARDS

To extend outside himself the Church founded in his body, and to lead that Church to the fullness of the Redemption, the Christ of Easter is equipped with organs whose function it is to communicate the mystery of his resurrection to men.

During his life on earth, he went about preaching, and enabling men to profit by the saving power of his body through sensible contact with it. But once he had his full messianic powers, he stopped preaching and refused that contact (John xx. 17); he was still present to save the world (Matt. xxviii. 20) but present in a different form, present only because he had left it. He had entered a new existence that did not conform with the life of the world and of the Church on earth. In order that men might hear him and that he might act upon them in a connatural way, he would therefore thenceforth make use of earthly instruments to make them aware of his presence.

Among the means whereby "the power of the Resurrection" is applied to us, we may distinguish between those by which the Christ of Easter communicates himself—the Apostles and the sacraments—and those by which the faithful receive him—faith, the moral effort of conforming with his death and resurrection, and the acceptance of suffering and death.

1. THE INSTRUMENTS OF THE RISEN CHRIST

1. THE APOSTLES

(a) The Synoptics

In the Synoptics, the apostolate seems to be perfectly established even during Christ's life on earth: the group of Apostles is formed, and its members entrusted with a mission and given certain powers—though on a closer study it appears that they are still only on the threshold of the apostolate.

As long as their Master remains with them, their real work has not begun. Our Lord makes it clear that there are two distinct phases in the apostolate. The first is strictly limited in its development. "Go ye not into the way of the Gentiles, and into the city of the Samaritans enter ye not But go ye rather to the lost sheep of the house of Israel." (Matt. x. 5–6) The Twelve set out as obedient and untroubled children, armed only with their trust in God. (Matt. x. 5–15.) This mission lasted a few days—a few weeks at most. The Apostles bore witness neither to the person of Christ nor to the coming of the Kingdom; they preached penance and the Kingdom that was in the future. (Matt. x. 7.) Our Lord gave them power over devils and power to heal (Luke ix. 1); but spiritual power and authority over the Church were promised them only for the future. (Matt. xvi. 18–19; xviii. 18.)

The second phase would see the Apostles' message carried to all nations, and the Apostles themselves brought before the thrones of pagan kings (Matt. x. 18; xxiv 9; Mark xiii. 9–10.) Their mission was now to take a tragic course. It was no longer the apostolic idyll it had been; henceforth the simplicity of the dove must go with the cunning of the serpent (Matt x. 16),[1] and whereas before, they need not take even a stick, now, whoever has not got a sword, must sell his coat and buy one. (Luke xxii. 35–6.)

Christ's entry into glory marks the beginning of this new phase. After his resurrection, he gave the Apostles a new mission: "All power is given to me in heaven and in earth. Go therefore and make disciples of all nations." (Matt. xxviii. 18–19.)

This time the apostolate is limited only by the boundaries of the world. Our Lord stresses this several times (Mark xvi. 15; Luke xxiv. 47); this universal object specifies the nature of this mission and sets it apart from the earlier apostolic efforts whose objectives were of their nature limited.

Some critics[2] reject these universalist texts as Pauline interpolations, but they are wrong to do so. The apostolate is transformed because it is developing in Christ who dies and rises again. Our

---

[1] Matt x. 16–23 is not a continuation of Matt x 5–10. The first consists in counsels for the Galilean mission, the second for the mission after the Passion. This is indicated both by the nature of the texts themselves, and comparison with Mark xiii 9–13 The tendency to synthesize which marks the first gospel caused the two to be placed together

[2] Following Reimarus in 1778, there have been such names as Strauss, Wellhausen, Harnack, J Weiss, Loisy, and others.

Lord relates the expansion of the goals of the apostolate to his passion and glorification. "It is written that thus it behoved Christ to suffer and to rise again ... that penance and the remission of sins should be preached in his name unto all nations." (Luke xxiv. 46–7.) At first he had been sent only to "the sheep that were lost of the house of Israel"; to give the Gentiles even a crumb of this activity, limited by its nature, adapted to a narrow goal, would be to rob the children of their bread. (Matt. xv. 26.)[3] The sending of the Twelve into Galilee derived from that provisional power, whereas the universal apostolate is bound up with an unlimited power: "All power is given to me. Go, therefore, preach." The unlimited jurisdiction of the Apostles corresponds with that of Christ, who has become Lord of all things.

The Resurrection brings a new theme to their preaching. Christ on earth had said: "The Kingdom is at hand", and the Apostles had echoed him. Now the Apostles were announcing salvation as already present. (Mark xvi. 15–16.) The person of Christ, not previously put forward, was now the central point of the message, and it became essential that the Apostles should be personally pledged to him (Matt. x. 32–5); penance is demanded in his name, and remission of sins granted in it. (Luke xxiv. 47.)

The content of the *kerygma* is Christ, who has died and risen again: "You are witnesses of these things." (Luke xxiv. 48.) It seems a long time since our Lord said, "An evil and adulterous generation seeketh a sign: and a sign shall not be given it, but the sign of Jonah the Prophet." (Matt. xii. 39; xvi. 4.)

The nature of this "sign of Jonah" is not entirely clear; we cannot be sure which episode in the prophet's story our Lord means to tell us he is fulfilling and presents as an authentication of his mission[4]: is it his voluntary sacrifice, his miraculous survival, or his equally

---

[3] The messianic influence of Christ on earth, circumscribed as it was by the limits of the flesh, touched only the area immediately around it, both in space and in time To give any part of it to the Gentiles would be to snatch it from the Jews.

[4] Maldonatus and many other critics think "the sign of Jonah" was an argument for the condemnation of the Jews, since they remained incredulous where the Ninevites had believed in a lesser prophet. Thus our Lord was refusing to give any sign at all to authenticate his mission. But though Christ was not giving the Jews the sort of sign they wanted, it is clear that he was promising a sign that could guarantee him. The example of the Queen of Sheba was equally damning to the Jews (Matt. xii. 42), but there is no question of a "sign of the Queen of Sheba".

astonishing success? Probably all three. "The sign of Jonah gives us
the essential features of Christ's career as underlying the history of
the prophet ... But the major episode of that sign, the thing that
divided the world in apostolic times, was the message of the Resurrection, the Son of Man being in the belly of the earth three days
and three nights, and Christ, the new Jonah, loosed from the
shadows of the tomb and the clasp of death."[5]

This whole train of thought is summed up in Luke xi. 30: "As
Jonah was a sign to the Ninevites, so shall the Son of Man also be
to this generation." Like "Jonah, wearing the halo of miracle",[6]
whose hearers must be converted or lost, so will the Son of Man,
risen from the dead, appear—a sign set up in Israel.

The sign is more than something that happened in the past, more
than preaching, more than resurrection the sign of Jonah is the
risen Christ preaching to the world.

After his resurrection, it was his disciples who were sent out to
preach in Christ's name The sign of Jonah, the risen Christ, was
set before all nations in the person of the Apostles. Borne by their
preaching, our Lord goes through the Nineveh of the world, heralding salvation or ruin.

The Apostles are the envoys of the risen Christ and his presence
in the world.

(b) The Acts

In the Acts, the whole apostolate is bathed in the glow of Easter.

The definition of an Apostle is that he is a witness of the Resurrection: "One of these men must be made a witness with us of the
resurrection." (i. 22.) This witness which they are to bear before the
people and the rulers (v. 29–32) is the entire *raison d'être* of the
Apostles. (ii. 32; iii. 15; v. 32; x. 41.)[7] "They gave the testimony of
the Resurrection" (iv. 33), *the* testimony, the testimony proper to
their apostolic function. Christ wanted, by appearing to them, to

---

[5] L. de Grandmaison, *Jesus Christ*, vol. iii, pp 231–2

[6] Lagrange, *L'Évangile selon saint Luc*, Paris, 1921, p 337: the miracle "is
supposed to have been known to the Ninivites".

[7] St Ignatius the martyr explained why an Apostle goes to meet death·
"Even after the Resurrection, I know and believe that Christ still had a real
body And when he came to Peter and the others, he told them to touch him
that they might see that he was not a disembodied spirit   That is why they
scorned to fear death   ." (*Smyrn.*, iii, 1ff)

make them his witnesses. (xiii 31; xxii. 15; xxvi. 16) They are not teachers of a body of doctrine, but declarers of something that has happened: "In the year 60, the Christian religion could appear to one Roman functionary as a dispute among the Jews concerning 'one Jesus deceased, whom Paul affirmed to be alive' (Acts xxv. 19)."[8]

Furthermore, there is less question of the Resurrection as an event, than of the risen Christ himself The Apostles are the witnesses of Jesus (i. 8; xiii. 31) by affirming the Resurrection. In the name of the Resurrection, they take up Christ's cause before the people who have rejected him.[9] They bear witness to his messiahship (v. 30–32; x. 42), to his lordship of grace and of justice as revealed in the Resurrection.

Because they stand for the Messiah, they attract the hatred of his adversaries. The revolt of the Gentiles against Christ, foretold in Psalm II, is identified with the persecution stirred up against the Apostles. (iv. 23–30.)

If their being his witnesses draws down upon them the blows directed against our Lord, it also gives them the messianic power of the risen Christ. The Twelve receive from him their equipment, as it were, for the apostolate, the power of the Spirit that enables them to bear witness. (i. 8.) So violent is the energy with which they are filled, that the Apostles' carnal nature is quite overset by it: "They are full of new wine", which inflames them and enables them to speak, a force as unlimited as the world it is to conquer: "The Holy Ghost will come upon you, giving you power, and you shall be witnesses unto me in Jerusalem, and in all Judea, and Samaria, and even to the uttermost part of the earth." (i. 8.) The Spirit, the power, the whole earth as a sphere of the Apostles' zeal— all this goes with the glory of the risen Christ.[10]

[8] *Christus, Manuel d'histoire des religions*, Paris, 1913, p 677. The Athenians said of Paul, "What is it that this word-sower would say?" and concluded that he was a preacher of strange divinities, vowed to a new pair of gods whose names were Jesus and Anastasis ('Resurrection') (cf. Acts xvii 18). This clumsy mistake shows what an inattentive listener might make of Paul's preaching· he was speaking of Christ and the resurrection from the dead
[9] Cf L. Cerfaux, "Témoins du Christ d'après le livre des Actes", *Angelicum*, xx, 1943, 167–8
[10] This text from the Acts corresponds point by point with the order of the mission given in Matt xxviii 18. But the Acts add the further precision that the omnipotence claimed by the risen Christ in the Gospel is that of the Spirit, and states explicitly that that Spirit was conferred in Christ's glorification.

Christ's own apostolate was consecrated in the Resurrection. "... that he should be the first that should rise from the dead, and should show light to the people and to the Gentiles" (xxvi. 23), and come to bless them with the blessing of Abraham. (iii. 26.) The Apostles are the agents of the salvation contained in the risen Christ.

They are sent by the risen Christ, worked upon by his power; they are his witnesses before the world, the bearers of his salvation.

(c) St. John

According to the fourth gospel, the apostolate is rooted in the incarnation of the Word of God: "As the Father hath sent me, I also shall send you." (xx. 21.) But during Christ's life on earth, Christ himself was God's only apostle. Before Easter no-one but him had been sent; this is implicit in the statement of the sending on Easter evening. (xx. 21.)

Christ's apostolic function rests on a consecration and a sending— "him whom the Father hath sanctified and sent into the world ..." (x. 36.) The sanctifying and sending are identified with the Incarnation, since our Lord argues from them to his divine Sonship. (x. 36.) His coming into the world is the part Christ plays that corresponds to his sending. The object of the incarnate Word's apostolate is to bring into the world the light of life and salvation; its aim is not to bring judgement, yet the coming of the Son does in fact constitute a judgement for the unbelieving world.

As long as Christ is in the world, he is wholly engaged in carrying out his mission; the glory proper to the Father's Son must be given him in order that eternal life be extended to "all flesh". (xvii. 1-2.) The sanctification upon which Christ's apostolate is based needs to be increased by a more total dedication to God and a more intense compenetration by the divine nature; it becomes clear, in fact, that the hour which is the culmination of his coming (xii. 27), and the culmination therefore also of his apostolate, is a sanctification: "I sanctify myself." (xvii. 19.)[11]

But at the very moment of that sanctification, the Son passes out of this world (xvii. 11) and breaks his natural bonds with it. (Cf. xx. 17.) The "coming", enriched in redemptive power, loses contact with the world to be redeemed. So, from the very day of his resurrection, our Lord creates organs of contact; these are the Apostles,

[11] For an explanation of this text see above, p 64

who carry on his own mission as his Father's Apostle in the world
(xx. 21), and through these means, he effects the greater things
which his return to the Father gives him the power to effect. (xiv.
12.)

As the organs of Christ who has now attained to the perfection
of his apostolate, the disciples undergo their investiture through a
sharing in the twofold sanctification of the Son, through the first
Incarnation, and through the Incarnation in glory: "Sanctify them
in thy truth. Thy word is truth. As thou hast sent me into the world,
I also have sent them into the world.[12] And for them do I sanctify
myself that they also may be sanctified in truth." (xvii. 17-19.)

The Apostles' sanctification, like Christ's, is a setting apart for
God (xvii. 14-16) and a consecration. It will take place in truth, as
an environment which will penetrate and transform them
(Lagrange), that truth which is the luminous holiness of God. Christ
asks for this sanctification in the name of truth: "As thou hast sent
me into the world, I also have sent them into the world." This
transformation in the light is necessary, for their mission is a continuation of the Incarnation, which is the coming of the light.

The consecration of the Apostles in the holiness of the Incarnation is the effect of our Lord's death and resurrection. "I sanctify
myself", said our Lord, "that they also may be sanctified in truth."
The sanctification of Christ is completed in his death and resurrection, in the immolation and oblation to the Father. It perfects the
initial consecration and brings the first, and as yet hidden, glory to
full flowering. (xvii. 5.) The Apostle, who participates in the paschal
sanctification of him whom the Father has sent, is linked to its first
and essential element, the Incarnation, for it has now become communicable at the same time as radiating glory.

The Apostle carries the Incarnation on from the moment when
the incarnate Word attained the culminating point of his coming
into the world. His role is a magnificent one. He is to make the
light that has come into the world present to men; he is to give life
to some and leave others in darkness; he will judge and divide the
world. (xx. 23.) And the world will turn on him the hatred it
bears Christ. (xv. 18-22.)

As in the Acts, the Apostles are given the power of the Spirit.
On the day of the Resurrection, Christ "breathed on them and he

---

[12] The sending already appears to be in the past This is a vision of things
sub specie aeternitatis.

said to them: Receive ye the Holy Ghost". (xx. 22.) The Spirit's hovering over our Lord was the sign of his holiness as Son and of his mission: "He upon whom thou shalt see the Spirit descending and remaining, he it is that baptizeth with the Holy Ghost. And I saw, and I gave testimony that this is the Son of God." (i. 33–4.) The communication of that holiness and the transmission of that power are accompanied by a giving of the Spirit Indeed, we must go further, and say that it is the outpouring of the Spirit which creates the Apostles. In the fourth gospel, our Lord generally gives a commentary upon what he is going to do beforehand.[13] To the man born blind, he declares, "I am the light of the world", and having said it, gives sight to his eyes. He declares to his disciples, "As my Father hath sent me, I also send you"; ". . . and having said this, he breathed on them" the Holy Spirit, as God had in the past breathed the breath of life into the nostrils of Adam.

It is from Christ's belly that the Spirit flows out, from his bodily humanity, which becomes a spiritual principle only when it is glorified. (vii. 37–9.) That is why the Apostles cannot be consecrated until Christ has first been consecrated by the Resurrection: "I sanctify myself.that they also may be sanctified."

The Spirit of holiness and of truth, can "sanctify them in truth" as Christ demands.[14]

The apostolate, born out of Christ's death and resurrection, bears the imprint of sacrifice. These men are oblations to God, set apart from the use of the profane world (xvii. 16); though they remain in the world, they are borne with Christ into the holiness of the Father.

(d) St. Paul

According to St. Paul, his own apostolate is grounded upon the same thing as the apostolate of the Twelve, namely the resurrection of Christ.

(a) Though he has never seen Christ in the flesh, he still fulfils the essential condition of the apostolate: "Am not I an apostle? Have not I seen Christ Jesus our Lord?" (1 Cor. ix. 1; cf. xv. 8–9.) Outside Damascus he witnessed a blinding "apocalypse" of our Lord.

[13] ix 5–6; ch xvii gives the theology of the Passion.
[14] St. John Chrysostom, *Hom. in Jo.*, *P.G.*, lix, 443, comments on xvii 17 thus: "Sanctify them by the gift of the Spirit and by Christ's true teaching."

He has had the essential experience, has seen with his own eyes the glorified Christ, the manifestation of the Son of Man which is known to be the advent of the end of time. In St. Paul's eyes, what happened at Damascus was not so much a conversion as a vocation. (Gal. 1 15.)[15]

More than five hundred brethren saw the glorified Christ without this giving them any claim to the title of Apostle; therefore being a witness can be no more than a prerequisite. St. Paul received, over and above this, a divine power that operates in the resurrection of Christ The Galatians questioned their Apostle's right to set himself up alongside the Twelve. In a laconic greeting indicative of displeasure, St. Paul declares himself "an Apostle, not of men, neither by man, but by Jesus Christ, and God the Father who raised him from the dead". (Gal. i. 1.) His consecration as an Apostle is due to Christ and depends, through the risen Christ, upon the raising action of the Father. The implication is clear enough, and most valuable: the apostolate is an effect of the Resurrection; it is a grace of the risen Christ (Rom. i. 3–5), a mandate given by the God-Saviour and the Christ of the *parousia* (1 Tim. i. 1.) This is what St. Paul has in common with the Twelve.

(b) The Apostles are, first of all, preachers: "Christ sent me not to baptize, but to preach the Gospel " (1 Cor. 1. 17.) They are as it were posting an announcement in the world, the announcement of the death and resurrection of Christ· "I delivered unto you first of all . . . how that Christ died for our sins . . . and that he rose again the third day." (1 Cor. xv 3–4.) "We preach Christ crucified . . . the power of God and the wisdom of God." (1 Cor. i. 23–4.)

(c) They are not merely relaying good news. Their function is more real than that: by their profession of faith and their very presence in the world, they bring men face to face with the death of Christ and the power of his resurrection.

The power of God that raises Christ and makes him able to subject all things to himself dwells in them. (Phil. iii. 21.) They compel the nations to obedience (Rom. i. 5); their preaching is a kind of war machine which drives all before it. "The weapons of our warfare are not carnal, but mighty to God unto the pulling down of fortifications; we destroy counsels and every height that exalteth

---

[15] Cf L. Cerfaux, "L'Antinomie paulinienne de la vie apostolique", *Rech. Sc. Rel.*, xxxix, 1951, 224ff ; J. Giblet, "Saint Paul, serviteur de Dieu et apôtre de Jésus-Christ", *La Vie Spir* , lxxxix (1953), 246

itself against the knowledge of God, and we bring into captivity every understanding unto the obedience of Christ." (2 Cor. x. 4–5.)

This force unleashed upon the world is the power of the Spirit which, "by virtue of signs and wonders", has beaten out a path for St. Paul from Jerusalem to Illyria. (Rom. xv. 19; 1 Thess. 1. 5; 1 Cor. 11. 4–5.) The apostolate is the first of the charismata, those often tremendous gifts of the Spirit (1 Cor. xii. 28); it is not surprising that the pagans took the Apostles for gods come down to earth. (Acts xiv. 11.)

The power of God acts in them for the salvation of the world, being none other than the saving life of the risen Christ: "The life also of Jesus is made manifest in our mortal flesh." (2 Cor. iv. 11.) The light shining on the face of Christ glows in their hearts. (2 Cor. iv 6.)

At the same time as his life, Christ's death also dwells in them, for it is only in his death that the force of God raises him up: "We bear about in our body the mortification of Jesus, that the life also of Jesus may be made manifest ..." (2 Cor. iv. 10; xiii. 4). Their existence in weakness, surrounded by suffering, continually exposed to death, forms the vessel of clay that contains the glory of their ministry. (2 Cor. iv. 7–12.) They are "separated" (Rom. 1. 1), using the things of this world so little that they are deemed unhappy (2 Cor. vi. 10); they are cut off from all the means of assuring worldly success. (1 Cor. ii. 3–4). But they are dead in the fashion of the risen Christ and drawn along with him in the triumphal force of God. (2 Cor. ii. 14.) Even the Apostle's speech is patterned on the death and life of Christ: devoid of all human wisdom (1 Cor. i. 17; ii. 4), exposed to the derision of the world (1 Cor. 1. 18), but filled with divine energy so that it becomes the very force of God. (1 Cor. i. 18; ii. 4.)

The Apostles speak in concepts and preach a doctrine, but what they are bringing into the world is a presence. They are themselves sacraments of the presence of the dead and risen Christ, and the organs whereby he is in contact with the world.

(d) They must go right through the world as living signs of the redeeming Christ, signs of his death and resurrection, in order to extend the mystery of that death and resurrection over the entire world.

Their words do not simply convey the news, they bear the life of the risen Christ and the faith they give rise to is a possession. Paul speaks of himself as "an apostle ... according to the promise of life which is in Christ Jesus" (2 Tim. 1. 1), whose object is to implement that promise (Meinertz) inscribed in the risen Christ. A life is brought into the world through the vehicle of speech; the Gospel is a force (Rom. i. 15–16), a reality in which men participate (1 Cor. ix. 23), which joins Jew and Gentile in a single body (Eph. iii. 6), whereby death is destroyed, life shines forth (2 Tim. 1. 10), and final glory is won. (2 Thess. ii. 14.) That is why the Apostles speak of themselves as ministers of God's mystery; it is through their ministry that the great plan of universal redemption is carried out (Col 1. 25–6; 1 Cor. iv 1.)

God's raising action in Christ attains its objectives gradually. Man need only accept the word preached to him to be saved. It is claimed for Christ that he is Lord of the world. (Rom. i. 5.) The Apostles' preaching is a sword-blade, a word that judges. The Apostles are an emanation from Christ, giving life to some, but destroying others. (2 Cor. ii. 15–16.) They force mankind, till then undecided, to make a choice, and apply to them the justice manifested in Christ's death and resurrection. Through them the world is divided into two, for life and for death.

The apostolate is at the very heart of the mystery of Easter and has a world-wide part to play. It is the open door through which the mystery of the Redemption comes into the world.

ii. THE SACRAMENTS

Man's contact with the risen Christ, established by the preaching of the Apostles, is completed by the ritual of worship. The two sacraments of which we know most, baptism and the Eucharist, are both linked to the Resurrection.

(a) Baptism
(1) The Synoptics

According to John the Baptist, all the saving work of the Messiah is summed up in the giving of a baptism: "I indeed baptize you in water unto penance, but he that shall come after me ... shall baptize you in the Holy Ghost and fire." (Matt. iii. 11–12; Luke iii. 16.)

The forerunner's work was to prepare the people to sustain the coming of the Messiah as judge, for this is how he is announced;

he is coming as a winnower, to separate the grain for the granary, and the chaff for the fire. Malachi has compared his coming to the fire of the foundry and the bleach of the fuller (iii. 2). The water the Baptist used cleansed the surface without scouring the bottom, but the Judge will baptize in the Holy Spirit, a divine principle that penetrates, devours and transforms; his judgement will be a baptism of fire which will consume impurity and those who are impure, and from this terrible cleansing will emerge the community of saints foretold for the last days. (Isa. iv. 3–5)

It does not appear that John connected this immersion in the Spirit with a ritual of water. His was a total vision with no distinctions of perspective, separating the first purification from the Last Judgement.

John's foretelling of this baptism in the Spirit was always vividly remembered (Acts i. 5; xi. 15), but it soon came to have a more restricted meaning. Our Lord himself seems to conceive this messianic baptism as depending upon a rite of ablution, for, as soon as he has come into the fullness of his messianic power, he commands the Apostles to administer a baptism of water. (Matt. xxviii 18–19.) The Apostles had begun to baptize while still with him (John iv. 1–2), and it was by baptizing with water that they thought the messianic outpouring of Pentecost was to be extended to the people (Acts ii. 38.)[16]

From this sacramental interpretation of the Messiah's baptism in the Holy Ghost, we may conclude that the water of Christian baptism was taken by Christ and his disciples to be a symbol of the Holy Ghost.[17] Whereas the forerunner baptized in water alone, Christ baptizes in the Spirit while also using water. The Christian

---

[16] St. Mark seems even to attribute to the Forerunner a prophecy of the Christian rite, for he takes away the eschatological sense of his words by omitting the prophecy of the judgement which forms the framework for the rest (Mark i. 8) In the fourth gospel, the sacramental gospel, it is quite clear that this baptism in the Holy Ghost (i. 26, 33) is the same as the rite whereby one is born of water and the Spirit (iii. 5.)

[17] This view does not seem to be that of the author of the Acts. For him the outpouring of the Spirit does not generally come with baptism, but precedes or follows it (viii 15, ix. 17–18; x. 44–8, xi. 15; xix 1–6) and does not appear to belong to the rite of ablution Cf J Coppens, "Baptême", *D.B Suppl*, col 889. The consistent way in which he dissociates baptism from the descent of the Spirit reveals an idea quite special to him In the same way, Luke shows an interval between our Lord's baptism and the descending of the Spirit (iii 21), and says that the latter took place while he was praying, whereas Matthew and Mark put the two together In Acts i 1–14, which is

institution still uses the symbolism used by prophecy in the past, whereby the messianic gift, the Holy Spirit, is a gushing or out-pouring of water. The early Churches might vary the way in which the water was applied,[18] but all were conscious of this essential symbolism

Two sayings of our Lord's (Mark x. 38; Luke xii 50) relate the idea of baptism to that of the Passion, and face the Synoptics with the problem of the relationship between baptism and the death and resurrection of Jesus.[19]

One very old tradition, on the other hand, interpreted the Synop-tics' account as placing the institution of Christian baptism at Christ's baptism in the Jordan, and making that the prototype of it, thus cutting across the doctrinal teaching of St. Paul and the con-nexion of the sacrament with Christ's death and resurrection.[20]

Our Lord's baptism was certainly a prefiguring of the Christian rite, but did not mark its institution as a sacrament; it is, as we can see from the context of events, itself directed towards the act of the Redemption and explained by it in the mind of Christ

The theophany of the Jordan marks the beginning of Christ's public life. God guarantees Jesus of Nazareth: the voice from heaven shows that he is the Son; the presence of the Holy Spirit shows that

wholly his own composition (whereas the succeeding pericopes reproduce sources, L Cerfaux, "La Composition de la première partie du Livre des Actes", *Eph Theol. Lov.*, xiii, 1936, 667–91), he sees the announcement of baptism in the Spirit as fulfilled by the outpouring of Pentecost

He wishes to stress, and indeed his theology includes only the post-baptismal outpouring, complete and charismatic, resulting from a new rite It does not appear that this would enable us to deny the connexion between baptism and the Spirit in the mind of the primitive Churches In xix. 1–6, the author speaks only of a post-baptismal outpouring, and yet St. Paul must have held at the beginning of his visit to Ephesus the theology of the Spirit of baptism which he set out during that visit (1 Cor vi 11; xii 13) And this text from the Acts does show a connexion in St. Paul's mind between baptism and the Spirit, just as Acts ii 38 does with St Peter.

[18] Acts ii 41 assumes baptism by pouring or even sprinkling, Acts xvi 33, baptism by pouring.

[19] J. Coppens, "Baptême", col 888, thinks that these texts are enough to prove that the water of baptism was linked with Christ's death and resurrec-tion even earlier than St Paul

[20] Cf A d'Alès, "Baptême", *Dict Bib. Suppl*, col 856 St. Chromatius of Aquileia even says. "For the waters of baptism would never have had the power to cleanse the sins of the faithful, unless they had been sanctified by the touch of the Lord's body " (*In Matth Tract*, 1, *P.L*, xx, 329.) This tradi-tion is contradicted by St Leo the Great, who sees the baptism in the Jordan as a purely Old Testament rite (*Ep. XVI*, 6, *P L*, liv, 701ff.)

he is the Messiah, the Anointed One of Iahweh, upon whom the power of God rests. Like the heroes of old, Christ enters upon his career by the impetus of the Holy Spirit. (Luke iv. 1, 14.)

This is the meaning of the theophany But the baptism of our Lord, taken as a whole, has a larger and more complex significance.

When John the Baptist first found himself in the presence of him whose terrible greatness he had so long contemplated (iii. 11), he cried out: "I ought to be baptized by thee, and comest thou to me?" And our Lord replied: "Suffer it to be so now. For so it becometh us to fulfil all justice." (Matt. iii. 14–15.) What was this justice they must both fulfil? John was the herald going ahead to open the road, the friend leading the way. The justice he must fulfil was preparing the road, and ushering in his greater friend. The justice Christ must fulfil was to be the Saviour of the sinful people (Matt. i. 21; Luke i. 77.) The meeting between them brought John to the culminating point of his mission as he, as it were, ushered Christ into his work of redemption. And Christ entered upon that work. The baptism was the prelude to the Redemption, and there lies the mystery of it.[21]

It was a prelude in symbol as well as in reality, for the whole act of redemption was reflected in it and begun in it. Our Lord must place himself among sinners and submit to "Baptism unto penance". He was later to submit to another baptism: "I have a baptism wherewith I am to be baptized." (Luke xii. 50.) "Can you . . . be baptized with the baptism wherewith I am to be baptized?" (Mark x 38.) His immersion in the water of penance was an anticipation and a figure of the blood and suffering of that other baptism. Corresponding to that momentary humiliation there was a glorification: "And Jesus, being baptized, forthwith came up out of the water; and lo, the heavens were opened to him: and he saw the Spirit of God descending as a dove, and coming upon him. And behold a voice from heaven saying: This is my beloved Son, in whom I am well pleased." (Matt. iii. 16–17; Mark i. 10–11.) Jesus came up out of the Jordan as later he was to rise from the dead, in the glory of the Spirit, in the manifestation of the divine sonship; the new creation which was to be fulfilled in the Resurrection was already promised.[22]

---

[21] J. Huby, *Évangile selon saint Marc*, 22nd ed , Paris, 1929, p 20. "The baptism which opened the preaching of the gospel, also opened the public work of expiation and reparation."

[22] Cf. above, p 251.

The baptism of water to which Christ had to submit himself was, therefore, related to his essential work of death and resurrection it was as it were a preliminary sketch of the work of redemption. From then onwards, John the Baptist, who had not known him before except as a judge to be feared (John i. 33), called him "the Lamb of God, he who taketh away the sin of the world". (i. 29.)[23] It is also significant that this anticipation of the drama of the Redemption took place in a ritual of water: Christ was rehearsing for his death and resurrection by entering the waters of baptism and emerging from them.

Thus the baptismal teaching of the Synoptics offers many suggestions. Christian baptism is linked with the tremendous promises of the Prophets and of John the Baptist, and with that eschatological baptism in the Spirit out of which the messianic people are to be born. Only later was theology to relate this outpouring of the Spirit to the glorification of Christ. But the account of his baptism even as it stands brings to mind the whole drama of the Redemption, and enables Christians to see the sacrament of water as an extending to them of the great eschatological event, of our Lord's death and resurrection.[24]

(2) The Acts

According to the Acts, baptism incorporates us into the Church, the expression in the world of that Kingdom of God that was set up when Christ was glorified. (ii. 41.) Administered in the name of Jesus (ii. 38; viii. 16; x. 48), it sets the seal of the Lord's possession upon those who believe; it confers remission of sins (ii 38), and the right to receive the Holy Ghost (ii. 38), which are graces that belong to the risen Christ (v. 31-2). But it seems as though only the *right* to receive the Spirit is given; though water symbolizes the outpouring of the Spirit in the messianic prophecies, even those actually quoted in the Acts (ii. 17-18, ἐκχεῶ), the author does not make it actually coincide with the rite itself. And there is nothing to suggest that baptism brings the believer into contact with the action of Christ in dying and rising again.

[23] Cf. O. Cullmann, *Die Tauflehre des N.T.*, Zürich, 1948, pp 11-16
[24] It seems as though the relationship between baptism and the act of redemption was recognized before St. Paul came to teach it Cf Rom. vi 3: "Know you not that all we who are baptized in Christ Jesus, are baptized in his death?"

(3) St. John

The fourth gospel does not relate baptism to Christ's death and resurrection in so many words.

The baptism in the Spirit which John the Baptist spoke of as bringing in the Kingdom, is given in the sacrament of water. (iii. 5.) To enter the Kingdom, a man must be born of water and of the Spirit the water symbolizes. The doctrine of baptism fits into the Johannine theology of the water come down from the heights of heaven and gushing out of the glorified body of Christ to give eternal life. (vii. 37; iv. 14.)

The cure of the man born blind (ix) gives us a clear symbol of the illumination of baptism. "I am the light of the world", Christ says, and immediately sends the blind man to wash in the pool of Siloam. The water of the pool removes the clay from the man's eyes and enlightens them. John understands the mystery of this, for he adds, "Siloam is interpreted Sent." This is not the meaning given by the philologists; but this was the popular interpretation, and John adopts it because it was so well fitted to express the symbol: the water of purification and illumination is drawn from Christ. Christ sent the blind man to find light in Christ.[25] According to vii. 37-9, the messianic water bestowed by Christ is the Spirit, and it flows from the belly of the glorified Christ The efficaciousness of baptism presupposes contact with Christ, with his glorified body. Baptism produces the same effect as Christ's glorification: the divine life, which is divine knowledge. (xvii. 1-3; ix. 38.)

(4) St. Paul

St. Paul gives as it were a three-dimensional development of the bare doctrinal outline.

Its central point is the traditional idea that baptism subjects man to the working of the Spirit: "In one Spirit were we all baptized into one body." (1 Cor. xii. 13.)

The word "baptize" has come to have a specialized meaning—its etymological sense ("immerse") is hardly thought of; it now means to administer baptism. However, water still remains the symbol of the Spirit by whom man is purified: ". . . but you are washed, but

---

[25] St. Augustine, *In Jo. Tract*, xliv, ii, *P L*, xxxv, 1714 "Thus he washed his eyes in that pool which was interpreted Sent, he was baptized in Christ "

ou are sanctified, but you are justified, in the name of our Lord
esus Christ, and the Spirit of our God." (1 Cor. vi. 11.) The immer-
ion of baptism washes the believer in the Holy Spirit. Baptism is
a laver of regeneration and renovation of the Holy Ghost". (Tit.
i. 5.) Paul retains the original symbolism of the messianic water.

Some have thought that he deviates from this traditional concept,
nd sees the immersion of baptism as immersing us in Christ as in
n element[26]; he writes, after all, "You have been baptized in [εἰς]
Christ." (Gal. iii. 27; Rom. vi. 3.) But he is not thinking of the
tymological sense of the word, and the preposition εἰς is not
estricted to a solely spatial meaning· there are similar phrases which
annot possibly be taken to indicate locality.[27] If, however, immersion
neant to St. Paul a burial (Rom. vi. 4), then the believer is not
mmersed in Christ but in death with Christ; and similarly, he
merges not from Christ, but from death *with* Christ. The rite of
ntering and leaving the water adds an additional significance,[28] but
loes not do away with the first symbolism; baptism remains an
utpouring of the Spirit.

Though baptism does not immerse the believer in Christ in any
patial sense, it does join him to Christ in his very being. The rite of
blution, by means of the Holy Spirit, attaches the believer organi-
ally to the bodily Christ, grafting him onto Christ (Rom. vi. 5),
lothing him with Christ (Gal. iii. 27), identifying him with Christ's
)ody: "In one Spirit were we all baptized into one body." (1 Cor.
ii. 13.) It is a Spirit of incorporation, of "Christification", as we
night say.

Thus baptism unites us to Christ's body, not primarily because
if the symbolic act of entering and leaving the water, but because
)f the ritual of water which communicates the Spirit. However, this
ontact with our Saviour does take place as we enter and leave the
vater, in the moment of Christ's death from which life flows, and
n a sharing in that act of redemption. (Rom. vi. 3–4; Col. ii. 12.)[29]

[26] Cf F Prat, *Theology*, vol ii, p. 462, J. Huby, *Épître aux Romains*,
rd ed , Paris, 1940, pp 207ff.

[27] 1 Cor x 2. "All in Moses were baptized."

[28] P. Plummer, in "Baptism", Hastings' *Dictionary of the Bible*, p 243:
'   a desirable symbol rather than an essential".

[29] This way in which the believer participates in the act of redemption is
)rought out well by St Leo the Great: ". . that being received by Christ
nd receiving Christ, he may not be the same after being cleansed as he was
)efore baptism, but that the body of him who is regenerated may become the
lesh of the Crucified"

The ritual of the water, by placing us actually in Christ's death and resurrection, the archetype of baptism, gains for us the holiness of the Spirit, for it is in the act of redemption that the Spirit flows out for us in the bodily Christ.

The twofold symbolism of baptism corresponds to the twofold origin of Christian life. The ablution with water indicates sanctification in the Spirit; the rite of entering and leaving the water shows our identification with Christ's body in his death and resurrection.

Once again we find this working together of Christ and the Spirit we have noted so often before. The two principles act in concert, in a single action, just as the single rite of baptism bears its twofold symbolism.

The application to us of the sanctifying Spirit, and our contact with the dead and risen body by identification, remain actual, though the rite only takes place once. For the Spirit, imprinted, as it were, in us (Eph. 1. 13-14) preserves our identification with Christ (Rom. viii. 9-10), and our identification with Christ maintains the presence of the Spirit. (1 Cor. vi. 17.)

The Epistle to the Hebrews, though it gives us only the barest outline, presents a remarkable baptismal teaching, for it envisages baptism in the framework of sacrifice.

Baptism is set alongside the old rite of communion by sprinkling: "Let us draw near with a true heart in fullness of faith, having our hearts sprinkled from an evil conscience, and our bodies washed with clean water." (x. 22.) A clean water which "is not simply fresh water from a spring, but water actually consecrated",[30] is poured over the body, while the heart is purified by being sprinkled with blood. The Jews were sanctified by the blood of the victim after the sacrifice of the covenant; so are Christians. (Cf. ix. 13-14, 19.) Baptism is the sacramental expression of that sprinkling.[31]

St. Peter (1, i. 2) takes up the same idea. The faithful are "elect

We cannot, however, say that the rite of baptism makes Christ's death and resurrection present, any more than it makes his body present It draws man into the act of redemption because it unites him to the body of Christ If the mystery of Christ is made present to our era because of baptism, it is in the Church that it is made present, for in this sacrament the Church is born, the dead and risen body of Christ

[30] J Bonsirven, L'Épître aux Hébreux, p. 440.

[31] Another text, though this is less clear, speaks of "the sprinkling of blood which speaketh better than that of Abel" (xii. 24; J Bonsirven, L'Épître aux Hébreux, p. 80)

. . according to the foreknowledge of God the Father . . . unto obedience [of faith] and sprinkling of blood." Faith makes them subject to Christ, and the sacrament sprinkles them with his blood.[32]

This doctrine of baptism is extremely close to St. Paul's; "We are baptized into one body" (1 Cor. xii. 13), he says, "You are baptized in his death" (Rom. vi. 3), united by baptism to the body of Christ in his immolation. The Pauline texts make it clear that this sprinkling of blood we receive in baptism is more than merely a symbol; and the Epistle to the Hebrews in turn illuminates St. Paul's thought in the light of the doctrine of sacrifice: baptism is a rite of communion in the immolated body of Christ.

If baptism is taken as being sacrificial then it will naturally be interpreted as a paschal rite. St. Peter, who sees baptism as a sprinkling of blood and a communion, attributes its effects to the Resurrection. This must be so, for our Lord himself communicates in his own sacrifice in his glorification, which is the principle of all Christian communion.

Theologians will certainly find the idea of sacrifice the ideal framework in which to synthesize the doctrine of baptism. Our communion in Christ's sacrifice explains our union with his immolated and glorified body; it explains the communication to us of the Holy Spirit, in whom the body of Christ was sanctified by the life-giving acceptance of the Father; it explains the bond existing between all the feasters at the table. One baptism, one body, one Spirit and the bond of peace. (Cf. Eph. iv. 3-4.) Baptism extends to the believer the Easter mystery, which is a mystery of communion.

(b) The Eucharist

The Eucharist is also a paschal sacrament.

The words of institution link the Eucharist to the Cross alone: "Take. This is my body [Matt., Mark], given for you [Luke, 1 Cor.]." "Drink ye all of this for [Matt.] this is my blood, the blood of the testament, shed for many [Matt., Mark]—the new testament in my blood. [Luke, 1 Cor.]"

Yet from the earliest times, the Church had a ritual meal with nothing to indicate any relation to the Cross, and much actually to detach it from the Cross and relate it to the Resurrection: the Breaking of Bread. (Acts ii. 42; xx. 7.) There was nothing profane about

[32] A. Médebielle, "Expiation", D B. Suppl., col 242ff.

this meal. Its ritual nature is clear from the consistent use of that rather strange name[33] for it, and St. Paul uses the term for a meal of a quite definitely religious nature. (1 Cor. x. 16.)

This duality has been taken to prove the existence of two types of ritual meal, the primitive breaking of bread, and another resulting from St. Paul's reforms (1 Cor. xi. 17–34), whereby the primitive meal was joined to the memory of the Last Supper and the death of Christ[34]

Despite the differences between the Breaking of Bread, and the Pauline Eucharist which reproduces the Last Supper, careful study will reveal places where the two sorts of meal meet and in fact become a single meal of communion with the dead and risen Christ.

(1) The Last Supper and the Breaking of Bread

The Breaking of Bread is linked to the meal the Apostles shared with the risen Christ.[35]

Christ was accustomed to appear during meals, and eat with the disciples (Mark xvi 14; Luke xxiv. 30, 41ff.; Acts x. 41.) "A remarkable feature of the Acts is the importance attached to this sharing of food with the glorified Lord "[36] St. Peter characterizes the witnesses of the Resurrection as those who "did eat and drink with him after he arose again from the dead". (Acts x 41.) This is what guarantees their authority. One must therefore consider "the fact that they took place during a meal as a characteristic element of those apparitions".[37]

As soon as Christ had ascended to the Father, the disciples who had so often rejoiced in his presence in the close community of a meal, once again gathered together to break bread. This could be explained by Christ's command, "Do this in commemoration of

---

[33] The expression seems never to have been used by the Jews to mean a meal. Cf. J Jeremias, *Die Abendmahlsworte Jesu*, 2nd ed , Göttingen, 1949, p 65

[34] H Lietzmann, *Messe und Herrenmahl*, Bonn, 1925

[35] For this we are indebted to O Cullmann, "La Signification de la sainte Cène dans le christianisme primitif", *Rev. Hist. Phil. Rel.*, 1936, pp. 1–22; *Christian Worship*, pp. 15–16; "Le Culte dans l'Église primitive", *Cahiers théol de l'actualité protest*, viii, 1945, Neuchâtel

[36] Y. de Montcheuil, "Signification eschatologique du repas eucharistique", *Rech Sc Rel*, xxxiii, 1946, 21

[37] O. Cullmann, "La Signification de la Cène", p 8.

me." But these meals were more directly connected with the meals of the forty days after Easter, an extension of the joy of that time.

One of the essential marks of these meals was "gladness in simplicity of heart" (Acts ii. 46), that gladness so characteristic in the Church of the risen Christ. (Acts v. 41; viii. 39; xi. 23; xiii. 48; John xx. 20.) Psychologically, therefore, the Breaking of Bread is connected with the meals eaten with the risen Christ rather than with the memory of the Last Supper.[38] Though, at the beginning, the meeting of the messianic community may have been more frequent (Acts ii. 46),[39] they came later to be fixed for the first day of the week (Acts xx. 7), the day of the resurrection—a further indication of the significance of this breaking of bread.

The story of the supper at Emmaus stresses the relationship between the ritual meal and the apparitions of the risen Christ That supper was different from the ordinary meals eaten during Christ's life on earth; it partook of the mystery of the risen Christ. The disciples recognized Christ, not because the act of blessing and breaking bread was particularly characteristic of him, but because "their eyes were opened", because during that meal they were enlightened with new knowledge and "they knew him in the breaking of bread". (Luke xxiv. 31, 35.) The confused sense they already had of being caught up in the mystery of Christ (verse 32) was sharpened and made clear during the meal· by it they were introduced into the sphere of the risen Christ. And St. Luke uses the same term for this meal with the risen Christ as for the ritual meals of the Church— the breaking of bread.[40]

In a Pauline Church. at Corinth, the merriment was so uncontrolled as to degenerate, and Paul found it necessary to impose a reform. With this object he sets out the relationship between the

---

[38] Cf O Cullmann, "La Signification de la Cène", p 4, *Christian Worship*, pp 14–15.

[39] The text does not, however, say they took place every day. "They were all assiduous in frequenting the Temple daily, but it was at home that they broke bread "

[40] It has been thought that the fact of there being no mention of wine is a further proof that the breaking of bread was related not so much to the Last Supper as to the meals of the risen Christ (O Cullmann, *Christian Worship*, pp 14–15) Wrongly, however. The wine need not be mentioned to have been there The argument from silence proves nothing here. The expression, "breaking of bread", having become a technical one, does not necessarily involve a statement of all the elements of the meal Bread is sometimes used as a name for the entire meal (Matt xv. 2; Mark iii. 20; John xiii. 18.)

meal of worship and Christ's last supper and death. (1 Cor. xi. 17-
34) From this moment on, according to Lietzmann, two sorts of
ritual meals divided the Church, the first without reference to
Christ's death, and the second, linked to his last supper and his
death, resulting from the Pauline reform; this dualism, he thinks,
remained through all the liturgy of the early centuries.

But it would be wrong to draw any such clear-cut conclusion The
Pauline Eucharist remains firmly in continuity with the primitive
Breaking of Bread.

Indeed, Paul had no sense of innovating, when he linked the meal
of the community to the Last Supper. He had told the Church at
Corinth this from the beginning (1 Cor. xi. 23); and the common
meal is mentioned before Chapter XI, which is supposed to give it
such a new orientation. In this previous reference, the technical
term, the breaking of bread, is recalled, but as well as the bread
the wine and chalice are also brought in quite naturally (1 Cor. x.
16), thus linking the Breaking of Bread to the Last Supper and the
Cross.[41]

The stress laid on the Last Supper in 1 Cor. xi. is explained by
the fact that it brings out an aspect which was certainly known, but
very much under-emphasized in primitive tradition, which had little
consciousness of the redemptive value of the Cross. The deepening
of the sense of the Cross so peculiarly St. Paul's, his theology of a
resurrection inseparable from a death, led him to stress the relationship between the ritual meal and the last supper and sacrifice. His
reform was not concerned with the rite, but with underlining the
sacrificial aspect which was in itself the best possible condemnation
of the abuses he mentions.

The Pauline Eucharist, then, made no break with the ritual meal
at which the primitive community recalled the appearances of the
risen Christ. And furthermore, the Breaking of Bread was linked,
by a real and probably fully recognized bond, to the Lord's Supper
referred to by St. Paul.

---

[41] Some time after this epistle was written, St. Paul was in Troas, and sum-
moned the community on Sunday for the breaking of bread (Acts xx 7)
The chalice is not mentioned, yet this was a Pauline community; the gathering
and the meal were religious; and the very wording of the account relates it
to 1 Cor. xi Cf Behm, *Th. W N T*, vol iii, p. 729. From this we must conclude that the ritual meal could include the cup without mention being made
of it, and that the Pauline Eucharist was in continuity with the primitive
ritual meal, the breaking of bread.

Towards the end of the paschal meal, our Lord had said: "I will not drink from henceforth of this fruit of the vine, until that day when I shall drink it with you new in the kingdom of my Father " (Matt. xxvi. 29; Mark xiv 25.) St. Luke puts this text in its proper place, before the institution of the Eucharist.[42] At that moment, Christ was preparing the table for a meal belonging to another world, a replica of the paschal lamb, in which he was to give himself in mystery in a state of immolation. Luke realized that the meal in the joy of the Kingdom was beginning at the Last Supper. That is why he modified the text from Mark, bringing it back from the eschatological distance to make it the prophecy of an immediate reality· "I will not drink of the fruit of the vine till the Kingdom of God come." (xxii. 18.) His Kingdom of God "at once suggests the sphere in which the new paschal rite was to unfold, that is, the Church".[43] In giving us to understand that our Lord would eat and drink again in the Kingdom, he must have had in mind the meals of the risen Christ which he, alone of the Evangelists, lays such stress upon.[44] To him, Christ's last supper was certainly related to the mysterious meals he had with the disciples after entering the kingdom.

The Apostles must have felt a continuity between those meals and the Last Supper The latter, so strange and intimate, belonged as much to another world as did the meals they had with their Master when he had returned from death and entered upon a new existence, in the glory of the Kingdom (Luke xxiv. 26). These were almost like a dream. The foretelling of the mysterious meal in the Kingdom applied to them and yet went beyond them, and brought them all together in one eschatological atmosphere.

We may conclude that the apostolic communities had only one ritual meal with different aspects—all of which may not always have been perceived simultaneously and clearly. The same Eucharist brings together two streams flowing from separate sources—one from Christ's last supper and death, and the other from the Resurrection and the meals that followed it.

[42] P. Benoit, "Le Récit de la cène dans Luc xxii, 15–20", *R B*, xlviii (1939), 382, 386
[43] P Benoit, "Le Récit de la Cène", p 388.
[44] Cf. Benoit, p 389

(2) The Meaning of the Eucharist

If we consider the significance the Eucharist gets from this double orientation, we shall realize that, far from being mutually exclusive, the two aspects in fact complement each other.

(a) The Presence of the Glorified Christ

The Breaking of Bread prolonged for the disciples, in the intimate communion of a meal, the experience of the presence of the glorified Christ. This, historically, is the first sense of the Eucharistic celebration· the Saviour was alive in the midst of the disciples when they gathered for the Breaking of Bread.

This presence of the glorified Christ which characterized the meals after the Resurrection, was also realized in the commemoration of the Last Supper. The Pauline Eucharist was "the Lord's table" (1 Cor. x. 21), "the Lord's supper" (xi. 20), and Christ presided over it as at the last supper he had on earth. Christ was the rock present in the midst of the people, as they were fed with spiritual food and drink. (x. 4.) Our Lord had, after all, foretold this gathering of the disciples round him at a meal: "From this time I will not eat the pasch, till it be fulfilled in the Kingdom of God." (Luke xxii. 16.) He was to celebrate the Pasch again with his own, a perfect pasch, a communion in the true sacrifice of the Lamb. In that mysterious banquet begun in the Eucharist, Christ himself was to drink the new wine (Matt., Mark) among the Apostles (Matt), once he had entered into his kingdom.

(b) The Sacrificial Meal

The Last Supper and its commemoration, however, appear primarily as the sacrificial meal of the Cross.

Our Lord invites those who believe in him to his table, for what he offers them is his "body which is delivered for you", his "blood shed for the remission of your sins". He offers the bread and the chalice, not merely because they are his body and blood, but because they are that body and blood offered to God, and offered for them. The High Priest of the Cross calls the faithful to communion in his sacrifice. Because it is a sacrificial meal, Christ appears in the victim state. He gives them to drink "the blood of the new testament, shed for many" (Matt., Mark), blood of sacrifice as the establishment of the old covenant required (Exod. xxiv. 8), shed at the moment of drinking.

Despite this victim state, the body of Christ in the Eucharist is no longer subject to the ultimate *kenosis* of the death on the Cross. To St. Paul it is spiritual food: "I would not have you ignorant, brethren, that our fathers . . . did all eat the same spiritual food and all drank the same spiritual drink." (1 Cor. x. 1–4.) Israel possessed a figure of the one spiritual bread which feeds and unifies the new people of God. The bread of the desert could be called spiritual because of its origin and because of the reality it reflected. But the Church's bread is spiritual in itself, for what nourishes in it is the Spirit; it is the body of Christ vivified by the Spirit.

In this way the Eucharist fulfils another condition of the sacrificial meal. God only invites those who are to offer it to his table after he has received the victim and established him in the divine sphere. The victim cannot become sacred food until it has attained the end of the sacrifice and entered into the Divinity. The Gentile, offering sacrifice to devils and then eating at their table, is uniting himself to them, for all victims become the property of the divinities who accept them and bear the imprint of their presence; in one case they are transformed into the holiness of God, in another consecrated to demons. The believer who eats and drinks at the Lord's table thus assimilates a divinized food. The bread and the chalice of benediction are a communion in an immolated body, but a body consecrated in the Godhead. (1 Cor. x. 14–21.)

Now in St. Paul's teaching, the body of Christ was divinized[45] in the Holy Spirit of resurrection. We eat "a spiritual bread", the body of the risen Christ.

Thus communion in the sacrifice of the Cross is effected by the presence both of the immolated body and of the glorified body.[46]

This paradox of Christ's death and glory being present together appears in the very elements of the Eucharist. The symbolism of the separate bread and wine, confirmed by Christ's words, "This is my body . . . this is my blood . ." relates to the immolation. But these elements are food and drink, a principle of life. Bread satisfies and wine elates, and both produce joy; the joy of all as individuals is

---

[45] That is to say, caught up by the glorifying power of God

[46] St. Ignatius of Antioch defines the Eucharist as "the flesh . . which suffered for our sins and which the Father through his goodness resurrected" (*Smyrn.*, vii, 1)

multiplied by the joy of all as a whole, and must find expression: "They took their meal with gladness and simplicity of heart." (Acts ii. 46.) The symbolism of the meal is basically of life and of joy, and yet it carries within itself the immolation, for the two elements are a single food, a sign of life, before being a reminder of the death, and it is as a meal that the Eucharist is a sacrifice: it is a sacrificial meal. The immolated body is given to the faithful in life and joy. In the Eucharist, as elsewhere, it is only in Christ's glory that we make contact with his death.

Thus it is in Christ's glory that believers sit down at the table of his sacrifice. He himself is present among the feasters, eating and drinking at the true festival of the Lamb. (Cf. Luke xxii. 16; Mark xiv. 25.) In his glory, he communicates in his own sacrifice, and all who are united to his glorified body communicate in it as well. The Eucharist is the archetype for all communion in the Cross, for it gathers the faithful up into the glorification of Christ.

The messianic community is formed and expresses itself in that meal: "This chalice is the new testament." (Luke xxii. 20; 1 Cor. xi. 25.) The Kingdom of God is revealed in it, promised as a banquet, as a fulfilment of the Pasch. In it the Church strengthens her unity, for every sacrificial meal creates bonds among the partakers that cannot be broken, and even in the past the eating of the lamb confirmed the unity of the people of God. (Exod. xii. 43-8.) All eat the one bread which is Christ's body, and all form one body which is the body of Christ. (1 Cor. x. 17.)

(c) Sacrament of Death and Resurrection

Like baptism, the Eucharist is a taking hold of the death and resurrection of Jesus. It unites the believer to Christ's death by associating him with the Resurrection.

But the Eucharist does more even than baptism. While the sign of baptism makes us present to Christ's sacrifice, that sacrifice is itself present in the Eucharist; it is not simply laid open to our era through the sign, but actually comes into it.

For the death of Christ is made present in the meal, in mystery of course, but in reality. To judge from the words of consecration, the blood is shed at the moment of being given us to drink: ". . . the blood of the testament shed for many . . ." (Matt., Mark.) In making the participle future ("shall be shed"), the Vulgate blurs the shades of meaning, for while referring to his own death, Christ was formally relating the eucharistic chalice to the blood which Moses caught as it poured from the victim, to pour out to seal the covenant of Sinai. "It is as blood poured out that the blood of Christ figures in the chalice."[47] St. Luke says so in so many words—unless he is making a grammatical error which would seem impossible to him[48] According to St. Paul, every celebration of the Last Supper announces the death of the Lord. (1 Cor. xi. 26)

But, though the death becomes present in the meal, it is not repeated like the death of the god in the mystery religions. The death announced by the Eucharist is the death that took place after the Last Supper, the death on Calvary to which Christ referred in the words of its institution (1 Cor. xi. 26, 23–4.) It is one event of history, Christ's death under Pontius Pilate, which is introduced among the feasters at the meal. It does not appear in the same way as it originally happened, for that is fixed in the past; it could only do this by being reproduced in a new death, and it is not reproduced It comes into our present history without happening again itself: the rite of the Last Supper gives no hint of any offering that would cause the sacrifice to happen again.

It is in the paschal meal, under the form of bread and wine, which signify life, in joy, in the life of glory, that Christ's death becomes present, present in the glorious end in which it is fixed, now and forever, by the Spirit of the Resurrection.

Immovably fixed in its heavenly goal, the sacrifice is made outwardly present in our age at the same time as the body of Christ in which it is present[49]; it is translated once again into the history of

[47] Lagrange, *Evangile selon saint Marc*, Paris, 1920, pp 355ff.

[48] "Poured out" agrees in case with "chalice", not with "blood"

[49] The doctrine set out here and in chapters iv and vi differs from that of Dom Odo Casel who, if I understand him correctly, holds that the liturgical rite, as a rite, has power to make the death and resurrection of the Lord present. The same would apply, according to him, to all the sacraments and rites, to the prayer of the community, for instance, or the consecration of virgins

But in fact the rite has not got this power of itself, simply by the power of symbolism, but only because it unites the believer to Christ in the act of the Redemption. Even apart from the liturgical celebration, the believer lives in this mystery (Gal ii 19–20), in that he is united to Christ.

It is in Christ himself, fixed forever at the summit of his redemptive activity, that the mystery is present—this is the truth on which everything else rests. It is present to us in as much as Christ is present to us The Church is in Christ and Christ is in her. The other sacraments bring us into that mystery

this world by the intermediary of the sacrament, and therefore becomes once more earthly and temporal. This translation into signs is necessary, for the sacrifice of Christ is essentially heavenly in its consummation, and cannot come back into our history in the form proper to it.

The Eucharist brings the fullness of Christ's sacrifice into his earthly body, the Church, in whom the sacrifice is still not complete; and it draws her towards that fullness, for it makes all men together the one body of Christ (1 Cor. x. 17), dead and risen, so that those who are fed by it are also offered in sacrifice.

Unique and never to be repeated, the death as it took place in history becomes present as it is now, in its everlasting fullness, in its goal of glory. It is made part of our history without happening again. The only sense in which it may be said to "happen" again is in the Church, which is as it were infected by the one sacrifice in the Eucharist Thus, the only new element in Christ's sacrifice is its sacramental reappearance in our time and its extension to the community of believers.

(d) Sacrament of the *Parousia*

This ritual meal, which is the perfect realization of the Church on earth, bears within it all the eschatological force that belongs to God's people on earth. It is a meal of the end of time, taken with the risen Christ in whom is the end of the world. The presence of

at the same time as uniting us to the body of Christ. They do not really bring his death and resurrection back into our era, except in so far as they identify the Church with the body of Christ in his death and resurrection. Only the Eucharist introduces the Easter mystery as it is in Christ into our era, because it makes Christ himself really present.

The other liturgical acts also unite us to the mystery, but they do so by uniting us to Christ The prayer of the community, for instance, gathers the faithful together in Christ This is because the Church is gathered together in Christ, in his death and resurrection, and therefore, the community of believers, praying together, is caught up in the mystery of Easter

The consecration of virgins is a total consecration to Christ We are consecrated to Christ only in his death and resurrection Such a consecration is the most effective way of achieving death to this world and the life of the next world in Christ

Again, it is not the rite as such which makes the death present, as it is supposed to in the mystery religions to which Dom Casel refers. The only exception is the Eucharist, for in it the body of Christ is itself present. The mystery of Easter is present in the body of Christ, and in the Church which is that body.

Christ means the arrival of the *parousia*; until then, the Saviour comes as it were incognito,[50] but it is a real coming, similar in all essentials to the final one; the eucharistic coming brings a judgement (1 Cor. xi. 29–34) based on the same criterion as the judgement of the Last Day Christ's body and man's position in regard to it. Anyone unworthy of the body of Christ eats and drinks his own damnation.

Despite the fact that this is a real coming, and, indeed, because of it, the Church's straining towards the final coming is nowhere so intense. The *Didache* tells us (x. 6) that what the early Christians thought as they broke bread could be expressed in the exclamation: "Maranatha—Come, Lord!" While the death of Christ was being announced in its midst, the community proclaimed its longing: "You shall announce the death of the Lord until he come." (1 Cor. xi. 26.)[51] The announcement of Christ's death is necessarily also the announcement of his resurrection, and therefore of the *parousia*.

Thus the Eucharist is both a pasch already present, and a parasceve, a vigil of the feast. It is adapted to our interlude between two eras, a *parousia* which exists alongside our carnal state and at the same time a presence which looks forward with longing, a food which increases the hunger it satisfies It is a goal attained in anticipation, and at the same time a setting on the way; it accompanies God's people, feeding them, the viaticum of the Exodus and the rock gushing with water, present at every stage of the journey. (1 Cor. x. 3–4.)

The Eucharist is a complex mystery, uniting the believer to both ends of history, to the Lord's resurrection and his *parousia*. You shall eat the whole lamb, commanded Moses, "the head with the feet" (Exod. xii. 9); in other words, you shall communicate in the whole mystery of Christ, one ancient writer explains, in Christ at both extremities of time [52] The Church is not torn apart by being thus orientated towards the opposite ends of her time, for she is linked to a single fact expressed at both ends of her history on earth, at one end as inauguration, at the other as consummation, and every Eucharist is a revelation of it for the time that lies between.

[50] The phrase is used by E. Walter, *Das Kommen des Herrn*, Freiburg-i-B , 1942, p. 33
[51] The Greek sentence expresses a finality Cf. F. Blass-Debrunner, *Grammatik des ntl. Griechisch*, 7th ed., 1943, § 383, 2; J Jeremias, *Die Abendmahlsworte Jesu*, 2nd ed., Göttingen, 1949, p. 118
[52] Cf *In Pascha II, P.G.*, lix, 728

(3) The Eucharist in St. John

(1) St John must be considered separately. Even apart from the explicit statement of it in Chapter VI, the idea of the Eucharist appears throughout the gospel in allusion and symbol, just as it is present in the whole of Chapter VI, though actually stated only at the end. It seems as though the Apostle, in this clearly sacramental gospel, was reconsidering all that Christ said and did in the light of his eucharistic experience [53]

St. John's doctrine of the Eucharist bears the same general character as his gospel.

Whereas the Synoptics stress the social nature of messianic salvation, come into the world as a kingdom, St. John gives more attention to its meaning for individuals. Similarly, for him the Eucharist is not so much a banquet as food given individually: "he that eateth my flesh" (vi. 54) suggests an intimate supping of the individual with Christ. (Cf. Apoc. iii. 20.)

The early liturgy was linked with the Cross and Resurrection; the Johannine Eucharist is traceable back to the Incarnation: it is the bread of God come down from heaven to give life to the world. (vi. 33.)

But, though it is the mystery on which all else rests, the Incarnation will only develop fully, through death, in glory, to yield all its power to save us, and Christ's flesh will not become our food till it has been given up to death and to glory. It is almost true to say, "The idea of the Passion and that of the Eucharist are as closely connected in this gospel as they are in Paul and the accounts of the Synoptics." [54] After all, "the bread that I will give is my flesh [given] for the life of the world". (vi. 51.)

The fact that the eucharistic discourse is preceded by the multiplication of the loaves and fishes and the walking on the water, suggests that the bread to be given by Christ was not his body in its earthly condition. To the Jews, who thought they were being invited to a cannibal feast, Christ answered· "Doth this scandalize you? If then you shall see the Son of Man ascend up where he was before? It is the Spirit that quickeneth; the flesh profiteth nothing." (vi. 61-3.) He was setting them on the road to understanding. Christ's flesh as one could see and touch it, and any physical eating of it, would profit nothing. The Spirit is the principle of eternal life

---

[53] O Cullmann, *Christian Worship*, pt. ii.
[54] A Loisy, *Le Quatrième Évangile*, Paris, 1921, p. 242.

(iii. 5–6), and Christ's body is as well in as much as the Spirit acts through it. Christ's glorification would make it possible for him to give himself as such food. The whispering could stop. In my glorification, says our Lord, you will understand[55]; you will know that it is my flesh quickened in the Spirit which I will give as food, for the Spirit alone is the principle of life. "My words—the things I am proposing—are [realities of] spirit and life." (vi. 63)

This doctrine of the Eucharist fits in with the declaration at the Feast of Tabernacles. By faith, the believer comes to the body of Christ, and there quenches his thirst with the water of the Spirit; but that water flows only after the glorification. (vii 37–9; vi. 35.)

Thus the Eucharist is a paschal sacrament for St. John. But, like the whole paschal theme in the fourth gospel, it remains in continuity with the Incarnation.[56] The Resurrection brings Christ to the fullness of his life as Son, and gives him the power to quicken all flesh (xvii. 1–2); and it is through the Eucharist that he exercises that power. (vi. 54.)

If we bring together all that Scripture has to tell us, we come to the conclusion that baptism and the Eucharist achieve basically the same effects. Both rites cause the paschal life of Christ to extend to the faithful, opening for them in his body an entry into the act of redemption.[57]

A number of texts suggest that baptism is to be considered as a rite of communion in the sacrifice; the Eucharist is clearly indicated as being such a rite, and the close relationship between the two sacraments extends that indication to baptism.[58] In both the believer

[55] The exaltation was not merely mentioned as a miracle to support the genuineness of Christ's words—any other miracle would have served this purpose—but as a demonstration of the truth, for by it Christ's flesh was to be established in that spiritual state which would give it the power to save and answer all the objections being made

[56] The Eucharist effects an interpenetration between Christ and the believer (vi. 56) parallel with the identification of the believer with Christ in the teaching of St. Paul. But this interpenetration does not appear to impress Christ's death upon the believer as well as his life

[57] It is not surprising that the man who, believing in the Redemption, receives the sacrament, should be justified by that sacrament (*ex opere operato*), since the sacrament is applying to the believer the justifying action which operates in the body of Christ.

[58] From this point of view, too, the sacrament works *ex opere operato*. The ancients thought they entered the society of God because they sat down at God's table and ate divine food. And in Christian communion the victim

is united to the body of Christ, immolated in the flesh and consecrated in the Spirit of God; by both he takes part in Christ's own
communion in his sacrifice—the Resurrection. In this communion
he is himself sacrificed, for he becomes joined to a body in which
the sacrifice is forever actual.

2. THE CHURCH'S ASSIMILATION OF THE EASTER MYSTERY

The Easter mystery opens out upon men by way of the apostolate
and the sacraments; through them it becomes communicable and is
communicated. But it remains for men to come to it and take it to
themselves. This they do by means of faith, by their effort to live
a Christian life, and by their acceptance of suffering and death.

i. FAITH

We begin with St. Paul, for he has a doctrinal synthesis on this
subject. But once we have set out his system, we may well wonder
whether he is not in fact continuing along the lines already indicated
by the Gospels.

(a) The Object of Faith

The object of Christian faith is not simply God, but God who
raises up Christ.[59] The Jews accepted the Mosaic faith (Deut. vi. 4),
yet they are numbered among the infidels (2 Cor. iv. 4), for they
do not believe in God who raised up Christ.

To St. Paul, the faith of Abraham was a kind of prophetic outline of our faith. The object of Paul's faith, as of Abraham's, was
the power of God who gave life to the dead: "Abraham is the father
of us all . . . He believeth God who quickeneth the dead, and calleth
those things that are not into being." He believed the promise made
of his seed, "nor did he consider his own body now dead . . . nor the
dead womb of Sara . . . and therefore it was reputed to him unto
justice". (Rom. iv. 16–22.)

Our faith is similar· "It is written not only for him [Abraham]

eaten has not been divinized merely symbolically; the banquet is divine in
the literal sense

[59] Rom. iv 24; vi. 4; viii 11; Col ii. 12; 1 Pet. 1. 21; cf. Polycarp, *Phil.*,
iii 1 "The characteristic title the Apostle gives God from now on is 'God
the Father who raised Jesus Christ from the dead'." (J. M. Shaw, "Resurrection of Christ", *Dictionary of the Apostolic Church*, p. 330; E Stauffer, *Theologie des neuen Testaments*, pp 221–2.)

that it was reputed to him unto justice, but also for us, to whom it shall be reputed, if we believe in him, that raised up Jesus Christ our Lord from the dead, who was delivered up for our sins, and rose again for our justification." (Rom. iv. 23–5.)

Despite the resemblance, our faith is enormously superior to that of Abraham. Whereas our ancestor believed in a human life being raised from a dead womb, our "faith in the operation of God who raises up" is concerned with a gift of heavenly life: God raised up a man, Christ Jesus, for our salvation, lifting him to his true divine life, in the total gift of the Holy Ghost.

The believer's entire faith centres upon this divine fact. It is briefly defined as "faith in the operation of God who hath raised him up from the dead" (Col. ii. 12; cf. Rom. x. 9; 1 Cor. xv. 2ff.; 2 Cor. iv. 13–14; Eph. i. 19; 1 Thess. iv. 14.) It believes in God whose will to save us is affirmed in the resurrection of Christ and who judges the world in Christ.[60] So essential is Christ's resurrection to our faith, that if he had not risen, that faith would be simply a dream, void of meaning. (1 Cor. xv. 14–15.)

Thus the object of our faith is not God in his serene essence, a God standing in motionless perfection, but the person of God who breaks into our history through the justifying and judgement-giving act of the Resurrection, who obliges us to make a decision, and radically changes the course of our destiny.

This revelation of God's salvation is effected in the person of Christ. The Christian faith is wholly centred upon Christ the Lord, Christ risen from the dead. "Christ is the Lord " (1 Cor. xii. 3; Phil. ii. 11; Rom. x 9.) formulates the earliest professions of faith.[61] This contains the whole Christian faith, and the whole Creed grows out of it.[62]

Thus the object of faith is essentially soteriological: Christ, Lord of the world to be saved and judged. In the risen Christ faith finds the Father who engenders Christ for us, and gives us the Holy Spirit for our own.

[60] In the double sense of justification and condemnation

[61] Cf. O Cullmann, *Les Premières Confessions de foi chrétiennes*, 2nd ed., Paris, 1948.

[62] As Cullmann points out (*Les Premières Confessions*, p 42), faith in the Trinity, to take one instance, starts with the Easter revelation, for in the Resurrection the Father engenders the Son in the Holy Spirit, and through the Son whom he engenders, he communicates the Spirit to us In Rom x. 6–9, St. Paul sums up faith in the Incarnation and the Redemption as confession of the resurrection and lordship of Christ.

Hope comes so close to faith that the two are hardly distinguishable—hope is faith as a driving force. Abraham believed against all appearances and hoped against hope (Rom. iv. 18–19); Christians are those who believe, and also those who "hope in Christ". (1 Cor. xv. 19.)

For the power of God effecting the salvation of the world in Christ, which constitutes the object of faith, is also the motive of hope; one cannot be committed to that faith without also having hope. (Cf. Tit 1. 1–2.)[63]

Other writers give us outlines and sometimes even exact formulations of this doctrine of faith. For the Synoptics, faith bears upon God in his power to establish the Kingdom, and it is inseparable from hope. In the Acts, faith is the response to the announcement of Christ's messianic exaltation, and those who believe call upon the name of the Lord. (ii. 21; ix. 14.) To St. John the object of faith is "that Jesus is the Christ, the Son of God" (xx. 31); the idea of Christ as Messiah and Redeemer is essential to it. "I am the Resurrection and the Life ... Believest thou this? ... Yes, Lord, I have believed that thou art Christ the Son of God who art come into this world." (xi. 25–7) The act of faith consists in believing that Christ has been sent by the Father (xvii. 8, 21), "that I am he" (viii. 24, 28; xiii. 19), in other words that he is Jesus who is to come (cf. Mark xiii. 6), he who, clearly from the context of viii. 24, is come to save from death; that he is the bread come down from heaven to feed the world (vi.). The object of faith is the Son of God, saviour of the world. Above all is that faith demanded and imposed by the exaltation (iii. 14–15; viii. 28); the beloved disciple "believed" when he saw the empty tomb (xx. 8); it is to the glorified Christ that the believer must adhere if he is to draw the Spirit from him. (vii. 37–9.)

If we leave out the shades of meaning each author supplies, we may conclude that the Christian faith bears upon the redeeming action of God in Christ, an action which culminates in the Resurrection.

[63] Faith is a dynamic virtue, attempting everything, never hesitating To believe in the resurrection of Christ is to believe that henceforward nothing is impossible Man enters upon the divine process of justification with complete assurance, the Apostle is never daunted, for the Gospel is the power of God (Rom. i 16), and he works with unshakable certainty for the complete conquest of the world

(b) Faith as Contact with the Mystery

The believer cannot fail to come in contact with this salvation of God towards which faith moves by its own inner necessity.

The saving mystery of Easter is opened wide and offered to man in the Apostles and in the sacraments; by faith, man is borne towards that mystery, lays himself open to it and welcomes it.

It is in this that the virtue of faith consists: it lays man open to the Easter mystery and enables him to take it to himself. "The exceeding greatness of his power [working in the resurrection of Christ is exercised] towards us, who believe." (Eph. i. 19.) "We have been buried with him in baptism, and we are risen again with him and in him, by the faith in the operation of God, who hath raised him up from the dead." (Col. ii. 12.)[64]

Where he is not explicitly saying this, St. Paul implies it by what he does say. Our risen life is defined as life "in the faith of the Son of God . . . who delivered himself up". (Gal. ii. 20.) The promise of the Spirit, fulfilled in the resurrection of Christ, is made effective for us by means of faith: "that we might receive the promise of the Spirit by faith". (Gal. iii. 14; cf. v. 5.) The presence of Christ in us, that permanent communion in the Resurrection, is the effect of faith: "Christ dwells by faith in your hearts." (Eph. iii. 17.) And similarly our presence in Christ: "That I may be found in him, not having my own justice . . . but that which is of the faith" which brings experience of his death and resurrection. (Phil. iii. 9–10) Christ's divine sonship, made manifest in his resurrection, and the privileges flowing from it—such as the freedom of the sons—are all communicated by faith: "After the faith is come, we are no longer under a pedagogue. For you are all the children of God by faith, which is in Christ Jesus " (Gal. iii. 25–6.)

According to the fourth gospel, faith is man's movement towards Christ, the possessor of life. To believe is to come. (v. 40; vi. 35; and *passim*.) In his glorified body Christ bears the well-spring of life (vii. 39; vi. 62–3), and man comes to him by faith to drink of the Spirit flowing from his pierced side

Faith has this power of opening man to the mystery of the paschal

[64] There are two means working together to link the believer to the fact of the Redemption From the believer's point of view, one is, as it were, the surroundings (ἐν) in which the contact is established, baptism; the other, faith, is an active instrument for taking possession of the Resurrection (διά).

Christ because it is not merely an intellectual assent but a handing-over of man to God in his total adherence to the risen Christ; it is man's living assent, in his inmost being, to another principle of life.

(c) Faith as a Death and a Resurrection

All knowledge presupposes a certain likeness in nature to the thing known, and all adherence to another demands a harmony. The risen Christ, the object of faith, is dead to the flesh and lives in the Spirit. In order to establish contact with him, faith makes man undergo a certain death, and it is in that death that it makes him adhere to the living Christ. It is thus a re-birth.

By faith, man gives up making himself the centre of his own life, the basis of his own salvation, and places that centre and basis outside himself, in God who gives life to Christ. Whereas the Jew relies upon the privileges of his race and upon his works, and remains bounded by the sufficiency of his own justice (Phil. iii. 9; Rom. ix. 32; x. 3), the believer considers everything that seemed gain according to the flesh as valueless and even harmful (Phil. iii. 8); he comes out of himself to seek a justice he has not merited by any works. (Rom. iii. 28; iv. 5; Gal. ii. 16; Eph. ii. 8–9; Phil. iii. 9.) He believes in the justice of God which is communicated in Christ, and he is in turn glorified, but not for his works, for his glory is in God alone. (2 Cor. x. 17; Phil. iii. 9.) He has crazily cast his anchor of certainty beyond all the assurances of the flesh to fix it in the death and resurrection of Jesus Christ. (Phil. iii. 3–11)

Intellectual adherence to the teaching of the Apostles is an immediate renunciation of one's own autonomy of thought, and of the security one finds in one's own understanding, by which one lays oneself open to invasion by another's thought. And at a deeper level, it is a complete renunciation of man's right to command himself: faith is obedience (Rom. i. 5), it makes man truly captive to God. (2 Cor. x. 5; Rom. vi. 17–18.) The believer opens himself to God, becomes linked to God, which means the death of the flesh. There is an anguish for man in making this complete reversal, in recognizing his fundamental powerlessness, in handing himself over to another, in delivering himself totally over to the salvific will of God. He lets go the certitudes within his grasp (Phil. iii. 3–7), abandons the ground he feels beneath his feet, in order to believe in a world he cannot see; he trusts his weight to something whose very existence (naturally speaking, impossible) he knows only by God's word. He risks all upon the word of God in Christ.

St Paul speaks of the "sacrificial oblation of faith". (Phil. ii. 17; Rom. xv. 16.) We say this sacrifice is metaphorical, but we must not therefore miss seeing its real analogy with the sacrifice of Christ [65]

(d) Faith an Effect of the Resurrection

This faith which subjects man to the raising action of God is itself an effect of that action.

The apostolic preaching which produces it is laden with the raising force of God. Once man has received it, it acts as from God and opens him to faith: "It has been given you as a gift ... to believe in Christ." (Phil. i. 29.) The confession of faith in the Lord Jesus which assures man the salvation of the Messiah (Rom. x. 9–11), is itself a result of the Spirit of the glorified Christ, who is the gift we receive from the Messiah: "No man can say Jesus is the Lord, but by the Holy Ghost." (1 Cor. xii. 3.) Faith which involves a death must presuppose a gift of the Spirit; for if it is a death to the flesh it can only be a death with Christ, and one can only die in this way in union with the life of our Saviour

Faith, therefore, not only opens man to the paschal mystery, but itself belongs to that mystery; it is an effect of the Father's action in glorifying Christ. It is at once cause and effect, creating the contact with the Resurrection that it demands. It is numbered both among the means whereby the risen Christ expands, and among the means whereby man assimilates the Resurrection.

Because God's raising force is at work in faith, it exercises a real causality in our justification. It is more than simply "an indispensable prerequisite" [66] for sacramental justification; its action complements the work of baptism: "... buried with him in baptism, in which [or "in him"] also you are risen again by faith in the operation of God". (Col. ii. 12.) Justification results from the combined action of the sacrament and faith.

Though he affirms quite definitely the efficacy inherent in the very administration of baptism, St. Paul attributes to man himself

[65] The martyr is the perfect type of the believer He lets go the life he has for life in Christ, in which he believes though he cannot see it.

[66] A. Wikenhauser, *Die Christusmystik des hl. Paulus*, pp. 81–2.

a part in his sacramental sanctification: "You are washed
[ἀπελούσασθε]" by baptism. (1 Cor. vi. 11.) "They that are Christ's,
have crucified their flesh with its vices and concupiscences." (Gal.
v. 24.) This crucifixion dates from baptism (the verb is in the aorist);
but unlike the parallel text, Rom. vi. 3–4, this one does not attribute
the death to the sacramental rite, but stresses the act of the will
whereby the believer effects, at the conscious level, the death of his
flesh at the moment of baptism.[67]

The efficaciousness of this human activity could hardly be in the
order of merit—such an idea would go counter to all Paul's teaching. Yet man does bring his co-operation to God's action in the
sacrament. His activity is not set alongside God's: the two activities
interpenetrate, for man's faith is itself due to the Spirit, and the
Spirit is given in the sacrament.[68] Yet man does play an important
part. By a positive will, expressed through faith, he puts himself at
the disposal of God who justifies the world in the dead and risen
Christ. He lets life be implanted in him, consciously submitting to
the death of Christ which the sacrament mysteriously achieves.[69]

ii. CHRISTIAN EFFORT

Baptismal faith is only the beginning of the long effort the believer
must bring to join the raising power of God.

[67] Cf. A. Steinmann and F. Tillmann, *Der Galaterbrief*, Bonn, 1935, p 160;
St. Zeno of Verona, *Tract XXXI, Invit. ad fontem II*, P.L., xi, 477: "You
are born by your judgement, for we know that whoever shall believe more
will make himself nobler" Greater faith means greater nobility.

[68] It does not seem as though St Paul ever envisages justification being
effected by faith alone, without baptism. Cf A Loisy, "L'Initiation
chrétienne", *Rev. d'hist. e litt rel.*, 1914, pp. 198–9, quoted with approval by
Lagrange, except in the case "where perfect faith comes before baptism, or
baptism cannot be administered" (*Épître aux Romains*, 3rd ed , Paris, 1922,
p. 152)

[69] The fourth gospel throws a similar light on the relationship between
faith and the sacrament On the one hand, Christ attributes to faith the power
of gaining eternal life: "Every one who seeth the Son and believeth in him
hath life everlasting, and I will raise him up in the last day." (vi. 40) Elsewhere the saving power of the heavenly bread is described in identical terms:
"He that eateth my flesh and drinketh my blood hath everlasting life, and
I will raise him up in the last day." (vi. 54) Faith and the sacraments bring
about eternal life The whole eucharistic discourse is contained in this statement: Christ gives the bread of life, which is himself, man assimilates it by
adhering to Christ in faith, an adherence which is expressed by the eating
of the sacramental bread The nourishing power is in the bread, but it is
by faith that it is eaten

(a) *The Need for It*

In the Pauline system, Christian effort is needed because the redemption is not yet complete either in the baptized person himself, in the Church or in the world.

The death and resurrection of baptism, although real, have taken place in mystery, leaving the whole field of events of human existence still at the disposal of the carnal order. There remains a lot of the past, an "old man", unrejuvenated by grace, an "outward man", superimposed on the "inward man". The need for Christian effort in our sanctification is based on this fact, coupled with the complete condemnation passed on the flesh in baptism; for it is the whole man who has died with Christ in baptism, and he is called on to live henceforth only according to the Spirit, despite all that remains in him of the flesh. Everything in him that resists must be made subject to the Spirit: "Mortify therefore your members which are upon the earth; fornication, uncleanness . . . For you have stripped off the old man with his deeds, and put on the new." (Col. iii. 5, 9–10.)

Every action of our conscious lives offers the opportunity for doing this, for the inward man comes to grips with the flesh in everything we do. The flesh opposes the Spirit both with its own instincts and with the weight of its inertia; the former constantly pull the believer back to his old ways, and the latter hampers the growth of the new life.

There must be an asceticism of restraint to curb "the members of the earthly man", to kill in order to give life: "For if you live according to the flesh, you shall die; but if by the Spirit you mortify the deeds of the flesh, you shall live." (Rom. viii. 13.) And there must be a positive asceticism to help forward the thrust of the Spirit, to bring human nature, weighed down with the flesh, into step with the Spirit· "that we also may walk in newness of life". (Rom. vi. 4.) "So run that you may obtain the prize." (1 Cor. ix. 24.) Both asceticisms are "mortifications" of the old man, and both are at work in every act performed in the Spirit.

The incompleteness of the Redemption and the struggle within man have their repercussions throughout the universe.

The baptized man is still fixed in "this world", though it is condemned, and yet he is in principle cut off from it. And though he is fixed in it, he must live as cut off from it because of that condemnation, "they that use this world as if they used it not", those who are married, who rejoice or who weep according to the world, must be as if they were not married, or as if they do not laugh or weep, because this world is passing away. (1 Cor. vii. 29–31.)

It is not a question of any withdrawal, but of strife and struggle on a world-wide scale. (Eph. vi. 12.) In the believer who is as yet incompletely caught up in the glory of Christ, the world below and the new creation meet and clash, "the rulers of this world of darkness" (Eph. vi. 12) join cause with what remains of hidden force in the flesh, and form with it a massive resistance which Christ will destroy in his Day, when he raises the dead.

(b) Its Nature

The goal of this asceticism characterizes its nature, and is what differentiates the Christian struggle from all other ascetic efforts. Only the ascesis that is directed towards resurrection in the Spirit is Christian.

It is a labour which would not find the Spirit at the end of its efforts if he had not been there at the beginning. The Spirit is as much its principle as its goal: "If by the Spirit you mortify the deeds of the flesh, you shall live." (Rom. viii. 13.) No asceticism could succeed in opening man's inmost self to Christ without the Spirit, for he is both the principle whereby Christ becomes universalized, and the principle whereby man's personality is compenetrated by Christ's.

Asceticism, which is an effort of spiritualization, also presupposes a communion with the glorified Christ, for he alone is the source of the Spirit. This does not mean just bearing similar sufferings, but like the baptismal death of which it is the development, it is the death of Christ himself, borne by the believer in order that Christ's resurrection may grow in him. The believer "suffers with" Christ (Rom. viii. 17), just as he "dies with" him in baptism.

Mortification is a declaration of love. It starts from communion with Christ and seeks a greater communion; the Spirit who is its principle and who is enabled by it to increase in us, is the love of God (Rom. v. 5); love is the alpha and omega of mortification. The Synoptics had, earlier on, characterized self-denial thus: "He that shall lose his life for my sake shall find it." (Matt. xvi. 25.) To be a

Christian and to find life, the loss we submit to must be for Christ's sake.

St Paul is giving the words their full richness when he describes abnegation as a sacrifice, with the body of the believer as the offering. (Rom. xii. 1.) Where it is merely the struggle against a bad instinct, it is a slight enough matter, but in the believer it is the death of Christ, a participation in the sacrifice in which Christ offered himself to the glory of God.

This is what mortification must be to stand among the means whereby we take possession of the Resurrection. Any other attempt to mortify nature will only result in creating a further obstacle to the Spirit's dominion.

Our Lord had long ago condemned the superficial asceticism of the Jews which they had wanted to impose on his disciples, and declared the superiority of interior worship. (Matt. ix. 13; xii. 7.) St. Paul had to fight against the dangerous return of asceticisms left behind by Judaism or the pagan philosophies among his communities. The faithful were told, "Touch not, taste not, handle not." (Col. ii. 21.) Those around them tried to force them to be circumcised, to abstain from certain food, to observe days and months and seasons. (Gal., *passim*.) The gnostic tendencies mentioned in the pastoral epistles (1 Tim. iv. 3) forbade marriage and certain foods. False ascetics thought they could find a purity and perfection which union with Christ by itself could not confer.

St. Paul instinctively felt this asceticism to be a negation of the Cross and Resurrection: "If then you be dead with Christ to the elements of this world, why as though you were living in the world do you let yourselves decree: Touch not, taste not, handle not? . . . If you be risen with Christ, seek the things that are above." (Col. ii. 20–iii. 1.) Such practices, instead of subjugating the flesh, help to strengthen it; under the guise of humility, they "puff up with vain pride" and result only in "honour to the satisfaction of the flesh". (Col. ii. 18, 23.) The liberties won in Christ are endangered; man falls back under the dominion of the Law (Gal. iv. 21), of the elements of this world (Gal. iv. 9; Col. ii. 8) and the angelic powers. (Col. ii. 18.) He becomes detached from the head (Col. ii. 19) by adhering to other principles, and the whole order of the flesh becomes re-established. "Are you so foolish that, whereas you began in the Spirit, you would now be made perfect by the flesh?" (Gal. iii. 3)

Though there is but one Christian mortification, which seeks the life of the Spirit in Christ, it is in practice expressed in a hundred different ways. The effort concerned with defending the life is not clearly distinguished from the effort concerned with developing it. There is frontal attack—"I chastize my body" (1 Cor. ix. 27); there is flight—"Fly fornication" (1 Cor. vi. 18), a flight best effected by seeking the things that are above (Col. iii. 1); there is inward renunciation of natural goods. (Phil. iii. 8.) To practise outward mortification does not involve any specific exercise, for "every creature of God is good" (1 Tim. iv. 4) and their use is indifferent as regards salvation. (1 Cor. viii. 8.) Nothing is forbidden, and there is nothing that cannot be sanctified. (Rom. xiv. 6, 1 Cor x 31.) The principle of mortification lies not in things, but in the heart of the believer, in the Spirit who supplants the flesh, in one love triumphing over another.

(c) Its Effectiveness

Mortification, as thus defined, has the splendid task of making the way clear for the Resurrection.

When St. Paul renounces all human advantages, it is in order to win Christ and gain "the excellent knowledge of Jesus Christ my Lord" which is the experience of the divine life. (Phil iii. 8.) The goal of the transformation that is brought about by putting to death the natural man, is total glorification. The Apostle conforms himself to the death of Christ in the hope of attaining bodily resurrection: "We are joint-heirs with Christ, if we suffer with him, that we may be also glorified with him." (Rom. viii. 17.)

Christian effort, as well as tending towards life, also effects that death of the flesh which no other asceticism can achieve: "They that are Christ's, have crucified their flesh with its vices and concupiscences." (Gal. v. 24.)

The believer has the power to mortify his earthly members (Col. iii. 5) because he bears his weapons in the Spirit (Rom. viii. 13), and because the death that enters his body is simply the coming into it of the risen life. Mortification kills by giving life.

Like faith, mortification, which is a means of assimilating the Easter mystery, belongs to the mystery itself. By it the Spirit, who raises up Christ and consecrates his death, extends that life and that death to us.

iii. CHRISTIAN SUFFERING AND DEATH

In this progressive putting to death of the carnal man, there is a limit beyond which asceticism cannot go; for the weakness of the flesh is an existential weakness, rooted in our earthly being.

As well as the mortification we freely undergo, St Paul recognizes another putting to death of the carnal man in which we do not take the initiative, but which we accept, and whose spiritualizing effectiveness goes far beyond that of any ascetic effort. suffering and death.

(a) Suffering

The suffering and physical weakness of the flesh sometimes figure as a cause of our future resurrection (Rom. viii. 17), and sometimes as an atmosphere favourable to the expansion of the power of the Resurrection now taking place. (2 Cor. xii. 9.) They are always accompanied with joy (2 Cor. i. 5), and an overflowing divine life: we are seen "as dying, and behold we live; as chastized and not killed; as sorrowful, yet always rejoicing; as needy, yet enriching many; as having nothing, yet possessing all things". (2 Cor. vi. 9–10.)[70]

Suffering has this power of grappling man to the process of Christ's glorification, because it is nothing other than the passion of Christ extended to man: it is "the sufferings of Christ that abound in us" (2 Cor. i. 5), it is "the mortification of Jesus borne in our body" (2 Cor. iv. 10), the passion of Christ experienced by the Apostle (Phil. iii. 10), and it is in Christ that he is weak (2 Cor. xiii. 4.) And, we must add if we are faithful to Paul's mind, this suffering is only Christ's if it is borne in the Spirit.

Death had destroyed the flesh in the individual humanity of Christ, and had brought that humanity into the glory of the Resurrection; and beyond this, it was the cause of the resurrection of all mankind. The same is true, in a lesser way, of the suffering of the faithful; and St. Paul stresses the social importance of suffering in the Church even more than its efficacy in the individual.

This was revealed to him by the Lord. The angel of Satan buffeted

[70] According to 1 Pet iv. 1–2, suffering endured in Christ's name destroys sin in the believer: "Christ therefore having suffered in the flesh, be ye also armed with the same thought [of the necessity of suffering for salvation—iii 18], for he that hath suffered in the flesh hath ceased from sins."

him, his infirmity humiliated him and seemed to hinder his apostolic work, and he "thrice besought the Lord that it should depart". And then he heard Christ saying, "My grace is sufficient for thee, for power is made perfect in infirmity." (2 Cor. xii 9.) The power of the Spirit, the divine life of Christ, develops and expands amid the destruction of the flesh. Where man has to admit his powerlessness, the power of God appears.[71] Because of the void it creates in his natural energies, suffering fills the Apostle with the glorious life of Christ and with an abundance of the charismata that enable him to win souls· "We always bear about in our bodies the death of Jesus, that the life also of Jesus may be made manifest in our bodies " (2 Cor. iv. 10.) Through the trials and weaknesses which unite him to Christ's death, the Apostle takes hold of the triumphant power of Christ risen· "Although he was crucified through weakness, yet he liveth by the power of God. For we also are weak in him: but we shall live with him by the power of God in our behaviour towards you." (2 Cor. xiii. 4.)

Strange paradoxes here: weakness is strength, disgrace is grandeur, and when a life has been condemned to sterility by lack of all human advantage, it bears fruit. Overwhelmed by this revelation, St. Paul declares his new and wonderful discovery: "Gladly therefore, will I glory in my infirmities, that the power of Christ may dwell in me. For which cause I please myself in my infirmities, in reproaches, in necessities, in persecutions, in distresses, for Christ; For when I am weak, then I am powerful." (2 Cor. xii. 9–10.)

He is referring here to the indirect effect on the world around. But suffering also exercises a direct action of sanctification upon the Church. When death takes place in the Apostle, life flows into the whole Church: "Death worketh in us and life in you." (2 Cor. iv. 12.) While infirmity and persecution are gradually bringing about the destruction of the man of flesh and blood in their Apostle, the level of life is rising in the faithful. That is why St. Paul rejoices in his sufferings (Col. 1. 24) and becomes strong enough to bear whatever may happen: "Therefore I endure all things for the sake

[71] This weakness of the flesh which, once it has been recognized and accepted, lays man open to the power of God, is simply the weakness of sinful man Of course we must not "do evil that there may come good" (Rom. iii 8), for sin cannot exercise the justice of God Yet the author declares that the justice of God is given to man because he is sinful and recognizes himself as such Christ himself entered into that living justice by accepting the weakness of sinful flesh even to its ultimate consequence, death

of the elect, that they also may obtain the salvation which is in Christ Jesus, with heavenly glory " (2 Tim. ii. 10.)

Col. i. 24 explains why it is necessary for an Apostle to suffer· "I fill up those things that are wanting of the sufferings of Christ, in my flesh, for his body, which is the Church, whereof I am made a minister."[72]

In Christ the sufferings are complete and can assure the justification of all mankind—St. Paul's thought admits of no argument on this point. It is in the Church that Christ's sufferings are deficient for man's salvation; it is in her that Christ's passion has yet to achieve full realization. The one death whereby Christ entered into life must be effected in his mystical body, for it is to be the *pleroma* (in the receptive sense) not merely of his glory, but also of his death; it is to be the dead and risen body of Christ.

It seems, then, as though Christ's death is not redemptive in actual fact unless it is made present in the world through the Church.

As the minister of the community (Col. i. 25), the Apostle has the task of perfecting in his own person the Church's communion in the sufferings of her Saviour. That is why he welcomes those sufferings, that they may all come together in his flesh, and that, as death is effected in him, life may work in the Church. (2 Cor. iv. 12) "I think that God hath set forth us Apostles as the last of men, as it were men appointed to death" (1 Cor. iv 9), men whose

[72] There are two possible renderings for this verse "I make up what is lacking to the sufferings of Christ", or " . what is lacking of the sufferings of Christ"

The first would mean that the sum of Christ's sufferings does not add up to the measure needed for the salvation of all men The second would mean simply that the measure was incomplete in the apostle

The word ὑστέρημα is contrasted with περίσσευμα as want with abundance. (2 Cor viii 14) Apart from its use in 1 Thess iii 10, it means not the insufficient nature of an object, but the partial lack of that object Thus, in 1 Cor. xvi 17, ὑμέτερον ὑστέρημα is translated not as "your need", but rather "what I am deprived of in you", or "what is partially lacking on your part" And Phil ii 30, as "that he might fulfil that which on your part was wanting towards my service". Therefore I prefer the translation "what is lacking of the sufferings of Christ" O Cullmann, *Königsherrschaft Christi und Kirche im N T.*, Zürich, 1941, p. 30, gives the same rendering

If it is preferred to keep the rendering "what is lacking to the sufferings", then rather than reading, "I make up in my flesh what is lacking to the sufferings of Christ", we must read, "I make up what in my flesh is lacking to the sufferings . " This would imply that it is the Church which is deficient; to the sufferings of Christ, which are complete in themselves, the Church's participation must be added Cf T K Abbott, *Colossians*, Edinburgh, 1897, p 232.

profession is suffering. These men are destined to propagate the divine life which, in them, can flow only from their Saviour's death.[73]

Suffering, so senseless in the eyes of the world, becomes in Christ a most rational means that "worketh for us . . . an eternal weight of glory". (2 Cor. iv 17)

(b) Death

One day the development of Christ's death will be perfect in us and the Resurrection will be complete.

Bodily death, more than anything else in our lives, does the work Scripture attributes to mortification. "It is a certain saying that if we be dead with him, we shall live also with him " (2 Tim. ii. 11.) This text is no longer referring to the death of baptism, or even to the gradual mortifying of the outward man; St. Paul is thinking of death at the hands of the executioner outside his prison. And how blessed is death which can open that door upon the life in Christ! Even in his first captivity, he was obsessed with his longing to lay aside the flesh that kept him at a distance from his Lord: "To me, to die is gain . . . I have a desire to be dissolved and to be with Christ." (Phil 1. 21, 23.)[74]

In this latter text, the two infinitives, "to be dissolved and to be with Christ", are bracketed together. Paul sees his martyrdom and reunion with Christ "as two interlinked events, or even as two facets of a single event".[75]

Of itself, death is simply the end of life, it is carnal existence, which is a road towards death, reaching its goal. For the believer it "changes sign", it abolishes the flesh and welcomes everlasting life.

This is the ultimate paradox of divine life being manifest through

---

[73] This explains the contrast we find in the life of the Apostles. During Christ's time on earth, they were surrounded with a special providence (Matt x 9–10); their Master watched over their lives with care (John xviii. 8–9.) This was their time of joy (Matt ix 15); persecution and the witness of blood would come later (Luke xxii 35–6, xxi. 12; Matt. x 16–17.) Beforehand, why should there be sufferings without any purpose? The Apostle's passion begins once his suffering has been united to the death of Christ, for from then on it becomes redemptive.

[74] Though, in all these texts, the death that brings beatitude is martyrdom, it is not "stretching them too far to conclude that the same direct reunion with Christ awaits those who die in the same dispositions as Paul, whether they are put to death for Christ like him, or simply animated with an equally perfect charity " (J. Huby, *Les Épîtres de la captivité*, 3rd ed , p. 285, *n* 4.)

[75] J Huby, *Épîtres de la captivité*, p. 284

weakness. The believer's death is a continuation of the mortification brought about by accepting the weakness of the flesh; it brings that mortification to its conclusion through complete acceptance.

The believer's last breath has the power of destroying the flesh and inaugurating life, because it is breathed out in the death of Christ himself. "If we die with him..." (2 Tim. ii 11), says St Paul, and he uses here a phrase which generally indicates the communion the faithful attain by baptism in the death that redeems them. Physical death consummates sacramental death[76]; it completes our incorporation into Christ in his redemptive act. The summit, as it were, of carnal man's weakness, becomes, in his acceptance of it, the supreme means of being caught up with the Saviour in his death and also therefore of his triumph. Man is then wholly possessed by the Easter mystery, Christ's death is now complete in him; it remains for the Father to complete the Resurrection.[77]

Pauline theology does not provide a single argument to show why the individual believer's resurrection should be delayed beyond death.[78] In his case it is indeed true that "he that is dead is justified from sin" (Rom. vi. 7),[79] for death is now complete.

Thus physical death completes sacramental death and all the other deaths in a Christian's life, all of which open out into the Resurrection.

Because it holds destruction for the human creature, it remains a punishment for sin (Rom. viii. 10), the supreme enemy. (1 Cor. xv. 26.) But for the Christian who accepts the fact that he is condemned to it, it provides the antidote for its own poison; it destroys its own work of destruction by the life it calls into being. It comes, as the

---

[76] Christian death, or at least martyrdom, which is the Christian death *par excellence*, is called by Tertullian the second baptism, the baptism of blood following the baptism of water (*De Baptismo*, xvi, *P L*, 1 1217.)

[77] The mere fact of this dying together, this "dying with" someone else, indicates the essential newness of Christian death, and the presence in it of the life of the Spirit. For the flesh is closed in on itself, carnal man is completely alone, and for him death, which brings the weaknesses of the flesh to their final paroxysm, takes place in utter loneliness But the believer dies with Christ; for him death is a communion.

[78] In Christ's case there was no cause to delay his resurrection after the moment of death Similarly with the individual believer, as long as his death is truly Christian. But the final resurrection is a universal judgement, the manifestation of the mystery of Christ in the whole Church, the re-creation of the universe.

[79] The Apostle applies this truism to baptism, yet man remains partially under condemnation (Rom viii. 10), because sacramental death does not wholly destroy the flesh by total incorporation in Christ's death.

last thing of all, to help in our effort towards God in Christ.[80] It is our final friend.

God's love and wisdom are indeed immeasurable. He has permitted sin, and willed that it be punished—by hard labour, by suffering and by death. But in Christ, the acceptance of this law of labour and of death brings man out of his sins, and places him in a life more splendid than any the first man could have bequeathed him

Man has had to pass through sin to enter into glory.

Death, we know, is at the origin of Christ's resurrection, not in himself alone, but in the whole Church. Any affirmation of human values, any love of life or of joy, which does not look beyond those values, beyond human life and pleasure, can only impede man's redemption and serve to extend the power of the flesh as against the Resurrection. Christ and those who believe in him live only in death; (like the Lamb in the Apocalypse) they "are standing, as it were slain", to themselves.

But this death is to be found only in the life of Christ. An apostle conforms himself to Christ's death and becomes an organ of salvation through the power the risen Christ exercises upon him; the sacraments extend the death of Christ upon us, by uniting us to his glorified body; faith, Christian effort, and mortification bring death about because of the Spirit, who is the life of Christ. If anyone tries to die to himself in any way other than living by Christ in glory, he will merely succeed in establishing in himself the rule of the flesh.

[80] St Ignatius (in his epistle to the Romans) gives us the formulae, "to die in [εἰς] Christ Jesus" (vi. 1), in which the preposition indicates the movement of union with Christ, and "to die to the world towards God". (ii 2.)

IX

THE EASTER MYSTERY IN ITS HEAVENLY CONSUMMATION

The Easter mystery will be consummated in the Church with the *parousia* of Christ. Will that be the end of it? Will it then be replaced by a further mystery for which it has been simply the preparation? Or is not the eternal life in fact precisely the Easter mystery as it remains forever fixed at its time of consummation?

1. THE SYNOPTICS

Several of the synoptic parables present the Kingdom of the world to come as something completely different from the time before the return of our Lord; so much so that his return seems to be merely a preparation for it.

Elsewhere, however, the Kingdom is in such perfect continuity with Christ's glorification that it is impossible to detect any transition between the entry of Christ into glory and the inauguration of the Kingdom of Heaven; and it seems then that it must only be the inadequacy of the analogy of a departure and a return which makes those parables appear to be contrasting two essentially distinct phases

The one and only Kingdom, the Kingdom of the end of the world, came into the world in the person of Christ when the hour of Christ's messianic glorification struck. Christ in glory is its corner-stone. (Matt. xxi 42.) He is its king; around him, as he comes upon the clouds (Matt. xxvi. 64), are gathered his elect (Matt xxiv. 31); he will have someone sitting on his right and on his left when he has come into his glory. (Mark x 35-40.) The banquet is prepared for the Son (Matt. xxii. 2); those invited will share it with him, they will share "the joy [of the banquet] of the Lord". (Matt. xxv. 21.)

When our Lord, fastened to the Cross, said to the thief, "This day shalt thou be *with me* in paradise" (Luke xxiii 43), he was stating the essential characteristic of the Kingdom: man finds his salvation, his happiness in heaven, by sharing in the glory of Christ.[1]

The Father has prepared a banquet for Christ, the banquet of the Kingdom: "Enter thou into the joy of the Lord", into the feasting hall, the Lord will say to the good and faithful servant. (Matt. xxv. 21.) "Blessed are those servants whom the Lord . . . shall find watching Amen I say to you, that he will gird himself, and make them sit down to meat, and passing will minister unto them." (Luke xii. 37.) He will share with them the glory prepared for him: "I dispose to you, as my Father hath disposed to me, a kingdom; that you may eat and drink at my table, in my kingdom." (Luke xxii. 29–30.)

The Jewish people looked forward with love and longing to the marriage feast of the Messiah, which would, like all marriage feasts, last a week, but in this week each day would be a millennium. The banquet of glory awaiting Christ is a wedding feast. (Matt. xxii. 2.) At present the community is keeping watch, and going to meet the bridegroom. At midnight he will arrive unexpectedly, the virgins whose lamps are ready will go with him into the marriage hall (Matt. xxv. 1–13).

If, for the Synoptics, heaven is a sharing in the wedding banquet of Christ, hell is being excluded from it, it is being cast out of the brightly-lighted hall into exterior darkness (Matt. xxii. 13), far from the face of Christ. (Matt. vii. 23; xxv. 41.)

In the Upper Room, Christ brought the synoptic revelation of his kingdom to its close. He spoke of the feast of the Last Day, the wedding banquet in the Kingdom, as a sublime paschal meal. Having foretold it, he instituted the sign of it on earth, the Eucharist, to be a hidden presence and revelation of the banquet to come. The feasters in heaven were to gather round the Christ of Easter, and he was himself to be their food.[2]

He himself will have prepared the table for this feast in the other world, as he has promised; he himself will go from one to another,

---

[1] St Ambrose, *Exp. Ev sec Lucam*, x, *P L*, xv, 1834. "For life is to be with Christ; therefore where Christ is, there is life, there is the kingdom."
[2] St Ignatius of Antioch, *Rom.*, vii, 3, envisages our eternal union with Christ as a eucharistic meal The Council of Trent, sess. xiii, ch. 8, says: "They will eat undisguised that same bread of angels which they now eat under the veil of the sacrament", *D B*, 882

giving them food; he will give himself to his own in the gift of his body.[3]

2. St. John

To St. John, eternal life consists in the knowledge of God communicated by Christ.

Even on earth, the Son revealed the Father's image to the disciple who watched him closely; to see him was to see the Father. (xiv. 9.) But as long as the Son remained lacking his full glory, man's knowledge of him remained incomplete, along with his knowledge of the Father and the life he was to receive.

Before his death, our Lord asked for his full glory in order that all men might know him and his Father, and might be given life in that knowledge. (xvii. 1-3)

The disciples, gathered round Christ, were to contemplate this paschal glory in heaven (xvii. 24); in that knowledge they were to find life and, no doubt, as on earth, in that knowledge they would also see the Father. Two texts seem to suggest this: 1 John iii. 2, and Apoc. xxi. 23. If the first is to be translated, "When he [Christ] shall appear, we shall be like to him, because we shall see him as he is", it implies that the vision of God is seen in the Son.[4] According to the Apocalypse, the heavenly city is lit by the glory of God, and "the Lamb is the lamp thereof". If the image is to be taken strictly, it is Christ who sheds the light of God. This means that the Incarnation has achieved its object of bringing the Word into the world, to enlighten all men with the life-giving knowledge of the Father.

I have shown that in St. John's soteriology, the doctrine of salvation through knowledge stands alongside the importance of our Lord's bodily humanity, and the sacramental idea. This divine life, which is a sublime knowledge, is given through contact with Christ's body, immolated and glorified. (vi. 51; vii. 37-9.)

[3] In biblical theology, the happiness of heaven is not simply a seeing God face to face, which might equally be the ideal of a spiritualist philosophy Heaven is a "Christian" reality, a paschal reality, with Christ as its necessary centre. Other sacred writers see beatitude as direct experience of God, an intimate knowledge of him, but for the Synoptics, it is Christ's banquet The theologian making a synthesis of biblical sayings on the subject, would say that the intimate experience of God is achieved by the faithful in their union with the glorified Christ.

Because of this mediation which Christ exercises actually by his body, the happiness of heaven appears more concrete and closer to the heart of man, even though that very closeness makes the mystery of heaven deeper still

[4] Cf. J. Bonsirven, *Épîtres de saint Jean*, Paris, 1936, p 163, *n* 1.

It would not appear that the faithful lose that contact in heaven. The branches of the vine remain attached to the main stem, for beyond it lies only the fire. The Apocalypse envisages the eternal life of heaven as a continuation of the eternal life we draw on earth from the Eucharist. In heaven and on earth the author makes no distinction between the two—he "that overcometh   . will eat of the fruit of the Tree of Life, which is in the paradise of God" (ii. 7); he eats the hidden manna (ii. 17), he is given the morning star, which is of the "root and stock of David" (ii. 28; xxii. 16); after his arrival Christ will come and sup with him. (iii 20) All these are eucharistic allusions. Just as the water of the Spirit springs from the side of the glorified Christ for the believer on earth, so the river of life flows for the heavenly city—from the throne of God, certainly, but also from the Lamb. (xxii. 1.)

What little St. John tells us about the life of heaven shows it as an effect of the mystery of the Incarnation in its paschal fullness.

3. St. Paul

When Christ has brought down the principalities and destroyed death, he will, according to St. Paul, hand over the kingship to his God and Father. He will himself submit to him to whom he has made the universe subject, that God may be all in all. (1 Cor. xv 24, 28.)

This handing over of the kingdom might be interpreted as an abdication to give the Father sole kingship, and some authors do interpret it thus. Christ's lordship is thus set between two limits in time—Easter and the *parousia*.[5] Beyond these, the Kingdom of God extends on either side, imperfect in its first phase, but after Christ's redemption, become perfect.

But if Christ were to abandon his universal kingship, the Father's plan would be completely upset, and the whole of the new creation of which Christ the Lord is corner-stone would collapse. The text does not support any such interpretation. It is not from the moment when all the powers are brought down to be a footstool for his feet, when God makes all things subject to his power (1 Cor. xv. 25, 28),

[5] Cf for instance, O. Cullmann, *Konigsherrschaft Christi und Kirche im N T*, Zürich, 1941, pp 11–14, 24ff ; *Christ and Time*, pp. 151ff ; E Stauffer, *Die Theologie des N.T.*, p. 198.

that Christ will cease to rule over them.[6] That day "of his coming and of his kingdom" (2 Tim. iv. 1) will certainly bring Christ's activity as king to its end, but only in the sense of completing his conquests. All will then return to the Father, because all returns to Christ, and the Kingdom of Christ is the Father's. (Eph. v. 5.)[7]

Then there are those who think that the whole system of relationship between the faithful and Christ will be reorganized in a new pattern and that, in the consummation, the faithful will be centred no longer "in him", but "with him" upon the Father. This idea comes from the Apostle's use of the two phases—"in Christ" and "with Christ". The first, belonging to the time between baptism and the *parousia*, is thus used to characterize Christian life in its incomplete state on earth, the second, used only of the baptismal act and the life of glory, applies to the believer's presence with Christ in the next world, both in the union with him effected on earth by the sacrament, and in the eternal union of heaven.[8] The believer who has lived "in Christ" during his time of development, would thus be detached from the living centre in which he had grown on earth, to live an adult life in heaven "in company with Christ", in a body like his.

But the evidence would have to be more positive before we could admit that the Apostle envisaged any such evolution. St. Paul might never speak of a heavenly life "in Christ" and yet not intend to deny such a thing. On earth the believer is identified with Christ; he lives *in* him, but not in company with him. It is that living in company with him that makes heaven so desirable; Paul speaks with longing of the happiness of "being with Christ" (Phil. i 23; 1 Thess. iv. 17), without mentioning the life "in Christ" which he already possesses on earth and which he therefore does not need to hope for; but his not mentioning it does not mean that he will not have it there too.[9]

---

[6] "Surely we cannot think . that he will cease to rule once all things have been placed under his feet, for that is when he will begin to rule more powerfully than ever" (St Jerome, *Adv. Helv* , vi, *P.L* , xxiii, 189)

[7] The eternity of Christ's kingship is expressly affirmed in 2 Pet 1. 11. (Cf Heb xiii. 8) This conviction is also clear from the certitude that "we shall reign with him". (2 Tim ii 12)

[8] E Lohmeyer, Σύν Χριστῷ, *Festgabe fur A Deissmann*, Tubingen, 1927, pp 221, 248–53 Lohmeyer's study convinced several other writers, cf A Wikenhauser, *Die Christusmystik des hl Paulus*, p 35

[9] Lohmeyer makes several mistakes He gives the phrase and all the phrases equivalent to it (verbs composed with σύν) a single meaning, whether they

There are several indications to suggest that St. Paul thought of Christ's living possession of the faithful as continuing when they are consummated. All will be brought to life "in Christ". (1 Cor. xv. 22.) It is St. Paul's invariable idea that whatever causes the beginning of any life is prolonged throughout that life; baptized and raised in Christ and in the Spirit, we continue to live by both. Then too, it is written that God "hath raised us up together [with Christ], and hath made us sit with him in the heavenly places, in Jesus Christ". (Eph. ii. 6) If in anticipation our presence in heaven is in Christ, will it be otherwise when it achieves realization? At that moment the Church will be the perfect *pleroma* of Christ (Eph. iv. 13), Christ in his fullness, the bearer of all his riches; she will hardly at that moment be placed outside him.

The Saviour will not abandon the function of corner-stone of the new universe, nor will he abandon that of head, which makes him the principle of life for the faithful. For them to cease to be "in him" would be to cease to live.

Again it has been claimed that, unlike the phase of life on earth, life in heaven will no longer be connected to the double centre of Christ's death and resurrection, but related only to the resurrection and determined by it.[10] This notion is supported by no textual evidence, and rests on a mistaken vision of the death to which the believer's life is linked.[11]

There is nothing to suggest that this relationship with Christ's

apply to the sacraments or to life in heaven But there is in fact a great difference In the sacramental texts, the phrase indicates participation in the redemptive act of death and resurrection. In those concerned with life in heaven, the phrase indicates life in company with Christ.

Furthermore, Lohmeyer does not point out that our death and resurrection with Christ are effected in Christ, in our union with Christ (Col. ii 11–12), and that being with Christ lasts throughout our life on earth (Col. iii 3, Gal ii 19), so that there is in fact no contradiction between the two phrases

It is true that Paul never says that in heaven we shall live in Christ as well as with him To the reason I have given in the text, one might add this further one. we may say that we die "in him" and rise again "with him", but we do not say, though it may in fact be so, that "in him" we live in his company.

[10] W. T. Hahn, *Das Mitsterben und Mitauferstehen mit Christus bei Paulus*, pp. 163, 177, 181

[11] Paul does not see two different aspects in Christ's death—the death as directed towards glory (whereby it is death to the flesh, is salvific, and remains permanent in Christ), and the death as a weakness of the flesh which is of itself valueless for salvation and belongs only to the past For him it is purely of the order of the flesh

death will stop in heaven, essential as it is to the believer's life, for the life is the goal of the death and necessarily involves death to the flesh. Union with Christ in glory sets an eternal seal upon our union with him in death. It is not a painful death, for it is no longer taking place; it has attained its goal in the glory of which it has become part; it is the end of the life of the flesh, of exile and of weakness, because it is spirit, contact and power. The Church will remain the dead and risen body of Christ, and the more complete the death, the more complete will be the resurrection. Because man's renunciation of self for God is total, it will no longer be called death, but life.

Life in its consummation means spiritual fullness, for newness of life and the death of the flesh both have their source in the Spirit. On earth the Spirit was present rather like a sum on account against the full amount; in heaven the Spirit's possession of the believer will be total.

As on earth, that life will be governed by the love filling men's hearts. While the knowledge we have on earth will be transformed (1 Cor. xiii. 12), charity will remain the same, for it is the imprint on man of the eternal Spirit, the mark made by his presence. (Cf. Rom. v. 5.)

The knowledge we have on earth will disappear, but only in the way a child's knowledge disappears with maturity to give place to an adult's (1 Cor. xiii. 8–11). Even on earth it is spiritual and alive, born of its living union with the object of knowledge in charity. (Cf. Eph. iii 17–18.) But it is adapted to the intermediate phase we are in, and is for that very reason imperfect. Later on it will be a complete cognitive experience; we shall see face to face (1 Cor. xiii. 12), we shall live in the vision of the Lord. (2 Cor. v. 7.) And this must surely be because then our living union in love will be complete. Since the love of the Spirit is the root of knowledge on earth, it will surely be in the Spirit that the knowledge of heaven will enlighten us also.

On earth, the object of our knowledge is Christ, to whom the believer is united in the Spirit, Christ the image of the invisible God, whose face radiates God's glory. (Col 1. 15; 2 Cor. iv. 4, 6.) According to 2 Cor. v. 7–8, the vision of heaven which is contrasted with faith will also be of Christ. However, our knowledge of God will not then be indirect, a reflection in a mirror, even with Christ as the mirror: the believer will see God's face. If all these things are true, then it would seem as though the believer will receive the vision of God as a result of his being united in life and in knowledge with Christ in the Spirit, of a certain identification with the Son who sees the Father.[12] St. Paul does not say this, but it could very well follow what he does say.

Thus, when he writes that Christ will submit himself to the Father and hand over his kingdom to him, that submission and handing over do not mean a renunciation of the title "Lord" and of the work of redemption, but their consummation. God has become all in all because Christ has brought all things into subjection to him and has filled the whole Church with his life.

In Christ himself, God was all from the moment of the Resurrection. In Christ's body the Church, God's all is only attained slowly as the Resurrection advances in it. Indeed, Christ's activity as conqueror might even have distorted the picture so as to cause our eyes to stop at Christ rather than going on to the Father, whereas in reality, since he is wholly possessed by God, any submission to Christ must be also submission to the Father. But from now on, the Son will simply let God rule in his divinized humanity which embraces within it the Church and, through the Church, the entire universe.

According to the Epistle to the Hebrews, heaven is a sanctuary, consecrated by Christ's blood, where the one great sacrifice continues forever with Christ as its high priest. The life of heaven is sacrificial in character: in Christ it is a life blossoming from the perfection of his oblation and forever fixed at that perfection, a life of sacrificial consummation. For the faithful, life in heaven shares this character, for their way into the sanctuary lies through the immolated flesh of the Saviour. (x. 20.) Christ's death, therefore, is not forgotten; it belongs as much to the life of the high priest and his faithful as the door to the sanctuary.

And the sanctuary itself is simply the glorified body of Christ.

In a great many texts, heaven appears to be a place. Theological reflexion makes allowance for the necessary materialization of spiritual concepts, and can distinguish the reality from the image used to make it clear to us.[13] Heaven for the faithful is the new

---

[12] Cf. along these lines L. Malevez, "Quelques enseignements de l'encyclique Mystici Corporis Christi", *Nouv Rev Théol.*, lxvii, 1945, 393ff.

[13] Cf. P. Benoit, "L'Ascension", *R B*, lvi, 1949, 202 The texts themselves suggest this distinction. One group presents the reality of heaven under a form which is clearly adapted to fit popular imagination. (Cf Matt iii 16-17;

world established with Christ's glorification. Our Lord had left our world here below and, at Easter, accomplished his ascent to the Father.[14]

It is in him that "the world to come", the Kingdom of Heaven, has come; that the "perfection" sought in vain by the ancients (Heb. xi. 40) is attained, and the heaven of the faithful established.

The glorified body of Christ is "the first room"[15] of the house on high When God gives the faithful glorified bodies to dwell in, they in their turn will enter their "eternal habitation" (2 Cor. v. 1–2), and the temple in which God resides will be complete.

Christ's body is the first room, but it is also the whole dwelling, the whole homeland. In him we sit in the heavenly places (Eph. ii. 6), in him we are citizens of heaven (Phil. iii. 20); the place of our existence in heaven is *in Christ*. Christ is the Temple of the new age, in succession to the Temple of Moses (John ii. 19) which, according to Heb. viii. is the figure of our heavenly dwelling; the inhabitants of the holy Jerusalem are gathered in it and in God. (Apoc xxi 22.) The way to this sanctuary lies not through space, but through the immolated body of Christ, a living way, a veil torn aside. (Heb. x. 20.) In its immolation, Christ's body is the way into the tabernacle, and the home to which that "living way" leads is the glory of that same body.

The Prophets did not locate the Kingdom of God somewhere in the sky. They saw God dwelling with his saints in their own glorified Temple, in a sanctified Zion, set amid a world renewed and at peace.[16] The New Testament sees the Temple and Sion of the Prophets as Christ and his Church· a living heaven, an edifice made up of men joined together by the Spirit[17]

---

xxviii 2; Luke ii. 14; John 1 51; 1 Thess iv. 16–17, 2 Cor xii. 2) Other texts definitely suggest that heaven is not a place but a higher kind of reality. Christ is the bread that came down from heaven (John vi. 33), he came down from heaven by the Incarnation. (John iii 13) Cf H Bietenhard, *Die himmlische Welt im Urchristentum und Spatjudentum*, Tubingen, 1951.

[14] Cf. above, p 38, p 48, *n* 26.

[15] P. Benoit, "L'Ascension", p 203.

[16] Cf. Apoc. xxi. 10 Rabbinic teaching also placed the world to come on earth (Strack and Billerbeck, *Kommentar*, vol iv, pp. 1145–6)

[17] Thus heaven is not simply a state of beatitude, as is often said in reaction to the popular idea of heaven as a place. It is a reality in itself, "but it is useless to ask where, just as it is wrong to imagine it far away This new world, where Christ rules and waits for us, is not far from us, nor outside this world, but transcends it It is of a different order   " (P Benoit, "L'Ascension", p. 203.)

4. SUMMING-UP

The sacrificial conception of eternal life, set out in the Epistle to the Hebrews, gives us the framework for a final synthesis. It makes God's taking possession of redeemed mankind appear as the fire of the sacrifice taking possession of the victim.

In the past man lived where sin had placed him, far from God. He offered himself in Christ, and by the immolation of his sinful being came forward from that distance where he had existed; God, by accepting his offering, sanctified him, receiving him into the holiness of his Spirit.

God is in heaven with the victim in whom God is all by the fire of his Spirit. But that victim does not lie motionless before God, but stands upright in sacrifice; his death is filled with life, for it is in the life of God that human life is immolated and absorbed. Man is given over to God; he is only immolated because the gift of self to God is an immolation of sinful man; he is expropriated from himself in the love of the Spirit who possesses him, who opens his being and presents him to the Father as a true son in the Son.

Man is not the only one who gives in this sacrifice. God gives himself in return, and man's life in heaven is a communion. God gives himself to Christ first, and in Christ, who comprises the faithful as well in his body and in his sacrifice, the faithful share in the communion. It is the paschal feast promised long ago, at which Christ eats and drinks with his disciples at his Father's table, at which they eat the Lamb, for it is in the immolated Christ that God gives himself to the faithful.

All the life of the world to come, then, is fixed at Easter. In this life, the faithful have come, one by one, to inscribe their names in the world to come, by inscribing themselves in Christ at the moment of his being glorified, even while remaining involved in the unfolding of time on earth. The *parousia* completes their union with Christ in that act and in that moment; they are contemporary with each other and with Christ in the Easter mystery.

The Spirit, who sets the faithful free of their carnal self-imprisonment and lays them open to God, undoubtedly also opens them to one another, just as he has been the bond of their incomplete union even on earth. Adam, the man of earth, knew Eve his wife, and formed with her a single body in the flesh. Christ in heaven knows his Church, forming but one body with her, in a union that is physical though in the Spirit Unhampered by the limitations imposed on their being by life in the flesh, the faithful will be close and loving to each other, in the one body of Christ and the one Spirit. Carnal love was a prefiguring of this love of heaven; but the latter is very different, for it can only exist precisely because it is no longer carnal; it is far closer, for what was the means of union to the former, the flesh, is actually an obstacle to be overcome.

It is the marriage feast, a feast at the foot of the Cross, begun in the last eucharistic supper, all are united in the immolated body of Christ, and in that body are united to each other. The indestructible society, which every sacrificial meal has aimed at bringing about, is now perfected.

Thus God is all in all, as it is his nature to be; he impresses upon all, in the Holy Ghost, his form of life, which is love.

The centre from which this living love radiates is the Lamb, the paschal victim. The end of a study of Christ's glorification will bring our minds back to his death and fix them there. For that is where his glory began, and still begins, even in heaven. The Lamb stands slain (Apoc. v. 6), and the faithful, in turn, triumph only in death—their death which is Christ's death communicated to them. The glory is marked by the stigmata of his five wounds The immolation remains inscribed in it, not as a memory, but as a reality, and proclaims for all eternity the death the Lamb submitted to for love of his Father.

He came down to live in the world of sin and slavery, in order that that world might receive a mortal blow in his body. He left the world below and entered heaven through the wounding of his body. But he has left his body, slain and brought back to life, among men, to be the living way along which they can go to the Father. In him men take their departure, in him they attain their end. When that end is achieved all the sons will then have rejoined their Father. Honour and glory to the Lamb!

*

INDEX OF SCRIPTURE REFERENCES

This index only covers texts actually commented on

INDEX OF AUTHORS CITED

SUBJECT INDEX

CPSIA information can be obtained
at www.ICGtesting.com
Printed in the USA
LVHW081509260922
729314LV00009B/308